Systematic Supervision for Physical Education

Lynda E. Randall, PhD
California State University, Fullerton

Human Kinetics Publishers
Champaign, Illinois

Library of Congress Cataloging-in-Publication Data

Randall, Lynda E.
      Systematic supervision for physical education / Lynda E. Randall.
         p.   cm.
      Includes bibliographical references (p.) and index.
      ISBN 0-87322-363-2
      1. Physical education teachers--Training of.   I. Title.
GV363.R28 1992   92-2930
613.7'1'07--dc20   CIP

ISBN: 0-87322-363-2

Acquisitions Editor: Rick Frey, PhD
Developmental Editor: Christine Drews
Assistant Editors: Elizabeth Bridgett, Moyra Knight,
   Dawn Levy, and Julie Swadener
Copyeditor: Julie Anderson
Proofreader: Kari Nelson
Indexer: Theresa J. Schaefer
Production Director: Ernie Noa
Typesetter: Julie Overholt
Text Design: Keith Blomberg
Text Layout: Denise Peters
Cover Design: Jack Davis
Cover Photo: Will Zehr
Illustrations: Kathy Fuoss
Printer: Braun-Brumfield, Inc.

Printed in the United States of America

10 9 8 7 6 5 4 3 2 1

Human Kinetics Publishers
Box 5076, Champaign, IL 61825-5076
1-800-747-4457

Canada Office:
Human Kinetics Publishers, Inc.
P.O. Box 2503, Windsor, ON N8Y 4S2
1-800-465-7301 (in Canada only)

Europe Office:
Human Kinetics Publishers (Europe) Ltd.
P.O. Box IW14
Leeds LS16 6TR
England
0532-781708

To my niece, Sheri,
who will carry the tradition of physical education
into the next generation of our family.

Congratulations on the completion of your degree.

Contents

Preface

Think back to your days of student teaching, and see what memories you can conjure up. If you are like me, you still have vivid recollections of the feelings associated with the student teaching experience—excitement, uncertainty, enthusiasm, fear of the unknown, and lots of anxiety. Each year, student and beginning teachers enter the "real world" of teaching, looking forward to putting their education into practice. But after 2 weeks of struggling in the gymnasium or classroom, those teachers sometimes redirect their goals to survival. They are uncertain of their roles and how to carry out their responsibilities. Moreover, they experience the powerful effects of occupational socialization and wonder if what they learned in methods classes has any relevance to reality.

The Systematic Supervision Model for physical education was designed to help the beginning teacher avoid the "staying afloat" syndrome; the model helps the teacher systematically establish specific goals and work toward them. Guided practice and feedback allow the novice teacher to apply theory to practice. As the teacher develops confidence and attains mastery, he or she is encouraged to maintain a broad repertoire of teaching skills introduced in undergraduate preparation. It is hoped that this will minimize the rejection of theory.

In addition to nurturing the fledgling teacher, the Systematic Supervision Model is a resource for professionals involved in the initial or ongoing training of physical education teachers. This target group includes professional preparation faculty and graduate students in colleges and universities, as well as administrators, department heads, and teachers in public schools.

The book serves three major functions. First, it reviews the current theory and research of effective teaching and effective supervision. Second, it proposes a comprehensive model of systematic supervision that is specific to physical education. Last, it reviews a variety of related issues that might support the delivery of systematic supervision, including in-service implications and educational reform movements. A second book, *The Student Teacher's Handbook for Physical Education*, contains an abbreviated version of the model and instruments to be used directly by student teachers and their cooperating teachers.

The model provides systematic reinforcement of desired teaching behaviors, which are defined in objective and observable terms. These target behaviors are presented as planned, sequential progressions that allow teachers to concentrate on one major objective at a time. The progressions are presented in 15 components, which are organized in 3 phases (Phase 1: Gaining Confidence and Establishing Control, Phase 2: Planning for Maximum Learning, and Phase 3: Refining Teaching Skills). These progressions are organized in a developmental framework to facilitate mastery of simple to complex teaching skills.

Prescribed tasks help the student teacher concentrate on developing specific competencies each week, while providing a clear observational focus for both the cooperating teacher in the school and the university supervisor.

The Systematic Supervision Model was developed initially for use by student teachers. It may also be a useful tool for the induction of beginning teachers and the ongoing professional development of in-service teachers, or as a model for peer coaching and self-analysis supervision. The accompanying handbook is a concise resource for the structuring of professional development activities at all of these levels.

The use of the Systematic Supervision Model requires an in-depth review and understanding of the entire model. It is not intended to be used in fragmented pieces, although some of the strategies might enhance an existing supervision model. Nor is the model intended to be a cure-all for all of the evils of teaching. Its scope is limited to those characteristics of effective teaching that are supported by research and activities that might help to promote the transfer of theory into practice.

The book is organized to provide a thorough description of the model and its evolution. Part I, which includes chapters 1 through 5, describes the current status of supervision and reviews the principles of effective teaching and effective supervision that undergird the model. Part II encompasses a comprehensive review of the model. Chapter 6 outlines the Systematic Supervision Model, and chapters 7 through 9 present the 3 phases of the model and their components. Part III reviews issues related to systematic supervision. Chapter 10 provides guidelines for implementing the model for maximum effectiveness. Chapters 11 and 12 provide supplementary resources related to supervision as in-service development and state-mandated educational reforms that effect the delivery of supervision.

Acknowledgments

A number of individuals have been instrumental in the development of this project. My initial inspiration for developing a model of supervision emerged from 10 years of experience in supervising student teachers and preinterns at Springfield College, San Diego State University, and Florida State University. Once I began actually creating and using the model, many student teachers, cooperating teachers, and university supervisors provided valuable input and feedback along the way. Doctoral students at Florida State University who were colleagues in research and development gave particularly important assistance. I extend grateful appreciation to Jeanette Askins, Joseph Cole, Carol Conkell, and Chuck Duncan. Mark Leroux at California State University, Fullerton, has been very helpful in the final stages of production.

A group of undergraduates at Florida State University gave their time and effort to replace a large number of research documents that were lost. Special thanks to Johnny Rainwater, Melissa Dawson, Tony DeWeese, Chrissie Droz, George Romans, Jennifer Matheson, and Susan Haygood.

For their interest in piloting the model internationally, I thank Rolando Herrera, Ledys Aragón, Carmen Umaña, and Elisa Salazar-Solis at Escuela de Ciencias del Deporte, Universidad Nacional, Costa Rica; and Myung-Hee Youn at Korea National University of Education, Seoul.

I owe a special debt of gratitude to Mary Alice Kowalski who assisted me with the tedious task of proofreading this manuscript.

I am especially thankful for the expert guidance and direction of my editors, Rick Frey, Chris Drews, and Julie Anderson, at Human Kinetics Publishers. Their consistent encouragement was particularly important to me in this first book.

Finally, I'd like to thank my colleagues at California State University, Fullerton, for supporting my work and giving me the opportunity to explore new horizons.

Credits

Figures 5.1 and 5.2 are adapted with permission from B.E. Long and L. Deture, 1986, Tallahassee: Florida State University. Copyright 1982 by B.E. Long and L. Deture.

Figures 5.3 and 7.11 are adapted with permission from unpublished material by T. Ratliffe, 1990.

Figure 7.1 is reprinted with permission from *Discipline and Behaviors Management* (pp. 36 and 41) by D. Sabatino, A. Sabatino, and L. Mann, 1983. Gaithersburg, MD: Aspen Publishers, Inc. Copyright 1983 by D. Sabatino, A. Sabatino, and L. Mann.

Figure 8.4 is adapted by permission of Merrill, an imprint of Macmillan Publishing Company from *Teaching Physical Education, 3rd edition*, by Muska Mosston and Sara Ashworth. Copyright © 1986 (New York: Macmillan Publishing Company).

Figure 9.1 is from Marlene J. Adrian and John M. Cooper, *Biomechanics of Human Movement*. Copyright © 1989 by Benchmark Press, Inc. Reprinted by permission of Wm. C. Brown Communications, Inc., Dubuque, Iowa. All rights reserved.

Figure 9.5 is reprinted with permission. Copyright by the American Association of Colleges for Teacher Education. D.R. Cruickshank, 1985, "Applying Research on Teacher Clarity." *Journal of Teacher Education* **36**(2): p. 46.

Figure 9.8 is reprinted with permission from *Essential Performance Objectives for Physical Education* (p. 9) by Michigan Department of Education, 1984. East Lansing, MI: Michigan Department of Education. Copyright 1984 by the Michigan Department of Education.

Photos on pages 1, 3, 11, 43, 79, 81, 89, 125, 183, 185, and 211 by Michael Riley.

Photos on pages 23 and 157 by Rich DeLong.

Photos on pages 59 and 201 by Deborah Thomas.

Author photo by Michelle Iversen.

Part I

Supervision and Evaluation: The Research Base

This part provides an empirical base for the development of the Systematic Supervision Model. The empirical base encompasses a broad review of research related to generic models of supervision, supervisory effectiveness, teacher effectiveness, and measurement-based observation. From this base, we can draw a number of implications for the development of an eclectic model of supervision for physical education. Based on the synthesis of a large body of research, this model must be planned, comprehensive, systematic, collaborative, analytical, and behaviorally based. It should also reflect the unique demands of teaching in a movement setting.

Chapter 1 provides a rationale for the use of systematic supervision. This rationale is based on three major premises:

- Traditional programs of supervision have failed to impact the quality of teaching.

- Shortcomings in undergraduate preparation have led to weak transfer of training.
- Beginning teachers as learners have unique needs for supervision.

Chapter 2 entails an overview of generic models of supervision. The five models selected were those most often cited in the literature. The models include clinical supervision, supervision as counseling, peer supervision, self-analysis, and competency-based supervision. Each of the models has distinctive features that educators should consider in developing an eclectic model.

Chapter 3 synthesizes a broad review of research on supervisory effectiveness. It examines empirical support for the generic models introduced in chapter 2 and outlines general conclusions for their utility. Research on supervision in physical education extends this review to content-specific applications of supervision. Research on general supervisory practices analyzes factors related to supervisory styles, skills and competencies, and overall effectiveness.

Chapter 4 describes a research base for the improvement of teaching. The chapter summarizes several decades of research findings with respect to instructional time, direct instruction, classroom management, classroom climate, feedback, expectancy, lesson presentation, and questioning. This research base includes both generic and physical education literature.

Chapter 5 introduces the concept of measurement-based evaluation. The chapter includes a general contrast and review of subjective and objective measures of teacher evaluation. It also describes the processes entailed in measurement-based evaluation of performance and proposes a framework for systematic observation of teaching.

Part I is designed to provide the supervisor with a basis for decision making. Effective supervision requires a strong foundation of current research related to effective teaching and supervision. This knowledge base makes up the scientific basis for the art of supervision and addresses these major questions:

- What is effective supervision, and how is it best delivered?
- What is effective teaching, and how is it best observed?

Chapter 1

A Rationale for the Use of Systematic Supervision

The Systematic Supervision Model was initially developed to facilitate the progress of student teachers in physical education. The rationale for the use of systematic supervision is based upon the following beliefs:

- Traditional programs of supervision have failed to significantly impact the quality of teaching.
- Supervisory programs typically do not reinforce, in any systematic manner, the teaching behaviors that student teachers learn in undergraduate preparation.
- Undergraduate professional preparation programs generally comprise a weak treatment (Locke, 1983), in that their effects are quickly washed out by school experiences (Zeichner & Tabachnik, 1981).
- The low impact of undergraduate teacher preparation, combined with the lack of substantive supervision, contributes to the rejection of theory by novice teachers and the widening of the theory/practice gap.
- Beginning teachers face a variety of unique conditions that can lead to transition shock (Corcoran, 1981). Systematic supervision can help alleviate some of the anxiety that results

from this transition by providing an element of structure.

Impetus for the model came from my experiences in supervising student teachers for 10 years. These experiences led me to awareness of and concern about the lack of transfer of theory into practice and the need to provide beginning teachers with a planned sequence of progressions for applying what they learned in undergraduate programs. I discerned a need to provide systematic reinforcement for student teachers, who began their internships with a mixture of confidence in their knowledge and uncertainty about their abilities to survive the rigors of the real world of teaching.

The strategies outlined in this text are based upon an eclectic model of systematic supervision. The model is eclectic in the sense that it derives its components from a wide variety of theoretical and empirical approaches to effective teaching. Before developing this model, I conducted an extensive review of the literature to identify elements of other supervisory models that could be practically combined and to establish a sound framework for applying current theory of effective teaching to practice. The resultant model applies this framework to a planned, comprehensive, and developmental approach to supervision, with emphasis on direct observation of teaching through systematic observation.

The model provides systematic reinforcement of desired teaching behaviors that are defined in objective and observable terms. These target behaviors are presented as planned, sequential progressions that allow the student teacher to concentrate on one major objective at a time. The progressions follow an order of simple to complex skills and are organized in 3 phases:

- Phase 1: Gaining Confidence and Establishing Control
- Phase 2: Planning for Maximum Learning
- Phase 3: Refining Teaching Skills

Prescribed tasks help the student teacher concentrate on developing specific competencies each week; the tasks also provide a clear observational focus for both the cooperating teacher and the university supervisor.

In addition to structuring the internship of student teachers, systematic supervision can facilitate the induction of beginning teachers into the 1st year of teaching. In this case, a program supervisor, peer teacher, or departmental administrator can observe the beginning teacher's progress in mastering the competencies. Similarly, specific components of the model can be implemented in in-service training to provide a clear frame of reference for improving teaching.

Failures of Traditional Supervision

The fact that traditional programs of supervision have failed to impact the quality of supervision is strongly supported in the literature. Supervision has been characterized as "suffer[ing] from the same limitations which bedeviled it 50 years ago" (Locke, 1979, p. 3); "a relatively dormant activity" (Sergiovanni & Starratt, 1979, p. 1); and "a ritualized, sterile process that bears little relationship to the learning of youngsters" (Blumberg, 1980, p. 5). Research consistently shows that the supervisor has virtually no influence on teaching (McIntyre, 1984), but rather the cooperating teacher provides the most important influence (Evans, 1976; Freibus, 1977; Karmos & Jacko, 1977; Seperson & Joyce, 1981).

The static nature of supervisory practice is one of the major reasons for its continuing ineffective-

ness. Analysis of the historical evolution of supervisory processes demonstrates that some shifts in emphasis have occurred. Traditional forms of supervision can be traced to their emergence in the Massachusetts Bay Colonies in 1642 (Eye, 1975), and research shows that those practices in the mid-1950s did not differ significantly (Gwynn, 1961). The major function of traditional supervision was inspection of the teacher, and this was authoritarian and poorly planned (Burton & Brueckner, 1955). The influence of scientific supervision in subsequent years led to the evolution of modern supervision. This approach was rooted in a research base and emphasized analysis of all aspects of the teaching-learning environment. However, these changes failed to significantly improve supervisory effectiveness, because the research methods typically used in studying teacher effectiveness were vastly insufficient.

In a summary of research on classroom teaching and student achievement, Graham and Heimerer (1981) described 3 phases of research paradigms. Phase 1 consisted of attempts to identify the qualities of good teachers; researchers accomplished this primarily by asking principals to identify good teachers and by attempting to determine the similarities among these teachers. Researchers selected traits such as warmth, openness, loyalty, energy, sincerity, and honesty from descriptions of those teachers judged to be most effective. This paradigm was prevalent in teacher education research conducted before 1950.

Dunkin and Biddle (1974) noted four major shortcomings of these early research efforts:

- failure to observe teaching activities,
- theoretical impoverishment,
- use of inadequate criteria of effectiveness, and
- lack of concern for contextual effects.

Phase 2 of the study of teacher effectiveness, termed the "search for a perfect method of teaching" (Graham & Heimerer, 1981, p. 15), characterized the teacher education literature of the 1960s and 1970s. Research designs in this phase were constructed to compare the effectiveness of various methods (e.g., traditional physical education vs. movement education) in terms of average gains of knowledge or skill. These methods, like those in Phase 1, involved no observation of teachers actually teaching. The majority of studies found no significant differences in student achievement.

The type of research conducted in Phase 3 placed emphasis on observing the teaching process in order to determine its relationship to learning. These process-product studies, prevalent in 1960s and 1970s, were influenced by classroom studies involving the successful teaching of reading and math. Researchers described teaching processes through direct observation of teaching behaviors in the teacher's natural setting.

During the 1980s, research on teacher effectiveness in physical education was extended to include qualitative designs. These studies used techniques of case study, interview, and ethnography to obtain descriptions of activity within a given context. Qualitative designs entail the study of the classroom in its naturalistic setting, allowing the researcher to discover phenomena in the absence of preconceived hypotheses. This approach provides a rich, objective, and holistic picture of the complex nature of the classroom.

Since the 1970s, a tremendous volume of research has been conducted within the area of teacher effectiveness for physical education. Literally hundreds of studies have been conducted, but their findings have largely failed to impact the quality of teaching (Placek & Locke, 1986). One particular research program was a series of student teaching studies directed by Siedentop (1981) at Ohio State University. These studies systematically demonstrated that researchers could objectively define and reliably observe teaching behavior and supervisors could influence the behavior of student teachers through systematic supervision.

Currently, a large number of instruments are available for systematic observation of teaching behavior within the specific context of a movement setting. The majority of these instruments were developed by graduate students in thesis and dissertation work. The body of research related to teacher effectiveness in physical education has grown to voluminous proportions. Yet, these efforts have had little effect on updating supervisory practices. There is a continuing lack of comprehensive models of supervision, despite extensive research evidence that effective teaching can be increased through systematic supervision. Consequently, the process of supervision frequently consists of little more than a tour through the gym (Locke, 1974).

A lack of consensus about the role of supervisors may be a major factor in their ineffectiveness. In outlining the scope of supervisory functions, Locke (1979) made the following observations:

> Supervision has several possible purposes. As evaluation it is an ubiquitous process designed to make sure somebody else is doing a good job. As skill development it is helping someone else learn how to do a better job. In education we apply the word as a generic term to cover (1) evaluative inspection of school teachers in order to generate information used in such decisions as hiring, firing, tenure, promotion and rewards, (2) efforts by administrators and subject matter specialists to improve the instructional effectiveness of teachers, (3) the oversight and tutelage provided by a cooperating practitioner during the apprenticeship of a student teacher, and (4) the visitations of a training program representative during that same exercise. Each of these variations of supervision involves the roles of "observer" and "observed," but the similarity ends there. (p. 4)

The practical realities of implementing supervision in an applied setting pose almost insurmountable obstacles to the production of significant change. Among the problems that contribute to this demise are serious time constraints, lack of administrative support, socialization effects of the school environment, tenacity of experienced teachers who cling to familiar routines, and stereotyped images of the supervisor's role (e.g., the "Snoopervisor" [Brodbelt, 1976]). The end result is that the supervisor typically plays no role at all in the improvement of teaching. Systematic supervision can greatly enhance the perceptions of teachers toward supervisors, as well as improve supervisory effectiveness in general, by providing a planned, sequential, and theoretically sound structure for the improvement of teaching.

Traditional programs of supervision generally have been ineffective. This failure is attributed to the static nature of supervisory practice, the ambiguous definitions of supervisory roles, and the lack of comprehensive models for implementing theory into practice. The end result of these shortcomings is that supervisory programs fail to systematically reinforce the teaching behaviors that student teachers learn in undergraduate preparation.

Students involved in teacher preparation typically take a variety of courses dealing with teaching methods and have a few opportunities to practice teaching styles in microteaching episodes. These experiences are often followed by preinternships, which allow the students to gain hands-on practice at implementing specified competencies. This combination of peer teaching and early field experiences exposes the student to a wide variety of teaching styles and methods, but does little to help the prospective teacher truly master a broad repertoire of competencies. Consequently, the student teacher begins the final internship with limited understanding of a lot of theory and insufficient experience with actually applying that theory.

Most student teachers begin the internship with serious intent. They hope to apply a variety of strategies for maximizing time on task, reducing management time, preventing disciplinary problems, designing appropriate activities, objectively evaluating learning, and using a variety of teaching styles. However, they may feel overwhelmed by the scope of the skills to be mastered and confused and discouraged by their inabilities to do everything at once. The result is that the student teacher often rejects recommended practices that do not meet with immediate success, and the repertoire of available teaching skills is quickly reduced.

This dilemma is further compounded by the failure of both the cooperating teacher and the university supervisor to systematically reinforce what the student teacher has previously learned. At this critical point in teacher preparation the process breaks down, and the bridge between theory and practice is not linked. The cooperating teacher, without the benefit of a structured plan, is unable to determine what the teacher preparation program has emphasized and what level of performance the student teacher should attain. If the university supervisor appears without a plan of supervision, and randomly identifies the competencies to be emphasized, then the effect of that supervision will be minimal.

Convincing evidence indicates that teachers need many opportunities to try out new teaching behaviors before they feel sufficiently comfortable to adopt them. A series of studies conducted by B.R. Joyce, Brown, and Peck (1981) and B.R. Joyce and Showers (1981) supported this notion. In summarizing this research, B.R. Joyce and Weil (1986) noted that:

> Teachers could acquire skill by studying the theories of various models of teaching or skills, seeing them demonstrated a number of times (fifteen or twenty. . .), and practicing them about a dozen times with carefully articulated feedback. However, as teachers attempted to use approaches new to them they experienced considerable discomfort. Only a small percentage (about 5 or 10 percent) of the teachers who had learned teaching strategies new to their repertoires were able to handle the discomfort without assistance. Most teachers never tried an unfamiliar strategy at all unless support personnel were available. (p. 438)

The transfer of teaching skills from theory into practice can be improved through a process of mentoring that B.R. Joyce and Showers (1982) call coaching. According to these researchers, peer coaching is a cyclic process that serves five essential functions: It (a) provides companionship, (b) produces technical feedback, (c) extends executive control through analysis of application, (d) helps teachers adapt to diverse students, and (e) provides personal support and facilitation. In some instances, supervisors use a structured observation form to assess the lesson.

Research clearly indicates that the coaching of teaching can enhance transfer of training, and that coached teachers, as compared to uncoached, practice new strategies more often and acquire greater skill after initial training, can more readily apply strategies to their own objectives and teaching styles, show greater retention of theoretical and practical aspects of strategies, are more likely to teach students about purposes of new models and their roles as learners, and have greater understanding of the purposes and applications of teaching strategies (B.R. Joyce & Showers, 1988).

Supervision of student teachers must provide for systematic reinforcement of critical teaching skills that student teachers learn in undergraduate preparation. Initial stages of skill acquisition inherently provide a period of discomfort for the learner regardless of the nature of the skill. Supervisors must provide the novice teacher with a clear description of what is expected and ensure that he or she receives abundant feedback about attaining those objectives. The precise definition of target behaviors in observable forms, combined with objective and data-based feedback, can greatly improve the supervisory process.

Shortcomings in Undergraduate Preparation

Studies of the socialization of teachers demonstrate that undergraduate preparation is "a weak treatment" (Locke, 1983) and "a low impact enterprise" (Lortie, 1975). Teacher preparation fails to substantively impact attitudes toward teaching because training cannot overcome the inertia of competing social influences. Among the proposed reasons for this dilemma are the progressive–traditional shift (Zeichner & Tabachnik, 1981), the apprenticeship of observation (Lortie, 1975), the notion of impression management (Shipman, 1967), occupational socialization (Templin, 1979), the washout effect produced by socializing agents in the school, and the conservative influence of university faculty and programs (Tabachnik, Popkewitz, & Zeichner, 1980).

The progressive–traditional shift occurs as a result of the liberalizing effects of university education, followed by the conservative socializing effects of the public school teaching experience. Teacher educators assume that undergraduate students take on the progressive beliefs about education and then adopt the conservative attitudes of the schools during the induction process. Researchers describe conservative attitudes as custodial, bureaucratic, and conforming, as opposed to humanistic and personalized (Hoy, 1967, 1968, 1969; Hoy & Rees, 1977). Occupational socialization further compounds the traditional shift, as the realities of the student teaching environment influence student teachers to shift their attitudes and behaviors toward occupational norms (Templin, 1979).

Some researchers have challenged these theories of teacher socialization on the basis that university education may have little impact on the liberalization of attitudes, and rather the ''biography'' of experiences that the student brings into the program is of much greater consequence (Lortie, 1975). In this view, teacher socialization occurs primarily in the years before training. The prospective teacher completes an apprenticeship of observation (Lortie, 1975) throughout many years of observation as a student. The attitudes toward education that the student develops during this apprenticeship (biography) are not greatly affected by teacher training. Therefore, the prospective teacher does not adopt the liberal ideas proposed in formal training but merely works at impression management, or the maintenance of a facade, for the duration of the training (Shipman, 1967).

Researchers often overlook the conservative influence of university faculty and teacher preparation programs as a factor in the failure of theory to translate to improved practice. However, the impact of theories espoused by university faculty is severely negated when the theories do not coincide with observable teaching practices. To this end, Locke (1983) contends that teacher education is a ''strong treatment,'' because many ineffective teaching practices are implicitly modeled and reinforced by university professors.

Teacher education programs may be strong treatments which promote precisely the effects commonly observed during the years of induction. The problem is that the really effective forces of teacher education are covert and unintended. At the overt level the trainees are taught to make good use of class time for a maximum of instruction and a minimum of waste. At the covert level, as conveyed by the actions and subtly expressed attitudes of teacher educators, students learn that waste is the norm and while efficient management must be learned, it need not be practiced. (Locke, 1983, p. 43)

In fact, the university may wash out liberalizing effects of teacher preparation and reinforce conservatism (Zeichner & Tabachnik, 1981). Although most studies of teacher socialization have focused on the schools, researchers need to extend this to examine the impact of university preparation. ''The question of how teachers are socialized cannot be addressed adequately without linking the processes of teacher education to on-going patterns of schooling and to the social, economic, and political contexts within which both universities and schools exist'' (Zeichner & Tabachnik, 1981, p. 10). Clearly, teacher educators must put their own houses in order (Rogus & Schuttenberg, 1979) before prescribing major reforms for the public schools.

A 1986 report of the Holmes Group emphasized the need for sweeping reforms in undergraduate teacher preparation. This group of education deans and academic officers from major research institutions in 50 states cited substantial evidence of inadequate professional education. The writers called for improved clinical experiences that ''build upon the general principles and theories emphasized in earlier university study'' (p. 61). We can no longer assume that clinical experiences invariably contribute to improved quality in teaching. Supervisors need comprehensive programs and planned supervisory models to identify and reinforce critical teaching competencies.

The lack of transfer of theory into practice supports the need for substantial improvements in clinical experiences. Two prevailing myths have traditionally supported clinical experiences (Zeichner, 1980). The first myth assumes that ''practical school experience necessarily contributes to the development of better teachers'' (p. 45). In documenting research to the contrary, Zeichner (1980) revealed that these experiences often promote purposes (e.g., rejection of theory and cynicism) that directly oppose the explicit goals of teacher preparation and thus are frequently miseducative. The second prevalent myth is that "teacher education's institutional structures are totally coercive; students passively conform to school bureaucracies and conservative norms" (Zeichner, 1980, p. 46). Pointing to conflicting and ambiguous results from a large body of studies in this area, Zeichner (1980) rejected this "social puppet" view. He found that student teachers are indeed active agents, playing an interactive role in the socializing environment of the school. In dispelling both of these myths, Zeichner concluded that field-based experiences produce a variety of complex consequences, both positive and negative, that may not be readily apparent.

Zeichner strongly endorsed the view that *more* is not *better* in terms of field-based experiences in teacher preparation. Noting the need for additional research, he admonished:

> It is naive to think that we now know all there is to know about field-based experiences, but from the little that we do know, there are definitely decrements indicated by the attitudes, behaviors, and perspectives of student teachers. Consequently, proposals which "solve" problems of teacher education by merely scheduling more student time in classrooms rest upon the apparently untenable assumption that more time spent in that way will automatically make better teachers. (p. 51)

The low impact of undergraduate teacher preparation is further mitigated by the lack of substantive supervision during all phases of teaching (preservice, induction or early years, and inservice). Ultimately, this contributes to the rejection of theory by novice teachers and the widening of the theory/practice gap. Research has clearly documented the existence of a large theory/practice gap (Kelley, 1974; Kelley & Kalenak, 1975; Kelley & Lindsay, 1977, 1980; Kelley & Miller, 1976; Kneer, 1986).

In one series of studies, Kelley and his associates assessed the extent of knowledge obsolescence of coaches, athletic trainers, practicing high school physical educators, and graduating college seniors in physical eduction. Through the use of paper-and-pencil knowledge tests, the researchers found that 85 percent of coaches tested failed to achieve a score of 70 percent in knowledge of training and conditioning (Kelley & Kalenak, 1975); 85 percent of athletic trainers failed the same measure (Kelley & Miller, 1976); more than 75 percent of

high school physical educators fell below competency level in five areas of disciplinary knowledge (Kelley & Lindsay, 1977); and graduating college seniors could not be distinguished from the practicing high school physical educators in terms of the adequacy of their disciplinary knowledge base (Kelley & Lindsay 1980). On the basis of these findings, Kelley & Lindsay (1980) raised the issue of academic credentials versus competence. We cannot assume that attainment of an academic credential (e.g., academic degree or teaching certificate) ensures competence (i.e., acquisition and retention of an adequate knowledge base).

Kneer (1986) illuminated additional causes for concern in her extensive study of the theory/practice gap as it exists in secondary school physical education. She studied a sample of 128 teachers selected from 20 randomly selected Illinois secondary schools to determine their use of recommended practices in six areas (planning, skill practice, teaching approach, communication techniques, evaluation, and teaching/learning environments). Disappointingly, but not unexpectedly, the results showed a large gap between theoretical prescriptions and actual applications of instructional practices. Among the significant findings were that only about 30 percent of the teachers studied used lesson plans; about 64 percent used only a group approach to teaching, whereas only about 4 percent used individualized instruction; and 36 percent rejected recommended practice procedures because they were too time consuming, whereas 29 percent believed they were unnecessary. The good news was that "only 3.57% of the teachers identified 'inability' as a reason for not using these procedures, [and] teachers with high in-service ratings had the smallest theory/practice gap" (Kneer, 1986, p. 105).

Beginning Teachers as Learners: Surviving Transition Shock

The failure of traditional supervision to meet the needs of beginning teachers can be partially attributed to neglect of the unique conditions that new teachers face. Beginning teachers frequently experience a high degree of anticipatory anxiety, heightened dramatically by the transition shock that results from exposure to the school environment. This phenomenon, termed "reality shock" by Veenman (1984), "indicates the collapse of missionary ideals formed during teacher training by the harsh and rude reality of everyday classroom life'' (p. 143). This dissonance may cause changes in behavior, attitude, and perception, or ultimately, exit from the teaching profession.

The empirical literature consistently documents the unique nature of the needs of beginning teachers. In a meta-analysis of 83 studies, Veenman (1984) identified eight areas of concern experienced most often by beginning teachers. These are listed in rank order:

1. Maintaining classroom discipline
2. Motivating students
3. Dealing with individual differences
4. Assessing students' work
5. Maintaining relations with parents
6. Organizing class work
7. Dealing with insufficient materials and supplies
8. Dealing with problems of individual students

The work of Fuller and her colleagues (Fuller, 1969, 1971; Fuller & Bown, 1975; Fuller, Parsons, & Watkins, 1974) contributed greatly to the understanding of developmental aspects of teacher concerns. In her classic Concerns Model, she illustrated changes in the focus of teacher concerns that occur over time. The concerns of beginning teachers center on survival as they strive to determine self-adequacy through the perceptions of administrators and other teachers. More experienced and more effective teachers tend to focus on task impact (student gains), and the determination of adequacy shifts toward self-analysis. Teachers evaluated as superior are primarily absorbed with concerns of student gains.

Given the unique nature of beginning teachers' concerns, and particularly the prevalence of anxiety related to transitional stages of teaching, supervisors need to address these concerns in a planned and comprehensive manner, identifying and organizing critical teaching competencies in the form of logical progressions. This systematic approach to supervision can help to reduce transition shock through attainment of six goals. Systematic supervision

- helps beginning teachers concentrate on one thing at a time, providing a focus while reinforcing a repertoire of skills that the teacher developed in undergraduate programs;
- reduces anxiety by removing the mystery and

providing a clear model of what is expected;
- helps involve and even educate or retrain the cooperating teacher;
- reinforces desired teaching behaviors through systematic, objective, and data-based observation;
- minimizes the rejection of theory and the development of cynicism; and
- reduces the negative effects of transition shock.

Summary and Implications

This chapter has introduced the concept of systematic supervision, outlined a rationale for its use in physical education settings, and proposed a specific Systematic Supervision Model, based on the general concepts of systematic supervision. The Systematic Supervision Model is eclectic and is based on empirical research, theory, and clinical experience. Although developed primarily for use with beginning teachers, the model also provides a framework for conducting structured in-service training for experienced teachers. The model is designed to provide for the systematic reinforcement of effective teaching behaviors that were selected on the basis of empirical support. These behaviors are defined in observable and measurable terms and are presented in the form of planned sequential progressions. Implementation of the model involves the use of systematic observation, completion of structured tasks, and attainment of specific competencies.

Research conducted during the past 2 decades has projected a clearer picture of effective teaching behavior, and researchers have developed hundreds of objective instruments for observing these behaviors. In addition, research has clearly shown that comprehensive supervision can significantly impact the quality of teaching. However, these findings have failed to influence the nature of supervision as it is generally practiced. Failures of traditional supervision, shortcomings of undergraduate preparation, and the rigors of transition shock are dynamically interacting factors that lead beginning teachers to reject theory. Those of us involved in teacher preparation can no longer simply present teaching styles and strategies and hope that these skills will naturally transfer to practice. The Systematic Supervision Model is a comprehensive model with potential for bridging the theory/practice gap.

Chapter 2

An Overview of Generic Models of Supervision

Before we adopt a model of supervision for physical education, we should examine the existing models developed for use in diverse settings and the nature of the theory and practice from which they evolved. The models described in this chapter are generic; they may be applied across subject matter contexts and grade levels. Although they do not consider the unique characteristics of teaching in a movement setting, they all have useful and practical applications that contribute to an eclectic model.

Historical trends in public school supervision in America provide evidence of three theoretical or philosophic thrusts. Scientific management, human relations, and neoscientific management are traditional images of supervision that were popular at times during this century. Conflicting historical accounts make it difficult to see a clear delineation of trends, but we can find some consensus in general terms.

Scientific management (scientific supervision) was ascribed primarily to the 1920s, a period in which the goals of supervision were to develop a research base for effective teaching, to discover "laws" of education, and to help teachers apply these findings (Lucio & McNeil, 1979). Early impetus for the thrust came from organizational theorists who were concerned with industrial efficiency.

Bobbitt (1912, 1913) was one of the first educational theorists to transfer this concern to the schools. This movement arose out of concern for the lack of standards for instruction and confusion about what constitutes best practice. The supervisor's role in this approach was essentially autocratic, and theorists emphasized relationships of control, accountability, and efficiency (Sergiovanni & Starrat, 1979).

Resistance to scientific supervision emerged in the late 1920s, giving rise to a new view of supervisory function. Protests called for a definition of supervision based on democratic principles and the recognition of teachers as individuals. Theorists emphasized developing the teacher as a person instead of manipulating the individual as an object. The supervisor and teacher have an egalitarian relationship in this approach. George Kyte (1930) defined supervision during this era as "the maximum development of the teacher into the most professionally efficient person she is capable of becoming" (p. 45). The resultant trend was popular throughout the 1930s and 1940s and was termed "supervision as democratic human relations" (Lucio & McNeil, 1979, p. 11). Goals of this approach included wider participation in decision making by teachers, cooperative determination of goals, recognition of the feelings and emotions of teachers, and the development of personal satis-factions. Although human relations supervision is still advocated by some theorists, it has failed to gain widespread acceptance or empirical support. Sergiovanni & Starratt (1979) alleged that "human relations promised much but delivered little" (p. 4). They attributed its failure to theoretical short-comings, permissive supervision, and an overem-phasis on winning friends.

A third phase in the development of supervision was launched by the proposal of a revisionist view combining aspects of both scientific management and human relations supervision. Neoscientific management, outlined in the 1967 Association for Supervision and Curriculum Development docu-ment, *Supervision: Perspectives and Propositions* (Lucio, 1967), evolved as a reaction to two concerns. The first was the failure of human relations super-vision to extend its attention to the teacher in the classroom; the second was a desire to return to earlier images of control, accountability, and effi-ciency (Sergiovanni & Starratt, 1979). Neoscientific management emphasized determining objective standards, performance objectives, and competen-cies that could be externally imposed without direct, in-class supervision. This orientation received only transitory attention from a small number of proponents and failed to garner any form of widespread or ongoing support by super-visors.

Clinical Supervision

Despite the abundance of literature generated, none of these theories have produced a compre-hensive model or prescription for supervisory practice. Little evidence suggests that any of the theories, or the writings of their proponents, have significantly impacted either the practice of super-vision or its intended outcome, the improvement of teaching. In documenting this failure, Cogan (1973) noted that traditional supervision has failed to provide consistent support for adapting new teaching strategies. Educational reforms have traditionally failed to provide sufficient levels of understanding and resures for innovation, and therefore implementation efforts are frequently delayed or unsuccessful. Cogan advocated a focus on comprehensive, in-class supervision that pro-vides an ongoing support system for teachers as they try out new behaviors. Cogan endorsed this emphasis on in-class, or *clinical*, supervision "be-

cause the American experience so far indicates that it is in the classroom, at the point of application, that new methods break down" (Cogan, 1973, p. 4).

Development of the Clinical Model

Clinical supervision, generally acknowledged as the best existing practice (Mosher & Purpel, 1972), traces its roots to the mid-1950s work of Morris Co-gan and his associates. In the process of supervis-ing student teachers in Harvard's master of arts in teaching program, Cogan developed the model to provide a powerful system of supervision with potential for significantly improving the quality of teaching. In Cogan's (1973) classic text, he made an important distinction between general super-vision ("supervisory operations that take place principally outside the classroom") and clinical supervision ("focused upon the improvement of the teacher's classroom instruction") (p. 9). Clini-cal supervision focuses on observable teaching be-haviors, instructional content, and student behaviors, and relies heavily on strategies of plan-ning, observing, and analyzing.

The rationale for clinical supervision is based upon several basic assumptions about the nature of teaching and learning. First, clinical supervision assumes that teaching is behavior, that is, "what the teacher does and what the pupils do, observ-ably, in interaction" (Mosher & Purpel, 1972, p. 79.) Second, teaching is inseparable from its results, thus we may study teaching and learning by the in-class collection of data on teacher–student interactions. Third, Cogan posited that teaching behavior is subject to identifiable patterns, and these teaching patterns are linked to the nature of learning that takes place. Finally, clinical supervi-sion assumes that teaching behavior is amenable to understanding and modification, and instruc-tion can be improved through modification of teaching behaviors (Mosher & Purpel, 1972, p. 80).

The effective implementation of clinical super-vision relies upon a positive teacher–supervisor relationship in which the goal is to change behav-ior, as opposed to changing personality, attitudes, and beliefs. The term that best describes this rela-tionship, as defined by Cogan (1973), is *colleague-ship*, a situation in which

> the teacher and clinical supervisor work together as associates and equals, and they are bound together by a common purpose. This purpose is the improvement of students' learning through

the improvement of teacher instruction, and it does not diminish the autonomy and independence the teacher should have. (p. 68)

An essential element of clinical supervision is shared decision making. Throughout the process, the teacher and supervisor jointly determine objectives, content, and methods of instruction; formulate hypotheses about the end results; specify the nature of data to be collected during in-class observations; analyze the data that are obtained; and plan for needed changes as they are identified. In this manner, the teacher and supervisor avoid unilateral decisions and, it is hoped, achieve a greater commitment toward full participation of both parties.

Clinical supervision, as defined by Cogan (1973), consists of a cycle of 8 phases:

Phase 1—Establishing the teacher–supervisor relationship
Phase 2—Planning with the teacher
Phase 3—Planning the strategy of observation
Phase 4—Observing instruction
Phase 5—Analyzing the teaching-learning process
Phase 6—Planning the strategy of the conference
Phase 7—The conference
Phase 8—Renewed planning

The cyclic aspect of the process represents, in Cogan's (1973) view, the developmental (as opposed to episodic or discontinuous) nature of acquiring new teaching skills. The process represents an ongoing commitment of resources and time devoted to the one-to-one interaction of teacher and supervisor, as well as to direct observation of teaching. Continuity of the teacher's development, as well as ample time for the teacher to unlearn and reacquire teaching patterns, is essential. Cogan (1973) rejected "the naive view of educators about what it really takes to improve teaching" (p. 14) and the common practice of providing random, cursory, and isolated classroom visits in the name of supervision.

An equally important, although less frequently acknowledged contribution to the concept of clinical supervision is the 1969 text of Robert Goldhammer, which actually preceded Cogan's work in publication. *Clinical Supervision: Special Methods for the Supervision of Teachers* (Goldhammer, 1969) described a similar model of five stages that the author developed from his work with Cogan at Harvard. Cogan's first 3 phases are encompassed

in Goldhammer's Stage 1, whereas Phases 5 and 6 are incorporated in Stage 3. Goldhammer's model appears as follows:

Stage 1—Preobservation conference
Stage 2—Observation
Stage 3—Analysis and Strategy
Stage 4—Supervision conference
Stage 5—Postconference analysis ("postmortem")

In a second edition of the text, revised by colleagues after Goldhammer's death, the authors made an effort to strengthen the conceptual basis for clinical supervision (Goldhammer, Anderson, & Krajewski, 1980). This change was a response to criticisms that appeared in the literature related to the original Cogan-Goldhammer models and their general failure to impact the practice of supervision in public schools (Harris, 1976; Hoy & Forsyth, 1986; Sergiovanni, 1976). In this edition the authors expanded upon the concepts of clinical supervision as distinguished from the process or method. They described clinical supervision as a subset of general supervision, and affirmed the appropriateness of the clinic as the classroom. In expanding the conceptual background, they identified nine characteristics associated with clinical supervision: It

- serves as a technology for improving instruction;
- acts as a deliberate intervention with the instructional process;
- is goal oriented, combining school and personal growth needs;
- assumes a working relationship between teachers and supervisors;
- requires mutual trust, as reflected in understanding, support, and commitment for growth;
- is systematic, yet requires a flexible and continuously changing methodology;
- creates productive tension for bridging the real–ideal gap;
- assumes the supervisor knows more about instruction and learning than the teachers; and
- requires training for the supervisor.

Collectively, these characteristics describe the clinical aspects of supervision as a teaching function.

In essence, the models of clinical supervision described by Cogan and Goldhammer are similar. They share the common elements of collegiality, collaboration, skilled service, and ethical conduct

(Garman, 1982) in a cycle of continuous support. Both of the models acknowledge that teaching is observable behavior, and they extensively use systematic observation instruments in the collection and analysis of data related to classroom events.

One of the systems used most frequently in clinical supervision is the Flanders Interaction Analysis System (FIAS) (Flanders, 1970). This system categorizes teacher verbal behaviors as indirect influence (accepting feelings, praising or encouraging, accepting or using ideas of students, asking questions) or direct influence (lecturing, giving directions, criticizing or justifying authority) in relation to student behaviors (responding, initiating). In a comprehensive discussion, Flanders (1976) elaborated on the use of interaction analysis in clinical supervision. Interaction analysis lends itself naturally to the process, because it involves the quality of human interactions occurring within the classroom context and allows an examination of the relationship between teaching patterns and classroom events. Ultimately, it seeks to help the teacher modify teaching patterns to accomplish self-selected goals.

An Extension of the Clinical Model

A model that has come to be associated with the term *clinical supervision* is Madeline Hunter's (1982) work on clinical instruction of teaching. The Hunter model describes essential elements of teaching and supervision as follows: selecting objectives at the correct level of difficulty, teaching to those objectives, monitoring student progress, adjusting teaching, and using principles of learning. The model includes a process of supervision to help teachers use seven essential elements of teaching and to ensure that supervisors provide feedback, reinforcement, and prescriptions for achieving and maintaining desired levels of performance (Pavan, 1985). Hunter presents these seven elements (anticipatory set, objective and purpose, input, modeling, checking for understanding, guided practice, and independent practice) as ''a basic white sauce of teaching'' (Hunter, 1984).

A major premise of this clinical theory of instruction is that the teacher is a decision maker (Hunter, 1985). Teaching involves an ongoing process of decision making regarding content, learner behavior, and teacher behavior, for which the ultimate goal is increasing the probability of learning (Hunter, 1982). The model, therefore, is designed to provide *propositional knowledge* (research-based generalizations about teaching behaviors that affect learning), *procedural knowledge* (ability to translate knowledge into procedures) and *conditional knowledge* (knowing when and why to apply the proposition). Hunter believes that this model is generic (applicable to all subject matter contexts, teaching styles, and learner characteristics) and encompasses all decisions that a teacher must make.

In a substantial deviation from the generic clinical model, Hunter (1986) recommended elimination of the preobservation conference. She believes that this process is unnecessary in current practice, because research provides a clear focus of cause–effect relationship in teaching and learning. In addition, she contends that the preobservation conference may be counterproductive because it creates biases in both the teacher and the observer.

Hunter (1984) provided three alternative frameworks for evaluating the design and implementation of instruction. One, the analysis of decisions in teaching, examines the nature of teacher decisions related to content, learner behavior, and teacher behavior decisions. A supervisor might question, for example, whether the selected content is at an appropriate level of difficulty for the learner, whether the learner's behavior is likely to produce the desired results, and whether the teacher appropriately applies learning principles to promote learning. A second framework, the analysis of lesson design, examines the lesson with respect to the seven essential elements (anticipatory set, objective and purpose, input, modeling, checking for understanding, guided practice, closure, and independent practice). The third proposed alternative for analyzing performance is the Teaching Appraisal for Instructional Improvement Instrument (TAIII), a process that involves the use of script tapes (anecdotal records of events that transpire in the lesson, recorded in temporal order). The instrument describes teacher decisions and behaviors (to help the supervisor identify productive behaviors), self-analysis of teaching, remediation, and evaluative conferences. The supervisor uses data from the observation to address the following questions (Hunter, 1984):

- Are teacher and learner effort and energy directed to learning?
- Is the learning objective at the correct level of difficulty for these students?
- Does the teacher monitor students' learning and adjust teacher and learner behaviors as a result of information revealed?
- Does the teacher use principles of learning effectively?
- How will the observer help the teacher to continue to grow?

Hunter (1985) cautioned against a number of abuses of her model that can result from incomplete understanding of its intent. The first abuse occurs when supervisors expect all seven elements of effective supervision to be present in every lesson. Hunter rejected this "white sauce recipe" conception, observing that teachers may select or omit elements to match specific learning objectives. A second abuse is the idea that more is better, which can result in the supervisor giving undue attention to measures of time spent in effective teaching behaviors. "Frequency counts are no more useful to teachers than to doctors. The number of times pills or surgery are prescribed cannot tell you if a doctor is making valid medical decisions" (Hunter, 1985, p. 59). Other abuses of the model include judging teacher decisions without full understanding of their objectives, expecting too much too soon, promoting the model at the level of teacher training before adequately educating central administrators, and inadequately training the staff at all levels.

A number of additional models of clinical supervision incorporate the basic Cogan-Goldhammer processes. In addition, a substantial amount of research has been conducted to determine the efficacy of clinical supervision in achieving its major purpose. These studies are summarized in chapter 3 of this text.

Supervision as Counseling

In contrast to clinical supervision, which seeks to improve instruction by focusing on the in-class behaviors of teachers (what the teacher does), counseling models of supervision share the goals of improved instruction achieved by promoting teacher self-growth and self-knowledge (what the teacher is). These models focus on the personality dimensions of teaching and are thus concerned primarily with feelings, attitudes, and values. Proponents of counseling models of supervision assume that the relationship between the student and the teacher is the most critical factor in learning. Consequently, the processes involved in supervision as counseling take place primarily outside the classroom. The relationship between supervisor and supervisee is equated to that of counselor and client.

Counseling techniques employed in supervision models include Rogerian therapy (C.R. Rogers, 1959, 1961), ego-therapy (Hummel, 1962), and Gestalt counseling (Nisenholz & McCarty, 1976).

The literature regarding application of counseling in general is considerably sparse, consisting essentially of one classic theory, a handful of empirical articles, and several theoretical articles offering general guidelines for enhancing personal development. Dussault (1970), a noted advocate of counseling models, described a middle-range theory of supervision for teacher education programs based on Rogerian principles, "middle-range" in that the theory deals only with supervision as teaching, as distinguished from the evaluative function. Dussault analyzed the similarities and differences between therapy and supervision in order to determine which elements should be transferred.

Rogerian Therapy

In addressing the supervision of student teachers, Dussault (1970) proposed that the supervisory conference should emphasize the development of congruence, empathy, and reciprocal positive regard. Specifically, it is essential to establish five conditions in order to facilitate changes in the personalities (and ultimately, the behaviors) of supervisees. These conditions are as follows (Dussault, 1970):

- The supervisor and supervisee are in contact.
- The supervisor is congruent in his or her relationship with the supervisee.
- The supervisor experiences unconditional positive regard toward the supervisee.
- The supervisor empathizes with the supervisee's internal frame of reference.
- The student teacher perceives, at least to a minimal degree, Conditions 3 and 4, the unconditional positive regard of the supervisor, and the empathetic understanding of the supervisor.

Dussault (1970) then hypothesized, in 17 statements, predicted changes in the supervisee's personality and behavior: The supervisee

- becomes more congruent (or, equivalently, more open to experience, less defensive);
- approaches optimum psychological adjustment;
- perceives his or her own professional activities and teaching performances more objectively and realistically;
- perceives that his or her ideal teaching self is more realistic and more achievable;
- perceives that his or her ideal self is more realistic and more achievable;
- perceives that his or her teaching self is more congruent with his or her ideal teaching self;

- perceives that his or her self is more congruent with his or her ideal self;
- has fewer professional fears and apprehensions;
- has less anxiety;
- has an increased degree of positive regard for himself or herself as a teacher;
- has an increased degree of positive self-regard;
- perceives other persons in the professional environment more realistically and accurately;
- more easily accepts other persons in the professional environment, having in particular more positive regard toward pupils;
- more easily accepts others in general;
- in making and evaluating professional decisions and choices resorts more often to the judgments and values of other members of the profession;
- changes teaching behaviors in various ways, limiting imitations of the supervisor's practices and methods and moving toward a more idiosyncratic style; and
- develops a teaching behavior that is more creative, more flexible, more uniquely adaptive to each new situation and each new problem.

Dussault (1970) further specified 22 dependent variables that will be affected if these conditions are established and continued throughout the supervisory process. These include

congruence, openness to experience, defensiveness, psychological adjustment, perception of one's own professional activities, perception of one's own teaching performance, ideal-teaching-self, ideal self, teaching-self, self, professional fears and apprehensions, anxiety, esteem for the self-as-teacher, self-esteem, perception of the other persons in the professional environment, acceptance of others in professional environment, positive attitudes toward pupils, acceptance of others, professional self-evaluation, professional self-decision making, teaching behavior, and creative teaching behavior.[1] (pp. 198-199)

Gestalt Counseling

Nisenholz and McCarty (1976) propose Gestalt counseling as an alternative technique in the supervision of student teachers. This approach also assumes that student teachers should be treated as individual, adult learners who are capable of learning from their experiences. The researchers deemed the counseling approach most important

during student teaching because it is often a period of "peak anxiety." Gestalt counseling helps the clients (supervisees) develop awareness of their own behavior patterns (gestalts) and assume responsibility for their own solutions.

Wolfe (1973) attempted to translate theory into practice within the counseling supervision mode by developing a series of activities for the cognitive and affective training of student teachers. His goal was to achieve confluence in teacher preparation through a blending of cognitive and humanistic education. Among the guidelines he suggested for affective training are

- confronting anxiety and anger,
- making education meaningful (e.g., extending relevance through weekly seminars and meetings on pertinent topics), and
- encouraging innovation.

To effectively use counseling models, the supervisor must acquire effective skills for dialogic communication. Blumberg (1977) defined the supervisor as an "interpersonal interventionist" and advocated the development of a "supportive interpersonal climate which allows the authentic 'reaching out' to the teacher as a person" (p. 23). Research findings indicate that when supervision is carried out in such a climate, teachers are more satisfied with and derive greater benefit from the process. Blumberg (1974, 1980) expanded upon his philosophies in a text that focused on dyadic relationships of the supervisor and teacher in inservice contexts.

Blumberg and Cusick (1970) reported an analysis of supervisory conferences that showed a low incidence of supportive climates. Using an interaction analysis instrument developed for this purpose (Blumberg, 1970), the investigators analyzed the audiotaped verbal interactions of supervisors and teachers in 50 separate conferences. Categories for supervisor teacher behavior reflected 10 kinds of verbalization (support-inducing communications, praising, accepting or using teacher ideas, asking for information, giving information, asking for opinions, asking for suggestions, giving opinions, giving suggestions, criticizing). Researchers coded teacher verbalizations in 15 similar categories. Analysis showed that supervisor talk comprised 45 percent of total conference time, teacher talk contributed 53 percent, and 2 percent was spent in silence or confusion. Supervisors also gave information five times as often as they solicited it and exhibited direct to indirect behaviors at a proportion of 0.65. The investigators concluded, "Supervisor-teacher interaction seems to be pretty much of a 'telling' affair, with the bulk of the supervisor's behavior being the giving of information'' (Blumberg & Cusick, 1970, p. 132).

Beatty (1977) addressed some general guidelines for implementing humanistic supervision in an essay that identified requisite knowledge, skills, and attitudes. Foremost among the essential competencies is the need for supervisors to be "dialogic rather than monologic communicators'' (p. 226). Beatty characterized the monologic communicator as one who works to exert power and influence over others (telling, controlling), while the dialogic communicator demonstrates unconditional positive regard, love, directness, genuineness, empathy, equality, and involvement. Dialogic communication is a critical element in establishing a growth-oriented environment for teachers and supervisors.

Ego-Therapy

A third counseling technique is ego-therapy or ego-counseling. Ego-analysis extends the psychoanalytic theories of Freud by considering the environmental influences of behavior (George & Cristiani, 1986). As applied to supervision, ego-therapy entails a collaborative relationship between supervisor and supervisee, with an emphasis on identifying defense mechanisms and coping positively with the school environment and personal needs.

Impact of Counseling-Based Supervision Models

With the exception of sensitizing the supervisor to the importance of interpersonal skills, the previously described literature does little to provide a clear, working model for the application of counseling models of supervision. This shortcoming has limited the general utility of these models to a small bit of "lip service" and little enduring value.

Peer Supervision

The peer supervision model extends the concept of human development by removing the hierarchical relationship, resulting in a new definition of collegiality. The responsibility for professional- and self-

development is shifted to teachers working in collaborative roles. This approach seeks to overcome the barriers of isolation imposed by the school environment, in a sense moving back the walls to allow teachers to experience "the view from next door'' (Bang-Jensen, 1986). The concept of peer supervision gained some momentum from a 1971 publication of the Association of Teacher Educators entitled *The Teaching Clinic: A Team Approach to the Improvement of Instruction* (Olsen, 1971). Theory and practice in this area are presently quite underdeveloped (Alfonso & Goldsberry, 1982), but some of the identified advantages merit consideration here.

Traditional supervision consists of little more than sporadic and unplanned visits and often provides little or no feedback. Alfonso and Goldsberry (1982) provided a graphic description of this problem:

> In many school systems, formal feedback on teaching performance may come no more than once a year and then in a quite perfunctory way. One of the tragedies of American education is that teachers work in isolation. Their immediate superiors often have only a rather generalized perception of their teaching performance. Teaching is still largely a solo act, observed, appreciated, and evaluated primarily by students. There is little contact among colleagues, classroom doors are seldom opened to each other, and teachers who are members of the same staff in the same school, even in the same grade or discipline, maintain a collusive and almost deliberate ignorance of the work of their peers. It is essential that such barriers be broken down and that teachers feel responsible for improving their instruction and for assisting their colleagues in their own self-improvement; this concept characterizes other professions. Although there is little contact or mutual responsibility among teachers, studies still show that teachers report other colleagues to be their first source of professional help, even when supervisory assistance is available. (p. 92)

Valerie Bang-Jensen (1986) outlined a number of factors that facilitate peer collaboration. She related these advantages to her personal experiences as a peer supervisor in the implementation of a writing program. First, the peer supervisor should be an expert in the given subject matter whose authority is based solely on the colleague's perception that the peer supervisor can help. Second, the supervisory processes should be initiated by the colleague or colleagues who wish to benefit, as opposed to being externally imposed; self-initiated improvement provides a considerably greater likelihood that real change will occur. Third, the peer supervisor must have empathy, credibility, and a clear understanding of the colleague's working conditions. Fourth, the peer supervisor must be provided release time and ample opportunity for in-class contacts. Last, the peer supervisor should focus on instructional improvement and should entirely omit evaluation.

Critics of peer supervision doubt its sufficiency as an operational model for supervision. Alfonso and Goldsberry (1982) theorized that this insufficiency is due in part to the loose definition of peer supervision, or the lack of differentiation between peer supervision (formal and authoritative function) and colleagueship in supervision (supportive function). The spectrum of possible functions of peer supervisors ranges from informal participation in limited aspects of supervision to full responsibility for the evaluation of teaching effectiveness. To the extent that supervision connotes formal responsibilities and authoritative function, peer supervision and colleague supervision are contradictory terms. Supervision in the pure sense involves superordinate–subordinate relationships, which do not exist in peer supervision. Alfonso and Goldsberry (1982) did, however, endorse the use of peer supervision as an adjunct to formal supervision (professional development resources). They cited three major advantages of colleagueship. First, it maximizes the use of human resources within the school toward the end of improved instruction. Second, it acknowledges that teachers can contribute substantively to these efforts, thereby deriving motivating factors of recognition, responsibility, and achievement. These factors are particularly important in increasing job satisfaction and fending off impending burnout. Lastly, colleagueship increases the likelihood of instructional innovations because it improves working relationships and enhances professional efficacy.

To successfully implement peer supervision in any form, educators must overcome some very pervasive obstacles. First, the physical barriers of the classroom and the lack of interaction among teachers present challenges. "If teachers are to be resources in a program of instructional supervision, barriers of time and distance and the tradition of privacy will have to be overcome" (Alfonso & Goldsberry, 1982, p. 103). Physical fragmentation may be more counterproductive at the secondary school level, where the departmental structure area is more delineated. A second obstacle is the

nature of teacher interactions within schools. The school climate fosters competition and mistrust, yet effective peer supervision requires a great deal of sharing, openness, and trust (Alfonso, 1977). Lastly, administrative barriers may pose problems in the form of collective bargaining restrictions or the resistance of supervisors in giving up their turf (Alfonso, 1977; Alfonso & Goldsberry, 1982).

In interpreting the scant amount of available literature, we can safely conclude that peer supervision as an adjunct to formal supervision can make valuable contributions to the overall process. We should note a further distinction in the ways in which peer supervision takes an evaluative function. Research indicates that peer evaluations lack sufficient reliability for use as summative evaluation and are subject to a positive bias that further contributes to this lack of reliability (French-Lazovik, 1981). Thus, peer supervision might be best directed at formative evaluation efforts (improving instruction) as opposed to summative evaluation (making decisions about merit, tenure, and promotion).

Self-Analysis in Supervision

An extension of increased autonomy in supervision is the self-analysis approach. The literature regarding this approach is extremely thin, and it consists essentially of a small number of studies and programs describing efforts to engage teachers in the processes of reflection and self-analysis. Self-analysis does not exist as a supervisory model per se, but rather as a loose concept of introspective processes. In fact, "self-analysis supervision" is probably a misnomer, because it is virtually impossible to initiate an analytical approach to one's own teaching without the help of some guiding principles or an individual with specific expertise (i.e., a facilitator). However, if we accept the basic notion that teachers are capable of independent learning and can best commit themselves to improved teaching when they make decisions independently, then the concept is worthy of continued investigation.

The rationale for self-supervision was concisely summarized by Dillon-Peterson (1986):

Almost all teachers and administrators care about students and genuinely want them to be capable adults who will live satisfying lives.

Given encouragement and appropriate opportunity, almost all educators want to continue learning how to do their work more effectively and will work enthusiastically toward that end.

Because teachers tend to teach as they were taught, significant change is difficult, but it can be facilitated through their own personal analysis, determination of direction, and commitment to specific efforts that are supported over time with adequate resources.

Teachers have much undifferentiated knowledge about how to accomplish improvement goals. They need the opportunity to reflect, focus, and plan with adequate human, financial, and time-resource support in order to draw on this knowledge.

Significant behavior change is most likely to occur when it is introduced, practiced, and self-critiqued in the context of the work situation and applied to real problems with appropriate outside support as needed.

Effective, long-term change results most often in relation to an effective planning process rather than in relation to isolated, miscellaneous, short-term activities, however interesting and pertinent they may be.

There are within any school district however small, staff development resources, primarily within the individuals themselves, to solve almost any instructional problem.

Adults learn better when they are treated as autonomous decision makers.

A self-developed or self-selected structure for identifying direction and assessing needs usually provides a better basis for substantive improvement than one that is imposed from outside. (pp. 34-35)

Dillon-Peterson (1986) concluded her argument with this:

The power lies in having those who must actually work to solve the problem describe and own both the problem and its solution and to rejoice in that solution. Basically, it comes down to a philosophical question: Do we trust each other to be true professionals, or don't we?[2] (p. 35)

Although self-analysis remains a relatively unexplored model of supervision, the literature thus far supports its utility as a further adjunct to formal supervision. Self-analysis is a desirable component of supervision because it fosters introspection, increased understanding, and commitment.

Proponents of self-analysis believe that people learn best by thoughtful analysis of their own behaviors, and that self-initiated changes are most likely to succeed. Continued application of self-analysis models of supervision through the development of practical models and empirical investigation should yield positive results.

Competency-Based Supervision

All of the previously described models of supervision (clinical, counseling, peer, and self-analysis) are similar in that the teacher is the primary focus of observation. Supervisory effectiveness is evaluated by its ability to produce changes in the behaviors or affective qualities of teachers, changes that we assume transfer to improved teaching. A contrasting approach to supervision is the competency-based or performance-based model, which employs as its measure of effectiveness observable changes in teacher behavior and student performance. Theoretically, this model is linked to social learning theory and behavioral psychology.

Competency-based supervision evolved naturally out of the 1970s movement toward competency-based education (CBE) and competency-based teacher education (CBTE). The emphasis on performance assessment was shaped largely by two cultural trends of that decade: accountability and personalization (Houston, 1974). A concise definition provided by Houston and Howsam (1972) illustrates the incorporation of these needs:

Competency based instruction is a simple, straightforward concept with the following characteristics: (a) specification of learner objectives in behavioral terms; (b) specification of the means for determining whether performance meets the indicated criterion levels; (c) provision of one or more modes for instruction pertinent to the objectives, through which the learning activities may take place; (d) public sharing of the objectives, criteria, means of assessment, and alternative activities; (e) assessment of the learning experience in terms of competency criteria; (f) placement on the learner of the accountability for meeting the criteria. Other concepts and procedures—such as modularized packaging, the systems approach, educational technology, and guidance and management support—are employed as means in implementing the competency based commitment. For the most part, these contributory concepts are related to individualization. (pp. 5-6)

In the context of teacher education or supervision, the measure of program effectiveness is observable teacher behavior. Teaching acts are viewed as observable performances of skill in matching perceptions, interpretations, and decisions to intended effects (F.J. McDonald, 1974). Teaching competence, therefore, requires that the teacher possess a broad repertoire of strategies and the ability to apply them to dynamic contexts. This definition does not preclude unique applications, because competence is construed as situational (contextual) (Houston, 1974). The following hypotheses summarize the situational qualities of teacher competence:

(1) While a competency core may exist, the varied teacher personalities, styles, and stances preclude definitions of a single set of requirements for all teachers; and (2) the more a person is proficient as a teacher, the more likely his or her professional style is to be unique. (pp. 36-37)

In his 1971 text, *Toward Accountable Teachers*, McNeil proposed a prescriptive model of supervision based on competency or performance assessment. His rationale for that approach took on a quality slightly different from the generic definition of competency-based education. Noting the inadequacy of the research base in teacher effectiveness, the author observed that "it is even doubtful that there exists a single variable of instruction that applies to all teaching for all pupils, in all subject matters and for all objectives" (p. 25). Consequently, he advocated a focus on student achievement (student gain) as a measure of teacher competence. An added qualification of this model is that criteria of teacher effectiveness should reflect the integrated goals and direction of the district, the school, and the teacher.

McNeil's (1971) model, termed Supervision by Objectives, is a behavioral approach to evaluating teacher effectiveness. Two basic assumptions are essential to the rationale for this model. First, it is assumed that "learning is evidenced by a change in behavior," and it is impossible to determine when learning has occurred without observing behavior. "Second, teaching is only successful when the instructor's predetermined and intentional change in the learner actually occurs" (p. 36). An important aspect of Supervision by Objectives is the prior determination of goals and performance objectives. This process helps to establish con-

gruency between the role expectations of supervisors and teachers and the integration of external (supervisor) and internal (teacher) control. McNeil (1971) summarized the rationale for joint planning of objectives as follows:

Learning theory and empirical data support the view that when there are clear statements of objectives learning is more efficient and objectives are attained more readily. Differences in objectives between supervisor and teacher are resolved before instruction under the contract plan, in contrast to those situations where teachers have been successful in producing changes in learners (have been successful teachers) but have failed their ratings as teachers because the supervisor did not concur in the desirability of the results produced. The teacher and supervisor become partners in the enterprise. Advice and suggestions from the supervisor are then valued by the teacher, because they are related to the teacher's own desired changes in learners. When there is no agreement on goals, suggestions from supervisors tend to be viewed as irrelevant, as the supervisor's personal impositions upon the teacher. (pp. 36-37)

Four phases of supervision for the improvement of instruction are preobservation, observation, analysis and strategy, and postobservation. In the preobservation conference, the supervisor and teacher agree on what learner behaviors are to be achieved, what evidence will indicate achievement of those objectives, and what the role of the supervisor is to be in classroom observations. Observation entails the recording of pupil–teacher interactions within the classroom. The analysis and strategy phase requires looking at the results in terms of stated objectives and then planning for modifications as needed. In the postobservation conference, the teacher and supervisor compare attained to desired results, develop new objectives, and design new teaching strategies.

Summary and Implications

Collectively, five generic models of supervision have produced a voluminous amount of literature during the past 20 years: These models are clinical supervision, supervision as counseling, peer supervision, self-analysis, and competency-based supervision. The generic models reflect varying degrees of theoretical and empirical support as well as practical utility. Clinical supervision has garnered the greatest amount of attention in the literature but does not contribute significantly to the general practice of supervision in the public schools. There is a need for an eclectic model that combines the desirable features of each, a model that is planned, comprehensive, systematic, collaborative, analytical, and empirically based. Further, that model should reflect the unique demands of teaching within a movement setting.

Chapter 3

A Review of Research on Supervisory Effectiveness

A great deal of recent research tests the merits of specific supervisory models and describes and evaluates the status of general supervisory practices as they exist. Of the generic models described in chapter 2, clinical and peer clinical supervision have received the greatest research focus. In summarizing this vast knowledge base, we come to two general conclusions. First, any planned, structured, and comprehensive model can potentially produce definitive improvements in teacher effectiveness and student achievement. Supervision can achieve positive results, provided that the selected model involves formative evaluation, direct (in class) observation, clear objectives, precise feedback, joint decision making, and follow-up. Second, this level of comprehensive supervision is not the norm, and teachers are continually evaluated on the basis of sporadic visits and subjective criteria.

Traditional supervisory practices provide few opportunities for feedback, and that which is provided is often vague and unhelpful. These practices are not positively perceived by preservice, student, beginning, or experienced teachers. Results of one survey revealed that 80 percent of teachers surveyed received only one in-class supervisory visit every 2 or 3 years, followed by a subjective and nebulous rating (McCarty, Kaufman, & Stafford, 1986). The words of one teacher were particularly descriptive: "I could care less what the principal says. He doesn't spend enough time in my classroom to know what is going on" (p. 352).

The inadequacy of traditional supervision, as aptly described by Goldsberry (1984), results primarily from insufficient time and insufficient understanding of the mechanics of comprehensive models:

> When . . . scarce time is parceled out over the many teachers to be supervised, the observations frequently resemble polaroid snapshots— single perspectives, frozen in time, often posed, and seemingly objective, but actually depending on the photographer's ability to frame, focus, aim the camera in the proper direction, and capture relevant background. (p. 12)

Despite the potential benefits of comprehensive supervision models, little strong evidence indicates that these models consistently produce measurable gains. Although research demonstrates that administrators, supervisors, and teachers can be trained to follow the processes of given models, there is little documentation of substantial differences in products. The real test for any model is whether it can produce verifiable increases in teacher effectiveness or student learning. The research, despite its abundance, demonstrates that not one of the comprehensive models is a panacea, and none can boast definitive evidence of its utility or link its application strongly to increased learning. All of the models require of the supervisor substantial time, training, and commitment in order to be successful.

This chapter summarizes research in order to identify general guidelines for effective implementation of supervision; the chapter also reviews evidence of support and rejection of the existing models. In selection of a model for implementation, we must consider the following criteria identified by Thompson (1979):

> The model must be based on a sound theory of education. It must provide teachers with latitude for decision making. Its philosophy must be congruous to professional treatment of teachers. To expect any measurable degree of success, the process must be acceptable to those receiving the supervision. Its operational implementation must be feasible for teachers in the field, and not limited in practicality to preservice programs. Finally, the supervision model must be supported by results of research. (p. 3)

This review provides an overview of current research efforts to document the utility of clinical supervision, peer supervision, self-analysis, and competency-based supervision. Because a research base for the counseling model of supervision is virtually nonexistent, this model is not included in the review. The review does include research related to supervision of student teachers, supervision in physical education, and general supervisory practices. The discussion is based on a comprehensive review of the literature conducted over the past 10 years, especially dissertations, studies, and research papers completed between 1984 and 1989.

Research on Clinical Supervision

This model has unequivocably captured the focus of attention of supervision research, both theoretical and empirical, during the past decade. Proponents have described it as the "best practice in in-service education" (Hutson, 1981, p. 1) and the "optimum approach to supervision" (Lerch, 1982, p. 238). It has been widely implemented across grade levels and content areas throughout the United States and around the world. McFaul & Cooper (1984, p. 6) suggested that "the clinical supervision model, with its emphasis on collegial analysis of observational data, seems to have face validity in teachers' eyes and offers the potential of raising teachers' awareness levels." However, the model suffers from a number of practical limitations and a weak research base.

Two reasons for its popularity, despite the absence of empirical support, are its spirit and form. Clinical supervision is attractive because of its democratic spirit and its focus on collaborative decision making. Also, its clearly defined and concrete observation and analysis techniques are appealing (McFaul & Cooper, 1984 p. 5).

On the basis of the available literature, we can conclude that clinical supervision is a theoretically well developed model but is often inadequately implemented. It offers the advantages of emphasis on collegiality, human relations, data-based observations, clear and concrete stages, and prompt feedback. However, it suffers from some serious limitations and has little value unless implementation is well developed and well directed. Clinical supervision is an expensive and time-consuming process, requiring that supervisors and staff are extensively trained and able to provide frequent observations and conferences. Acheson and Gall (1987) recommend that in order to achieve substantial improvements in instructional effectiveness, each teacher complete at least six cycles of clinical supervision each year. This makes it difficult for school districts to meet the budgetary and staffing demands required for implementation.

Implementation of the Clinical Model

Researchers cannot clearly document that clinical supervision, in the comprehensive format defined originally by Goldhammer and Cogan, is extensively practiced. McFaul and Cooper (1984) alleged that the model is preached more than practiced. One survey of urban teachers showed that only 15 percent had any experience with clinical supervision (Cawelti & Reavis, 1980). Another survey showed that 20 percent of a surveyed group were supervised by a clinical model (McCarty, Kaufman, & Stafford, 1986). Clinical supervision in its true form seems to be highly acclaimed but seldom practiced (McFaul & Cooper, 1984).

A number of studies show that teachers and administrators favor the concepts of clinical supervision but that the actual implementation falls short. Most of the literature that describes implementation efforts involves work with preservice and student teachers carried out in university programs, and a limited amount of literature deals with public school settings. Supervisors can generally perform the cycles required in clinical supervision but complete the various subprocesses (e.g., developing preobservation contracts, analyzing data, and generating alternative solutions in postobservation conferences) with varying degrees of comprehensiveness and quality. Extensive inservice training is required to ensure that supervisors understand all of the concepts and processes required of clinical supervision (Goldsberry, 1984).

Sullivan noted in her 1980 review that both the quantity and quality of research on clinical supervision were insufficient to support any general conclusions at that time. In summarizing the results of 13 studies, she noted a number of design weaknesses that limit generalizability and tentatively indicated that the model is valid and can potentially make positive contributions.

Empirical Support for Clinical Supervision

The current research base in support of clinical supervision is considerably more substantial, but not more definitive. A review of doctoral dissertations and published studies completed between 1984 and 1989 revealed 26 studies (primarily doctoral dissertations) dealing specifically with clinical supervision in its original form and 10 devoted to Hunter's Instructional Skills and Clinical Supervision method. The scope of these included the concepts, processes, and products of clinical supervision. In addition, a host of theoretical articles described varying levels of success with implementation efforts, or argued for or against its merits. Following is a synthesis of the most salient findings.

Recent studies of clinical supervision have used a variety of research designs, including descriptive, survey, correlational, and applied behavior analysis, as well as naturalistic methods and experimental comparison. Subjects included principals, supervisors, department coordinators, teachers at all levels (elementary through community college), elementary school students, student teachers, and cooperating teachers. The investigations assessed (a) attitudes, perceptions, and affects; (b)

changes in behaviors or outcomes; (c) applications with student teachers; (d) factors related to implementation; and (e) workshop evaluations. These studies provide a mixed picture of the merits of clinical supervision, with some studies supporting and others negating its values.

Studies focusing on affective dimensions of clinical supervision show that it is generally well received by principals (Deakin, 1986), teachers (Bartlett, 1987; Chamberlain, 1988; Foley, 1987; Kamiya, 1986; G.R. Smith, 1985; Steinhaus, 1987), and student teachers (Berg, Harders, Malian, & Nagel, 1986; Whitehead, 1984). However, it is likely that teachers and principals would be more comfortable with almost any structured model than with the random supervisory practices that typically prevail. Thus the question seems not to be whether principals and teachers like it, but whether it works.

Research has produced some fragmented and conflicting findings relative to the value of clinical supervision. Limited evidence shows that clinical supervision can modify the supervisory practices of principals (L.A. Anderson, 1987; Holodick, 1989; Kopecky, 1986). One study that examined the impact of clinical supervision on the instructional behaviors of teachers found no significant changes (Gibson, 1986). With respect to producing significant changes in student achievement, the jury is still out. Two experimental comparisons found little impact of clinical supervision on student outcomes; one involved second grade students (Young 1986) and the other community college students (Andreotti, 1987).

The primary difficulty in investigating the impact of this model has been ensuring a full and comprehensive implementation of the model and its components. Young's (1986) description of a treatment condition indicated a weakness in the design. She notes that time constraints allowed only one preobservation conference per teacher, and teachers received between two and four cycles of observation and conferencing. Theoretically, one cycle equals a single completion of the established phases of clinical supervision. This raises the question of whether the cycles of clinical supervision Young observed were adequately planned and implemented to provide a true test of the model. Note, Acheson and Gall (1987) recommended that teachers complete a minimum of six clinical supervision cycles in order to produce change.

A similar question remains of whether the clinical model studied by Andreotti (1987) was adequately implemented. The clinical supervision treatment in this study consisted of four 20-minute observations and four postobservation conferences. No preobservation conferences were conducted. Based on this limited research base, we can make no definitive conclusions about the relationship of clinical supervision to student achievement.

It seems that principals, in-service teachers, and preservice teachers value the general constructs of clinical supervision. However, implementing this model requires extensive in-service training and a great commitment of time. The model may indeed be preached more than practiced, and typical applications may not entail the full scope of the recommended cycles. These shortcomings apparently have reduced the impact of clinical supervision on teacher and student outcomes and have compromised the designs of studies that examine these relationships.

Specific Applications of the Hunter Supervision Model

A number of investigations target Hunter's model for specific application in supervisory settings. This clinical supervision model provides three alternatives for evaluating teaching: analysis of decisions in teaching, analysis of lesson design, and use of the Teaching Appraisal for Instructional Improvement Instrument. Pavan (1985) synthesized a number of studies in schools using comparative measures, dividing her discussion into effects of training and student achievement. She reported three studies of training in Hunter's Instructional Skills and Clinical Supervision method, in which researchers provided varying degrees of support. Use of Hunter's clinical supervision by four elementary principals seemed to be related to the use of her instructional model (R.M.G. Joyce, 1982). Saldana (1983) noted small differences between knowledge scores for educational concepts of teachers and administrators trained in the Hunter system and those who were untrained. Gerald (1984) reported evidence that teachers and principals trained in the Hunter model reported increased knowledge and skills; principals recorded more criterion-based observations on written teacher evaluations following the training.

In interpreting the research on the Hunter model and student achievement, Pavan (1985) recognized the difficulties inherent in controlling for a host of extraneous variables. Of the four studies included in this portion of the analysis, one (Congdon, 1980) reported no significant differences in student reading performance and one (Mayfield, 1983) attributed significant gains in reading comprehension. However, Pavan noted design deficiencies in the latter. She included in this discussion Spaulding's

(1984) study of the implementation of clinical supervision by principals in 10 elementary schools; these principals received 8 days of training before implementing the model. Pavan raised questions of terminology and protocol concerning the Spaulding (1984) investigation, because the clinical supervision consisted merely of monitoring for the presence of the Hunter 7-Step Lesson Model.

A final study that Pavan (1985) reported is Stallings' (1985), longitudinal assessment of the Hunter model by 13 teachers at two elementary schools. Data from the 1st of 4 planned phases indicated that clinical supervision produced increases in instructional effectiveness, student engagement, and student achievement. However, Pavan acknowledged many uncontrolled intervening variables.

Implementation in South Carolina of Hunter's Program for Effective Teaching (PET) failed to produce significant gains in student achievement (Mandeville & Rivers, 1988). Analysis of achievement data showed that the students achieved at similar levels regardless of whether their teachers were trained in the Hunter model. These findings sparked complaints from Hunter (1989) that the study was seriously flawed and allegations that the program was poorly implemented. Her criticisms centered on inadequate teacher training and insufficient coaching (observation and feedback).

Acknowledging Hunter's belief in the need for a minimum of two years of coaching, Mandeville and Rivers (1989) conducted a follow-up study to test this assertion. The researchers used a survey to collect data from teachers on the quality and quantity of coaching received following initial PET training. Student achievement scores were then matched for these teachers and a comparable group of untrained teachers. Teachers who had received the training were generally very positive about its utility and reported regular use of its components. Only 57 percent of the trainees received a minimum of one coaching observation per year; only 7 percent reported receiving five or more per year. Although coaches generally adhered to recommended practices, the researchers identified shortcomings in the coaches' attention to "facilitating a teacher's analysis of a lesson, encouraging development of alternative approaches, and conducting the conference in a nonjudgmental way" (p. 41). The researchers found no relationship between student achievement and either the quantity or perceived quality of coaching overall. However, coaching provided by both a principal and a PET trainer produced significant gains in mathematics achievement. The factor of equivocation, or "items dealing with the coach's tendency to point out mistakes immediately and to offer unsolicited opinions about how the lesson should have been taught" (pp. 40-41), was also positively related to mathematics achievement. These findings supported the need for comprehensive training of clinical coaches, and the need for "ample high-quality coaching" (p. 42).

In summarizing the efficacy of the Hunter model, Koehler (1986) emphasized the absence of strong evidence that can improve the quality of supervision. Although administrators and teachers adopt the model readily, they soon tire of its inflexibility. The inflexibility of routines limits growth, because participants focus on a set of rigid processes rather than diverse alternatives. She concluded that "the model . . . does not empower the supervisor or teacher to adapt it or attain a continuing level of intellectual pleasure in understanding more about teaching and supervision" (p. 4).

Summary of Research on Clinical Supervision

At present, there is still no definitive support for the effectiveness of clinical supervision in improving instruction or increasing learning. A reasonable amount of evidence shows that principals and teachers like the model and that it enhances positive attitudes. The difficulties in providing research support result from the complexities of designing studies to control for many extraneous variables. In particular, researchers must ensure that ample time is provided for the mastery of both the skills and concepts of clinical supervision and must closely monitor the supervisory process to see that it is completely and correctly implemented. The extent of implementation must be considered carefully in the conduct of process-product studies.

Clinical supervision is not a Band-Aid, and it cannot quickly remedy the shortcomings of public schools. It is especially unrealistic to assume that cooperating teachers can easily perform the functions of clinical supervision without substantial training, incentive, and time. It is a time-consuming and costly endeavor that can likely pay off if competently directed and if the appropriate conditions (e.g., funding, staffing, and release time for teachers) and climate (trust, collegiality, and support) are present.

Research on Peer Supervision

Peer supervision most often takes the form of peer clinical supervision, wherein participants undertake some structured form of the phases with teachers as supervisors. Some professionals have proposed peer supervision as a solution to the problems of clinical supervision (funding, time, and staffing), but peer supervision seems to suffer from many of the same pitfalls. Among the reported benefits are the encouragement of reflective practice among teachers (Russell & Spafford, 1986), reduction of the theory/practice gap (Smyth, 1982), reduced isolation and fragmentation, and increased risk taking (Heller, 1988). A particularly appealing notion is that peers are safe observers, allowing teachers to try out new strategies and risk failure without losing face to supervisors (Heller, 1988).

Smyth (1982) took the extreme position that clinical supervision administered by supervisors is not clinical supervision but some kind of look-alike; that is, clinical supervision must involve peers. This view asserts that teachers possess the authority and expertise to help each other, and teacher autonomy, collegiality, and collaboration can only occur in this fully nonthreatening scenario.

The research base for peer supervision is very scant, despite the abundance of theoretical articles and model descriptions touting its virtues. It may be equated to, but is not synonymous with, the concept of peer coaching — an arrangement by which teachers lend support in the adoption of new strategies through shared planning, observation, and analysis. The distinction is that peer supervision involves at least some aspect of evaluation or targeting of areas for improvement (though probably formative), whereas peer coaching is geared toward lending support and collaboration. B.R. Joyce and Showers (1982) identified five major functions of peer coaching: "provision of companionship, giving of technical feedback, analysis of application: extending executive control, adaptation to the students, and personal facilitation" (p. 6). Hunter's model, however, uses the term *coaching* in a supervisory sense — referring to providing formative feedback through observation and conferencing. However, this function might be fulfilled by a teacher, administrator, or supervisor.

Of the recent research reported in the literature, half provided a measure of support for the use of peer supervision at some level (Hanna, 1988; Hosack-Curlin, 1989; Little, 1985; and Meyers, 1988). However, the remaining studies (Clark & Richardson, 1986; P.S. Dodds, 1985; Hamilton, 1987; and Pierce, 1989) raised considerable skepticism, and one in particular (McFaul & Cooper, 1984) invited the defense of peer clinical advocates.

The study that seems most provocative to advocates of peer supervision is McFaul and Cooper (1984). The authors used a qualitative design to describe and evaluate processes and outcomes of implementing peer clinical supervision in an urban elementary school. Subjects were elementary school teachers participating in a graduate course on clinical supervision. Ethnographic field notes, self-reports, and conference audiotapes provided data. Although all teachers were able to implement the model and felt generally positive, they reported feeling harried about time. Analysis of preobservation contracts and audiotapes showed a lack of in-depth application. The researchers concluded that "the underlying assumptions of the peer clinical supervision model were incongruent with the school context" (p. 7).

Goldsberry (1984) and Krajewski (1984) launched vehement responses to McFaul and Cooper (1984). Both alleged that weaknesses in the design and delivery of the intervention, as opposed to shortcomings in peer supervision, accounted for the failure of the teachers to fully implement the model. Goldsberry pointed out that the intervention provided only 4 weeks for teachers to complete 8 clinical supervision cycles, and suggested that the teachers were inadequately prepared by the intervention to carry out truly meaningful analysis of teaching. Krajewski noted that the study "(1) appeared to ask the impossible of teachers, (2) afforded an unfair test of clinical supervision, (3) asked for too much in too short a time, and (4) thus assured a negative outcome" (p. 11).

The logical synthesis of this research is that peer supervision is most appropriate as an adjunct to supervision, and not as a model in itself. Supervisors should strive to involve teachers in collaborative kinds of relationships, and all in-service training should certainly be followed by extensive peer coaching. Peer supervision can help to increase collegiality and shared decision making but will probably not produce lasting and substantial changes in teaching behaviors. Teachers have reported concerns about insufficient time, limited understanding, and lack of confidence in identifying observation tools. For social reasons or for expediency, teachers are reluctant to tackle in-depth analysis and generate alternative solutions. Although beginning teachers are receptive, substantive, critical analysis is least likely to occur when senior faculty are involved. Peer supervision is untenable as a singular supervision model.

Research on Self-Analysis Supervision

Some proponents see self-analysis approaches to supervision as good ways of increasing the amount of available feedback to teachers. Because traditional feedback channels (principals, supervisors, and cooperating teachers) are limited in quality and quantity (Freiberg & Waxman, 1988), self-analysis can fill an existing gap. Self-analysis has been most often applied in research designs involving student teachers.

One important issue that must be resolved is whether student teachers, in their situations of transition and survival, can reliably and accurately apply the techniques of self-analysis. Queen and Mallen (1982) argued that this application is paradoxical:

The assumption that the student teacher can successfully evaluate personal teaching capacities and techniques in the available field period is improbable. Motivating the student teacher to employ a truly critical examination of personal capacity is negated by the potential loss engendered by an analysis fostered during what is the final transition of the teacher's becoming. (p. 56)

In elaborating on this inconsistency, these authors questioned whether student teachers have sufficient motivation, insight, and experience to evaluate themselves. Acceptance of this notion requires the following assumptions (Queen & Mallen, 1982, p. 57):

- Objectives (beyond the goal of becoming a teacher) have been classified and sanctioned by those responsible for the student's becoming.
- The interactive-communicative process responsible for establishing a competent teacher operates effectively and is based on sound theoretical, yet practical, concepts.
- The student unequivocally desires to assert what is most profitable and productive in terms of academic competency and social relevancy.
- Specific enabling tasks and understandings are assumed to have been tested and thus generalizable to the teaching situation potentially confronting the student teacher.
- The teacher knows specifically the type and direction of activities needed to attain the primary objective — becoming a teacher.

One way of resolving this question is to study the accuracy of self-report measures as applied by student teachers. A number of researchers have examined this issue and have reported conflicting findings. An additional study examined the accuracy of self-reports given by in-service teachers (Koziol & Burns, 1986). Although two studies (Chiu, 1975; Pease, 1975) found similarities between the self-assessments of student teachers and those of their supervisors, two others (Briggs, Richardson, & Sefzik, 1986; Wheeler & Knoop, 1982) showed that student teachers tend to rate themselves significantly higher. In comparing the self-reports of in-service teachers to direct observations of teaching behavior, Koziol and Burns (1986) found high percentages of agreement. These inconsistencies point to the need for continued investigation of the accuracy of student teacher and in-service teacher self-reports.

Several studies support the value of training as a means of enhancing the self-evaluation of student teachers. Reported outcomes include reliability of self-evaluation (Jalbert, 1966), increased self-awareness, and improved teaching (O.P. Johnston, 1969; Stallings, 1985). The use of these strategies in combination with a comprehensive, overall supervision model could yield substantial benefits.

Dessecker (1975) applied self-analysis to a physical education context. In this study, the author investigated self-management in student teaching by having interns collect data about their own performances. Student teachers used microcassette recorders to record their verbal behaviors, then used a systematic observation instrument to code behaviors. Follow-up analysis and goal-setting were facilitated through weekly, on-campus seminars. The author found the technique to be useful in improving the verbal behaviors of student teachers. A similar study conducted by Paese (1984a) replicated these findings.

Some evidence shows that teachers feel positively about the strategies of self-analysis supervision and can be trained to implement it effectively. However, the use of self-analysis as a singular approach to supervision is not warranted; the abilities of teachers to carry out reflective processes have been justifiably questioned. Self-analysis is particularly problematic for student teachers, who are unlikely to identify shortcomings in their own performance at this critical stage of entrance into the teaching profession. However, self-analysis strategies may be useful as part of a larger and more comprehensive supervisory process. This usefulness depends on the clear identification of effective teaching practices and the provision of adequate teacher training in self-evaluation techniques. Self-analysis can provide useful feedback and increase the amount of available feedback, primarily through formative evaluation.

Competency-Based Supervision

Evidence shows a growing trend toward performance- or competency-based approaches to super-

vision and evaluation, at least in higher education. One review (McIntyre & Norris, 1980a) noted that almost half of 710 survey universities in 50 states reported the use of such programs in the supervision of preservice and student teachers. Researchers have frequently used competency-based assessments (of both knowledge and performance) in designing follow-up studies to evaluate teacher education programs (Stolworthy, 1986). Also, many of the beginning teacher evaluation programs and teacher effectiveness assessments developed through educational reforms across the country use competency-based methods. A 1984 report of the National Center for Education Information identified 16 states that mandated periodic state-wide performance evaluations of teachers (Feistritzer, 1984). At that time, an additional 13 states were considering adoption of such measures, and this trend is certain to continue. A sampling of criteria used in selected state-mandated instruments is presented in chapter 12.

General Implications for Competency-Based Supervision

Soar, Medley, and Coker (1983) advocated the use of performance-based criteria in evaluating teachers. Labeling traditional methods of evaluating teachers as inadequate, the authors called for increased attention to "identifying competent teachers, diagnosing incompetence, and measuring changes in competence validly and reliably" (p. 239). Such a focus would then allow participants to discuss strengths and weaknesses in light of a clear set of expectations. The ultimate goal of this approach is to help the professional or preprofessional develop a clear picture of the kinds of teaching behaviors that are desired and to translate that knowledge into self-assessment. In turn, effective teaching would contribute to increased student performance, the ultimate goal of competency-based supervision.

Researchers have strongly advocated performance-based evaluation as a model for student teachers. Proponents believe that the provision of immediate and objective feedback, based on identified criteria, is essential for the effective supervision of student teachers. Weller (1984) asserted that the goal of developing a "highly competent, successful, practicing professional . . . [could] best be achieved by infusing identified competencies into the profession" (p. 213). Objective observations can be documented through the use of observation checklists, Likert-type ratings of competency statements, and audio recordings and video tapings. Baseline data and graphic information can also assist the student teacher in self-analysis. However, quantitative methods can be appropriately augmented through the use of anecdotal records and other qualitative or subjective observations.

Competency-based supervision can also improve communication between interns, cooperating teachers, and university supervisors. Hoover, O'Shea, and Carroll (1988, p. 23) advanced this thesis, observing that "the definition and monitoring of clearly stated performance standards is . . . often absent from internship programs." Emphasis is more often given to the affective dimensions of the experience, and evaluations show minimal variation from one intern to another (Griffin et al., 1983). Development of specific skills is not facilitated when competencies are not clearly defined and their mastery is not systematically monitored (Hoover, O'Shea, & Carroll, 1988).

Implementation of performance-based criteria should reduce two kinds of systematic rater biases: the *leniency effect*, which occurs when raters are reluctant to assign negative ratings, and the *halo effect*, which results when one trait or behavior positively affects the rating of other traits (Allison, 1978). Another limitation of traditional assessments is that "cooperating teachers tend to reduce their evaluations to a single overall impression rather than specific areas of competence" (Chang & Ferre, 1988, p. 493). However, one study designed to test the effect of "carefully formulated behavioral anchors" revealed subjective rating errors; cooperating teachers' summative assessments of student teacher performance evidenced both halo and leniency effects (Phelps, Schmitz, & Wade, 1986).

Critics of competency-based supervision claim the following limitations (Gitlin, 1981):

- It focuses more on how the teacher performs, but not enough on how the standards should be established.
- It makes the assumption that effective teaching requires the assimilation of "a set of technical skills" (focus on practice), and ignores the perspective that teaching is an art.
- It does not link teaching to reflective processes (focus on purpose), and therefore does not allow recipients to become students of teaching. (p. 47)

Specific Applications of Competency-Based Supervision

Tinning (1988) argued that "the . . . teacher [in this approach] is regarded as a passive recipient of professional knowledge, and the educational and social contexts in which teacher education is embedded tend to be accepted as given" (p. 88). These criticisms, however, do not seem tenable unless competencies are applied with total inflexibility and absence of attention to affective and cognitive aspects of learning to teach.

One of the most thoroughly developed models for the implementation of competency-based supervision is Woolever's (1983) Hierarchy of Generic Teaching Skills. This approach to supervision of student teachers is based upon the identification of generic teaching competencies and provides systematic appraisal of these competencies with structured classroom observation guides. The model assumes that "desired teaching behaviors should be stated as behavioral competencies and should be explicitly communicated to the student before formal observations begin" (p. 3). The author selected the competencies included in the model on the basis of four criteria: common sense, research evidence, established educational practice, and educational philosophy of the training institution. The competencies are arranged into six hierarchical categories: "general professional criteria; beginning skills in gaining and holding pupil attention; using reinforcement theory to increase learning and develop productive behavior; increasing student motivation to learn; lesson planning, implementation, and evaluation; and leading a classroom discussion" (p. 5). Both the university supervisor and the cooperating teacher apply these criteria through systematic observations, rating selected competencies as *honors*, *pass*, *needs improvement*, and *unsatisfactory*. Student teachers progress upward in the hierarchy at their own rates. Evaluations collected from 130 graduates of the program have yielded "overwhelmingly positive" comments.

Despite the extent of its theoretical support and practical application, the current literature provides little empirical information about competency-based supervision. The growing trend toward performance-based evaluation of teachers signals the need for continued research in the area of competency-based supervision. The competencies identified in performance-based observation systems provide a convenient focus for the design of competency-based supervisory approaches. Additional research is needed to determine what factors can increase the benefits of such approaches.

Competency-Based Supervision in Physical Education

A few theoretical articles and research reports have proposed applications of competency-based supervision to physical education settings. Cole (1983) endorsed it as an improvement over traditional forms of informal supervision in which observers randomly select and record what they choose to see on the basis of personal perspectives. Cole described behavioral feedback as essential to the acquisition, refinement, and maintenance of desirable teaching practices. She suggested that directing teachers and their interns discuss specific desired teaching behaviors and their application and utility to motor learning theory.

Coulon (1989) suggested a competency-based approach to the development of behavioral contracts among student teaching triads. The terms of the contract specify desired teaching behaviors in objective and observable terms and the roles of the triad members in mastering the behaviors. The behavioral contract can also strengthen the commitment of triad members to work collaboratively and can increase the specificity of feedback from supervisors.

Paese (1984b) suggested competencies for student teachers that relate to planning, classroom management, evaluation, feedback, knowledge of the school in relation to society, class routines and policies, and professionalism. The author provided eight competencies as a starting point, adding that participants could determine other competencies on an individual basis. Paese's basic competencies include abilities to

- systematically plan for instruction (unit and lesson plans);
- write terminal objectives for students and lead the students toward the objectives through a carefully planned progression of enabling objectives;
- manage and control individual students and groups using various techniques of classroom management;
- systematically evaluate students' progress in all three domains;
- provide constructive feedback to students in an environment that encourages maximum participation and utilizes minimal managerial activities;
- provide students with an introductory knowledge of the roles of school administration, teacher organizations, and the school in society;
- understand and carry out class routines and policies; and
- demonstrate professionalism and responsibility through a good attendance record, appropriate dress, punctuality, and following school rules for teachers.

Darst and Steeves (1980) reported a study of a competency-based approach to student teaching in physical education. The researchers observed seven secondary student teachers to obtain baseline and intervention data for seven student teacher behaviors and two student behaviors. An intervention training package contained a competency-based learning module, instructions, graphic feedback, cuing, reinforcement, weekly goals, and terminal goals. An analysis of behavior changes indicated that the competency-based approach was productive. These findings were consistent with those of a series of studies conducted at Ohio State University (Boehm, 1974; Darst, 1974; K. Hamilton, 1974).

O'Cansey (1987, 1988) and Coulon (1988) studied the impact of a behavioral model on the development of competencies in cooperating teachers. In the 1987 study, O'Cansey developed a personalized system of instruction (PSI) to improve post-teaching conferencing skills of cooperating teachers and university supervisors. The Behavioral Model of Supervision — Physical Education (BMS—PE) incorporates competencies targeted for improvement, including monitoring for academic learning time, four subskills of conferencing behavior, and follow-up monitoring. The general thrust of the intervention was to help supervisors (a) become more precise in identifying and observing effective teaching behaviors, (b) give more precise feedback, and (c) hold student teachers accountable in conferencing interactions. The author recorded supervisory verbal behaviors from audiotaped conferences and categorized these behaviors with respect to focus, explicitness, and accountability. Results of this analysis indicate that the model was successful in bringing about the desired increases in supervisory behaviors.

One element of O'Cansey's behavioral model is the Effective Supervision Guide (ESG), described in detail in his 1986 document. To improve conferencing behaviors, supervisors develop a plan based on the collection of baseline data with three systematic observation instruments. After establishing baseline measures, the supervisor then selects target behaviors for remediation or maintenance, specifies strategies to accomplish this, identifies performance criteria for evaluation, and establishes schedules for the mastery of the target behaviors. The ESG seems to be a useful strategy for helping supervisors collect objective and reliable data and use it to organize effective conferences.

Coulon (1988) used a modified version of BMS-PE and the basic ALT-PE system (S. Wilkinson & Taggart, 1985) to develop a self-instructional module for cooperating teachers. The author tested the effects of the module in four single subject designs by measuring specified cooperating teacher verbal behaviors, student teacher behaviors, and in-class pupil behaviors. The obtained data showed strong evidence of the efficacy of the module on cooperating teacher task statements (explicitness and accountability). Some evidence showed desired changes in student teacher behavior, but the author observed no substantial pupil behavior changes.

Gangstead (1983) used the behavioral approach to improving teaching to develop a comprehensive model for supervision of student teachers. The author adopted the rationale for this approach from a series of studies directed by Siedentop at Ohio State University, which indicated that applied behavior analysis can produce measurable improvements in the quality of student teaching experiences. Gangstead's model emphasizes formative evaluation and the provision of accurate feedback for joint analysis by the supervisor, cooperating teacher, and student teacher. Formative evaluation in this model allows the supervisor to

- identify and enhance desirable behaviors and skills during student teaching,
- determine weakness in or absence of desirable behaviors and skills during student teaching,
- prescribe instructional resources and training, and
- forecast summative results.

The Gangstead model provides a clear focus of effective teaching skills and reduces the student teacher's anxiety of guessing about evaluation criteria. The joint selection of target skills ensures that all members of the triad will work on the same premises and toward the same objectives. The model also affords the student teacher a level of colleagueship, and it respects his or her ability to make decisions about effective teaching. As a general behavioral model, it seems to have merit.

Although the research on competency-based supervision is less plentiful than that of clinical models, its findings are much more consistent. The use of competencies can improve supervision and quickly bring about desired changes in teacher behavior. In addition, competency-based supervision provides a clear picture of what is expected, facilitates consistent monitoring, allows a developmental and step-by-step approach to acquiring competence, and provides a basis for quantitative and graphic illustrations of observed teaching behaviors.

Research on Supervision of Student Teachers

Given the bulk of the literature available on this topic, this section is restricted to those studies and supportive articles that illuminate the most critical aspects of effective supervision of student teachers. The Educational Resources Information Clearing House (ERIC) data base for the years 1983 through 1989 produced 860 references on this subject. Of these, almost one-third involved data-driven research; the remainder involved theoretical treatises or practical guidelines for ensuring quality experiences. Though this data base is large, its fragmentary nature makes it difficult to deduce general findings. The literature selected for review represents that portion which was most logically cohesive or seemed to provide the most useful insights. In order for the reader to more clearly analyze this literature, this chapter is divided into sections discussing

- learning to teach,
- the supervisory triad, and
- obstacles to effective supervision of student teachers.

Learning to Teach

Understanding the process of learning to teach requires a thorough analysis of the development of cognitive (How do student teachers think?), affective (How do they feel?), and behavioral (How do they perform?) dimensions. The development of teaching skills is an ongoing and career-long process. However, the most dramatic changes and improvements occur during student teaching. Thus, student teaching is the most critical aspect of professional preparation and is a potential bridge for the theory/practice gap. Research has shown performance in student teaching to be the strongest predictor of success in in-service teaching (Day & Brightwell, 1978). Effective teaching skills that are clearly defined, systematically monitored, and frequently reinforced will have a greater chance of survival throughout induction and in-service years.

A few studies have focused on cognitive dimensions of student teaching. The quantity of this literature does not promote generalization of findings or conclusions. However, it does shed some light on pertinent aspects of student teacher thinking.

Studies of student teacher cognitions show shifting developmental trends from concrete to abstract and from a focus on mechanical aspects of teaching to a more reflective analytic style. These trends are evident in the nature of problems perceived by student teachers. They are also reflected in the nature of decision-making strategies used by student teachers at various phases of their internships. Student teachers tend to focus on aspects of teaching that contribute to success in daily lessons, taking a rather short-range look at what works.

The most comprehensive review of beginning teacher concerns was Veenman's (1984) meta-analysis, introduced in chapter 1. First on the list of commonly perceived problems were those related to classroom discipline. Recently, a study of common problems of secondary student teachers revealed that four of the most frequently reported problems were related to classroom management and discipline (Doebler & Rooberson, 1987). This finding is consistent with another study that focused specifically on perceived problems of preservice teachers (Purcell & Seifert, 1982).

It is unclear whether affective dimensions of learning to teach demonstrate the same developmental patterns of evolution as those related to cognitions. Two studies (Minehart, 1986; Richardson-Koehler, 1988) reported shifts during the term from concerns of self-survival to future concerns of employment and lifestyle. However, Fredericks (1987) found conflicting results from journal entries and the Fuller Teacher Concerns Statement (TCS). Journal entries showed a shift from task to impact (on student) concerns, whereas TCS data showed that student teachers were concerned with the task (mechanical) aspects of teaching throughout the two-semester practicum.

In view of the developmental nature of student teacher cognitions and affects, the application of contingency theory or situational leadership is a logical idea. Adopted from the business leadership theory of Fiedler (1967), contingency management assumes that the appropriate supervisory style will depend upon the maturity level or readiness of the student teacher (J.D. Phelps, 1985; Stalhut, 1987). *Situational leadership* is another term sometimes used for this approach.

Glickman (1985) applied this concept of differentiation when he conceptualized his developmental model of supervision. This model places three orientations of supervision (directive, collaborative, and nondirective) on a continuum from maximum supervisor responsibility to maximum teacher responsibility. Supervisors who apply directive styles of supervision will demonstrate more task behaviors, whereas those using nondirective styles will demonstrate heavier emphases on relationship behaviors.

Factors that contribute to readiness of teachers are abstract thinking ability (low, moderate, or high) and source of motivation (egocentric, group, or altruistic). These levels of motivation correspond roughly to Fuller's (1969) stages of concern—self-adequacy, task impact, and student impact. Beginning teachers tend to focus on survival or egocentric concerns. Once teachers attain levels of skill adequate for survival, they then shift toward adaptation of instruction for needs for their particular groups—task-impact concerns. Ultimately, superior teachers will concern themselves with providing improved instruction for all students—student impact (Glickman, 1985).

Table 3.1 is Glickman's (1985) graphic illustration of the relationship of teacher thought and motivation to developmental readiness for change. Teachers in cell Ia (concrete thought, egocentric motivation) are resistant to change, demonstrating rigid and invariant approaches to teaching and motivated primarily in maintaining their jobs. Box IIb represents the next level of teachers, who have increasing concerns about their classrooms but are still restricted in their thinking. They are willing to change and are interested in meeting the instructional needs of their students. However, this readiness is limited by insufficient knowledge and experience. Teachers at the highest level of maturity are capable of substantive change, able to perform abstract thinking, and motivated to effect wide-scale educational improvements.

The supervisor's logical progression with student teachers, therefore, is to use more direct supervision during the initial phase of the internship and more indirect stages during the terminal

Table 3.1 Thought and Motivation of Teachers

Type of motivation	Concrete thought	Restricted thought	Abstract thought
Egocentric	Ia (resistant)	Ib	Ic
Group	IIa	IIb (willing)	IIc
Altruistic	IIIa	IIIb	IIIc (capable)

Note. From Carl D. Glickman, *Supervision of instruction: A developmental approach*. Copyright by Allyn and Bacon. Reprinted by permission.

phase. Copeland (1982) supported this approach after surveying student teachers to determine their preferences across time.

Research on behavioral dimensions of learning to teach has consistently shown that supervisors can effect substantial changes in student teaching behavior within relatively short periods of time. Interventions that clearly identify desired behavior, provide adequate training and practice opportunities, and allow systematic monitoring and reinforcement should produce changes in the desired direction. Thus, planned interventions prior to or during the student teaching experience can dramatically impact the quality of teaching. Current research describes changes in classroom management patterns (Medrano, 1986; Seaborn, 1986), time management (Woolfolk & Woolfolk, 1984), and transfer of training (Howdyshell, 1987; Wynn, 1987).

Embrey (1987) conducted a particularly interesting qualitative study to describe the behavior of one student teacher in elementary physical education. The author observed changes in teaching behavior and analyzed them with respect to the socializing effects of the cooperating teacher, the program, and the context. Embrey acted as a participant observer, collecting field notes, audiotapes, interview notes, and a variety of data sources every morning over a 10-week period. Among other findings, two patterns of teaching behavior were described. The student teacher experienced a slump in performance during the midpoint of the semester and then demonstrated marked improvement. The student teacher also evidenced a pattern of ups and downs each week, with difficulties occurring early in the week and then ameliorating with the cooperating teacher's assistance later in the week.

The Supervisory Triad

The dynamics of the supervisory triad are critically important to the supervisory experience. Student teachers have consistently valued the practicum experience as contributing most to overall teacher training. Thus, it is essential to ensure the quality of this experience, and especially to facilitate positive relationships, clear role delineations, and productive interactions among the student teacher, cooperating teacher, and university supervisor. For the sake of clarity, note that a variety of terms are frequently used to name the public school teacher who supervises the internship. Among the terms are cooperating teacher, directing teacher, teaching assistant, colleague teacher, clinical teacher,

collaborating teacher, field supervisor, and supervising teacher.

Role Perspectives

To ensure clear communication within the triad, all parties must be clear about their roles and responsibilities, and role expectations must be congruent among the group. Logically, supervision works best when everyone understands his or her job and knows how to perform it. Unfortunately, this often is not the case. Grimmet and Ratzlaff (1986) contend that "the role of the cooperating teacher is poorly defined and that teachers generally are unprepared for the task of student teaching supervision" (p. 42). The role of the university supervisor varies substantially according to the philosophic orientation of the individual (Zahorik, 1988) and the activities performed (Koehler, 1984).

The Supervisor's Role

Zahorik (1988) demonstrated role ambiguity in a description of three types of behaviors evidenced in the observing-conferencing roles of university supervisors. The author categorized supervisors in light of their dominant goals of behavior prescription, idea interpretation, or person support. Behavior-prescription supervisors "told student teachers to use certain instructional and management acts and avoid others" (p. 11). The author subdivided this type into (a) the *scholar supervisor*, who supported effective teaching prescriptions by citing research; (b) the *master supervisor*, who based prescriptions on personal experience as an expert teacher; (c) the *mentor supervisor*, who acted as a sage; and (d) the *critic supervisor*, who focused on documenting teaching acts for analysis and interpretation, followed by prescription.

The second type of supervision, labeled *idea interpretation*, "consisted of presenting beliefs to the student teacher that the supervisor had about what classroom and schools ought to be like" (Zahorik, 1988, p. 11). The author subdivided this group into (a) the *humanist supervisor*, who focused on raising consciousness about questionable practices, and (b) the *reformer supervisor*, who was similar to the humanist supervisor but more confirmed in prescribing practices, even to the point of modeling desired behaviors.

The third type of supervision, termed *person-support*, "focused on facilitating student teacher decision making by creating a climate that permitted and encouraged student teachers to think for themselves" (Zahorik, 1988, p. 11). Subtypes included (a) the *therapist supervisor*, who focused on the student teachers reactions and provided support; (b) the *advocate supervisor*, who tried to create a better environment in which the student teacher could operate; and (c) the *inquirer supervisor*, who questioned the student teacher to encourage self-analysis and reflection.

In addition to goal differentiation, Zahorik's supervisors varied with respect to active and reactive styles. The active style consisted of prescribing (telling) and interpreting (analyzing), whereas the reactive (asking) style involved encouragement of reflective thinking by student teachers. The interrelationship of supervisor goals and styles is illustrated in Table 3.2.

The Cooperating Teacher's Role

Given the ambiguity of role definitions, it is not surprising that the influence of the university supervisor is generally negligible (Zahorik, 1988). Although the cooperating teacher seems to have the greatest influence over what takes place (Haberman & Harris, 1982; McIntyre & Norris, 1980b), that influence is not necessarily positive. The powerful impact of the cooperating teacher can actually negate the effect of previous undergraduate training when incongruent values are present (Emans, 1983).

Though conflicting findings exist, the bulk of the literature indicates that cooperating teachers are the dominant influence on the attitudes and behaviors of student teachers. This is a logical result of the arrangements that surround student teaching—the university supervisor can make only limited visits, whereas the cooperating teacher serves as a role model throughout the internship. The daily interactions of the student teacher and cooperating teacher place the university supervisor in the position of outsider (Zimpher, deVoss, & Nott, 1980). The university supervisor's limited observations and lack of time reduce the credibility of his or her feedback in the eyes of both cooperating teachers and student teachers. Consequently, teaching styles and attitudes of student teachers are primarily influenced through the direct "tutelage" and by "modeling" of cooperating teachers (B.R. Joyce, 1988b).

Observed Practices in Supervision of Student Teachers

Despite the importance of their respective roles, university supervisors and cooperating teachers typically fail to achieve their potential impact. Two common obstacles to effective supervision by

Table 3.2   Types of Supervision

| Goal | Style | | |
| | Active | | Reactive |
	Prescriptive	Interpretive	Supportive
Behavior	**Behavior prescription** Scholar Master Mentor Critic		
Idea		**Idea interpretation** Humanist Reformer	
Person			**Person support** Therapist Advocate Inquirer

Note. Reprinted by permission. Copyright by the American Association of Colleges for Teacher Education. J.A. Zahorik, "The observing conference role of university supervisors." *Journal of Teacher Education* 39(2), p. 12.

university supervisors are insufficient time and lack of formal training. Cooperating teachers demonstrate shortcomings in the nature of the feedback they provide for student teachers. They also tend to focus on the practical and mechanical aspects of teaching, overlooking the theoretical basis for effective practice.

Supervisory Practices of University Supervisors

Lack of time to sufficiently observe and lack of formal training of university supervisors are two dominant themes in the current literature. Although estimates of observation time vary according to the constraints of the program, they tend to be quite low. Bowman (1979) reported that

> typically, supervisors visit their student teachers five times and spend approximately six hours in the school; their visits include the ''amenities of greeting and exchanging pleasantries with the building principal [and] sitting through recess periods,'' with the actual observation of student teaching limited to about one hundred minutes during the entire student teaching experience. (pp. 29-30)

Johns and Cline (1985) found that sufficient length of observations and frequency of feedback were related to student teachers' satisfaction with the practices of university supervisors. The authors also linked positive perceptions to supervisor professional interest, the abilities of supervisors to address student concerns, diagnosis of learning problems, and the conduct of regular seminars. One factor contributing most to positive ratings of supervisors was assessed by this judgement: ''My college supervisor's interest in my professional improvement and growth was sincere and helpful'' (p. 22).

Surprisingly, most university supervisors lack formal training in supervisory practices (Koehler, 1984; Zahorik, 1988). They tend to rely on their own experiences as teachers and on informal contacts with other supervisors in evaluating student teachers (Koehler, 1984; Rust, 1988). To a more limited extent, supervisors apply current research and theory of effective teaching.

Supervisory Practices of Cooperating Teachers

Descriptions of typical practices of cooperating teachers have important implications for the improvement of the student teaching experience. Par-

ticular problems are apparent in the nature of feedback provided (Koehler, 1986) and evaluative skills (Chang & Ferre, 1988; L. Phelps, Schmitz, & Boatright, 1986) of cooperating teachers. Student teachers value high rates of immediate and specific feedback provided by cooperating teachers (Brunelle, Tousignant, & Piéron, 1981). In an analysis of feedback provided by cooperating teachers, Griffin et al. (1983) noted that student teachers received little specific information regarding evaluation of their behaviors or rationale for suggested practices. Feedback was situation-specific and tended to focus on isolated classroom events. The authors found little relationship between feedback and research or previously learned principles from theory coursework. In providing feedback regarding lessons, cooperating teachers avoided focusing on negative aspects and gave criticism in the form of pep talks (Zimpher, deVoss, & Nott, 1980).

Cooperating teachers are generally more oriented toward practical perspectives of teaching than toward theory, so they may not help the student teacher acquire general principles and reflective practices (V.R. Koehler, 1986). Cooperating teachers tend to focus their feedback on procedural skills such as classroom management and mechanical elements of teaching (Housego & Boldt, 1986) and are often weak in their abilities ''to provide an articulate analysis of [their] own teaching'' (Richardson-Koehler, 1988, p. 32). Cooperating teachers tend to be didactic and do not consistently encourage autonomy or decision making by student teachers (Mistretta, 1988).

One factor that minimizes the validity of cooperating teacher evaluations is that these teachers are reluctant to give low ratings. Halo and leniency effects, as previously discussed, are common in evaluations. The tendency to overrate student teachers makes it impossible for anyone making comparisons to identify substantial individual differences. It seems that cooperating teachers are influenced by the desire to enhance self-confidence of student teachers and are therefore overly disposed to superior ratings (L.A. Phelps, Schmitz, & Boatright, 1986).

A similar study documented the overabundance of superior ratings given by both university supervisors and cooperating teachers. Chang and Ferre (1988) attained mean ratings by university supervisors of 3.6 on a 5-point Likert-type scale for the categories *attitude, scholarship, instruction, discipline,* and *personality*. Analysis of written comments by cooperating teachers and university supervisors showed close similarities. Further, Frankiewicz (1988) showed that criteria used for evaluating student teachers show little application of teacher effectiveness research.

Cognitive Abilities of the Cooperating Teacher

The ability of the cooperating teacher to provide effective guidance to student teachers may be affected by the factor of conceptual level (CL). The conceptual levels of individuals vary from low to high, based on their abilities to integrate and apply abstract concepts (D. Hunt, 1977). Thies-Sprinthall (1980) hypothesized that cooperating teachers with low or moderate conceptual levels might produce negative experiences for student teachers, molding them to a narrow scope of teaching alternatives instead of broadening perspectives. Her study revealed, at one level of analysis, that mismatched supervisory pairs (high CL student teachers, low or moderate CL cooperating teachers) produced student teachers who performed well in teaching but were evaluated below average by their cooperating teachers. A possible implication is that "supervisors who themselves are at the modest levels of psychological development may misperceive or misunderstand the teaching performance of more developmentally advanced student teachers" (Thies-Sprinthall, 1980, p. 19).

Continuing research should address the identification of exemplary cooperating teachers for work with student teachers. In addition to motivation and effective modeling, cooperating teachers should ideally possess high conceptual levels. Failure to address these important factors will likely contribute to a less-than-satisfactory experience for the intern (and perhaps everyone involved). Thies-Sprinthall (1980) aptly summarized the importance of the selection process, as well as appropriate matching of cooperating and student teachers:

Supervisors clearly need a complex conceptual system as a basis for selecting appropriate learning experiences for beginning teachers. This means that the supervisors themselves need to accurately "read" individual differences in student teachers, employ a variety of supervision techniques, and provide a humane environment designed for positive growth. Effective supervisory behaviors may be direct concomitants of higher more complex stage functioning. A constructive developmental mismatch implies that the supervisor functions at a slightly higher stage than the low func-

tioning student teacher and at least at a level similar to the high student teacher. (p. 20)

Obstacles to Effective Supervision of Student Teachers

A number of factors pose potential pitfalls to supervision by both cooperating teachers and university supervisors. Lack of communication is the most formidable obstacle and that which is most commonly observed (Hoover, O'Shea, & Carroll, 1988). Others include inconsistent or undefined goals, lack of university support, contextual variables, defensive postures of cooperating teachers, and the need for overall school reform.

Communication among members of the supervisory triad can help to reduce many problems associated with the student teaching experience. One analysis of problems experienced by cooperating teachers in the supervision of student teachers provides some areas that need improved communication. Applegate and Lasley (1982) collected problem incidents and inventory data from a large sample of cooperating teachers. Analysis of the data revealed six factors related to the problems of cooperating teachers, as outlined in Table 3.3.

In a general overview of obstacles, Richardson-Koehler (1988) summarized barriers to effective supervision of student teaching. She derived these insights from a participant observation study in which she served as a university supervisor of elementary student teachers. Analysis of multiple data sources led her to three general conclusions. These conclusions concerned the normative values held by the cooperating teachers. First, teachers valued learning through experience, individualism, and egalitariansim. These values, an emphasis on trial and error, and unwillingness to allow student teachers to observe other classrooms posed serious limitations on the feedback provided. Second, teachers were unwilling or unable to reflect on and analyze their own teaching practices, thus leading to inadequate feedback and confusion and frustration of student teachers. Third, the university supervisor cannot break these norms by working with cooperating teachers and student teachers under the present circumstances; there simply is not enough time to overcome these forces.

Lack of communication can also contribute to the defensive reactions of cooperating teachers. These reactions are difficult to avoid, because student teachers tend to model the teaching behaviors of their cooperating teachers. Therefore, any criticism

Table 3.3 Problems of Cooperating Teachers

Factor 1: Problems with students' orientation to teaching
Cooperating teachers have problems when field experience students (FESs) are not prepared for their assignments, do not exhibit some basic understanding of student behavior, do not have skills in lesson preparation, or do not exhibit some curiosity about the process of becoming a teacher.

Factor 2: Problems understanding the partnership of teaching
Cooperating teachers have problems when they sense they are solely responsible for students' field work. Cooperating teachers want to see more active involvement on the part of the college or university.

Factor 3: Problems with professionalism
Cooperating teachers express concerns about the lack of interest by both the FES and the university supervisor about school norms and professional responsiblities.

Factor 4: Problems with field experience students' attitudes and skills
Cooperating teachers have problems with students who do not display a commitment to teaching. FESs do not always assume positive attitudes about doing such tasks as evaluating students' work, running errands, or operating audio-visual equipment.

Factor 5: Problems with enthusiasm for teaching
Cooperating teachers express concern with the lack of initiative and enthusiasm exhibited by FESs.

Factor 6: Problems with planning and organization
Cooperating teachers are concerned about FESs' organization and management abilities. They expect FESs to be able to teach lessons. This includes planning for instruction, organizing materials, asking appropriate questions, and carrying out activities to their logical conclusions.

Note. Reprinted by permission. Copyright by the American Association of Colleges for Teacher Education. J.H. Applegate and T.J. Lasley, "Cooperating teacher's problems with preservice field experience students." *Journal of Teacher Education*, 33(2), p. 16.

of the supervising teacher connotes criticism of the cooperating teacher (Richardson-Koehler, 1988; Zimpher, deVoss, & Nott, 1980).

Another potential pitfall of poor communication is the development of inconsistent goals for student teaching. Inconsistencies within the triad of beliefs regarding the purposes of student teaching and supervision can produce dissatisfaction and diminished performance. Inconsistencies are exacerbated when the priorities of the university

differ substantially from the realities of the school system (Hoover et al., 1988). It may be that substantive improvements of student teaching experiences cannot be achieved without major overall reforms of public schools.

General Conclusions

Research on supervision of student teachers encompasses a broad spectrum of topics and diverse findings. However, we can find a consensus of support for several basic conclusions. This literature provides some useful insights for optimizing the critical period of "learning to teach" in student teaching. Supervisors can facilitate the process by first recognizing the developmental trends of student teacher cognitions and affects. The initial, intermediate, and terminal phases of the internship may require different approaches to supervision, in line with the shift of student teacher concerns from survival to future considerations. Because cooperating teachers play a dominant role in influencing the student teacher, the selection of exemplary role models is essential. Finally, it is quite clear that the behaviors of student teachers and their supervisors can be easily affected within a short period in order to achieve desired objectives.

Research on Supervision in Physical Education

Research at Ohio State University has followed a clear focus of progressions for the training of student teachers in physical education. This program encompasses an ongoing series of interventions to upgrade the quality of student teaching experiences and to help cooperating teachers and student teachers assume more directed roles in the process. Siedentop (1981) published a summary report of this research effort from 1973 to 1977. This report chronicled eight steps in the process of developing the "behavior change supervision effort" (p. 31). These steps entailed the following:

Step 1—Deciding what to change and how to measure it (identifying target behaviors; developing the OSU Teacher Behavior Scale) (Siedentop & Hughley, 1975)

Step 2—Answering the initial question, Can changes in behavior be produced with a 10-week internship?

Step 3—Moving toward greater complexity and

more reality (adding behavior categories and reducing supervisory visits)

Step 4—Developing a systematic format (developing competency-based materials, training modules, and extended observation categories; developing target and maintenance goals)

Step 5—Increasing frequency of observation/feedback while reducing the supervisor's role (using peer observers)

Step 6—Using self-management in student teaching (e.g., self-audiotaping and weekly seminars)

Step 7—Training the cooperating teacher to be supervisor (workshop training in coding behavior, using alternative supervision strategies, contracting)

Step 8—Adding a behavior change project to the student teaching experience, with target behaviors selected by students

Studies undertaken at Ohio State University during the 1970s demonstrated the utility of systematic observation methods and established protocol for the use of increasingly sophisticated observation instruments and coding techniques. Researchers extensively used the multiple baseline design in testing the effects of interventions. Collectively, these studies laid a strong foundation for supervision research, demonstrating that the teaching behavior of student teachers can be readily changed through systematic supervision. The studies produced evidence that teaching behavior can be objectively defined and reliably observed (Siedentop & Hughley, 1975); changes in behavior can occur within a 10-week internship (Hughley, 1973); these changes can occur with reduced supervision (Rife, 1973); competency-based training modules can facilitate behavior change (Boehm, 1974; Darst, 1974; K. Hamilton, 1974); student teachers can be trained to successfully use peer supervision (P.A. Dodds, 1975); student teacher self-management is also a viable alternative (Cramer, 1977; Dessecker, 1975; Hutslar, 1977); and student teachers can implement their own behavior change projects (Currens, 1977; McKenzie, 1976; Siedentop, Rife, & Boehm, 1976).

Research conducted subsequently at Ohio State University has continued to broaden and extend this knowledge base. Two recent studies were reported previously in this chapter in the section on competenecy-based supervision. Essentially, these studies demonstrated that a behavioral model can be used to change the behaviors of cooperating teachers and university supervisors (O'Cansey, 1987)

and can be used in a self-instruction context to accomplish similar changes (Coulon, 1988). Simultaneously, Eldar (1988) determined that a self-management program can bring about desired changes in targeted verbal behaviors and time management of student teachers.

Researchers at Ithaca College have also implemented a focused series of studies, as reported by Mancini, Wuest, and van der Mars (1985). These studies employed a series of interventions based on systematic supervision and the use of systematic observation instruments in micropeer teaching. This approach to supervision begins in methods classes during the freshman year, as students view videotapes and receive systematic supervisory feedback. Experiences in the junior year provide more emphasis on systematic observation and on the coding of lessons taught by the students themselves and by their peers.

Interventions conducted in this program have compared systematic supervisory feedback (SSF) combined with conventional supervisory feedback to conventional supervisory feedback alone. Researchers have used a variety of instruments, and dependent variables have included behavioral and attitudinal dimensions of student teaching. Of the eight studies reported, all produced significant desired changes in student behavior and/or attitude, lending strong support for the use of systematic supervision in undergraduate training.

Tannehill and Zakrajsek have conducted several investigations that provide greater understanding of the role of the cooperating teacher in supervision of student teachers in physical education. Some insights were gained from a study that described how supervision of student teachers impacted perceptions of three selected elementary physical education cooperating teachers (Tannehill, 1989). The researcher used semistructured interviews to glean insights on a variety of topics. Among the pertinent findings was that these cooperating teachers perceived their primary purpose as providing a professional role model for student teachers. Reasons for serving as a cooperating teacher included professional exchange and renewal, professional responsibility, and ability to make a difference. All three of the cooperating teachers felt a professional bond with the university supervisor. Participation in supervision markedly impacted the professional lives of these individuals, contributing positively to their growth and development and allowing them to make valuable contributions.

In another descriptive study, Tannehill and Zakrajsek (1988) analyzed supervisory practices related to the frequency of observation and quality of feedback provided. Results showed that cooperating teachers gave extremely low rates of feedback, with many student teachers receiving fewer than one comment in each category per week. Cooperating teachers spent very little time observing or conferencing. Comments given in supervisory conferences dealt with a narrow spectrum of teaching behaviors and focused mostly on planning or classroom management. Comments consisted mainly of general praise, and cooperating teachers provided little specific praise or encouragement. The researchers theorized that "overuse of 'good' as a descriptor points to a lack of analytical skills for expressing feedback in qualitative and evaluative terminology" (p. 11). Student teachers consistently expressed the desire for increased amounts of specific feedback.

In response to these reported findings, Tannehill (1988) developed a tutorial manual for the self-directed training of cooperating teachers in physical education. Tannehill and Zakrajsek (1990) then tested the effects of this strategy on the supervisory behaviors and practices of a group of secondary cooperating teachers. In addition to the daily supervision log and weekly report, the authors used audiotaped supervisory conferences to collect data. Analysis of the resultant data showed that teachers trained with the program gave better feedback and observed more frequently than cooperating teachers in a control group. They also demonstrated more indirect and task-relevant behaviors in supervisory conferences.

Studies of supervision in physical education have typically applied the behavioral approach to modifying teaching behaviors. These studies have quite consistently shown that student teachers in physical education can readily benefit from structured supervision programs and can rather quickly modify their behaviors when essential elements of supervision are present. These elements include clear descriptions of desired teaching behaviors, close monitoring, and provision of specific feedback.

Additional research has shown that cooperating teachers and supervising teachers in physical education can be trained to provide more effective supervision to student teachers (Coulon, 1988; O'Cansey, 1987; Tannehill & Zakrajsek, 1990). Learning to teach in a movement setting has unique demands, and supervisors must be adequately prepared to assist in this difficult transition. Further attention is needed to develop training modules and packages for upgrading the

skills of cooperating teachers and university supervisors in physical education.

Research on General Supervisory Practices

The preceding sections of this chapter review research on generic models of supervision, supervision of student teachers, and supervision within the context of physical education. A number of additional studies provide useful information regarding general aspects of effective supervision. Again, these articles represent a comprehensive (but not exhaustive) coverage of the published resources. Topics of general supervisory practices are categorized according to supervisory styles, skills and competencies, and factors of effectiveness.

Supervisory Styles

Blumberg and Cusick (1970) first addressed the concept of supervisory styles, classifying styles as either direct or indirect according to the nature of supervisor–supervisee verbal interactions. Direct supervisory styles are characterized by a didactic, prescriptive, telling, or information-giving orientation. The directive style places great emphasis on the content of the supervision process and little on interpersonal relationship. The indirect style of supervision is characterized by asking, supporting, and praising, and it emphasizes developing collaborative interpersonal relationships.

Scales developed more recently by Sistrunk (1981) provide an additional method of analyzing supervisory style. The author developed two instruments (Forms 1 and 2) of the Supervisory Behavior Description Questionnaire to determine supervisors' preferences for very directive, collaborative, or very nondirective styles. Sistrunk (1986) used these instruments in a series of studies of supervisory behavior. Collectively, these studies demonstrated that Forms 1 and 2 of the instrument can be reliably used to assess supervisory behavior patterns and style preferences of supervisors and teachers.

Three studies examined teacher preferences for supervisory styles. Studies indicate that teachers prefer a collaborative style of supervision (Rossicone, 1985) and a supportive, collegial relationship with the supervisor (Al-Duaij, 1987; S.M. Taylor,

1985). These findings also parallel the basic elements of adult learning theory, in which participatory governance is generally desirable.

Supervisory Skills and Competencies

The effective supervisor, regardless of the level and context of his or her responsibilities, must demonstrate a variety of skills and competencies. In a broad sense, these skills may be categorized as *human relations, managerial,* and *technical* (Alfonso, Firth, & Neville, 1984). The three categories encompass a large spectrum of behaviors that have not been adequately defined and cannot be precisely prescribed. Just as there is no single best way to teach, there is also no single best approach to supervision. The artful supervisor is able to apply scientific principles and knowledge of effective teaching and supervision in a reflective and selective manner.

Supervisors are typically most effective in the area of managerial skills (those involving organization and decision making); the second most effective area is human relations (interpersonal) skills. Technical skills (involving specialized knowledge and abilities) tend to comprise the area of weakest development (Alfonso et al., 1984). Managerial skills, because of their very nature, often monopolize the supervisor's time and limit attention to the human relations and technical aspects of supervision.

Communication skills, specifically conferencing/listening skills, seem to receive the greatest amount of empirical attention. Studies show that supervisors can learn key skills of interpersonal communication with extended practice (C.A. Johnston, 1986; Taylor, Cook, Green, & Rogers, 1988). Research has identified conference climate, structure, and principal behavior meeting expectations as factors related to success of the postobservation conference (Spencer, 1986). Teachers perceive postobservation conferences as contributing to increased self-awareness of teaching behaviors (Sorrick, 1988).

Supervisory Effectiveness

Researchers have conducted a small amount of research to identify factors of general supervisory effectiveness. Various factors identified include frequency and duration of observations, supervisory behaviors/styles, and conceptual level of teachers.

Studies have examined these variables with respect to teacher satisfaction, teacher efficacy, and teacher organizational behavior. Although these studies are insufficient to produce definitive conclusions, some general implications are evident.

A reasonable amount of evidence shows that teacher satisfaction with supervision is related to the frequency of observation and feedback. Breton (1989) reported that resource teachers were more likely to experience satisfaction if supervision was frequent. Similarly, Hare (1987) reported that teacher perceptions of the accuracy of supervisory evaluations were positively related to the frequency of observation and the quantity of evaluation feedback. Schwartzberg (1987) found positive relationships among the variables of clarity of criteria and standards, frequency of observation and evaluation, and teacher perceptions of evaluation. Only one located study reported conflicting evidence. M.G. Rogers (1987), in studying a large sample of public school teachers, found that satisfaction was related to the extent to which the observed frequency of direct supervision matched the desired frequency of direct supervision, as opposed to the frequency of supervision per se.

Recent research has directed limited attention to the relationship of supervisory practices to selected teacher behaviors and perceptions. Osterman (1985) demonstrated that performance evaluation and distribution of authority were positively related to productive teacher behavior and teacher–principal interactions (cooperation, communication, and goal-oriented interaction). The author found that teachers valued four supervisory behaviors related to postobservation conferences: The supervisor (a) pointed out and built on strong points of the teacher, (b) developed a relationship of trust and confidence, (c) conducted the postobservation promptly after the observation, and (d) provided specific praise for effective teaching behaviors (Friend, 1987).

Calhoun (1986) studied the relationship of teacher conceptual level to the utilization of supervisory services. She hypothesized that teachers of high conceptual levels would demonstrate more extensive and effective uses of available resources and would produce more effective classroom instructional environments. Although she did not find evidence to support the first relationship, she did find a significant positive relationship between teacher conceptual level and involvement in professional development activities. High conceptual levels of teachers were also significantly correlated with effective classroom communication patterns.

It appears that frequent observations, clearly identified goals, and collaborative decision-making strategies are related to general supervisory effectiveness. Effective supervision requires mastery of skills related to a variety of functions. It also demands sufficient time and resources.

Summary and Implications

The research base on effective supervision is diverse and rich. Literally hundreds of studies have been conducted within recent years, producing a number of consistent findings and a far larger number of conflicting results. Collectively, these studies find that any structured model of supervision is superior to unstructured and unplanned approaches. Clinical supervision has yielded extensive research, indicating that its processes are appealing to teachers and administrators. However, its use requires a great deal of training, and the model is not often implemented in its true form. Peer supervision and self-analysis are attractive alternatives, though they do not comprise a singular approach to supervision of instruction. Competency-based supervision can contribute to the clear communication of expectations and to an objective and data-based approach to improving teaching. Although devoid of a research base, counseling models have merit in relation to the devlopmental readiness of teachers to acquire new skills.

General research on supervisory effectiveness has illuminated the deficiencies of current practice. Interventions in this area, however, have shown that planned supervision can positively impact the knowledge, attitudes, and behaviors of student teachers, in-service teachers, cooperating teachers, supervisors, and administrators. These studies and those relating to traditional models of supervision, when viewed collectively, have important implications for the development of a model of supervision for physical education. They support the need for an eclectic approach that adopts useful elements of a variety of generic models. Moreover, they point to the need for a planned, structured, and developmental model with specific application to movement settings.

Chapter 4

A Research Base for the Improvement of Teaching

Descriptive studies of supervisory practice indicate a need for increased formal training of both university supervisors and cooperating teachers. Formal training for both roles must include the study of effective supervision and effective teaching. Chapter 3 has synthesized a large body of research on supervisory effectiveness, studies that yield many useful implications for effective supervision. Chapter 4 reviews current research related to effective teaching, providing an empirical basis for the observation and analysis of instruction.

An Overview of Current Research

The past 30 to 40 years have yielded abundant information about principles of effective teaching in physical education. The first compendium of research on teaching, Gage's *Handbook of Research on Teaching* (1963), sparked a watershed of research. Following the trends of classroom research, physical education studies have primarily focused on process-product designs, attempting to determine relationships between teaching processes

(what teachers do) and student products (student outcomes, as measured by performance). These studies have been quantitative, describing variables in terms of measurable teacher and student behaviors.

A follow-up to process-product designs was the process-process paradigm. This perspective assumes that what the teacher does (teacher processes) will influence what students do (student processes), which in turn will influence learning. For example, teacher questioning techniques (processes) might influence student response patterns (processes) and ultimately student learning. Process-process paradigms have been evidenced primarily in the ALT-PE research, which views time on task at an appropriate level of difficulty as a criterion-process variable. ALT-PE (Academic Learning Time in Physical Education) is construed as a definable criterion providing direct evidence of student processes for which there is a strong likelihood of learning (i.e., motor skill acquisition) (Siedentop, 1991).

More recently, qualitative designs have focused on naturalistic investigations of teaching, studying firsthand the holistic teaching environment as it exists, without prior hypotheses or assumptions, in an effort to describe what is. Most often, these naturalistic studies use the method of participant observation, in which the researcher participates to some degree within the daily environment (Earls, 1986). Other naturalistic methods involve open-ended questionnaires, field notes of direct observations, formal and informal interviews, journals, and other document collections.

A central issue throughout the past decades of teacher effectiveness research has been whether teaching should be conceived as a science or an art, or as having elements of both. This leads to the question of whether knowledge or intuition forms the basis of teaching decisions. Teaching as a science is amenable to scientific inquiry and is capable of yielding scientific laws and principles for effective teaching. Teaching as an art assumes that effective teaching is far too complex to be subjected to scientific inquiry and the variables that affect it are too broad and diverse to allow generalizations. The reality is that teaching subsumes the characteristics of both science and art. Although extensive research and replication can identify general principles of effective teaching, the artful teacher must be able to apply these principles appropriately to a wide variety of contexts. Hosford (1984) termed this ability "the art of applying the science of education."

Hunter (1984) found that both science and art are essential to effective teaching. She wrote that teaching is a manifestation of science for these reasons:

- Identifiable cause-effect relationships exist between teaching and learning.
- Those relationships hold for all teaching and learning regardless of course content, and regardless of the learner's age and socioeconomic or ethnic characteristics.
- Although researchers identified many of these relationships in the static purity and potential sterility of the research laboratory, those relationships seem to hold in the dynamics inherent in a functioning classroom.
- Those relationships are stated in terms of probability, not certainty.
- The deliberate, intuitive, or inadvertant use of those cause-effect relationships can be observed and documented in the process of teaching.
- The principles derived from those relationships should also be incorporated in the process of planning and evaluating before and after teaching.
- The science of teaching can be taught to and predictably learned by most professionals who are willing to expend the required effort.

Hunter (1984) added that effective teaching also can be (not invariably is) an art that goes beyond proficiency, for these reasons:

- An aesthetic quality can exist in planning, in teaching, and in the evaluation of teaching performance.
- Those aesthetics can be observed, identified, labeled, and acquired but cannot be predictably taught.

Although teaching and learning are complex processes, and the research findings produced have been less than definitive, we can make some useful generalizations for the improvement of instruction. The competencies described here were selected on the basis of substantial empirical support by both generic and physical education research. They also represent a nucleus of skills that are achievable, though not consistently observed in physical education settings. Concentration on development of these skills should help student teachers and beginning teachers bridge the gap between theory and practice during the transition years. Practice at developing these competencies will provide a firm foundation for the in-service development, peer supervision, and self-analysis efforts of experienced teachers.

Time to Learn

This topic encompasses two of the most essential elements of effective teaching: the provision of time on task and opportunities for success with the criterion materials. *Time to Learn* is a review of the Beginning Teacher Evaluation Study (BTES) conducted at the Far West Laboratory in San Francisco, California (Denham & Lieberman, 1980). This series of investigations resulted in the concept of academic learning time and illustrated its critical relationship to learning. Academic learning time "is defined as the amount of time that a student spends engaged in an academic task and that s/he can perform with high success. The more ALT a student accumulates, the more the student is learning" (Fisher et al., 1980, p. 8).

The Evolution of Academic Learning Time

The California Commission for Teacher Preparation and Licensing initiated the BTES. It focused on second- and fifth-grade mathematics and reading and was initially designed to identify desirable generic competencies of beginning teachers and to provide follow-up evaluation of teacher preparation programs. Eventually, its goals were expanded to examine relationships between specific teaching behaviors and student outcomes and to disseminate this information to teachers and researchers. The project involved a series of studies occurring between 1973 and 1978 and used a variety of research techniques including stimulated recall, ethnography, interviews, teacher and student self-report, systematic observation, and testing (e.g., achievement).

What evolved from the studies was a model of classroom instruction that illustrated that we can measure student learning in two ways. We can measure learning directly, through student achievement test scores, or indirectly, through student classroom behavior. Observation of the classroom behaviors of students provides a more immediate and ongoing measure of learning (Fisher et al., 1980). This model is illustrated in Figure 4.1.

Two important quantitative aspects of ALT are allocated time (the amount of time designated for a particular content area, such as addition) and engaged time (the portion of allocated time during which the student pays attention). In addition to time, success is an important qualitative factor in student learning. Success depends upon an appropriate match between the student's skill or ability level and the learning task. Academic learning time involves the optimal allocation of time and appropriate time to maximize success (Block, 1980). Fisher et al. (1980) defined three rates of success:

High success—occurs when the student understands the material and makes only a few mistakes.

Medium success—occurs when the student partially understands and produces some correct responses and some errors.

Low success—occurs when the student does not understand the material and makes only a few correct answers by chance.

Thus, ALT involves the concepts of allocated time, student engagement, and student high success (balanced with some medium success). The model suggests that achievement increases in relation to time spent working with the criterion materials (academic tasks) at high success. It does not imply that all time should yield success, or that success will come easily, but that we need to strike a balance between medium and high success rates with an emphasis on the latter.

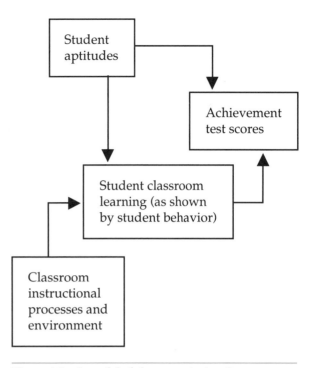

Figure 4.1 A model of classroom instruction.
Note: From "Teaching behaviors, academic learning time, and student achievement: An overview." By C. Fisher, D. Berliner, N. Filby, R. Marliave, L. Cahen, & M. Dishaw. In *Time to Learn* (1980), by C. Denham & A. Lieberman (Eds.), p. 8, Washington, DC: National Institute of Education. Copyright 1980 by California State Commission for Teacher Preparation and Licensing, Sacramento. (ERIC Document Reproduction Service No. ED 012-947).

Siedentop, Birdwell, and Metzler (1979) first described the measurement of academic learning time in a physical education setting. Their original instrument has been modified several times, but the most currently used version is the ALT-PE 1982 revision (Siedentop, Tousignant, & Parker, 1982). Adaptations of the model have added the dimension of teacher behavior (Birdwell, 1980) and have provided a simplified coding format for teaching and coaching settings (Wilkinson & Taggart, 1985). An ALT-PE Microcomputer Data Collection System (MCDCS) has also been developed by Metzler (1989a).

Academic Learning Time in Physical Education

In translating what has been learned from the BTES, researchers in physical education have studied the amount of ALT-PE provided by physical education teachers at elementary and secondary levels. In general, these studies show that ALT-PE is typically low, sometimes as low as 15 percent (Randall & Imwold, 1989). ALT-PE is a variable of which physical education teachers seem to be quite unaware, and which specialized training has failed to sufficiently address. One comparison of academic learning time provided by specialists and by nonspecialists in elementary physical education revealed no significant differences in this criterion (Placek & Randall, 1986).

Metzler (1979) described a phenomenon called the "funnel effect," which illustrates how allocated time gradually diminishes as it funnels down to engaged time, motor-engaged time, and ALT-PE. For example, a school might allocate 50 minutes for physical education class. Of that time, approximately 10 minutes is lopped off at the beginning and at the end for dressing, showering, taking roll, and other managerial activities. This leaves about 30 minutes of engaged time, the portion of allocated time devoted to physical education content. Of those 30 minutes, some time is devoted to cognitive and managerial activity (e.g., demonstrating, explaining, organizing groups, and transitioning), and motor-engaged time (purposeful movement) is further reduced to as little as 15 minutes (or less!). ALT-PE is that portion of motor-engaged time in which the student is engaged at an appropriate level of difficulty. ALT-PE is diminished if the task is not structured to provide many opportunities to practice (high engaged rates) or if the task is too easy or too difficult.

In a summary of research on ALT-PE, Metzler (1989b) reviewed more than 50 current studies and summary articles. The author synthesized findings into six areas of the literature: teacher time, student time, time and achievement, experimental manipulation of time, coaches' time, and players' time. Pertinent conclusions were that teachers spend too much time in noninstruction (management, monitoring, and organization) and too little time teaching. Consequently, students spend much of their time in unproductive activities (waiting, listening, and off-task). Higher rates of ALT are produced in sports settings than in physical education; coaches spend more time teaching than teachers, and players spend more time practicing than students.

Teacher conceptualizations of time focus on the activities of the class as a whole, as opposed to activities of individual students. The inherent nature of the activity contributes substantially to the production of ALT, which varies according to content (e.g., team sports vs. individual activities). Mounting evidence strongly links dimensions of

student time to increased learning. Research has focused attention also on the characteristics of effective intervention strategies for increasing rates of ALT-PE, and supports their general utility (Metzler, 1989b).

One recent study indicated that the interval recording technique used by the ALT-PE instruments (Versions 1 and 2) may not provide valid estimates of student engagement (Silverman & Zotos, 1987). When compared to an equivalent time sampling method and actual second-by-second engaged time coded by an instrument designed for that purpose (with each student coded for the entire 30 minutes), the ALT-PE time sampling formats provided considerably higher estimates of ALT-PE.

Silverman and Zotos (1987) interpreted this as evidence that a measurement error results from coding one behavior for an entire 6-second interval. However, the rank order of engaged times for six observed classes was the same for the ALT-PE instruments as the equivalent time sampling method and the actual engaged-time measure. Its usefulness as a general comparative measure, as opposed to a precise measure of engaged time, was judged tenable.

There are several limitations of ALT-PE that relate to Silverman's observations. Parker (1989) noted that ALT-PE is a time-based concept that utilizes interval recording techniques and is thus limited by the nature of that technique. ALT-PE does not distinguish activity-specific dimensions of motor performance, thus motor-engagement can take diverse forms. ALT-PE provides a limited perspective of what happens in physical education, ignores congruence between learner needs and content, is insensitive to the goals of a given lesson, and fails to indicate the quality of the practice.

Despite its limitations, ALT-PE is an extremely useful tool for gaining insight into the effective use of time in physical education. It can provide measures of the relative productivity of lessons and can act as an index for the improvement of instruction and the effectiveness of specific interventions. When ALT-PE is applied by trained observers and interpreted within its intended framework, the validity and reliability of the instrument seem more than adequate.

Time and success are two variables that are inextricably intertwined with student achievement. By increasing the amount of time in which students are engaged in the content with few errors, we can increase the amount of learning that takes place. Increases in allocated time alone will not necessarily ensure increased learning, and we gain no advantage by having a student repeatedly practice a task that is too easy or difficult.

Imagine what might happen if we asked a second-grade child to practice shooting basketballs at a 10-foot basket. Suppose that child practiced diligently for 20 minutes or more, successfully getting the ball in the basket once or twice within that period. What would be the net gain in student skill of that practice situation, even multiplied by 10 or 20 class periods? Certainly, it would be negligible. Any improvement the child might gain over time could probably be attributed more to growth and development (the child is taller and stronger) than to improved skill. The obvious solution is to choose a more appropriate skill, or at the very least, lower the basket. A guideline for increasing time and success variables is plenty of appropriate practice.

The concept of academic learning time provides an extremely important focus for observing and analyzing instruction. Its elements of allocated time, student engagement, and student success are inextricably linked to student learning. Although research clearly supports these relationships, many teaching environments demonstrate low levels of academic learning time. Educators must direct continued attention to intervention strategies for increasing rates of academic learning time, particularly in the area of physical education.

Direct Instruction

This concept has fairly recent origins and is attributed primarily to the work of Rosenshine and Furst (1971), who described a model of instruction that emphasizes a high degree of structure, academic focus, sequencing, and teacher direction. This model tends to incorporate large-group instruction more than individual instruction. Through a synthesis of 50 process-product studies, the authors identified 10 variables that seemed to be supported by the research as related to student achievement. The characteristics of direct instruction included the following (Rosenshine, 1979; Rosenshine & Furst, 1973):

- Clarity of the teacher's presentation
- Variability of activities during the lesson
- Enthusiasm of the teacher
- Task orientation or businesslike behaviors in the classroom
- Student opportunity to learn, or content covered

- Acknowledgment and encouragement of student ideas during discussion
- Criticism of the student (negatively correlated with achievement)
- Use of structuring comments at the start of and during a lesson
- Use of a variety of types of questions in terms of cognitive level
- Probing or encouragement for elaboration on responses by students

The following definition provides a clear summary of the characteristics of this model (Rosenshine, 1979):

Direct instruction refers to academically focused, teacher-directed classrooms using sequenced and structured materials. It refers to teaching activities where goals are clear to students, time allocated for instruction is sufficient and continuous, coverage of content is extensive, the performance of students is monitored, questions are at a low cognitive level so that students can produce many correct responses, and feedback to students is immediate and academically oriented. In direct instruction the teacher controls instructional goals, chooses materials appropriate for the student's ability, and paces the instructional episode. Interaction is characterized as structured, but not authoritarian. Learning takes place in a convivial atmosphere. The goal is to move the students through a sequenced set of materials or tasks. Such materials are common across classrooms and have a relatively strong congruence with the tasks on achievement tests. (p. 38)

The author proposed these variables of direct instruction on the basis of generic research involving classrooms of normal children. None of the studies attempted to isolate groups of students according to achievement, aptitude, or personality variables. The factors related to achievement were individually supported but were not collectively subjected to empirical scrutiny. Subsequent research on the model produced conflicting results, and it became apparent that a number of contextual variables (grade level, class size, content, and groupings) might affect the results of direct instruction. Two variables that did hold up to close scrutiny were *content covered* (opportunity to learn) and *task orientation* (academic focus, student engagement time, and attention). The author theorized that other variables were more important at upper grade levels (intermediate and above).

In an analysis of direct instruction, Peterson (1979a, 1979b) examined contextual variables (content, objectives) and individual variables (personal control, ability) that may limit the effectiveness of direct instruction. She conducted a meta-analysis of 200 studies, concluding that direct instruction produces larger gains in achievement whereas open instruction yields greater increases in creativity, curiosity, independence, and attitude toward school. The objectives of instruction therefore influence decisions about style, because direct instruction does not facilitate inquiry but may improve basic skills.

Peterson (1979a, 1979b) interpreted some studies to indicate that *locus of control* is an important variable, with students of external control benefiting most from direct instruction. Other variables of personal control that she found important were *degree of achievement* and *task orientation*. Ability was an apparent factor; low-ability students performed better in large groups, and the reverse was true for high-ability students.

Rosenshine (1987) used the term *explicit teaching* to denote "a systematic method of teaching that includes presenting material in smalls steps, pausing to check for student understanding, and requiring active and successful participation from all students" (p. 75). He acknowledged that this method is most appropriate for promoting skilled performance or mastery of specific knowledge (e.g., mathematical procedures, specific reading skills, science facts). Thus, the distinction is made between explicit and implicit skills.

For generic applications, the appropriateness of direct instruction depends upon the objectives of the teacher and the characteristics of the students. As applied to physical education, the general constructs of direct instruction (teacher directed, structured, task oriented, sufficient time allocated, closely monitored, clear goals, providing success, frequent feedback) will be effective when the objectives of the lesson involve convergent learning (e.g., acquiring specialized skills, developing fitness). When a teacher desires divergent outcomes (e.g., problem solving, exploration, guided discovery), he or she should employ more indirect styles of teaching.

A series of studies reported by Goldberger (1982) indicated that direct teaching styles might be effective for achieving specific learning outcomes in physical education, irrespective of SES and ability variables. The author investigated direct instruction in terms of Mosston and Ashworth's (1986) spectrum theory, with Styles A-E (command, practice, reciprocal, self-check, and inclusion) included in a "direct cluster." Goldberger found that Style B (practice), which most closely approximates the concept of direct instruction, consistently produced learning of a novel task across socioeconomic status (SES) settings and ability groupings. Goldberger found Style C, a reciprocal style that involves working in pairs, to be helpful in developing social interactions.

Oliver (1983) examined the impact of direct instruction on skill learning in physical education. This constituted the first empirical look at direct instruction in a physical education context. Results showed that direct instruction promoted acquisition of volleyball skills.

An instrument developed for the assessment of direct instruction in physical education is the Direct Instruction Behavior Analysis (DIBA) (Zakrajsek & Tannehill, 1989). The instrument uses an interval recording format and contains 15 categories for observing teacher and student behavior. Teacher behaviors are categorized as *informing*, *observing*, *structuring*, *questioning*, *praise/encouragement*, *feedback*, *controlling*, *none of the above* (noninstructional), *enthusiasm*, *clarity*, and *modeling*. Student behavior categories are *motor engaged*, *cognitive engaged*, *response preparing*, and *off task*. The supervisor observes teacher and student behaviors alternately throughout the lesson, providing an overall analysis of the effectiveness of direct instruction.

Classroom Management

Effective classroom management requires knowledge and application of general principles for communicating and reinforcing expectations for student behavior. The knowledge base for classroom management derives primarily from the work of Kounin (1970) and a series of studies described by Evertson and others.

Jacob Kounin's (1970) work in identifying variables of effective discipline is a classic reference. Essentially, it encompasses six strategies for the prevention of off-task behavior and the maintenance of a task-oriented learning environment. These variables are as follows:

With-it-ness—awareness of what is going on
Overlapping—ability to attend to two events simultaneously

Smoothness—"absence of dangles, flip-flops, and thrusts" (p. 74)

Momentum—maintenance of brisk pace

Group alerting—efforts to gain and maintain attention of the students as a whole; keeping them on task and "on their toes" (p. 117)

Accountability—extent to which the students are held responsible for their own behavior during the lesson

Although research has supported the first four variables, *group alerting* and *accountability* have not shown positive correlations with learning gains (Brophy, 1979). It appears that the application of the first 4 strategies will produce good results.

Carolyn Evertson and her associates have conducted a number of studies of classroom management at the University of Texas, Austin, Research and Development Center for Teacher Education. This work has involved correlational and descriptive studies of elementary and junior high school classes to determine how successful teachers effectively manage classrooms (Emmer, Evertson, & Anderson, 1980; Sanford & Evertson, 1981). Researchers also conducted an experimental study to determine the effect of training on classroom management (Evertson, Emmer, Sanford, & Clements, 1983). Results of the Classroom Management Improvement Study showed that training could help teachers establish and maintain productive classrooms.

These studies reveal that what happens at the beginning of the year is of paramount importance in establishing classroom management. In essense, the findings support the old teaching axiom of "don't smile until Christmas," although this should be interpreted somewhat loosely. Effective teachers in elementary and junior high schools spent more time at the beginning of the year explaining, monitoring, and reinforcing rules. Effective teachers demonstrated a stronger leadership role, clearly establishing consequences for misbehavior, and holding students accountable for their work.

The Classroom Organization Study, which focused on elementary classrooms, produced 11 prescriptions for classroom organization and management (Evertson, Emmer, Sanford, & Clements, (1983):

- *Readying the classroom*. The teacher ensures that classroom space and materials are ready for the beginning of the year.

- *Planning rules and procedures*. The teacher thinks about what procedures students must follow to function effectively in the classroom and in the school environment, decides what behaviors are acceptable, and develops a list of procedures and rules.
- *Establishing consequences*. Before the school year begins, the teacher decides on consequences for appropriate and inappropriate behavior in the classroom. The teacher communicates these to the students and follows through consistently.
- *Teaching rules and procedures*. The teacher includes sequences for systematically teaching rules and procedures in lesson plans for the beginning of school. The teacher decides when and how they will be taught and when practice and review will occur.
- *Developing beginning-of-school activities*. The teacher develops activities for the first few days of school that will involve students readily and maintain a whole-group focus.
- *Planning strategies for potential problems*. The teacher plans strategies to deal with potential problems that could upset classroom organization and management.
- *Monitoring*. The teacher monitors student behavior closely.
- *Stopping inappropriate behavior*. The teacher handles inappropriate and disruptive behavior promptly and consistently.
- *Organizing instruction*. The teacher organizes instruction to provide learning activities at suitable levels for all students in the class.
- *Developing student accountability*. The teacher develops procedures that keep the children responsible for their work.
- *Ensuring instructional clarity*. The teacher is clear when presenting information and giving directions to students.

These studies provide a clear conceptual framework for the establishment of effective classroom management. Timing is essential to both preventive classroom management (organizing to prevent disruptions) and discipline (dealing with disruptions as they occur). Effective classroom managers establish and reinforce rules at the beginning of the year (within the first 3 weeks) and apply them consistently throughout the year. Such managers promptly desist inappropriate behaviors when they occur and also signal appropriate behaviors. Some additional behaviors of effective teachers are eye contact and stating desired attitudes.

Classroom Climate

Classroom climate refers to the emotional dimensions of the learning environment, although the term could be broadly construed as the interaction of curriculum, instruction, and instructional materials (Talmage & Eash, 1979). The emotional climate of the classroom describes the nature of teacher and student interactions. Related factors include teacher directness/indirectness, student involvement in verbal discourse, and praise versus criticism. It would be handy if the research provided a neat package of guidelines for a positive or productive classroom climate. Unfortunately, the literature is somewhat ambiguous and controversial and does not necessarily support expected conclusions. Should teachers emphasize "critical demandingness" or patience and encouragement? Will praise produce increases in student learning? What is the impact of teacher expectations on student learning? Although many teaching methods texts stress the need for a positive classroom environment, the research does not support the belief that a warm emotional climate is essential for learning. A neutral classroom environment seems to be most conducive, but negative classroom climates should not be promoted (Soar & Soar, 1979).

One teaching behavior that can substantially impact the classroom climate is praise. According to Brophy (1981), praise entails commending the worth of a student or expressing approval or admiration. Praise is distinguished from positive feedback (acknowledgment of a correct response) by the element of teacher affect that is added (surprise, delight, excitement) or by information about the value of the specified behavior. In contrast, "criticism refers to negative teacher responses to student behavior which go beyond whatever level of simple feedback (negation) is needed to indicate that behavior is inappropriate or answers are incorrect. . . expressions of disapproval, disgust, or rejection" (p. 6).

Surprisingly, praise is weakly and inconsistently correlated with learning. Its value as a general strategy has been considerably overrated, but we should not reject it outright. Brophy (1979) suggested that praise should be given in moderation and should be as specific as possible. Ideally, teachers should praise students individually and privately, placing more emphasis on thinking and effort than on getting the correct answer. Praise may have more value for students of low ability or confidence, provided it is credible, genuine, and deserved. Criticism should also be specific and

should identify desirable alternative behaviors or responses.

A functional way of viewing praise and learning is as a curvilinear or inverted-U relationship. Although praise is essential to motivation, it cannot produce linear increases in student learning. In fact, excessive or lavish praise can actually inhibit learning, as aptly illustrated by Wildman et al. (1985):

> Under conditions of little or no praise, one can reasonably expect that a student's classroom performance will suffer. As the use of praise increases, so does performance. But the relationship is not linear — performance does not continue to improve with higher and higher levels of the treatment. Ultimately, under too much praise, performance will deteriorate, producing . . . [a] curvileaner relationship. (p. 81)

Evertson (1975) examined, with respect to student learning, a number of additional factors related to praise and criticism. For the elementary students studied, socioeconomic status (SES) seemed to be an important variable. Praise was more often positively correlated with learning in low-SES schools but was relatively unimportant in high-SES schools. Positive reinforcement and praise were more successful learning strategies for low-SES students, whereas critical demandingness and communicating high expectations were more successful with high-SES students. For both high and low socioeconomic students, symbolic rewards (e.g., stickers, smiling faces, and gold stars) were positively associated with learning gains, but verbal praise and special privileges (e.g., housekeeping chores and monitoring) were not.

The effect of criticism appeared to depend on the focus of the criticism. When the teacher criticized poor academic work, criticism tended to connote high expectations for student performance. Justified, appropriate, and gentle criticisms aimed at upgrading the quality of work were positively correlated with learning gains for high-achieving students.

One plausible explanation for the interaction of achievement motivation and praise/criticism was offered by Evertson (1975) in this analysis:

> In short, a student who is accustomed to success, expects success, and is capable of achieving success with reasonable effort tends to respond well, at least in terms of improved achievement, to chiding criticism for failure that results from lack of effort or persistent

application of skills. In contrast, the student who is accustomed to failure, and has difficulty mastering something even if he persists long and hard is much more likely to be positively affected by encouragement and praise, and more likely to be negatively affected by criticism. (p. 10)

Studies of teacher praise yield useful guidelines for establishing productive classroom climates. Brophy (1981) proposed 12 such guidelines on the basis of his functional analysis of the research. He proposed that effective praise

- is delivered contingently;
- specifies the particulars of the accomplishment;
- shows spontaneity, variety, and other signs of credibility and suggests clear attention to the student's accomplishment;
- rewards attainment of specific performance criteria (which can include effort);
- informs students about their competence or the value of their accomplishments;
- helps students better appreciate their own task-related behavior and problem-solving abilities;
- uses students' own prior accomplishments as the context for describing present accomplishments;
- is given in recognition of noteworthy effort or success at difficult tasks (difficult for the particular student);
- attributes success to effort and ability, implying that the student can expect similar success in the future;
- fosters endogenous attributions (students believe that they expend effort on the task because they enjoy the task and/or want to develop task-relevant skills);
- focuses students' attention on their own task-relevant behavior; and
- fosters appreciation of and desirable attributions about task-relevant behavior after the process is completed.

We must use caution in the strict interpretation of guidelines for effective praise. First, many of the studies reported were descriptive or correlational and therefore did not attempt to establish cause-and-effect relationships. Both praise and criticism occurred infrequently in the classrooms that were studied. Second, although praise has not been consistently correlated with student learning, research has shown that praise used as a contingent reinforcer affects specified student behaviors (Brophy,

1981). Third, we should consider the unique nature of the physical education environment.

One of our primary goals in physical education is to develop positive attitudes and approach tendencies so that students will be likely to engage in movement activities outside of school and throughout their lifetimes. Although lavish and insincere praise will probably not help, genuine and specific praise should enhance motivation. Praise will be particularly important for those students who lack confidence, experience, or ability in physical skills. In any event, the climate of physical education should not be negative.

Some all-too-common practices in physical education are very detrimental to classroom climate. For example, teachers may spend more time with athletes versus nonathletes and give more attention to boys versus girls. Other negative practices include allowing children to pick teams; overemphasis on competition; focus on product (e.g., winning) versus process (skill acquisition, knowledge, and attitudes); and use of games of elimination. A positive classroom climate, in which these practices are absent, is essential to motivation for all students, regardless of their abilities.

Feedback

Feedback is related to the emotional climate in a broader sense than is praise, because feedback may take the form of positive, corrective, negative, or neutral responses. Teachers can provide feedback in relation to the student's social behavior (conduct) or to aspects of the skill performance. Some important definitions and distinctions are essential to the concept of feedback in movement settings. The literature shows conflicting use of terminology; definitions presented here were adopted from Sage (1984).

Definitions Related to Feedback

Feedback refers to all of the information that is available during or after a movement. It may be derived as *intrinsic feedback* through information that is inherently available to the performer (kinesthetic, tactile, visual, or auditory sensations) or provided as *augmented feedback* (through external sources). Of primary interest here is teacher verbal feedback, which is information the teacher provides to the student about his or her performance.

Augmented feedback may be classified as verbal or nonverbal. It may also take the form of *knowledge of results* (information about the product or outcome of the performance, e.g., did the ball land in the service court?), or *knowledge of performance* (information about the movement pattern — did the racket reach the back-scratch position?).

In addition to its source, feedback can be categorized according to its valence (positive or corrective), its latency (immediate or delayed), its precision (general or specific), its timing (concurrent or terminal), its target (individual, group, or whole class), and its relevance (congruent or incongruent to the task).

No matter how it is construed, feedback is essential to learning. It is perhaps the most important variable in skill performance. Research shows that no improvement occurs without feedback, progressive improvement occurs with it, and deterioration occurs quickly after its withdrawal (Bilodeau & Bilodeau, 1961). Feedback fulfills the three basic functions of information, motivation, and reinforcement.

Descriptions of Feedback in Physical Education and Athletics

Studies show that physical educators are less than optimally efficient in providing feedback. They tend to provide low frequencies of feedback in general and disproportionately higher rates of corrective to positive feedback. This may result from a kind of coaching mentality with which athletic experiences influence physical educators to focus on errors as opposed to correct responses. Physical educators are more general in giving positive feedback and more specific in providing corrective feedback (Tobey, 1974). General feedback statements or ''global goods'' do not identify a specific element of that performance (e.g., ''nice,'' ''good job,'' ''that's it''). Specific feedback statements identify a specific aspect of the performance as correct or incorrect, or give a precise prescription for improvement (''good follow-through,'' ''bend your knees'') (P.A. Dodds, 1989).

The study of informational and motivational feedback provided by coaches in a youth sport setting has provided some interesting findings. Evaluations of coaches by Little League baseball players were positively related to provision of technical instruction and supportive coaching behaviors of reinforcement and mistake-contingent reinforcement. These behaviors also induced more positive attitudes toward the sport and toward

teammates and higher levels of self-esteem (Smoll & Smith, 1984).

Guidelines for Providing Augmented Teacher/Coach Feedback

The following guidelines are proposed tentatively, because this research has produced conflicting results. Much research derives from motor learning laboratory tasks, whereas some is based on animal studies. Studies of teacher feedback in applied settings have also produced controversy (Paese, 1987), and additional research is needed in this area. Consequently, it is difficult and even precarious to translate these findings to applied settings. However, there seems to be general consensus on the following points:

- Frequent feedback is desirable for skill acquisition and improved performance.
- Feedback should be sufficiently precise to identify relevant aspects of task performance, but not so precise as to confuse the learner.
- Feedback should be appropriate to the learner's development level. Feedback for novices should focus on gross aspects of the task, whereas feedback for skilled performers may be more complex. Similarly, young children lack the cognitive capacities to process complex feedback.
- Knowledge of performance (KP) is best for closed motor skills (those in which the environment is stable, e.g., hitting a ball off a stationary tee), whereas knowledge of results (KR) is more appropriate for open skills (those in which the environment is unstable, e.g., hitting a pitched ball).
- Feedback should be followed by opportunities to practice the skill and implement the prescription.
- Teachers should try to consistently reinforce both high- and low-skilled students.
- Teachers should correct errors when they become habitual.

Expectancy

Research interest in teacher expectations was sparked by the publication of Rosenthal and Jacobson's 1968 book, *Pygmalion in the Classroom*. The central thesis of that work was based on self-fulfilling prophecy, or specifically that teacher expectations can directly and indirectly influence student performance. This study showed that teacher expectation about student performance affected teacher behavior. Teachers showed different behavior patterns with students believed to be high and low achievers, and student achievement was affected by these differences. In short, students tend to perform in accordance with the expectations of their teachers.

Teacher expectations are inferences that teachers make about students' academic abilities and potential to benefit from instruction (Good, 1987). Expectations may involve entire classes, groups, or individual students and are frequently influenced by stereotyped beliefs about gender, race, ethnicity, or ability. Expectations may take the form of *self-fulfilling prophecy*, erroneous beliefs that lead to behaviors that produce outcomes consistent with those beliefs. They may also consist of *sustaining expectations*, failure of teachers to see student potential and to respond to students in ways that encourage fulfillment of that potential (Cooper & Good, 1983).

Teachers communicate expectations to students through classroom assignments, pacing, and interactions with students. Teachers may communicate expectations through overt or subtle behaviors, and expectations may affect the content of instruction or the way that it is presented. As a result, students form their own expectations that consequently affect effort and performance. The Brophy-Good model provides a clear description of the dynamics of this phenomenon (Good, 1987):

1. The teacher expects different types of behavior and achievement from different students.

2. Because of these varied expectations, the teacher behaves differently toward different students.

3. This treatment communicates to the students what behavior and achievement the teacher expects from them, and it affects their self-concepts, achievement motivation, and levels of aspiration.

4. If this treatment is consistent over time, and if the students do not resist or change it in some way, it will shape their achievement and behavior. High-expectation students will achieve at high levels, whereas the achievement of low-expectation students will decline.

5. With time, students' achievement and behavior will conform more and more closely to the behavior the teacher expects of them.

Research on the model has demonstrated a variety of overt differential behaviors that teachers might demonstrate. With respect to students perceived as high or low in ability, teachers may respond differentially in the following manners (Good, 1987):

- Provide low-expectation students less time to answer
- Give low-expectation students answers or call on someone else, rather than trying to improve responses of low-expectation students by giving clues or additional opportunities to respond
- Give inappropriate reinforcement: reward inappropriate behavior or incorrect answers by low-expectation students
- Criticize low-expectation students for failure more often
- Praise low-expectation students less frequently for success
- Fail to give feedback to the public responses of low-expectation students
- Pay less attention to low-expectation students generally or interact with them less frequently
- Call on low-expectation students less often to answer questions
- Seat low-expectation students farther from the teacher
- Demand less from low-expectation students
- Interact with low-expectation students more privately than publicly and monitor and structure their activities more closely
- Administer or grade tests and assignments differently, giving high-expectation students but not low-expectation students the benefit of the doubt in borderline cases
- Have fewer friendly interactions with low-expectation students, including less smiling and fewer other nonverbal indicators of support
- Give briefer and less informative feedback to low-expectation students' questions
- Use less eye contact and other nonverbal communication of attention and responsiveness with low-expectation students
- Use effective but time-consuming methods with low-expectation students when time is limited
- Interrupt low-expectation students more often when they make reading mistakes[3]

The research described previously derives from studies of elementary classrooms. However, Martinek (1981, 1982) applied pygmalion theory to physical education. A classic reference is *Pygmalion in the Gym*, published by Martinek, Crowe, and Rejeski in 1982. This study found that teacher expectations in physical education are affected by a number of interacting processes. First, teachers form expectations of students on the basis of impression cues such as somatotype, gender, and disabling conditions. Second, these interactions between the student and teacher are influenced by the teacher's expectations. Last, the student perceives these expectations through interactions and begins to respond in accordance (Martinek, 1982).

A classic example of expectancy occurs frequently in fitness testing, when the instructor arranges the girls in the class for one heat of the 1-mile run, and sends the boys off in the next heat. The expectation communicated is that boys perform better than girls. Teachers communicate this expectation early in elementary physical education and reinforce it consistently throughout secondary physical education.

Self-fulfilling prophecy and sustaining expectations are salient forces in physical education. Teachers may intentionally or unknowingly respond differently to boys and girls, high- and low-skill students, attractive and unattractive students, athletes and nonathletes, and students of varying racial and ethnic groups. Physical education teachers need to develop increased awareness of and sensitivity to this issue.

Lesson Presentation Skills

This area of research is included to facilitate physical education instruction primarily as it occurs in classroom settings. Classroom teaching is a fairly new area of endeavor for physical educators, whose efforts have typically been confined to the gymnasium or playing field. However, the trend toward incorporation of academic concepts (e.g., personal fitness, health, and life management), particularly in secondary schools, has placed some physical educators in the classroom for the first time. This transition to a foreign teaching environment can produce discomfort, and attention to a number of specialized skills can help reduce this feeling.

Research has shown that several components of lesson presentation influence learning. Two of these elements, set induction (or anticipatory set) and closure, relate to strategies for introducing and summarizing lesson content. Two others, pacing and structuring, relate to strategies for maintaining a productive flow of learning activities throughout the lesson. An additional element, task orientation, has been discussed previously with

respect to direct instruction. Task orientation is also relevant as a general characteristic of effective lesson presentation, particularly when the goal relates to content or skill mastery.

Effective teaching in the classroom follows the sequence of getting attention, giving information, engaging the students actively in the content, and summarizing what has been done. Such teaching begins, therefore, with set induction—actions of and statements made by the teacher to orient the students to the objectives of the lesson. Set induction focuses student attention on the lesson, creates an organizational framework or scaffolding for the content and activities to follow, enhances abstract thinking through the use of examples or analogies, and initiates the interest and involvement of students in the lesson (Shostak, 1990). Shostak (1990) suggested that the teacher use set induction

- to focus student attention on the teacher's presentation by employing an activity, event, object, or person that relates directly to student interest or previous experience;
- to provide a structure or framework that enables students to visualize the content or activities of the presentation;
- to clarify the goals of the lesson presentation;
- to provide a smooth transition from known or already covered material to new or unknown material by using examples (either verbal or nonverbal), analogies, and activities that students have interest in or experience with; and
- to evaluate previously covered material by involving students in activities, examples, and analogies that demonstrate understanding of content.

Another concept that relates to set induction is Ausubel's (1963) Model of Advance Organizers. In his theory of meaningful verbal learning, the author emphasized the importance of linking new material to previous learning through the use of introductory activities. A review of research conducted on the use of advance organizers revealed that they do contribute to recall of lower-order concepts (Rolheiser-Bennett, 1987). Advance organizers are effective in a variety of curriculum areas and for students of all ages, but particularly at the concrete operations stage (Stone, 1983).

Pacing is an important aspect of effective teaching that can apply specifically to the rate of content coverage within a given lesson or to the selection of curriculum content in the planning phase. Pacing affects content coverage with respect to the amount of material that the class can cover, and effective teachers tend to expose students to a large amount of developmentally appropriate material and move them through it at a fairly rapid pace (Harrison, 1987). Generally, a rapid pace of instruction is more effective than a leisurely one. However, in making pacing decisions teachers must consider the nature of the content and the readiness of the students. In content areas in which cumulative tasks are important (i.e., understanding of one element is essential to understanding the next), pacing must be more closely geared to individual student differences and mastery (Karweit, 1985).

It is unproductive for students to spend substantial amounts of time practicing and reviewing skills that they have already mastered. Likewise, it is not helpful to subject students to materials and activities that are too difficult to allow success. Roberton (1977) described two negative results that can occur when teachers expose students to skill practice situations for which they lack readiness. Substitution of motor skills occurs when students demonstrate alternative behaviors in game or practice situations that are too complex (e.g., running around the backhand side to use the forehand stroke in tennis). Regression of motor skills shows backward development or less mature performance than is possible in less dynamic situations (e.g., bouncing the ball far ahead in a dribbling relay race).

Researchers have also described pacing in terms of its active or passive nature. Gump (1982) characterized active pacing as "pulling" students along through the work, whereas passive pacing depends on student progress and motivation. Active pacing is designed to maintain momentum and involvement in classroom activities, and it helps the teacher maintain task orientation.

Task orientation involves a businesslike approach to teaching; the teacher focuses on academic content and wastes little time in noninstructional activity. Teachers with high task orientation will demonstrate subject orientation, avoid digression from the key points, and maintain student on-task behavior.

Structuring is a behavior that also helps to maintain academic focus, providing clarity and direction for activities to follow and helping students to understand what is expected of them. Structuring moves are verbal actions (initiatory moves) that teachers use to gain attention of students and to set the context for what is to follow (Bellack, Kliebard, Hyman, & Smith, 1966). Berliner (1987) proposed that structuring can help teachers enhance their students' learning by providing clear directions in introducing lessons, serving as advance organizers, or summarizing or reviewing material. Therefore, teachers may use structuring behaviors during set induction or closure or during the les-

son itself as a means of focusing attention on specifics.

A comprehensive model of classroom presentation, discussed previously as an outgrowth of direct instruction, is Rosenshine's (1987) conceptualization of explicit teaching. Using a summary of research in this area, he identified six teaching functions that involve decisions about content presentation. Within each of these functions, the author recommended effective teaching behaviors, as follows:

Teaching Functions

1. **Review**
   Review homework
   Review relevant previous learning
   Review prerequisite skills and
      knowledge for the lesson
2. **Presentation**
   State lesson goals and/or provide
      outline
   Teach in small steps
   Model procedures
   Provide concrete positive and
      negative examples
   Use clear language
   Check for student understanding
   Avoid digressions
3. **Guided practice**
   Provide ample time
   Provide ample frequency of questions
      or guided practice
   Ensure all students respond and
      receive feedback
   Aim for high success rate
   Continue practice until students are
      fluid
4. **Corrections and feedback**
   Give process feedback when answers
      are correct but hesitant
   Give sustaining feedback, clues, or re-
      teaching when answers are incorrect
   Reteach when necessary
5. **Independent practice**
   Help students during initial steps, or
      overview
   Continue practice until students are
      automatic (where relevant)
   Provide active supervision (where
      possible)
   Use routines to give help to slower
      students
6. **Weekly and monthly reviews**[4]

Closure, or the brief review and summarization of the lesson's activities, can also help to anchor learning. Shostak (1990) outlined the purposes of closure as (a) signaling the end of a lesson or calling attention to a particular lesson segment, (b) organizing student learning, and (c) summarizing and reinforcing the major points of learning. We can view closure as a complement of set induction that provides information about what has occurred with respect to the lesson's objectives. During closure the teacher may wish to identify areas in which students show progress or need further attention. The teacher may also point out particular mechanical aspects of skill performance, game strategies, or other elements of performance for review.

Questioning Skills

Although teachers can use lesson presentation skills to provide instructional input (give information), questioning skills are used to obtain information from students, to check for understanding, and to anchor important concepts. Effective questioning techniques involve using high- and low-order questions, providing wait time, probing, and verbally reinforcing responses. In a global sense, we can categorize questions as lower cognitive level (those involving fact recall) and higher cognitive level (those requiring students to think independently) (Gall, 1984). Basically, questions involving *what*? and *where*? are classified as low order, whereas those requiring *why*? responses are termed high order. In more precise terms, we can categorize questions according to six levels of Bloom's (1956) *Taxonomy of Educational Objectives*. These include knowledge, comprehension, application, analysis, synthesis, and evaluation. Chapter 9 contains definitions and examples of these categories. This conceptualization reflects a hierarchical view of the nature of thought process required for generating responses. Cognitive operations involved in knowledge or comprehension questions can be classified as low-order or convergent, whereas the remaining levels require high order or divergent responses (Winne, 1979).

Classroom observations show that, on the average, 60 percent of questions asked by teachers require only recall. High-order thinking is required by 20 percent of questions, whereas the remaining are procedural (Gall, 1970). This underemphasis of high order questions can also be observed in the nature of written tests used typically by teachers across curriculum areas and grade levels.

Process-product studies of the effect of questions on student learning have produced conflicting results about the efficacy of low-order and high-order questions. The prevailing belief has been that higher cognitive questions more effectively promote student learning. A meta-analysis of research on questioning conducted by Redfield and Rousseau (1981) supported this conclusion. However, others (Gall, 1970; Winne, 1979) believe that this conclusion is not tenable. Gall (1984) proposed a resolution of the conflict, suggesting that fact questions are most appropriate for developing mastery of basic skills among young, disadvantaged children. The author recommended higher cognitive questions for students of average and high abilities, especially in high school teaching, which should foster independent thinking.

Another important element of effective questioning is wait time, time for students to organize their thoughts. Most teachers ask questions at a very rapid rate, frequently asking multiple questions (some requiring higher-order cognitive processes) within a minute or two. Failure to provide think time (wait time) results in fewer and poorer student responses. Providing 3 to 5 minutes of wait time after asking a question allows students to organize their thoughts, produces more and longer responses, and helps initiate more student questions (Rowe, 1974a, 1974b; Tobin, 1986).

Research has found that probing, or stimulating students to think or to refine their responses, relates positively to student achievement (L. Anderson, Evertson, & Brophy, 1979). Teachers can use probing questions to extend, amplify, rephrase, or give information about why a student response is correct. For example, "So, John, you believe that people in America have become more sedentary. Why do you believe that is so?" Teachers, however, tend to use probing infrequently. More often than not, they respond to student answers with nebulous utterances, such as "uh-huh," "OK," or "no," or do not respond at all (Sadker & Sadker, 1990).

Several feedback strategies have application to questioning skills. Process feedback, given when students have incorrect or partial answers, helps them to derive the correct answers. Feedback may also be classified as terminal or sustaining. Sustaining feedback, which allows the student to revise or correct the answer, is generally preferable to terminal feedback, in which the teacher supplies the correct answer, calls on another student, or allows someone to call out the answer (L. Anderson et al., 1979).

Research on elementary reading instruction indicates that choral responses, which allow students to answer questions in unison, or "call outs," in which students answer questions without being acknowledged, can negatively impact learning (L. Anderson et al., 1979). This research positively correlated the use of ordered turns for individual responses with learning. The study found that to keep members of the group alert, teachers should occasionally and randomly select individual students to reinforce previous responses of other students.

These findings are in direct conflict with Hunter's (1982) theories of instructional practice. She recommends the use of choral responses as an effective way to reinforce learning and believes that this allows students who are confused to learn the correct response without embarrassment. We need additional research to examine the importance of individual and choral responses, particularly across grade levels and in varying content areas.

Reinforcement of student answers through verbal or nonverbal repsonses can also play an important role in learning. These responses may consist of short feedback statements, such as "correct" or "yes, good," or extended statements that build upon or apply student ideas. Nonverbal reinforcement can take the form of facial expressions, eye contact, and gestures that positively reinforce the student. Research shows that reinforcement of student responses increases student motivation to learn and contributes to more positive attitudes and higher achievement (Sadker & Sadker, 1990).

Summary and Implications

Several decades of research have provided useful guidelines for effective teaching across grade levels, subject areas, and ability levels. Although it is not possible to identify one best way to teach, the research supports a number of important elements of effective teaching. We might construe academic learning time as the most essential element of effective teaching/learning environments. The concept of direct instruction also encompasses a set of variables that should increase learning when convergent outcomes are desired. Additional research has produced some general implications for classroom management, classroom climate, feedback, expectancy, lesson presentation, and questioning.

In applying this research, we must use some level of caution. We should not construe research on effective teaching as providing strict rules for teaching behavior. Indeed, the artful teacher must use research findings and apply effective teaching behaviors appropriately for the given context. It is impossible to define a set of strict and rigid rules for effective teaching in all conditions. However, a broad knowledge of the research findings provides a broader repertoire of behaviors and allows teachers to make informed choices.

Chapter 5

Measurement-Based Evaluation of Teacher Performance

In order to implement systematic supervision, we must understand the concept of measurement-based evaluation and the strategies for its use. *Measurement-based evaluation* entails the assessment of teacher effectiveness based on performance. The supervisor directly measures teacher performance by observing teacher and student classroom behaviors and by using systematic observation instruments.

The alternatives to measurement-based evaluation are *subjective methods* (e.g., informal analysis, eyeballing, anecdotal records, checklists, and rating scales) and *measurement of outcomes* (student achievement). Both of these alternatives have serious limitations, which are outlined in this chapter. Although subjective methods alone do not suffice as evaluation methods, they can provide useful information to augment objective evaluation procedures.

This chapter emphasizes the objective processes used in measurement-based teacher evaluation. It also briefly describes subjective methods such as intuitive judgment and anecdotal records that have traditionally prevailed in supervision. Preinterns, interns, and beginning and experienced teachers are frequently subjected to unplanned and unreliable methods of evaluation and are judged on the

basis of whatever personal perspectives the observer chooses to emphasize. Because subjective measures rely heavily on inference, they have serious limitations. Objective measures of teacher and student outcomes offer face validity for evaluation of teaching. However, their applications are also limited by many practical constraints. Measurement-based evaluation through systematic observation of teacher behavior offers an alternative method of objective teacher assessment.

Subjective Methods of Evaluation

Teacher evaluation practices have historically relied on subjective methods of analysis, a tradition that has been woefully inadequate. Medley, Coker, and Soar (1984) summarized, ''The whole art of teacher evaluation up to the present consists of obtaining someone's subjective judgment of how 'good' a teacher is, a judgment based on the assumption that the judge knows what good teaching is and can recognize it when he sees it'' (p. 4). Although plumbers, mechanics, and other technicians are evaluated on the basis of what they do, teachers as professionals do not receive the same consideration. Medley, Coker, and Soar (1984) propose that teachers should be evaluated as professionals on the basis of whether they use "the best practice available at that time" (p. 6). The only teacher characteristics that are of concern are those "which we can observe, evaluate, and do something about" (p. 43).

Bohning (1978) uniquely categorized some limitations of subjective judgment, as applied to the evaluation of student teachers. When the university supervisor applies subjective ratings of criteria (e.g., objectives, teaching behaviors, or personal abilities), the implicit assumption is that he or she is able to accurately observe and evaluate the effectiveness of the student teacher in each of the designated areas. Further, subjective evaluators assume that the supervisor can make these judgments fairly on the basis of limited and informal observations. Consequently, the student teacher may receive a higher or lower evaluation than deserved. Table 5.1 summarizes factors that can contribute to these inequities.

Traditional observation (data collection methods) in general have many insufficiencies, the most serious of which is common to all of the following methods. Collectively, subjective evaluation

Table 5.1 Factors Contributing to Rating Inequities

A higher evaluation rating than deserved

Let the record stand. A past record of successful coursework and participation in campus activities at the university may favorably influence the present evaluation.

Encouragement. If a university supervisor thinks that a student teacher has the ability to succeed, the supervisor may rate according to potential rather than actual performance.

Blind faults. A university supervisor may not see certain faults in a student teacher because the supervisor has the same faults. For example, a university supervisor who is not well organized may give a high rating to a student teacher who is also not well organized; the supervisor is not aware that the behavior is a fault.

No news is good news. If the directing teacher or other school personnel have not complained, a university supervisor may tend to assume that all is well and give the student teacher a high rating.

Benefit of a doubt. A university supervisor may rate a student teacher higher if the supervisor is unfamiliar with the student teacher's particular expertise than if the supervisor is familiar with the area.

Compatibility. A university supervisor may tend to rate a student teacher he or she knows and likes higher than a student teacher the supervisor has not previously known.

A lower evaluation rating than deserved

Membership guilt. A student teacher on a weak teaching team or in a weak school situation is associated with the team or situation and may receive a lower rating than if working alone or with an effective team.

Perfection required. A university supervisor may set the interpretation of the master scale of standards so high that no student teacher can measure up to the standards.

Self-comparison. A lower rating may result when a student teacher doesn't teach the level or subject as well as the university supervisor remembers he or she once did.

Personality problem. A student teacher may be too meek or too aggressive or lack some trait that the university supervisor considers necessary; the student teacher may thus suffer in the evaluation. The trait may not be included on the evaluation form, but the importance the university supervisor attaches to the missing personality trait can lower the overall ratings for the student.

Nonconformist. The university supervisor who views the master list of standards as an obligation list may tend to rate the "boat rocker" or "oddball" lower than deserved because that student teacher is different.

"Can't see the trees for the forest." A university supervisor may be required to rate the student teaching competency of an individual who has more real teaching ability than the supervisor has. The supervisor may assign lower ratings if he or she does not recognize the student teacher's more subtle effective teaching behaviors.

Note. From "Subjective Judgment Pitfalls in Evaluating Student Teachers" by G. Bohning. *Teacher Educator*, 1978, 14(1), 13-14. Copyright 1982 by Teacher Educator. Adapted by permission.

methods are subject to the personal opinions and biases of the observer, and they thus lack objectivity and reliability. Consider, for example, the use of a rating scale in evaluating a given teacher. What is the likelihood that two observers, when simultaneously observing the same teaching events, will produce similar ratings (1-4) on a variety of elements? A degree of enthusiasm that one supervisor considers a 4 (*excellent*) may be rated by another as 2 (*fair*). Or, one observer evaluating the same teacher on two similar occasions may show fluctuating standards based on personal feelings at any given time.

In addition to these common shortcomings, traditional data collection methods suffer from specific limitations. A summary of traditional methods follows, with attention to the unique limitations of each.

Intuitive Judgment

This is what Siedentop (1991) called a global approach to supervision, in which an assumedly knowledgeable and experienced supervisor observes teaching and then forms a general judgment or evaluation of its merit. This method is inadequate because it fails to provide specific information for formative or summative evaluation, and because it focuses primarily on the teacher and too little on students (Siedentop, 1991).

Informal Analysis

This refers to unstructured observations of classes in which "observers simply 'sit in on a class' and watch what goes on" (W.G. Anderson, 1980, p. 6). Informal analysis involves no advance planning of what or how to watch. Observers typically record notes in the form of narrative descriptions or anecdotal records that are quite general in nature. Figure 5.1 is an example of an anecdotal record.

Although informal analysis is not without value, it does have limitations. W.G. Anderson (1980) succinctly summarized these shortcomings. First, informal analysis captures only "a small piece of the action" (p. 7), because the observer records only fragmentary events and perceptions. Second, observation and recording of events depend on a personal perspective, because "focal points for informal analysis are in large part subjectively determined" (p. 9). Choices about what to record or evaluate are based on the observer's personal biases and concepts of teaching. Third, the primary focus in informal analysis is the teacher, and observers largely neglect student behaviors as a data

source. Last, informal analysis produces "an inclination to evaluate" (p. 10), because it is difficult to chronicle classroom events without applying one's own value system.

Eyeballing

This method is basically the same as informal analysis, except the observer takes no written notes. It can be a useful adjunct to other forms of supervision but does not suffice as a singular approach to evaluation. This is what Locke (1974) referred to in physical education as a "tour through the gym," a commonly misused method in which the observer briefly passes through a class and relies on recall to make later observations and judgments.

Rating Scales

These consist of lists of objectives, traits, or skills that are deemed generally desirable. The observer rates the teacher with respect to each criterion, typically on a scale of 1 to 5 or a similar format. An example of a generic rating scale for student teachers is provided in Figure 5.2. The use of rating scales dates back to 1915, and few changes or improvements have been made in their applications since (Medley, et al., 1984). They are still commonly used, despite serious limitations in their validity and reliability, primarily because they are simple to construct and apply.

Dunkin and Biddle (1974) noted four problems that are inherent in the use of rating scales. First, these scales rely on *high-inference judgments* and frequently provide only minimal information about indicators of the criterion (e.g., enthusiasm). High-inference measures require a great deal of subjective judgment on the part of the rater and are thus subject to inaccuracy. A second problem is that observers often apply rating scales on a "one-time-only" basis, and single ratings cannot reflect variations in the qualities observed. Third, rating scales are often used by untrained raters or observers who may have natural biases resulting from established relationships (e.g., principals, teachers, or students). A fourth limitation is that the qualities included in rating scales are usually selected on the basis of arbitrary opinion and are not validated against objective measures. Thus, the validity of the scale depends entirely on what the developers of the scale view as effective teaching.

As in the case of informal analysis, rating scales are also affected by the personal biases of the observers (what they view as important). Rating scales are "notoriously unreliable" (Siedentop,

Figure 5.1

Sample Anecdotal Record

Student teacher _____ *Charles Cole* _____ Date _____ *March 9, 1992* _____

Supervising teacher _____ *Joseph Duncan* _____ Grade/period _____ *3* _____

School _____ *Seminole High School* _____ Activity _____ *Volleyball* _____

Commendations

> *Effective use of classroom routines in getting the class started*
> > *Use of a time-saving method for taking roll*
> > *Students begin warm-up while instructor records absences*
> > *Use of student leaders for warm-up activity*

> *Demonstration was effective*
> > *Brief, clear*
> > *Emphasized critical parts of the skill*
> > *Followed by immediate opportunities to practice with feedback*
> > *Use of teaching cues*

> *Practice opportunities*
> > *Drill provided for maximum participation*
> > *Should have positive transfer to the skill*

> *Classroom climate—very positive*
> > *High rates of positive, specific feedback*
> > *Use of first names*
> > *Students respond positively to teacher*

Recommendations

> *Perhaps a process measure would be effective in this skill assessment (looking at the form of the movement, in addition to or instead of the distance)*

> *Break the class into small groups for testing—engage waiting students in another skill practice*

> *Closure—was this given?*

Please keep designated copy:	
White—student teacher	Pink—observer
Canary—supervising teacher	Gold—observer

Observer _____ *Carol Askins* _____ *February 1, 1992* _____
(Date)

Title _____ *Assistant Professor* _____

Adapted from Long and Deture (1986) by permission.

Figure 5.2

Sample Rating Scale

Teacher _____ Date _____ Grade/period _____

School _____ Activity _____

Throughout the clinical experiences program, the student teacher should demonstrate growth. For the purpose of the periodic and final evaluations, the student teacher should be viewed as a beginning teacher.

Definition of rating terms

O   *Outstanding*—utilizes skills and abilities in a creative and highly effective way
E   *Effective*—utilizes skills and abilities in a most satisfactory way
A   *Acceptable*—exhibits skills and abilities at an adequate level
I   *Improving*—shows progress toward acquiring needed skills and abilities
NI   *Needs improvement*—requires assistance or guidance in this area
NA   *Not applicable*—not relevant at this time for this student teacher

I. Teaching competencies	O	E	A	I	NI	NA
A. Planning for instruction						
1. Uses long-range goals						
2. Employs measurable objectives						
3. Designs activities related to specific objectives						
4. Shows consistent evidence of advance planning						
5. Selects appropriate instructional aids						
B. Implementing instruction						
1. Uses time efficiently						
2. Implements smooth transitions						
3. Uses set induction to initiate lessons						
4. Delivers instruction in a logical coherent manner						
5. Reviews effectively and emphasizes key concepts						
6. Uses a variety of teaching methods						
7. Provides for student practice and participation						
8. Gives meaningful feedback						
9. Adapts lessons to students' individual needs						
10. Uses questioning techniques effectively						
11. Provides appropriate wait-time and response						
12. Gives clear sequential directions						
13. Sustains learner involvement and interest						
C. Management and communication						
1. Applies rules and routines consistently						
2. Identifies and stops deviant behavior quickly and appropriately						
3. Monitors activities simultaneously						
4. Implements an effective classroom management system						
5. Establishes effective rapport with students						
6. Listens carefully to students						
7. Uses positive reinforcement						
8. Uses language appropriate to the level of the students						
9. Demonstrates effective verbal and nonverbal behavior						
10. Promotes students' positive self-image						
D. Evaluation						
1. Uses an objective and accurate system for pupil evaluation						
2. Diagnoses the entry and performance level of each student						

(Cont.)

Figure 5.2   (Continued)

	O	E	A	I	NI	NA
3. Constructs tests that correspond to objectives						
4. Administers evaluation procedures fairly						
5. Interprets and uses evaluative results correctly						
6. Grades and returns test papers promptly						
II. Knowledge competencies						
A. Basic skills						
1. Uses standard english in oral communication						
2. Uses correct grammar and spelling in written communication						
3. Demonstrates the ability to work with fundamental math concepts						
4. Comprehends and interprets printed material accurately						
5. Comprehends and interprets oral messages						
B. Subject matter and methodology						
1. Demonstrates thorough knowledge of content area(s)						
2. Demonstrates knowledge of subject areas and grade level curriculum						
3. Uses appropriate methods to teach: concepts, laws, principles, academic rules, and value judgments						
C. Human development/relations						
1. Demonstrates knowledge of the stages of cognitive and physical development						
2. Comprehends the foundation of social and moral development						
3. Recognizes characteristics of exceptional children						
4. Demonstrates knowledge of human relations and effective social interactions						
III. Professional competencies						
A. Professional attitudes						
1. Shows enthusiasm for teaching						
2. Demonstrates initiative and a willingness to accept responsibility						
3. Is consistently reliable and punctual						
4. Demonstrates a commitment to continued professional growth						
B. Professional behavior						
1. Demonstrates flexibility and good judgment						
2. Accepts and uses suggestions from supervisors to improve performance						
3. Works effectively with peers, parents, and supervisors						
4. Attends to administrative policy and duties in a timely manner						

Evaluator's personal reactions
(Please use space below for supportive statements and recommendations for growth)

IV. Overall evaluation (to be completed only as part of final evaluation)

Additional growth needed   Adequate competence   Excellent performance

Evaluator _____ / _____
                                        (Signature)   (Title)

Student teacher _____ / _____
                                        (Signature)   (Date)

Please keep designated copy:	
White—student teacher	Pink—university supervisor
Canary—supervising teacher	Gold—observer/other

All data nonconfidential
Periodic evaluation   ☐
Final evaluation   ☐
(Check appropriate box)

Adapted from Long and Detvure (1986) by permission.

1991, p. 296), and their reliability is further compromised with the addition of a larger range of scores (e.g., a range of 1-10 produces lower reliability than 1-5). Thus, several observers using the same scale will produce different ratings depending on four factors: what each rater thinks the teacher should have done, what behaviors the rater takes into account, the importance the rater attaches to each behavior observed, and the reference standard with which the rater compares what he or she observed (Medley et al., 1984). Ultimately, the effectiveness of the teacher as determined by ratings will vary according to the rater.

Checklists

These contain descriptions of qualities similar to those on rating scales, except that the observer simply indicates whether or not the quality is present (e.g., yes/no; observed/not observed) and does not judge relative strength or weakness. Figure 5.3 is a sample checklist of indicators of effective classroom management. Like rating scales, checklists often contain descriptors that are not directly observable (e.g., enthusiasm or positive rapport) and thus depend on inference. Because the lists require only a check, they do not distinguish between desirable behaviors that occur once for short duration and those that are consistently present throughout the lesson. Teachers may tend to teach toward the checklist, deliberately exhibiting brief behaviors (e.g., telling a joke indicates use of humor) in order to obtain checks. Additional problems are posed by the recording of continuous teaching behaviors (e.g., monitoring, explaining), because they occur over a period of time.

Objective Measures of Teacher and Student Outcomes

During the past decade, educational reform measures have called attention to the need for greater teacher accountability. As a result, many states have adopted paper-and-pencil tests of teaching competence. In addition, student achievement testing has taken on increased significance in measuring the impact of curricular and instructional interventions. Although these assessments provide useful data, we cannot view them as definitive measures of teacher evaluation. The following sections outline the limitations of paper-and-pencil tests and student achievements as indicators of effective teaching.

Paper-and-Pencil Tests

These are written tests used to assess essential knowledges or characteristics of effective teachers. The National Teacher Examinations and various competency tests used for state certification are examples of this approach. Earlier research efforts also used personality and attitude inventories to identify characteristics of good teachers. In general, these measures demonstrate low correlation with teacher effectiveness as assessed by performance ratings or student achievement (Medley et al., 1984). They might be more appropriately used as general screening measures for teacher candidates (e.g., measures of basic literacy) than as evaluation tools.

Student Achievement

This approach assumes that student achievement as a measurable product is the most appropriate and direct indicator of teacher competence. The use of student achievement for teacher evaluation, particularly summative evaluation, is currently a very controversial topic. The National Education Association has staunchly opposed its use, and many teacher contracts exclude it as a basis of evaluation (Millman, 1987). Opponents have challenged the validity of this approach on the basis of three problems: "pupil variability, the regression effect, and the limitations of achievement tests presently available" (Medley et al., 1984, p. 33).

The productivity of a teacher is not analogous to that of a salesperson or factory worker, whose effectiveness is judged on the basis of the quantity and quality of his or her products. Teaching is uniquely challenging because it involves working with children versus adults, and because students vary in terms of their abilities (e.g., I.Q.) and experiences (e.g., home and peer-group influences). Pupil differences are compounded when students of varying abilities are randomly assigned to classes, and disproportionate ability groups result (Medley et al., 1984).

The regression effect is a statistical phenomenon that results from the tendency of extreme scores to regress toward the mean (Campbell & Stanley, 1966). On any given measure of achievement, students at extreme ends of the scoring continuum have potential for staying at the same level or moving toward the mean score. Students who perform well have increased likelihoods of doing more poorly on a subsequent measure, whereas students who perform poorly have increased chances of doing better. Therefore, a negative correlation

Figure 5.3

Management Strategies Checklist

Teacher _____ Date _____ Grade/period _____

School _____ Activity _____

Ø = Observed   O = Not observed   NA = Not applicble

Pre-class

_____ Exhibits proper punctuality and attendance
_____ Displays proper dress and appearance
_____ Writes lesson plans
_____ Prepares unit plan

Class management

_____ Starts activity quickly (less than 2 minutes)
_____ Ensures equipment and environment are safe
_____ Ensures equipment is easily accessible
_____ Establishes and reinforces stop and go signals
_____ Clearly communicates and reinforces behavior rules and expectations
_____ Quickly and consistently enforces consequences for inappropriate behavior
_____ Gives directions clearly and briefly
_____ Tells or demonstrates to students what to do before they get equipment
_____ Effectively uses demonstrations
_____ Observes class from the perimeter
_____ Moves around class and keeps students on task
_____ Ensures transitions are planned and efficient
_____ Speaks to students only when they are quiet and listening
_____ Conducts a lesson closure (less than 2 minutes)

Comments:

_____

_____

_____

Adapted from Ratliffe (1990) by permission.

will occur between scores on the pretest and the posttest (gain scores) (Medley et al., 1984). When evaluators do not consider this effect, regression can lead to incorrect conclusions about the effectiveness of instruction. The potential for error is particularly great when students are grouped and assigned to classes on the basis of test scores. In this case, marked improvements by remedial students give the false impression that these teachers are superior.

A third problem with the use of pupil gains in teacher evaluation is the limitation inherent in achievement tests. Because achievement tests are limited in their scope to a set of simple and defined outcomes, we cannot assess learning that occurs outside of that framework. Students may achieve a larger scope of complex and worthwhile goals and objectives, but these are not visible as products of effective teaching. These complex goals are also difficult to obtain within a limited time period. Standardized tests, then, are oriented more toward the measurement of "low-level gains" than "high-level gains" (Medley et al., 1984). These tests do not lend themselves to the valid and reliable evaluation of teaching.

Although we should not dismiss student learning as a useful focus, its use as a direct measure of teacher effectiveness is problematic. Pupil differences, regression, and limitations of achievement tests compound the results of such measurements, especially when instruction occurs in a variety of contexts. Because of these limitations, gain scores are not appropriate indicators of effective teaching unless the observer imposes rigorous statistical and design controls.

Measurement-Based Evaluation Through Systematic Observation

Measurement-based evaluation requires the use of systematic observation instruments, systems designed to reliably and objectively record measurable and observable behaviors. This approach is sometimes called *descriptive analysis* and can be used to record either teacher or student behavior (or both). Observers usually collect data through direct (live) observations of classroom teaching, though videotapes or audiotapes may be used. Structured observation systems are advantageous in providing objective and reliable data about

teaching events while minimizing the potential for observer bias. Supervisors can select systematic observation instruments to focus on dimensions of teacher behavior that are most essential to promoting learning and to provide a clear record of behavior for subsequent analysis.

Dougherty and Bonanno (1979, p. 83) identified four common features of systematic observation tools. We may view these features as advantages of the approach.

- All systems avoid qualitative or evaluative judgments. The intent is to present an accurate representation of actual occurrences without bias.
- Most systems view only a limited portion of the teaching/learning process. The totality of the teacher/pupil interactive process is simply too complex to be efficiently contained within a single recording instrument.
- Most systems classify behavior into categories. This provides a clear, systematized manner of viewing selected behaviors. It also allows for the development of mutually exclusive, clearly defined areas of interest that tend to increase objectivity.
- Most systems concentrate on verbal behavior only. Verbal behavior is more easily observed and less easily misinterpreted than nonverbal behavior, and most researchers have assumed that verbal behavior provides an accurate representation of a teacher's total behavior pattern.

While recognizing the advantages of systematic observation, we should note several limitations. In a recent overview, van der Mars (1989) judged four limitations crucial. First, systematic observation focuses only on observable and measurable events and behaviors that can be seen or heard (i.e., visual or audible). This limitation does not, however, preclude the use of systematic observation to describe affective qualities. It is possible to identify observable behaviors that are indicative of certain affective qualities (e.g., enthusiasm, enjoyment, and warmth). A second limitation is that systematic observation provides only descriptive (vs. evaluative) information. The individual who interprets the data must try to meaningfully apply them in the form of feedback (positive reinforcement or suggestions for improvement). A third and related limitation is that the generated data are not prescriptive (i.e., adjustments in teaching must be based on inferences of the data). Fourth, the data obtained through systematic observation must be viewed contextually (e.g., with regard to the unique environment, the teacher's objectives, and learner characteristics). Just as one cannot prescribe a best way to teach, one cannot evaluate a multitude of teaching contexts with one formula.

The Process of Measurement-Based Evaluation

The application of measurement-based evaluation through systematic observation entails four basic steps:

1. deciding what to observe (defining the task),
2. securing a permanent record of the behavior,
3. collecting the data, and
4. comparing the data to established criteria.

Each one of these steps has several substeps, which are defined in the following sections.

Defining the Task

This step involves deciding what dimensions of teacher effectiveness are important and what observable behaviors or criterion variables might be used to measure that dimension. After making those decisions, the observer will select, modify, or develop an instrument for the collection of data. Some examples of dimensions for concentration include the emotional climate of the classroom, classroom management, use of time, use of resources, or level of student involvement. The observer should select one or more dimensions for observation with the input of the teacher, though student teachers may lack the experience and insight to guide this process. In the case of the student teacher, the developmental level or stage of the internship, as defined in chapter 6, will give useful cues for selection of dimensions for observing students.

Informal analysis can also provide insight into dimensions of teaching for analysis. Having gained some information about the teacher's goals and the context of the learning environment, an observer may then observe informally to determine what areas of change are needed. For example, a teacher may wish to increase the level of participation within the class and find a way to motivate and reward students who continually disengage. Or, when teaching in a classroom situation, a teacher may desire to initiate more classroom discussion and involvement. Research on effective teaching

can also direct the selection of dimensions for observation and analysis.

After the observer identifies one or more dimensions for focus, he or she must decide what observable behaviors will be the best indicators of the desired goal. These might be teacher behaviors, student behaviors, or teacher–student interactions. They may be verbal or nonverbal behaviors. But they will always be observable and measurable, events that we can see or hear and count.

Observable teacher or student behaviors may be categorized as either discrete (having a distinct beginning or ending point) or continuous (having no distinct beginning or ending point). Discrete behaviors are most often recorded by their frequency of occurrence (e.g., number of feedback statements given or number of questions asked), whereas continuous behaviors lend themselves to duration recording (e.g., how long the student pays attention). We may also observe a series of discrete teaching behaviors in the form of analytic units. These are observed in group fashion because their occurrence tends to follow a sequential pattern (Dunkin & Biddle, 1974). Siedentop (1991) identified the managerial episode, consisting of "a sequence of time that is initiated by a teacher managerial behavior and culminates when the next instructional or practice activity begins" (p. 24), as a useful analytic unit.

Following are some examples of discrete teacher and student behaviors.

Teacher behaviors	Student behaviors
questions	asks
prompts	responds
praises	attempts skill
gives feedback	touches
stops off-task behavior	talks
smiles	smiles
frowns	frowns

The following are examples of continuous teacher and student behaviors.

Teacher behaviors	Student behaviors
managing	attending (listening)
demonstrating	watching
monitoring/observing	waiting
explaining	assisting
giving instructions	practicing

All of these behaviors are observable and measurable. They also describe processes, what teachers or students do. Occasionally, we may wish to observe and record a *criterion process variable*, which is an indirect measure of the product or outcome the observer assumes to be closely related to learning. The most commonly used criterion process variable is academic learning time (ALT), a method that analyzes teacher and student processes as indirect measures of student learning. Metzler (1979) designed an instrument for assessing academic learning time in physical education (ALT-PE), which was modified subsequently by Birdwell (1980) and Siedentop et al. (1982). Both of these instruments require that the user undergo a substantial amount of training in order to obtain reliability, and they are used essentially for research purposes. Wilkinson and Taggart (1985) developed a simplified instrument for use in teaching and coaching situations.

The selection of a structured observation instrument will depend on the nature of variables to be studied and the purpose of the observation. Some instruments provide complex data and sophisticated analyses and are intended for research purposes. They generally require that the user undergo a great deal of training in order to use the instruments properly. Other instruments are designed for the purpose of evaluation, usually formative (for instructional improvement) versus summative (for decision making). The instruments developed or selected for the Systematic Supervision Model fall into the latter category and can be easily applied with little training.

Securing a Permanent Record of the Behavior

We can classify systematic observation instruments according to their form as

- category systems,
- sign systems, or
- multiple coding systems.

Category systems record the presence of behaviors as they occur. These systems contain a small and manageable number of predefined categories that are independent and mutually exclusive. Categories are mutually exclusive when they are unambiguous, when a given behavior can only correctly be coded into one category. One example is the Flanders Interaction Analysis System (FIAS) (Flanders, 1970), which provided the initial impetus for the systematic observation movement. This system uses 10 categories of teacher and student verbal behavior to classify the nature of interactions patterns in the classroom (direct teacher influence or indirect teacher influence).

A second category of structured observation instruments comprises sign systems, which require the observer to decide whether or not, but not how often, a behavior occurs. A sign system contains a list of specific behaviors that the observer records (only once) as they are observed. The system divides observations into a number of short intervals (e.g., 2 to 5 minutes) and derives frequency information from the number of intervals in which a behavior is recorded.

The third major category of structured observations includes multiple coding systems, in which the observer records a given behavior in more than one category. One example of a multiple coding system contained in the Systematic Supervision Model is the Student Teacher Observation of Questioning Skills. Figure 5.4 contains a sample of this instrument. The general focus of the instrument is on teacher questioning skills, and the observer records questions verbatim as they occur. Questions might also be coded from recorded videotape or audiotape. In addition to writing the questions, the observer records three dimensions of the questioning behavior: (a) cognitive level — which level of Bloom's taxonomy does it reflect, or is high-order or low-order thinking required? (b) is unison or individual response required? and (c) does the teacher provide for wait time (3 to 5 seconds) so that students can structure their responses?

Coding Techniques for Systematic Observation. Structured observations require the use of established coding techniques for recording the data. Appropriateness of these techniques depends on the nature of the behavior to be observed and the design of the instrument to be used. Coding techniques typically used include event recording, duration recording, interval recording, and placheck (planned activity check) recording or group time sampling.

Event recording is a simple frequency count of events as they occur, typically recorded as checks or tallies. One might count the number of feedback statements provided by a teacher or the number of skill attempts. Event recording can provide a frequency count of observed behaviors, or it can provide the relative ratios, percentages, or proportions of behaviors observed within the given categories. When the observer also records duration of observation, he or she can translate frequency counts into average rates per minute (e.g., 5 skill attempts in a 10-minute period = 0.5 skill attempts per minute). Event recording is applicable when the behavior to be observed is discrete, as previously defined, and can therefore be counted.

Figure 5.4

Systematic Observation of Questioning Skills
Sample Data From Secondary Level

Teacher _____ *Ted Hughes* _____ Date _ *December 13, 1991* _ Grade/period __ *7* __

Class size ____ *27* ____

List the questions as they occur. Indicate within the boxes whether the responses required are individual or choral, whether the teacher provided 3 seconds or less of wait time, and the level of the taxonomy the questions reflect.

1. *Who can give me a definition of health-related fitness? What does that mean?*
2. *Mark, what is one component of health-related fitness?*
3. *Who can give me another component?*
4. *What kinds of sport activities require a lot of flexibility? Can you name some, Linda?*
5. *And why is flexibility important to the sport of swimming?*
6. *Now, who remembers the definition of skill-related fitness? What does that mean?*
7. *Is speed an example of a skill-related fitness component, Danielle?*
8. *Can you identify a sport skill that requires a lot of speed?*
9. *Now, is it possible for most people to increase their speed substantially?*
10. *Why do you think that health-related fitness is more important to us than skill-related fitness?*

Individual	Choral
‖‖‖ ////	/

Wait	No wait
‖‖‖ /	////

Place a tally in the space that reflects the level of the taxonomy corresponding to each question.

Low order (Knowledge, comprehension)	High order (Application, analysis, synthesis, evaluation)
‖‖‖ /	////

The instrument in Figure 5.5 is included in the Systematic Supervision Model and uses an event recording format for coding skill attempts by a selected target student. It provides an overall frequency count of skill attempts, as well as relative proportions or percentages of successful and unsuccessful skill attempts. On this form the observer records discrete skill attempts (events) as a circle, drawing a slash through the circle to indicate successful skill attempts [θ]. The observer can also combine the form with the element of observed time to illustrate the average number of skill attempts per minute.

Figure 5.5

Event Recording of Student Skill Attempts

Interval

1　θ O _____

2　O _____

3　_____

4　θ O O O _____

Total skill attempts	7
Total successful skill attempts	2
Percent success	28.6

Duration recording involves recording the length of time during which a given behavior occurs. In its simplest application, an observer can use a stopwatch to record the length of uninterrupted time during which a student is engaged in motor activity. By totaling all of the recorded durations, the observer can obtain a total duration of motor activity time. Duration recording is appropriate for continuous teacher and student behaviors, because it is amenable to timing. Its data are usually recorded in the form of minutes and seconds, as illustrated in Figure 5.6.

Interval recording designates short periods of time (intervals) during which the observer looks for and identifies the category that best describes the behavior of the teacher or student. The observation session is divided equally into short intervals ranging from 5 to 20 seconds. A typical interval format might be to observe for 6 seconds, then record for 6 seconds, repeated in sequence throughout the period of observation. Observers frequently use prerecorded audiotapes (cueing tapes) to observe and record intervals. When measures of student behavior are of interest, the observer may randomly select one or more target students and observe

Figure 5.6

Duration Recording— Student Use of Time

Non-instruction

1. waiting	2:16
3. getting equipment	:35
5. transitioning	:25
8. waiting	1:30
	Total = 4:46

Cognitive activity

2. demonstration	1:30
6. skill instruction	2:00
	Total = 3:30

Motor-Engaged Activity

4. guided practice	2:30
7. independent practice	5:30
8. partner activity	3:21
	Total = 11:21

them for short periods (e.g., 2 minutes) in sequence. The use of randomly selected target students prevents observer biases (e.g., selecting a high-skill student or one who is boisterous and off-task) and misrepresentative data (atypical students who do not reflect what is going on in general). Data obtained through interval recording are usually expressed in terms of the relative percentages of observed intervals for each of the defined categories.

One structured observation tool that uses an interval recording format is the ALT-PE instrument (Siedentop et al., 1982). This instrument requires the observer to make two decisions within each coded 6-second interval: (a) What is the context that the teacher has set up? (general content, subject matter knowledge, or subject matter motor), and (b) what is the learner involvement level of the target student at that time? (motor engaged, non–motor engaged). Ultimately, the instrument provides a measure of academic learning time in physical education, the amount of time in which learners are motor-engaged at an appropriate level of difficulty (successful). A sample of ALT-PE data collected over a 2-minute interval is contained in Figure 5.7.

A placheck (planned activity check) is the last coding technique typically employed in systematic observation. With this method, the observer quickly scans the class from left to right at a designated interval, counting the incidence of dichotomous variables (e.g., active/inactive or on-task/off-task). The observer counts each student only once during

Figure 5.7

Interval Data for Academic Learning Time in Physical Education

Subject 1

Context level

P	Tn	Tn	T	M	P	P	P	P	P	P	P	P	P	P	P	P	P	P	P

Learner involvement level

W	C	C	W	W	Ma	Ma	W	I	Ma	W	W	W	Ma	Mi	Of	Of	Ma	Ma	Mi

P	= Practice	C	= Cognitive	OF	= Off-task
T	= Transition	Ma	= Motor appropriate	W	= Waiting
Tn	= Technique	Mi	= Motor inappropriate		

Note: These representations represent only the ALT-PE categories coded for this sample observation.

a scan, which usually lasts about 10 seconds. Plachecks are spaced periodically throughout the class period to give a representative sample of the behaviors (e.g., every 5 minutes). Generally, it is easiest to count the least frequently occurring behavior (e.g., off-task) and subtract that from the total number of students in the class. The observer counts data from each of the dichotomous codings over the intervals, which provide information about the proportions of observed behaviors within the designated category. Figure 5.8 is an example of a planned activity check (group time sampling).

Reliability of Measurements. One last element of securing a record of the data is the ensurance of reliability. Reliability here can refer to *intraobserver agreement* (the extent to which one observer consistently uses a given instrument) and *interobserver agreement*, the extent to which two observers simultaneously coding the same events with a given instrument demonstrate agreement. To establish intraobserver agreement, an observer uses the same instrument to code the same videotaped episodes twice.

For event recording, duration recording, or time sampling formats, we can check the percentage of agreement with this formula:

$$\frac{\text{smallest number observed or shortest duration}}{\text{largest number observed or longest duration}} \times 100 = \text{percent agreement}$$

Figure 5.8

Planned Activity Check for Evaluating Lesson Effectiveness

Teacher _____ *Jessica Lee* _____

Date ___ *October 3, 1991* ___   Grade/period ___ *4* ___

Class size ___ *28* ___

Time	Number of students on-task	Number of students off-task
9:05	14	14
9:10	28	0
9:15	18	10
____	____	____
____	____	____
____	____	____

Number of observations for on-task = *60*
Number of observations for off-task = *24*

Percent on-task =

$$\frac{\text{Number on-task}}{\text{Number on-task + number off-task}} \times 100$$

$$= \frac{60}{60 + 24} \times 100 = \frac{60}{84} \times 100 = 71.4 \text{ percent on-task}$$

For interval recording, we check the percentage of agreement with the Interval-by-Interval (I-I) formula:

$$\frac{\text{number of agreements}}{\text{number of agreements} + \text{disagreements}} \times 100 = \frac{\text{percent}}{\text{agreement}}$$

(An agreement is any interval in which both observers score the same behavior, and a disagreement is any interval in which both observers score different behaviors. This same formula is appropriate when single or multiple behaviors are observed.)

We can establish interobserver agreement through either live or videotaped codings. When interval coding is used, a cueing tape (sometimes with split-jack to accommodate two earphones) is used to time the recordings. The previous formula is then applied to calculate the percentage of agreement.

$$\frac{25}{25 + 5} \times 100 = 83.33 \text{ percent agreement}$$

For purposes of research, it is appropriate to use a more rigorous method of calculation for interobserver agreement. The I-I method can produce deceptively high estimates of reliability in instances in which the observer codes very many or very few behaviors within a given category. The Scored-Interval (S-I) method (Hawkins & Dotson, 1975) is more sensitive to effects of the rate of behavior, adequacy of definitions, observer competency, and observer bias. This method disregards all intervals in which both observers scored a given behavior as absent. Only intervals in which at least one observer recorded a designated behavior as present are considered. In essence, the I-I method pools agreements and disagreements for each observed interval into an overall agreement estimate. The S-I method looks at agreements and disagreements for each behavior as they are scored, resulting in separate agreement scores for each behavior. The end result is a more rigorous measure of interobserver agreement.

Validity of Observation Instruments. The validity of the observation instrument describes the extent to which it measures what it purports to measure. To a great extent, we determine the validity of the instrument by the definition of mutually exclusive and mutually exhaustive categories. Categories are mutually exclusive when an observed event can correctly fall into only one category. This in turn depends on the precise definition of categories of behaviors, along with good examples. An instrument contains mutually exhaustive categories when all of the behaviors to be observed can be coded into one of the existing categories.

Collecting the Data

In this step the observer collects the data with the designated instrument or instruments through live (in-class) coding or occasionally through the use of audiotape or videotape. The observer must be as unobtrusive as possible so as not to disrupt the natural flow of events. In most cases, students will readily adjust to the presence of an observer or even recording equipment. The camcorder provides a relatively compact and portable videorecording device for classroom observation. The observer's role is simply to record the data in the most objective manner possible and to avoid interacting with the class or interjecting evaluations.

When teacher verbal behavior is the focus of observation, the teacher can use self-recorded audiotapes to collect the data. In a movement setting, the teacher accomplishes this by carrying a microcassette recorder in a pocket or on a belt. In the classroom, a stationary tape recorder should produce little distraction to normal classroom interactions.

When target students are used, the observer should select them randomly. For general purposes, it is acceptable for the observer to divide the total number of students in the class (e.g., 20) by the number of desired target students (e.g., 4) and then mentally count off and identify students; $20 \div 4 = 5$, so the observer will select every fifth student, scanning left to right or counting in line as students enter the gym. For research purposes, the observer should use a table of random numbers to select students.

Initially, the goal is to collect baseline data that will represent the status of events as they typically occur. Whenever possible, the observer should collect data over several observations in order to gain a representative picture of the behaviors in question. The observer will interpret and analyze data in the next step, allowing the observer and teacher to establish goals for future observations.

Comparing the Data to Established Criteria

There are no hard-and-fast rules or scientific principles for guiding this step of measurement-based evaluation. Because there is no single best way to teach, there can be no exact formulas for use as criteria of effective teaching. There are, however, some general principles that can guide the process.

The observer should begin by completing all of the calculations required of the instruments and translating raw data into frequencies, percentages, ratios, and rates per minute as appropriate. Whenever possible, the observer should also provide a graphic illustration of the data. For example, Figure 5.9 shows data an observer obtained concerning a teacher's use of instructional time. The instrument itself provides bar graphs for illustrating the amount of time devoted to management, instruction, and movement activities. The bar graphs clearly show that the teacher spent too much time in management. The supervisor might then discuss goals and strategies for reducing management and increasing movement time, identifying factors and events that contributed to the observed circumstances and those that could bring improvements. This supervisor should assume a nonjudgmental manner, emphasizing collaboration and joint decision making.

In the process of collaboration, the supervisor must consider the teacher's goals, level of experience, and developmental readiness to change (e.g., motivation, cognitive level, and confidence). It is helpful to begin by praising those observed elements of the lessons that were most effective. With beginning teachers or those experiencing problems, the supervisor should focus on the gross aspects of improvement (making basic changes) before considering the fine-tuning aspects. With beginning and experienced teachers, the supervisor should identify a small number of elements for improvement as opposed to overwhelming teachers with many. Just as a golfer could not improve a golf swing by concentrating simultaneously on the grip, the action of the trunk, the position of the club face, and weight transfer, a teacher cannot focus simultaneously on complex multiple objectives.

Research on effective teaching can provide additional guidelines for interpreting data. For example, it is generally desirable that the teacher provide

- clear directions,
- consistent reinforcement of expectations,
- high rates of positive, specific, and task-relevant feedback,
- short managerial episodes,
- teaching cues,
- many successful skill attempts for low- and high-skilled students,

- high rates of time on task, and
- brief and clear instructions and demonstrations.

Monitoring change in teaching behavior requires ongoing observation and analysis. The rates at which teachers progress will vary according to personal limitations as well as the contextual variables that are present (e.g., class size, time, equipment, space, facilities, curriculum, and teacher autonomy). Eventually, the teacher internalizes basic skills and practices them automatically. In a series of progressions, the observer and teacher will identify new goals and teaching competencies to master and will have many opportunities for observation and feedback.

Overview of Systematic Observation Instruments

Observation instruments for both generic and specific physical education contexts are almost limitless. Some excellent sources for locating instruments include the following.

Generic Instruments

Good, T.L., & Brophy, J.E. (1987). *Looking in classrooms* (4th ed.). New York: Harper & Row. (ISBN 0-06-042401X)

Simon, A., & Boyer, E.G. (Eds.) (1974). *Mirrors for behavior III: An anthology of observation instruments.* Philadelphia: Research for Better Schools, Inc. (ISBN 0-686-21804-5)

Physical Education Instruments

Anderson, W.G. (1980). *Analysis of teaching physical education.* St. Louis: C.V. Mosby. (ISBN 0-8016-0179-7)

Darst, P.W., Zakrasjsek, D.B., & Mancini, V.H. (Eds.) (1989). *Analyzing physical education and sport instruction* (2nd ed.). Champaign, IL: Human Kinetics. (ISBN 0-87322-216-4)

Rink, J.E. (1985). *Teaching physical education for learning.* St. Louis: Times Mirror/Mosby. (ISBN 0-8-16-4136-5)

Siedentop, D. (1991). *Developing teaching skills in physical education.* (3rd ed.). Palo Alto, CA: Mayfield. (ISBN 0-87484-550-5)

Figure 5.9

Systematic Observation of Time Management
Sample Data From Elementary Level

Teacher _____*Rod Kurtz*_____ Date *November 2, 1991* (Grade)/period ___5___

Class size ____19____

Provisions for reducing management time and increasing time on task:
- *Prepared equipment in advance*
- *Used a signal for attention*
- *Provided many stations*
- *Incorporated few transitions*

Managerial episodes		Cognitive activity		Motor-engaged time	
1. Taking roll	*5:00*	*2. Explains task*	*:45*	*4. Skill practice*	*5:00*
3. Arrange groups	*2:30*	*6. Technique*	*:15*	*7. Skill practice*	*4:00*
5. Transition	*:30*	*12. Closure*	*1:00*	*9. Skill practice*	*4:00*
8. Switch stations	*:35*			*11. Minigame*	*3:00*
10. Transition	*:25*				
	9:00		*2:00*		*16:00*

Percent of total time

100	100	100
80	80	80
60	60	60
40	40	40
20	20	20
0	0	0

33.3 percent   *7.4 percent*   *59.3 percent*

Summary and Implications

Measurement-based evaluation entails the assessment of teacher effectiveness based on performance, as measured directly with systematic observation instruments; as such, it offers objectivity and reliability. In contrast, subjective measures such as informal analysis, eyeballing, anecdotal records, checklists, and rating scales are subject to a number of limitations. Another alternative, the assessment of student outcomes, is also greatly influenced by situational variables. Primarily, subjective measures are influenced by the personal biases of the observer and are characterized by high inference. Objective measures are governed by factual decisions and are characterized by low inference.

Measurement-based evaluation uses systematic observation systems for the process of descriptive analysis. The observer uses these instruments to code observable behaviors and to categorize them according to established definitions. Techniques used in coding the data include event recording, duration recording, interval recording, and time sampling. The appropriateness of these techniques depends on the nature of the given variable to be observed. Two important considerations for the use of systematic observation are the validity of the scale, as determined by structure of the instrument; and the reliability of the scale, as affected by the data collection process.

A large number of systematic observation instruments are available for use in generic and physical education settings. Many of these require the user to undergo extensive training in order to obtain reliable coding. When a unique situation arises, a supervisor may need to construct an instrument to observe selected variables within a given context. The instruments designed for the Systematic Supervision Model were designed to be used with minimal training and to focus on limited aspects of the teaching-learning environment.

Although objective measures are advantageous, it is possible to combine subjective and objective measures of effective teaching in order to obtain a richer picture. The supervisor should not hesitate to augment the Systematic Supervision Model with a variety of subjective measures. In some instances, it may be necessary for the supervisor to put aside the systematic observation instrument and attend to the issue at hand.

Part II

The Systematic Supervision Model

This part provides a detailed look at the Systematic Supervision Model. The overall structure of the model, consisting of 3 phases and 15 components, is introduced initially. Separate chapters present each of the 3 phases of the model. These chapters provide a general theoretical overview, a knowledge base for the selected components, and specific steps for implementing the model. Steps for implementing the model include competencies to be attained, tasks for the student teacher, and observation and evaluation tools for the cooperating teacher.

Chapter 6 introduces the gross structure of the model and provides a conceptual framework for its implementation. The chapter draws relationships to illustrate the model's eclectic use of some generic principles of supervision. The chapter then defines the process of systematic supervision with respect to the proposed Systematic Supervision Model. The developmental nature of the model is explored with respect to the structure of 3 phases:

gaining confidence and establishing control, planning for maximum learning, and refining teaching.

Chapter 7 outlines Phase 1 of the Systematic Supervision Model, a sequence of 5 components related to gaining confidence and establishing control. This phase structures a gradual induction into teaching, helping the student teacher establish a foundation for further development of teaching skills. Components included in Phase 1 are using guided observation and inquiry, developing a discipline plan, communicating expectations and reinforcing desired behavior, improving classroom management, and developing a positive classroom climate.

Chapter 8 presents Phase 2 of the model, emphasizing teaching skills essential to planning for maximum learning. Professional preparation courses cover all of these skills, but the skills often fail to transfer into practice because they are not systematically reinforced during student teaching and induction. In a series of activities, this phase provides additional practice with developing performance objectives, using mechanical analysis and teaching cues, selecting skills at an appropriate level of difficulty, maximizing time on task, and evaluating the effectiveness of lessons.

Chapter 9 concludes this part with an overview of Phase 3 of the Systematic Supervision Model. This phase contains a variety of teaching skills that may require additional practice once the teacher has established a comfortable level of competence. Components in this phase include providing appropriate feedback, techniques for effective demonstration, lesson presentation skills, questioning skills, and assessing student performance.

Part II provides detailed information about the structure of the Systematic Supervision Model and how it can be used. Although the model is generally sequential, it does allow supervisors some flexibility to reorder the components to meet the needs of varied internship programs and individual student teachers. The model is intended to provide focus and direction for internship experiences, as contrasted to a lockstep and prescriptive approach.

The Student Teacher's Handbook for Physical Education, a resource that describes only information directly related to the model, is also available as a separate publication. This resource has all of the necessary materials for implementation of the model, including brief knowledge bases, target behaviors (competencies), tasks for the student teacher, and observation and evaluation instruments. This resource should provide a clear focus for all members of the supervisory triad—the student teacher, the cooperating teacher, and the university supervisor. Common goals, mutual understanding, and a clear direction should greatly enhance the chances for improved outcomes of supervision.

Chapter 6

A Proposed Model of Systematic Supervision

Systematic supervision is presented here as a 15-component model, which was initially designed for use with student teachers. However, the developmental nature of the model makes it equally appropriate for assisting the induction of beginning teachers. It may also be used as a structure for peer supervision, self-analysis, or in-service programs for experienced teachers. The 15 components correspond roughly to the weeks of a full semester of student teaching but can be completed over a shorter practicum period if necessary. The macrostructure of the model describes 3 phases of supervision. Phase 1 is designed to assist teachers in gaining confidence and establishing control. Phase 2 builds upon this solid framework by helping the teacher plan for maximum learning. Phase 3 extends the process of supervision to focus on refining teaching skills. These phases are illustrated in Table 6.1.

Although student teachers generally will cover 1 component per week, individuals will differ in the rates at which they acquire teaching skills. Unique circumstances of the school environment may also affect the student teacher's progress in mastering the competencies. For this reason, the supervisor may need to spend more than 1 week on a given component or revisit specific skills from time to time. Time constraints may necessitate eliminating some of the tasks within the competen-

cies. These minor modifications should not diminish the overall impact of the Systematic Supervision Model.

Systematic supervision entails identifying target behaviors deemed essential to effective teaching, developing these behaviors through a planned sequence of tasks, and directly observing teaching with systematic observation instruments. The observation instruments that the model uses were developed or selected to provide a narrow focus for teaching behaviors. Unlike many of the observation instruments developed for research purposes, these instruments require minimal training in order to obtain reliability. The student teacher and the cooperating teacher can use these instruments easily, and the instruments should help them both attain an objective and data-based style of analyzing teaching.

Table 6.1 Systematic Supervision Model

Phase 1	Phase 2	Phase 3
Gaining confidence/ establishing control	Planning for maximum learning	Refining teaching skills

The Systematic Supervision Model is eclectic in nature because it incorporates aspects of a variety of generic models of supervision. Drawing from the clinical model, the Systematic Supervision Model adopts several major assumptions about teaching and learning. The model assumes that teaching is behavior, that teaching and learning are inseparably intertwined, that the process of teaching is subject to objective analysis, and that modifications in teaching behavior will produce desired effects in learning. More importantly, the Systematic Supervision Model promotes a comprehensive and ongoing process, as opposed to random and intermittent visits. The model accepts the notion of ''colleagueship'' as essential to the process of supervision.

To the extent that it is concerned with the feelings, attitudes, values, and perceptions of the teacher, the Systematic Supervision Model incorporates the philosophic basis of counseling models. However, it stops short of a counseling approach, because the primary focus is on what the teacher does as opposed to what the teacher is. The Systematic Supervision Model contributes to the emotional well-being of the teacher by removing the mystique of supervision and reducing the inherent anxieties caused by unknown evaluation criteria.

We can easily apply aspects of peer supervision and self-analysis to the Systematic Supervision Model. The model clearly defines the general focus, target behaviors, tasks, and evaluation procedures for each component. For this reason, the model could be used by experienced and inexperienced teachers working together in a mentorshiping relationship, or by two or more teachers at any level of experience working in collusion. Similarly, an individual teacher may wish to concentrate on selected aspects of the model in a self-analytic approach.

In a general sense, the model identifies competencies for effective teaching behavior. The competency-based orientation offers the advantage of clearly defined teaching roles, systematic training to develop competencies for fulfilling roles, and a central focus on effective teaching research (B.R. Joyce, Soltis, & Weil, 1974). However, the Systematic Supervision Model adopts a broader definition of competencies in the form of ''generally stated goals reflecting various functions that teachers should be able to perform'' (Kay, 1975, p. 4). In the strictest sense, competencies define precise behavioral objectives and specify all of the knowledge, attitudes, and skills required for effective teaching. In addition, they specify criteria or standards of performance required to establish competence. The Systematic Supervision Model rejects this approach because it is impractical to specify levels of teaching behavior that are appropriate for all settings. Thus, the model defines competencies generally to facilitate a process rather than product approach. A general overview of the model is presented in Table 6.2.

Table 6.2 15-Component Model of Systematic Supervision

Phase 1: Gaining Confidence/Establishing Control

1. Using guided observation and inquiry
2. Establishing a discipline plan
3. Communicating expectations/reinforcing desired behaviors
4. Improving classroom management
5. Establishing a positive classroom climate

Phase 2: Planning for Maximum Learning

6. Developing performance objectives
7. Incorporating mechanical analysis and teaching cues
8. Selecting activities at an appropriate level of difficulty
9. Maximizing time on task
10. Evaluating lesson effectiveness

Phase 3: Refining Teaching Skills

11. Providing appropriate feedback
12. Using techniques for effective modeling
13. Developing lesson presentation skills
14. Enhancing questioning skills
15. Assessing student performance

Phase 1: Gaining Confidence and Establishing Control

A basic prerequisite to developing teaching competence is gaining confidence in the mechanics of classroom management and control. Consider the illogic of asking a student teacher to produce maximum time on task while he or she is still absorbed in the gross aspects of confronting a group of students (gaining attention, establishing authority, organizing people, and managing equipment). Although maximizing time on task is a worthwhile goal, it is not an element of immediate survival in the ''real world'' of teaching. A planned sequence of experiences can support the beginning teacher through the transition period. Phase 1 is designed to reduce anxiety by reinforcing teaching behaviors that are related to successful classroom management.

Two essential elements of effective classroom management are clear communication to students of behavioral expectations (clarity) and consistent reinforcement of these expectations (consistency). The teacher can best facilitate effective classroom management in a positive classroom climate. Classroom climate is primarily determined by the nature of verbal and nonverbal interactions between teacher and students.

Gradual induction into teaching roles allows the student teacher to assume greater responsibility as he or she gains confidence and experience. For this reason, the model provides for the student teacher to undertake guided observation and inquiry during the 1st week of student teaching, aided by systematic observation and structured interviews. The structured interviews provide a form of mentorship, allowing the cooperating teacher and a school counselor to present their philosophies and guidelines for effective management and control. Although observation and inquiry are the major activities, the student teacher should also assist with some activities related to management and instruction (e.g., taking roll, giving a demonstration, or working with individuals or small groups).

In the second component of Phase 1, the student teacher focuses on establishing definitive expectations for the conduct of students and writing these expectations in the form of a discipline plan. He or she will then begin to assume greater responsibility for teaching, adding one or two classes a week until a full teaching load is acquired. Having defined expectations for student behavior, the student teacher will focus on communicating expectations, reinforcing desired behaviors, and establishing a positive classroom climate during Components 3, 4, and 5. Figure 6.1 (p. 85) provides a summary of processes included in Phase 1.

Phase 2: Planning for Maximum Learning

Once the beginning teacher has established the preconditions for teaching (classroom management), he or she can then begin to acquire preactive and interactive decision-making skills for maximum student learning. Phase 2 reinforces critical teaching skills related to developing performance objectives, incorporating mechanical analysis

and teaching cues, selecting activities at an appropriate level of difficulty, maximizing time on task, and evaluating the effectiveness of lessons. Comprehensive written plans are pivotal to bringing about maximal learning.

Planning, despite its importance, seems to be one aspect of pedagogy that deteriorates rapidly in the early phases of teacher induction. Student teachers often begin their experiences with many conflicting ideas of what should constitute a lesson plan. These conflicts stem from major inconsistencies in models presented in the methods classes. In addition, student teachers seem to believe that lesson planning is an exercise reserved for practice in the laboratory and is not necessary once they begin teaching in the schools. The efficacy of lesson planning may be further demeaned when student teachers do not observe it in practice by experienced teachers.

The emphasis on planning for maximum learning throughout Phase 2 is designed to enhance introspection. The goal is for the student teacher to continually ask, ''Why am I doing this?'' ''Were my objectives achieved?'' and ''How can I do better?'' Intentionality, or ''doing something because it is believed that it will make a difference'' (B.R. Joyce & Showers, 1988, p. 96) is preferable to the arbitrary selection of content and methodologies. In addition, interactive decision making allows the teacher to modify the structure of the lesson to adjust to unique conditions, rather than dogmatically pursue the lesson just as it was planned.

Comprehensive lesson planning also improves the quality of teaching by providing a clear picture of the skills that students will perform. Performance objectives and mechanical analysis can sharpen this visual image of correct skill performance, thereby enhancing clinical diagnosis (Hoffman, 1983) and the provision of feedback. Careful skill analysis and identification of teaching cues should translate to precise instructional input and skill feedback. A summary of processes included in Phase 2 is provided in Figure 6.2 (p. 86).

Phase 3: Refining Teaching Skills

The experiences provided in the first 2 phases of the Systematic Supervision Model should provide a sound foundation for induction into teaching. After 10 weeks (components) of planned progressions for the basic skills, the model shifts to an

Figure 6.1

Phase 1:
Gaining Confidence and Establishing Control
Summary of Procedures

	Component 1	Component 2	Component 3	Component 4	Component 5
General focus	Using guided observation and inquiry	Establishing a discipline plan	Communicating expectations/ reinforcing desired behaviors	Improving classroom management	Establishing a positive classroom climate
Target behaviors	Cueing and reinforcing done by cooperating teacher	Plan rules, consequences, and rewards	Cue and reinforce	Begin and end class on time; use short transitions, brief instructions, and verbal prompts	Positive verbal behavior related to student behavior and skill attempts; use first names
Tasks for student teacher	Participate in interviews; systematically observe cooperating teacher	Complete a written discipline plan	Analyze verbal behavior from observation made by cooperating teacher	Develop a written plan for reducing management time	Make audiotaped self-analysis of verbal behavior
Observation/ evaluation strategies	Questionnaires; systematic observation form— Communicating Expectations	Discipline Plan form	Systematic observation form— Communicating Expectations	Plan for Improving Classroom Management; Classroom Management Observation Instrument	Classroom climate observation form

Figure 6.2

Phase 2:
Planning for Maximum Learning
Summary of Procedures

	Component 6	Component 7	Component 8	Component 9	Component 10
General focus	Developing performance objectives	Incorporating mechanical analysis and teaching cues	Selecting activities at an appropriate level of difficulty	Maximizing time on task	Evaluating lesson effectiveness
Target behaviors	Planning observable and measurable objectives for three learning domains	Skill analysis; use teaching cues and skill feedback	Student opportunity to respond and student success rates	Student engaged time in motor, cognitive, and management activities	Student rates of on-task/off-task, motor-engaged/non-motor-engaged activity
Tasks for student teacher	Develop and analyze performance objectives and lesson plans	Identify mechanics and teaching cues for skills to be taught in written lesson plan	Use Mosston & Ashworth's inclusion style to teach a lesson with multiple skill-entry levels	Utilize Lesson Plan Format B to plan for maximum time on task and success	Conduct self-analysis of placheck data; restructure lesson for reteach phase
Observation/ evaluation strategies	Performance Objectives Assessment Form; stimulated recall technique	Specialized Lesson Plan Format A; systematic observation of teaching cues and feedback	Event recording of skill attempts and success rates—high- and low-skilled students	Duration recording of motor-engaged time; systematic observation of time management	Planned activity check of student on-task/off-task, motor-engaged/non-motor-engaged behavior

emphasis on refining teaching skills. These skill areas include providing appropriate feedback, effective modeling (demonstrating), lesson presentation, questioning, and student performance assessment. Although these competencies do not involve a central theme, they constitute aspects of teaching effectiveness that are frequently overlooked or lost in the shuffle of basic survival concerns.

The student teacher initially practices providing appropriate feedback in Phase 1 as an aspect of establishing a positive classroom climate. Phase 3 extends the emphasis to an in-depth analysis of skill-related feedback. Because feedback plays an essential role in skill acquisition, it merits continued practice and refinement of factors related to its valence (positive or negative), specificity, timing, target, and task relevance.

Effective modeling or demonstration is important in providing students with a clear image of skills to be performed. Often, demonstrations conducted in physical education involve too much teacher talk and incorporate too much detailed information for students to process. The effectiveness of a demonstration is further negated if the teacher does not follow up immediately with practice opportunities and feedback. Thus, the cycle of demonstration, practice, and feedback is important to the acquisition of motor skills.

The teacher needs additional teaching competencies to expand his or her repertoire of effective teaching behaviors in a physical education setting.

Teacher preparation in physical education typically provides few opportunities for the prospective teacher to practice giving information or soliciting student responses. Completion of Phase 3 indicates that the teacher has acquired teaching skills that will transfer from the fields and gymnasia to the classroom. The teacher can apply lesson presentation and questioning skills to cognitive instruction, where the main objective is to help the student acquire and assimilate information. A summary of processes included in Phase 3 is included in Figure 6.3 (p. 87).

Summary and Implications

The Systematic Supervision Model provides a planned sequence of progressions for induction of the beginning teacher. The structure of the 3 phases — gaining confidence and establishing control, planning for maximum learning, and refining teaching skills — provides a clear developmental focus. The model helps the cooperating teacher and university supervisor provide consistent reinforcement of target behaviors and allows the student teacher the comfort of knowing exactly what is expected. The target behaviors included in the model do not comprise all the teaching behaviors required for effective teaching. However, the mastery of these skills should indicate more than satisfactory attainment of teaching competence.

Figure 6.3

Phase 3:
Refining Teaching Skills
Summary of Procedures

	Component 11	Component 12	Component 13	Component 14	Component 15
General focus	Providing appropriate skill feedback	Using techniques for effective demonstration	Developing lesson presentation skills	Enhancing questioning skills	Assessing student performance
Target behaviors	Positive, specific, and task-relevant feedback related to skill attempts	Criteria of an effective demonstration	Effective set induction, explanation, and closure	High-order questions; probe; prompt; provide wait time	Error detection, clinical diagnosis, and process assessment
Tasks for student teacher	Audiotape lessons and analyze feedback through systematic observation	Plan and implement skill demonstration to be videotaped; analyze videotape for set criteria	Develop a written lesson plan (Format C) for presenting cognitive content	Plan and implement a lesson to develop high-order thinking	Select and implement a process measure of skill development
Observation/ evaluation strategies	Systematic Observation of Teacher Verbal Skill Feedback	Videotape of lesson; effective demonstration checklist	Specialized Lesson Plan Format C; Lesson Clarity Observation Form	Systematic Observation of Questioning Skills	Videotape analysis

Chapter 7

Phase 1: Gaining Confidence and Establishing Control

This chapter introduces Phase 1 of the Systematic Supervision Model in three sections: a theoretical overview, a knowledge base for Phase 1 components, and specific steps for implementing Phase 1. The theoretical overview describes the broad scope of issues related to gaining confidence and establishing control, whereas the knowledge base reviews the literature related to each of its 5 components. The section containing specific steps for implementing Phase 1 describes target behaviors and competencies for the student teacher to attain, tasks for the student teacher, and observation/evaluation strategies for each of the 5 components.

A Theoretical Overview

The skills practiced in Phase 1 of the Systematic Supervision Model will help the teacher establish an environment that allows the teacher to teach and students to learn. The first prerequisite of that environment is an atmosphere in which students perceive the teacher as a leader and as having authority. This requires the teacher to use a "take-charge" approach that communicates positive ex-

pectations for all of the students. The assumption of a leadership role can be problematic in the initial stages of teaching or for teachers who lack confidence in their abilities to establish and maintain control. The school is a very complex and dynamic environment, reflecting many of the stresses and pressures in our society. Discipline currently ranks as the Number 1 problem in our schools nationally and has been consistently cited in this manner in Gallup polls conducted since 1969. Consequently, discipline and control issues are a primary concern of student teachers and beginning teachers. Indeed, discipline problems can challenge even the most experienced teacher in contemporary school settings. Particularly in the case of student teachers, supervisors should consider the developmental needs of teachers as they progress through the stages of induction. Beginning teachers in general will benefit from focused attention to skills needed for the establishment and maintenance of classroom management and control. This focus should help the teacher reduce anxieties and develop general confidence and teaching efficacy. The competencies in Phase 1 are supported by a large body of literature, much of which is reported as research evidence in chapter 4. Chapter 7 reviews the implications of that research, as well as specific guidelines and applications, as it relates to gaining confidence and establishing control. Components of this phase include using guided observation and inquiry, establishing a discipline plan, communicating expectations/reinforcing desired behaviors, improving classroom management, and establishing a positive classroom environment.

A Knowledge Base for Phase 1 Components

An expanded knowledge base will help us review the literature described in chapter 4, A Research Base for the Improvement of Teaching. This knowledge base provides a conceptual framework for the strategies that are described in the section concerning specific steps for implementing Phase 1.

Using Guided Observation and Inquiry

This component alerts the student teacher to a number of variables that may affect the school environment and his or her ability to function within it. Each school has a certain unique ecology, determined by interacting factors related to the school (size, geographic location, urban or rural setting, facilities, and equipment) and its student composition (socioeconomic status variables, race, ethnicity, and cultural norms and values). Other important variables depend on the institutional organization (administrative, faculty, staff, and parental interactions; policies; and rules) and parental factors (involvement and participation in school activities, and level of support concerning student disciplinary problems).

When student teachers and beginning teachers lack an established structure or plan, their observations may be random and fragmentary. Research has found that preservice teachers in their early training stages focus primarily on students in unguided observations (Bell, Barrett, & Allison, 1985), whereas teachers who have accumulated teaching experience can simultaneously attend to student, teacher, and lesson dimensions (Barrett, Allison, & Bell, 1987). The teacher's exposure to aspects of the school environment and interactions with individuals within it are often limited by the isolating effects of the physical environment—the distant locations of the gymnasium or playing field.

Key individuals in the school can provide valuable information to student and beginning teachers. At the administrative level, principals, assistant principals, deans, and guidance counselors are usually well apprised of relevant facts. Department heads, cooperating teachers, mentors, and peer teachers in physical education can also help to orient the novice teacher. Parent and citizen advisory groups are an untapped resource of information and support. Input from these individuals will be most useful if the novice teacher asks specific questions. Supplementary orientation will occur naturally through the daily processes of school interactions.

Two inquiry methods (structured interviews) used in this component are designed to help the student teacher acquire specific information from the cooperating teacher and from an administrator who regularly deals with disciplinary issues. In addition to providing objective data about the school, these people can provide information about their personal philosophies and about beliefs and strategies that they have found effective. The model contains two instruments for this purpose, which serve as guides; the student teacher can easily expand their use to other key individuals or with additional questions. In addition, this component includes a structured observation form to help the student teacher focus on specific aspects of the teacher's verbal behavior (cueing and reinforcing). The student teacher uses a verbal behavior grid to record data regarding the cooperating teacher's communication of expectations and reinforcement of verbal behavior.

Establishing a Discipline Plan

Teachers have many options in selecting an approach to discipline. A number of contextual variables identified in the previous component (e.g., existing rules and policies, laws, characteristics of the school environment, student composition, and parental support) will influence decisions. Decisions about discipline will also depend on the philosophies held by school boards, administrators, faculty, parents, and individual teachers. Formalized models of discipline cover a range of approaches to intervention such as relationship-listening, confronting-contracting, and rules/rewards-punishments. In line with the selected approach, teacher behaviors in response to disciplinary problems will fall on a continuum from silently looking on to physical intervention and isolation (Wolfgang & Glickman, 1986).

The focus on assertive discipline in this text is not intended to preclude the use of other approaches. To the contrary, an eclectic approach incorporating many schools of thought is practical. To facilitate this goal, the following section outlines general strategies for effective discipline. In addition, the text provides background information and key principles of several established theories of discipline, including Dreikurs' and Grey's (1968) logical consequences, Glasser's (1975) Reality Therapy, Gordon's (1975) Teacher Effectiveness Training, Behavior Modification, and Canter and Canter's (1976) Assertive Discipline model.

General Strategies of Effective Discipline

Individual student misbehaviors are generally motivated by one or more of the four basic motivations: seeking attention, seeking power, seeking revenge, and displaying inadequacy (disability as an excuse) (Dreikurs & Grey, 1968). In dealing with persistent behavior problems, the teacher must first determine the student's motives. Dreikurs and Grey (1968) outlined indicators of the student motives based on the teacher's emotional reaction. Teacher feelings of annoyance will probably indicate that the child is seeking attention. If the teacher feels angry or provoked, the child's behavior is probably motivated by a desire for power. If the teacher feels offended or hurt, the child's likely motivation is revenge. Teacher feelings of helplessness and exasperation indicate that the child is reacting to inadequacy.

Group behavior problems may stem from a variety of causes. It is important that the teacher try to analyze and consider all potential causes of the problem. Often, teachers look first to the student as the cause of behavior problems. However, group or individual behavior problems may stem from student issues, instructional behaviors, or content-related factors.

When behavior problems occur, the teacher must decide whether the problem at hand requires immediate attention, eventual attention, or monitoring (Weber, 1990). As a general rule, the teacher can ignore behavior problems that are minor and do not disturb the process of instruction. Behaviors that are persistent, are potentially dangerous, or disrupt learning should be dealt with immediately. Mild reprimands or corrective feedback statements remind the student that the displayed behavior is inappropriate and should be modified. The teacher should use harsh reprimands or loud verbal commands in situations in which serious misbehavior must be quickly curtailed (e.g., students fighting) but should not use

such methods under ordinary circumstances. Proximity control, or moving closer to a student who is off-task, can also help to prevent disruptions. For serious behavior problems, the teacher may need to remove the child temporarily from the environment (Weber, 1990).

Two general strategies can help to prevent disciplinary problems: planning carefully and comprehensively, and making lessons interesting and challenging. Particularly when learning to teach, the teacher should develop detailed plans for all of the managerial and instructional aspects of the lesson. Plans should consider the developmental needs and interests of the children and should structure the lesson to maintain momentum and student involvement.

Kounin's (1970) research findings concerning smoothness and momentum support the need for innovative lessons. This study linked effective classroom management to the teacher's ability to plan and implement lessons that maintain student interest and prevent misbehavior. The study found that successful teachers teach well-planned lessons that progress smoothly and at a fairly rapid pace. They also waste little time moving (transitioning) students from one activity to another and provide individual seat work at a level appropriate for the interests and abilities of individual students.

Long, Frye, and Long (1985) proposed some practical guidelines for the teacher to use in establishing effective relationships with students. These strategies should help the teacher maintain a sense of personal balance in dealing with disciplinary problems. The authors suggested 17 strategies for laying the foundation of a caring attitude and prompting desired behaviors: The teacher should

- believe in him- or herself (self-efficacy),
- think and speak positively about him- or herself,
- cultivate interests outside of school,
- listen to others (empathize),
- look for positive qualities in others,
- avoid labeling student conduct (a student is not inherently good or bad),
- respond more positively to others,
- put misbehavior in perspective (see misbehavior as a problem to be corrected as opposed to a personal affront),
- let students know what to expect,
- let students know the rules,
- give clear instructions (ask for questions for clarification, and give clarification only when students are listening),
- make the physical setting conducive to learning,

- provide appropriate materials,
- give students time on task,
- develop effective management behaviors,
- consider student interests, and
- reinforce desired behaviors.

One additional strategy that should not be used but requires attention is corporal punishment. Although 47 states allow corporal punishment, and the Supreme Court has upheld its use (*Ingraham v. Wright*, 1977), a number of problems are inherent in its use. Erlanger (1974) examined the myth that the only way some kids learn is by spanking, since it's the way they're taught at home. The author found that the use of corporal punishment by lower class parents is greatly exaggerated. In school, corporal punishment is most often used in primary grades and reinforces in young children the belief that aggressive behavior is a solution to problems. Corporal punishment is an ineffective way to discipline school children and usually requires many repetitions. It can potentially lead to low self-concepts, violent personalities, and suppressed aggressive behavior.

Established Theories of Discipline

Each of the following theories has important implications for effective discipline. By making teachers more aware of major principles for effective discipline, supervisors can inspire teachers to seek additional information and to incorporate these strategies into teaching repertoires. Because there can be no singular best approach to handling disciplinary problems, the teacher needs a broad repertoire of teaching behaviors. The application of these principals to appropriate situations is the artful or intuitive element of teaching. The principles are therefore offered not as prescriptions, but as ideas.

Logical Consequences

Dreikurs and Grey (1968) proposed the concept of logical consequences as an alternative to authoritarian approaches to discipline, in which the parent or teacher "knows best." We can classify it as a social democratic theory, because it emphasizes the importance of developing behavior patterns that are acceptable to society. Desired social outcomes are personal responsibility, respect for self and others, tolerance, understanding, and a sense of unity ("we" feeling) (Dreikurs, Grunwald, & Pepper, 1971).

A major premise of this theory is that parents and teachers should deal with children as equals, attempting to influence behavior by imposing logical consequences. Logical and natural consequences are central definitions of this theory. Spencer (1885) first defined natural consequences as the inevitable consequences or reactions that follow an individual's actions — the natural flow of events without intervention. A natural consequence for a child who breaks crayons is that he or she has to color with broken parts (Clarizio, 1980). Logical consequences are those imposed by parents or adults. Logical consequences are intrinsically related to the misbehavior, involve no element of moral judgment, and are involved only with the "here and now."

A pertinent example might be the misuse of equipment in physical education. Suppose a child breaks a racket by recklessly tossing it onto the floor. The natural consequence that follows is that he has no equipment to use. The logical consequence that the teacher might eventually impose is that the child should repair or replace the equipment. Or, suppose a child at home frequently spills her milk. Next time that happens, should the parent punish her by sending her away from the table, let her suffer the natural consequence of staying thirsty, or impose the logical consequence of having her mop it up?

Reality Therapy

Glasser's (1965) Reality Therapy is a clinical psychological approach that the author later applied to classroom learning in *Schools Without Failure* (Glasser, 1969) and *Control Theory in the Classroom* (Glasser, 1986). As applied to teaching and learning, Reality Therapy is a model of classroom discipline that focuses on personal development. The model incorporates the concept of realistic behaviors, or those that students select in terms of their consequences to themselves and others (Joyce & Weil, 1986). The model helps children develop responsible behavior through increased self-understanding.

A central assumption of reality therapy is that behavior problems stem from low self-esteem. Glasser (1975) proposed that all personal problems stem from a failure to meet one of two basic needs: the need for relatedness (love) and the need for respect (self-worth). Students adopt irrational or unrealistic behaviors in school when their efforts to achieve success are consistently blocked. A primary goal of reality therapy is to provide opportunities for students to feel good about themselves.

To increase self-awareness, the teacher helps students understand why problems occur in school. In confronting problems, the teacher asks the child to reflect on past behavior and develop and commit to a new approach. Through the use of questions, the teacher helps the child to accept responsibility for his or her behavior and does not permit rationalization or excuse making. "What did you do?" "How are you going to change your behavior?" and "How will you avoid this problem in the future?" are questions used to prompt the student toward self-responsibility.

A method for developing group responsibility in school settings is Glasser's (1969) classroom meeting. These meetings offer a climate in which students can discuss problems, examine personal values, propose solutions, and commit to alternative courses of action. In follow-up meetings, students evaluate proposed solutions and reinforce their commitments to action. A full discussion of this model and its applications is included in Joyce and Weil's (1986) *Models of Teaching*.

Teacher Effectiveness Training

Another approach to personal development in classroom settings is Gordon's (1975) Teacher Effectiveness Training (TET). This model emphasizes the development of effective dialogue between teachers and students, accomplished through the use of specific communication skills. The model evolved from Parent Effectiveness Training (Gordon, 1970), which is also primarily concerned with interpersonal communications. The approach involves finding out why students are misbehaving (what is bothering them?) through nondirective questioning. The teacher and student then identify solutions to the problem in a way that avoids blame. The teacher and student use joint problem solving to negotiate viable solutions. The role of the teacher is listener, counselor, and facilitator.

Specific teaching skills used in TET are I-messages, passive listening, and active listening. I-messages help students assume responsibility (ownership) for their behavior. An I-message is a direct statement, containing the word *I*, that describes how the student's behavior affects the teacher (e.g., "When you are talking, I am not able to give the directions"). Passive listening or silence provides the student an opportunity to express feelings and experience some level of catharsis. Passive listening is enhanced by cues that show

interest and attention: nonverbal cues (e.g., nodding, leaning forward, smiling, frowning), verbal cues ("Uh-huh," "Oh," "I see"), and "door openers," (which are verbal encouragements to talk more (e.g., "Do you want to talk about that?"). Active listening involves interacting with the student and providing feedback related to their concerns.

Gordon (1975) identified two kinds of verbal communication that can effect student behavior. Communication roadblocks pose obstacles to effective dialogue, while communication facilitators can enhance interactions. Following are verbal communications identified by Gordon (1975).

Communication Roadblocks

- Ordering, commanding, directing
- Warning, threatening
- Moralizing, preaching, giving, "shoulds and oughts"
- Advising, offering solutions or suggestions
- Teaching, lecturing, giving logical arguments
- Judging, criticizing, disagreeing, blaming
- Name-calling, stereotyping, labeling
- Interpreting, analyzing, diagnosing
- Praising, agreeing, giving positive evaluations
- Reassuring, sympathizing, consoling, supporting
- Questioning, probing, interrogating, cross-examining
- Withdrawing, distracting, being sarcastic, humoring, diverting

Communication Facilitators

- Passive listening (silence)
- Acknowledgment responses
- Door openers, invitations to talk
- Active listening (feedback)

Behavior Modification

Behaviorists believe that the ultimate goal of education is to "provide the student with the behaviors necessary for self-discipline" (Madsen & Madsen, 1981, p. 71). The basic assumption is that all behavior is learned as a result of reinforcement and can be modified by changing the environment. Thus when disciplinary problems occur, the behaviorist teacher looks for environmental circumstances that can be manipulated to modify behavior. The primary focus is on changing undesirable behavior, as opposed to understanding why it occurred. The teacher also deals with behavior at the time of the occurrence (focusing on the "here and now") and reacts immediately. The teacher rewards appropriate behavior with positive reinforcement.

Behavior modification originated in the conditioned reflexes research of Ivan Pavlov, the behavior therapy of John B. Watson, and the operant conditioning theories of B.F. Skinner. Essentially, operant conditioning states that the likelihood that a behavior will recur can be strengthened or diminished by reinforcing stimuli that follow. Positive reinforcers are those that, when delivered, strengthen a response that preceded. Positive reinforcers may take the form of reward. Negative reinforcers are those that, when removed, strengthen a response that preceded.

A behavioral definition of learning is change or modification in behavior. Behavior modification assumes that learning (in this case discipline) must first be externally imposed and can later be internalized by the learner (self-discipline). Behavior modification theory holds that learning is extrinsically motivated, and when learning does not occur it is simply because reinforcing consequences have not been identified by the learner.

Techniques involved in behavior modification alter the environment in order to bring about desired changes in behavior. These techniques involve four basic steps: pinpointing observable (undesirable) behaviors, recording behaviors in measurable terms, identifying cause-and-effect relationships, and evaluating causes by isolating (adding and removing) specific consequences (Madsen & Madsen, 1981). Behavior modification deals with overt and measurable behaviors as opposed to attitudes. Through behavioral observations, teachers can identify desirable and undesirable behaviors. By manipulating the environment, teachers can then determine which environmental conditions (antecedents) and which reinforcers (consequences) seem to have cause-and-effect relationships with given behaviors. In this manner, the A-B-C model demonstrates that behavior (B) is a function of its consequences (C) and its antecedents (A).

In establishing behavior management plans, teachers must specify contingencies between desired behaviors and their consequences. A preliminary analysis of the environment will reveal antecedents that can be manipulated (e.g., curriculum, physical/spatial arrangements, rules, and cues). The teacher must select reinforcers based on which stimuli are positive or negative for the students. For example, the removal of a student from physical education for a short time-out may be a negative reinforcer for some students and a positive reinforcer for others. Positive reinforcers (rewards) may take the form of tangible objects (tokens,

candy, toys), social experiences (verbal or written praise, physical closeness, approval, attention), activity (privileges), feedback (extrinsic knowledge of results), and success experiences (intrinsic satisfaction).

The teacher can impose four possible consequences in response to student behavior: introduction of a reward (positive reinforcement), introduction of a punishment (aversive stimulus), removal of a reward (extinction or time-out), and removal of punishment (negative reinforcement). To encourage good behavior, the teacher can use rewards (positive reinforcement) or removal of punishment (negative reinforcement). To discourage inappropriate behavior, he or she may use punishment (aversive stimulus) or removal of a reward (ignoring behavior or time-out) (Weber, 1990).

The following is a summary of guidelines for the application of reinforcement theory (Clarizio, 1980; Givner & Graubard, 1974):

- The strength of a reinforcer is determined by its ability to accelerate or decelerate a given behavior. The quality is unique to the individual child and may be influenced by developmental level and sociocultural factors.
- Reinforcers are most effective when given immediately after the student exhibits the desired behavior.
- A behavior that is not reinforced will be gradually extinguished (eliminated).
- Behavior modification requires the consistent and systematic application of reinforcers.
- The effects of punishment are generally short-term.
- Frequent reinforcement is essential for the student to acquire new behaviors. The teacher can use intermittent reinforcement schedules to maintain behaviors.
- When a desired level of behavior is not within range, the rewarding of small steps (progress toward the objective) can produce shaping of behavior.
- It is useful to reinforce desirable behaviors that are incompatible with undesirable behaviors (rewarding desired behaviors and ignoring undesired).
- Persistent or serious misbehavior may require some form of punishment.
- The combination of punishment and reward seems to be most effective (reward desired behavior, punish undesired behavior).
- The removal of rewards (e.g., time-out, response cost) can serve as a positive form of punishment.
- Time-out, or the temporary removal of a stu-

dent from reinforcing stimuli, is frequently used as a form of punishment.

Assertive Discipline

Assertive Discipline is an established behavioral model that Canter & Canter (1976) developed on the basis of assertion training. Assertion training acknowledges three styles by which people may express their wants and needs, two that are ineffective and one that should be systematically encouraged. The nonassertive individual is passive or wishy-washy and does not express or follow up on his or her wants and feelings, thus a nonassertive teacher ignores many inappropriate behaviors. The aggressive or hostile individual expresses needs but does so in a way that threatens or abuses the rights of others. An aggressive teacher attempts to rule by intimidation, often criticizing and berating students for their behaviors. Assertive individuals express their own wants and needs in a manner that is objective and clear, and they follow up with appropriate action when necessary. An assertive teacher firmly and consistently enforces rules and consequences that maintain an environment for learning.

Assertive Discipline emphasizes the clear communication of needs, expectations, and rules to students and parents and the consistent application of established consequences. It is designed to help teachers increase their own influence or power through assertive behavior. Canter and Canter (1976) summarized the role of assertion for teachers in this statement:

When a teacher is assertive, and clearly and firmly communicates her wants and feelings to a child, she sends a very clear message. This message says: ''I care too much about myself to allow you to take advantage of my wants and feelings! I care too much to allow you to act in an inappropriate manner without my responding! I, as well, care too much about you to allow your inappropriate behavior to go unnoticed by me!'' Simply stated, the assertive teacher lets the child know that she means what she says and says what she means. (p. 9)

This model proposes that teachers must influence the behaviors of children in order to meet their own needs. These needs are particularly paramount in the current context of the school environment, which includes diminished prestige for teachers, decreased parental support, and increased student behavior problems. The model identifies three rights of teachers that are essen-

tial to empowerment (Canter & Canter, 1976). The teacher has the right to

- establish a classroom structure and routine that provide the optimal learning environment in light of the teacher's strengths and weaknesses,
- determine and request appropriate student behaviors that meet the teacher's needs and encourage positive social and educational development of children, and
- ask for help from parents or the principal when the teacher needs assistance with a child.

The model asserts that children have the right to

- have a teacher who helps children limit inappropriate self-disruptive behavior,
- have a teacher who provides children with positive support for appropriate behavior, and
- choose how to behave and know the consequences that will follow.

To use Assertive Discipline, the teacher must possess six interpersonal communication skills. The teacher must be able to identify wants and feelings as related to interpersonal relationships, verbally communicate wants and feelings, persist in statements of wants and feelings, verbalize with a firm tone of voice, maintain eye contact while delivering assertions, and demonstrate congruent nonverbal gestures with verbal assertions.

Rules and consequences are two additional important elements of Assertive Discipline. Assertive Discipline assumes that children want and desire rules and limits to their behavior. The teacher must consistently reinforce rules through the application of rewards and (negative) consequences. The teacher develops rules and consequences by first identifying desirable and undesirable behaviors. Limiting rules to a small number helps teachers to reinforce them consistently, because one teacher cannot reasonably monitor and enforce a large number of rules. Typically, these rules are limited to a list of four or five essential behaviors that are stated positively. Following is an example.

- Stop on the signal.
- Listen when the teacher is talking.
- Stay in your own self-space.
- Take good care of the equipment.
- Be considerate of others.

The teacher should clearly communicate these rules or expectations to students. It is important that the teacher spend time teaching the rules at the beginning of the year, or at the beginning of a unit when specific rules apply. The teacher should post the rules so that students are reminded of them, and the teacher should check for understanding and review the rules regularly. It is also recommended that a formal notice of policies, stating rules, rewards, and consequences be sent to parents and returned with signatures.

Most importantly, expectations must be consistently reinforced. When teachers threaten to impose consequences but fail to follow through, students quickly learn to disregard these threats. Thus, follow-through is essential to effective discipline; the teacher should deliver a promise but not a threat. Students must clearly understand the consequences that will follow inappropriate behaviors, so the teacher must clearly define, communicate, and post consequences. Following are some examples of consequences, ordered in terms of occurrences.

1st time—verbal warning and name on clipboard

2nd time—short time-out (10 minutes)

3rd time—longer time-out (15 minutes)

4th time—phone call home

5th time—administrative action or parent/teacher conference

Serious misbehavior clause—removal to principal's office

Positive assertions and rewards are probably more important to effective discipline than are negative strategies. Positive assertions and rewards encourage the continuation of appropriate behaviors and let children know that they can earn attention through positive channels. Canter and Canter (1976) suggested that a teacher try to balance his or her attention to positive and negative behavior in order to maintain a positive classroom climate and discourage misbehavior for attention.

Positive responses should be meaningful in that they are carefully planned out, viewed positively by the teacher and the students, and provided immediately and frequently. The teacher can easily supply frequent responses through social reinforcers such as eye contact, touch, and the use of first names. Other suggested follow-through consequences include special attention, positive note or phone calls to parents, awards, special privileges, tangible rewards, and privileges at home.

Assertive discipline is most effective when it is implemented schoolwide. Administrators can establish rules, consequences, and rewards for the school overall, and teachers can define them specifically for each classroom or activities within the classroom. As of 1987, approximately 3,000 school

districts had implemented Assertive Discipline as a general model. Canter and Associates (1987) reported that more than 500,000 people had been trained in the principles of this method.

Some criticisms have arisen; Render, Padilla, and Krank (1989) criticized the model's small database and limited research evidence, and Hill (1990) wrote that the model is dehumanizing and humiliating. However, Assertive Discipline is still widely supported as a valuable model. Among the positive effects supported in the literature are increases in student self-perceptions, teacher satisfaction, time on task, student preparation, appreciation of the program by students and staff, and decreases in office referrals and classroom disruptions (McCormack, 1989).

Activities within Component 2 of the Systematic Supervision Model are designed to help the teacher plan promptly and comprehensively for effective discipline. Figure 7.6 provides a format for developing a discipline plan, specifying rules, consequences, and rewards. This format follows the basic structure of Assertive Discipline. However, the format can describe any comprehensive plan for implementing the principles of effective discipline. Teachers have many options for disciplinary approaches, ranging from packaged models to their own eclectic approaches.

The selection of a model will depend upon the contextual variables examined in the previous component (school, student, administrative, teacher, parental, and community factors). It will also depend upon the degree of autonomy that teachers wish to give students. Ultimately, the goal of all disciplinary approaches is to help students acquire self-discipline and an internal locus of control and to accept responsibility for their own successes and failures.

Developing a discipline plan helps teachers to be more consistent and decreases the likelihood that their reactions will be influenced by factors such as their mood, time of day, activity, or student. A plan also helps students to clearly understand what is expected of them and what will be the consequence of off-task behavior. Ultimately, the goal is to have students practice self-discipline as they assume more and more responsibility for their own behaviors.

Communicating Expectations/ Reinforcing Desired Behaviors

As a follow-up to the discipline plan, Component 3 focuses on the clarity and consistency of verbal communications. The following material outlines specific strategies and techniques for effective teacher verbal behavior and describes guidelines for establishing and reinforcing rules. Essentially, a teacher wants to let students know clearly what is expected of them and give them feedback about how their behaviors match the teacher's goals. Teacher verbal reinforcement patterns will help establish a positive classroom environment.

Clear Communication

Rules should be few in number and limited to those that are most essential to learning. When rules are excessive in number, they result in teacher nagging, student testing of and focusing of misbehavior on rules, and less overall behavioral change (Clarizio, 1980). Rules should deal with behaviors that are most important to the teacher and should of course be enforceable. Three criteria of good rules are that they are definable, reasonable, and enforceable (L.M. Smith & Smith, 1966). Rules are reasonable when they are appropriate for the developmental level of the child and are not too restrictive.

Verbal skills are important in communicating assertions regarding student behavior, because the manner of delivery is just as important as what is said. Canter and Canter (1976) described a variety of techniques for verbal limit setting that are designed to help teachers say what they mean and mean what they say. Four methods of requesting specific behavior include hints ("Everyone should be working"), I-messages ("I want you to open your book and get to work"), questions ("Would you please get to work?"), and demands ("Please get to work now"). The authors cautioned that teachers should only make demands that they are prepared to back up with consequences.

The teacher can use nonverbal cues (eye contact, hand gestures, touch) and can use names to emphasize words when setting limits. Although some children may not respond positively to eye contact or touch, these strategies are usually effective in showing that the teacher means what he or she says. So, to strengthen an assertion (e.g., "I want you to stay in your seat") the teacher might establish eye contact, point to the child, and use the child's first name, stating emphatically, "Susan, I want you to stay in your seat."

Clarity, in addition to making rules explicit, can also reduce behavior problems by making instructions very clear. When giving instructions about how to perform tasks, teachers should use precise language and ask for student feedback on the clarity of the instructions. One excellent strategy for checking understanding is for the teacher to have a student repeat the instructions. The teacher should give instructions only when students are listening; it may be necessary to wait for their attention.

Consistent Reinforcement

For reinforcing desired behaviors, teacher approval (feedback and praise) is the most useful tool. It is important that the teacher reward behavior frequently and consistently and observe those principles of effective praise identified in chapter 4. That is, praise should be specific, directed toward significant behaviors, sincere but not lavish, and given equitably. The teacher must give students immediate feedback on how their behavior matches his or her expectations. As opposed to only letting students know when they fail, the teacher should let them know when their behaviors are on task and productive for learning.

Consistency in enforcing rules and expectations means that the same expectations for appropriate behavior apply to all students under all circumstances. A lack of consistency confuses students, because they are never quite sure what is expected of them. It may also result in resentment by some students who feel unfairly treated. Teachers can avoid inconsistency by carefully planning the rules, monitoring student behavior (vigilance) and enforcing rules (Evertson, Emmer, Clements, Sanford, & Worsham, 1989).

In responding to rule infractions, the teacher should follow some basic principles to preserve a positive classroom climate. Sabatino (1983) summarized these principles into 10 rules for teacher responses. Teachers should

- avoid directing peer (classroom) pressure to a misbehavior when the matter can be handled gently and quietly;
- move toward the student, creating an aura of personal contact;
- develop nonverbal cues;
- identify the misbehavior after the reprimand and direct the student toward the activity;
- direct the sanction to a specific person;
- make mutual respect the rule, not the exception, for classroom management;
- give the students opportunities to experience decision making and outcomes;
- consciously plan decision-making opportunities and build them into the curriculum so

students can accept responsibility for their own behaviors;

- observe the critical difference between classroom control and authoritarian controlling of a student or group; and
- create a climate of meaningfulness, allowing students a sense of positive regard and control over the environment.

Some additional useful references provided by Sabatino are included in Figure 7.1 and Table 7.1. Figure 7.1 includes a teacher checklist for self-evaluation of effective use of reprimands. Table 7.1 is a list of nonverbal (body) cues and their meanings.

The broken record is a technique that allows teachers to persist in their demands without being sidetracked or manipulated by a student. Simply repeating the demand, in response to the student's protests or excuses, allows the teacher to remain calm and avoid a confrontation. In almost any case, arguing or debating with the student is futile. The teacher may need to deliver the broken record message as many as three times, in combination with eye contact, gestures, touch, and the use of the student's name. However, the teacher must also be prepared to follow through with a consequence if necessary.

The activities included in this component pertain to clear communication of expectations (rules and procedures) to students and the provision of appropriate feedback with respect to those expectations. One instrument is provided for the systematic observation of teacher behavior in communicating and reinforcing expectations. Additional instruments are included that the teacher can use as self-checks for the effective use of reprimands and consistent body language. The teacher's goal is to ensure clarity and consistency in dealing with behavior management.

Improving Classroom Management

Classroom management refers to any provisions that the teacher makes to create an appropriate environment for teaching and learning. Management strategies may be either preventive (the teacher avoids sources of disruption and maintains appropriate student behavior) or disciplinary (the teacher handles inappropriate student behaviors as they occur) (Siedentop, 1991). Ideally, teachers should limit managerial time, the total time spent in organizational, transitional, and nonacademic activities. The ultimate goal of classroom manage-

ment is to optimize the amount of time in which students are actively engaged in the content (essentially, purposeful movement). Preventive classroom management plays the most important role in this overall control process.

Effective preventive classroom management occurs when the teacher minimizes time spent in noninstructional activities and maximizes time devoted to content. Established classroom routines for organizing people, equipment, and activities can help the teacher optimize time by letting students know what is expected (Siedentop, 1991). As such, routines contribute to the ultimate goal of student self-management. Classroom routines can reduce teacher talk, because they require less explanation, and can capitalize on planned strategies for saving time. The teacher should establish classroom routines early in the year (or term); routines can include such activities as beginning the class, taking roll, distributing and collecting equipment, and transitioning (relocating between activities).

Effective classroom management does not simply happen. In fact, it requires comprehensive planning and consistent monitoring. The teacher can use a number of specific strategies to reduce management time, including

- beginning and ending class on time,
- incorporating short transitions between activities,
- reducing the number of transitions to maintain flow and momentum of the lesson,
- giving brief and precise instructions,
- using short demonstrations followed by immediate practice,
- teaching with enthusiasm, and
- using prompts (verbal cues) to keep students on task.

Planning for classroom management also requires that the teacher anticipate environmental changes that may affect teaching. The teacher should develop contingency plans for rainy days or scheduling changes and should keep several plans in reserve for instructing in the classroom or with limited space and equipment. For example, this is an excellent time to incorporate learning aids (e.g., posters, slides, paper-and-pencil activities, and learning games) for teaching concepts related to physical education.

Activities for Component 4 involve planning, implementation, and evaluation of classroom management. The student teacher uses a classroom management planning form to assist in the preactive phase of improving classroom management.

Figure 7.1

Teacher Checklist for Self-Evaluation

Teacher _____   Date _____   Grade/period _____

School _____

_____ During what type of class activities are most misbehaviors exhibited?
_____ What task—lecture, photocopied and workbook sheets, group discussion—restricts student and teacher movements, thus forcing the teacher to be highly visible when disciplining students?
_____ Is the teacher mobile in the room?
_____ Does the teacher handle nonconforming behavior privately or publicly?
_____ Does the teacher use nonverbal techniques effectively?
_____ Does the teacher usually reprimand verbally and publicly?
_____ Do students understand what inappropriate behaviors are?
_____ Does the teacher understand what inappropriate behaviors are?
_____ Does the teacher redirect the student to a more appropriate activity after reprimanding him or her?
_____ Are assignments clear? Do students understand the task?
_____ Does the teacher identify specific students when they misbehave?
_____ When the teacher reprimands, is it clear which students are misbehaving, or does the teacher criticize or penalize the entire class?
_____ Can the teacher punish less and praise more?
_____ Does the teacher realize different students have different values?
_____ Do the students believe the teacher is concerned about their personal and social concerns?
_____ Does the teacher limit the students' thinking?
       Example: "Were you happy when you did well on your paper?"
              Better: "How did you feel when you were so successful?"
_____ Does the teacher listen when the students talk?
_____ Does the teacher establish eye contact with the students?

Adapted from Sabatino, Sabatino, and Mann (1983) by permission.

Table 7.1 Body Cues and Their Meanings

Cue	Meaning
Fold arms across chest	Impatience
Sigh heavily	Tired
Place hands on hips	Get to work
Close and open thumb and forefinger rapidly	"I know you have gum."
Motion to wastebasket	"Spit it out."
Point to wristwatch	"Time to go."
Drop head and raise eyebrow	"I am watching you and I'm not happy."
Point pencil	"Get to work."
Shake head slowly	"I wouldn't do that."
Lift eyebrow	"Are you doing what you're supposed to be doing?"
Stare at student	"That's enough."
Stop talking	"I am becoming irritated."
Give special handshake	"You are outstanding!"
Wink at student	"Come on and do what I asked," or "I see you and we'll let it go this time."
Clear throat	"I'm tired of talking over your whispering," or "You have my attention and I want you to quit your mischief."
Hug	"Thanks," or "I like you."
Tap on desk	"May I have your attention?" or "Stop it."
Drop hand at student's desk	"Pay attention."
Deliver friendly pat on back	"Good try," "Now listen," "I like you," or "Help me."
Pat shoulder	"I see you working," or "Keep trying."
Place hand on student's shoulder	"Nice job," "I'm proud of you" (depends on atmosphere of moment and pressure exerted), or "You are to behave right now."
Move student close to teacher's desk.	"Don't make a scene. You misbehaved so I must put you near me where I have more control—away from your friends."

Note. From "Prevention: Teacher's Attitude and Adaptive Behavior — Suggested Techniques" (1983) by A.C. Sabatino. In *Discipline and Behavior Management* (p.41) by D.A. Sabatino, A.C. Sabatino, & L. Mann (Eds.). Rockville, MD: Aspen Systems Corporation. Adapted by permission.

The student teacher will plan and record strategies for the reduction of management time on this form. The cooperating teacher uses the Classroom Management Observation Instrument to collect data on managerial behaviors and to provide feedback on the effectiveness of the planned strategies.

Establishing a Positive Classroom Climate

The quality of teacher and student interactions within the classroom determines the nature of the classroom's emotional climate. Interactions include teacher–student, student–teacher, and student–student verbal and nonverbal behaviors, which may be positive, negative, or neutral. A positive emotional climate, for the purposes of this model,

is one that promotes learning and supports growth. It is not necessarily a climate of lavish praise but is more appropriately neutral in its balance of positive and corrective feedback in relation to student skill attempts and student conduct. Such a climate encourages students to do their best and feel comfortable in attempting new skills. A productive climate reinforces appropriate behaviors of students by promoting mutual respect and consideration for others. Last, it demonstrates equity of opportunities and responses to behaviors of all students — male and female, athletic and nonathletic, attractive and unattractive, abled and disabled, of high and low socioeconomic classes, and from varying ethnic and racial groups.

Encouragement is one element of a positive classroom climate that can impact student motivation. Encouragement is distinguished from praise in that it is needed most when a child fails, as opposed to when a child succeeds (Dreikurs et al., 1971). Encouragement places value on the child as he or she is, and it requires the teacher to accept deficiencies and work toward developing the child's full potential. Dinkmeyer and Dreikurs (1963) outlined nine principles for the use of encouragement. The person who encourages

- places value on children as they are,
- shows a faith in children that enables them to have faith in themselves,
- has faith in children's abilities and wins children's confidence while building their self-respect,
- recognizes effort as well as a job well done,
- utilizes the group so that children can be sure of their places in it,
- integrates the group to facilitate and enhance children's development,
- recognizes and focuses on strengths and assets, and
- utilizes children's interests to energize instruction.

The use of first names is another element of the productive classroom climate that is strongly linked to motivation. By learning and using the students' first names, the teacher shows a personal interest in each child, establishes equity among boys and girls, and holds students accountable. The use of first names with a verbal reprimand or desist indicates that the teacher is acutely aware of the student's behavior in the class and can easily identify students who misbehave.

Three additional techniques can enhance classroom emotional climate: boosting, hurdle help, and situation restructuring (Weber, 1990). A teacher can use boosting by showing concerted interest in a student's work when the student first exhibits boredom or frustration. Hurdle help is special assistance that the teacher gives to help the child overcome a difficult obstacle or frustrating situation. The goal is to facilitate success before the student's frustration leads to maladaptive behavior. Situational restructuring occurs when the teacher uses a given cue (one or two sentences) that changes or initiates a new activity, for example, when the teacher changes the purpose of a task in order to avoid student boredom.

Summary of Phase 1 Theory

The preceding theoretical overview synthesizes a large amount of literature related to the teacher's general goal of gaining confidence and establishing control. In the developmental sequence of learning to teach, survival concerns will be paramount for the beginning teacher during the 1st phase of student or in-service teaching. This material provides a foundation for the teacher to develop the teaching skills required for gaining confidence and establishing control.

Specific Steps for Implementing Phase 1

The competencies and target behaviors for Phase 1 are organized into five components: using guided observation and inquiry, establishing a discipline plan, communicating expectations/reinforcing desired behaviors, improving classroom management, and establishing a positive classroom climate. The following defines specific competencies for the respective components, as well as tasks for the student teacher and observation/evaluation tools for the cooperating teacher.

COMPONENT 1: Using Guided Observation and Inquiry

<table>
<tr><td colspan="2" align="right">**COMPONENT 1**</td></tr>
<tr><td>GENERAL FOCUS</td><td>Using guided observation and inquiry</td></tr>
<tr><td>TARGET BEHAVIORS</td><td>Cueing and reinforcing done by cooperating teacher</td></tr>
<tr><td>TASKS FOR
STUDENT TEACHER</td><td>Participate in interviews; systematically observe cooperating teacher</td></tr>
<tr><td>OBSERVATION/EVALUATION
STRATEGIES</td><td>Questionnaires; systematic observation form—Communicating Expectations</td></tr>
</table>

Competencies for the Student Teacher to Attain

1. Obtain information related to policies, practices, philosophies, and contextual factors of effective discipline by interviewing the cooperating teacher.

2. Identify and record cues the cooperating teacher uses to communicate expectations to students.

3. Systematically record augmented verbal feedback statements (positive and corrective) that the cooperating teacher uses to reinforce expected behaviors.

4. Obtain additional information related to districtwide or schoolwide disciplinary policies, philosophies, practices, and contextual factors by interviewing a counselor or administrator within the school (and outside of the physical education department).

Tasks for the Student Teacher

1. Interview the cooperating teacher using the form entitled Focused Questions for Interview of the Cooperating Teacher (Figure 7.2). Add any questions that you or the cooperating teacher feel are relevant. Record all of the responses in writing and review them at your earliest opportunity.

2. Use the systematic observation form entitled Communicating Expectations (Figure 7.3) to observe the cooperating teacher's verbal behavior. Observe and record for a minimum of two class periods, using separate copies of the same form. Then, summarize the data in terms of numbers of positive and corrective feedback statements given.

3. Use the form entitled Focused Questions for Interview of School Counselor or Administrator (Figure 7.4) to record, analyze, and review the responses of a selected individual.

Note: The order of completion of these tasks is not of great consequence. Sometimes it is difficult to get an appointment with the counselor or administrator, particularly at the beginning of the year. You can delay Task 3 if necessary but should complete Tasks 1 and 2 in the 1st week. Interviewing the cooperating teacher before observing may cue you to some particular points of observation.

Observation and Evaluation Strategies for the Student Teacher

Teacher verbal behavior is the focus of the systematic observation instrument entitled Communicating Expectations (Figure 7.3). Observe the cooperating teacher to determine what expectations he or she establishes for the conduct or social behavior of the students. List these expectations on the lines provided at the top of the page. Usually, the cooperating teacher will state these expectations at the beginning of the class but may add more as specific needs arise. The following are expectations for conduct that the cooperating teacher might state verbally:

"Please stop when the signal is given."

"Be careful to avoid collisions."

"Keep your own space on the mat."

"Do not begin rolling until the person in front of you has finished."

"Replace your equipment when I blow the whistle."

"Listen while the teacher is talking."

These are input (cueing) statements, given prior to student behavior for the purpose of establishing parameters, rules, and procedures. For the purpose of this instrument, they do not deal directly with instructions for skill performance (technique, strategy, or mechanical principles).

Once the cooperating teacher has communicated expectations, record teacher feedback statements related to the established expectations. The goal is to see how the teacher responds to the students by reinforcing desired expectations. For example, what is the frequency (total or rate per minute) of the verbal feedback statements? What proportions of the statements are general versus specific, or positive versus corrective?

In coding these statements, include only verbal (spoken) feedback and disregard nonverbal feedback (gestures). At a later date or in another observation, you may wish to include nonverbal feedback behaviors. In coding observations, use an event recording format, placing a checkmark or tally in the appropriate box each time the teacher verbally reinforces an established expectation for student conduct (e.g., "Good, thank you for listening"). Focus on student conduct feedback, not feedback given for skill attempts.

The coding of data requires two levels of decision making. First decide whether the feedback is positive or corrective. Positive feedback indicates approval of the student's conduct or social behavior. Examples of positive feedback are as follows.

"That's it."

"John is listening."

"Thanks for picking up your equipment."

"Good, you stopped quickly on the signal."

Corrective feedback indicates disapproval of the observed student conduct.

"Susan, you are not listening."

"Class, we cannot begin until everyone is ready to follow directions."

"No!"

"Stop that."

The next level of decision making requires you to determine if the feedback statement is general or specific. General feedback statements, sometimes called "global goods," simply indicate approval (''Great,'' ''Good,'' ''Way to go!'' or ''That's it'') or disapproval (''Nope,'' ''That's not it,'' ''Stop,'' or ''Wrong'') but do not indicate a specific aspect of behavior that is good or bad. Specific feedback statements tell what aspect of the behavior is good or bad, approved or disapproved (''Thanks for listening,'' ''Good job of getting ready quickly,'' ''Stop pushing, Jeff'').

At the end of the observation, tally the number of statements recorded in each of the four quadrants of the grid. Then, tally the checks in the top two boxes and record that number in the space beside *Number general*. Next, tally the bottom two boxes and record that number in the space marked *Number specific*. Repeat this process by totaling the checks in the left two boxes to determine the number of positive statements. By totaling the two right boxes, determine the number of corrective statements.

Follow up the observations with this instrument by having a planned discussion with the cooperating teacher. Try to learn more about how expectations are communicated and the teacher's intentions for reinforcing desired behaviors. Use this information later to assist you in your own teaching.

The remaining two instruments, Focused Questions for Interview of Cooperating Teacher (Figure 7.2) and Focused Questions for Interview of School Counselor or Administrator (Figure 7.4) are self-explanatory. Schedule a convenient time for the interviewee, allow ample time to address the questions, and discuss any pertinent concerns that may arise. The interviews will not be optimally effective if they are rushed or conducted impromptu. It is best to provide the individuals with a copy of the questions in advance, giving them time to organize their thoughts and to add any relevant items that they feel should be included.

Figure 7.2

Focused Questions for Interview of the Cooperating Teacher

Sample Data From Secondary Level

Interviewee _____ *Michael Tomlin* _____

Interviewer _____ *Kate Slusher* _____   Date of interview _____ *March 14, 1992* _____

1. What is your philosophy of disciplining students? In simple terms, what works best?

    This is a transition period in their lives. They are not children anymore, yet they are not quite adults. There is a wide range of maturity within all classes. For every one of their actions, they need to realize there are consequences.

2. What are some of the behavior problems that most frequently occur? How can they be prevented?

    1. Not dressing out—stress the impact this has on their total grade.
    2. Not participating—stress personal best! Explain in personal fitness sections why you do what you do.
    3. Trying to get away with something—if you catch students once or twice early, they will stop. Seek parental contact and counseling if necessary for all three.

3. What are some possible negative consequences for unacceptable behaviors? Give specific examples.

    The expected behavior is explained and described in the student code of conduct. If they deviate from the code, I give them a warning. If the misbehavior continues, I contact the parents; if misbehavior still continues, I contact the guidance counselor.

4. What kinds of positive consequences (rewards) do you use to encourage appropriate behavior?

    Most rewards are reflected in grades. Also, verbal praise is considered a reward. I improve their self-esteem by helping them realize self-improvement (self-awareness).

5. Is there a districtwide, schoolwide, or departmental disciplinary policy in place?

    Yes, districtwide. It serves as the county's chain of command. Anything done in the classroom must follow guidelines set by the district.

6. Specifically, how should I handle the following problems if they occur?

    Failure to dress out (if required).   *Find out why. Give or loan uniforms. Go to parents if necessary.*
    Failure to participate.   *Ask why? Be patient—try to encourage. Talk to parents. Then send failure notice.*
    Use of inappropriate language.   *Stress controlling emotions.*
    Insubordination/rudeness/talking back.   *Use code of conduct. Separate them from class. Send referral to office.*
    Fighting.   *Send immediately to the office. Implement mandatory suspension. Warn other teachers.*
    Carrying weapons.   *Automatic expulsion. Try to get the weapon if it is safe. If not, get the student's name and report to the office.*
    Others.   *Not applicable*

7. What other guidelines can you offer to help me become a more effective disciplinarian?

    Students need to learn to respect their peers. They need to know you are available for counseling. Give all students equal praise. Be honest with students. Help them get the answers to their questions.

Figure 7.3

Communicating Expectations
Systematic Observation of Teacher Verbal Behavior
Sample Data From Elementary Level

Teacher _____ *Miss Barrett* _____ Date ____ *January 3, 1992* ____ (Grade)/period ___ *1* ___

Class size _____ *31* _____

Expectations communicated

1. *Listen when the teacher is talking.*
2. *Start and stop on the signal.*
3. *Be careful to avoid collisions.*
4. *Put your equipment back when you are finished.*

ETC.

Feedback

Positive general	Corrective general
++++ ++++ ++++ ////	///
Positive specific	Corrective specific
////	++++ ////

Number positive ____ *23* ____   Number general ____ *22* ____

Number corrective ____ *12* ____   Number specific ____ *13* ____

Figure 7.4

Focused Questions for Interview
of School Counselor or Administrator
Sample Data From Elementary Level

Interviewee ___*Susan McCoy—Guidance Counselor*___

Interviewer _____*Christopher Collins*_____   Date of interview ___*September 8, 1991*___

1.   How does the nature of the community impact the learning environment within this school?

The neighborhood around the school is multicultural. The school has a population of 40 percent white, 40 percent black, and 20 percent other.

Only four buses come to the school. Most children walk or are driven.

This school does a lot of reaching out to the community.

2.   What is the range of socioeconomic groups represented within the school's population?

Over 40 percent of the students are on free lunch, which means they are low income. This is primarily a low-income school.

3.   What kinds of individual needs can I anticipate in working with a variety of students here?

There are a lot of emotionally needy children because of the large number of single-parent homes.

The children look for approval from the teacher, also nurturing guidance.

Some students will misbehave just to get attention.

Look for the good aspects of children's behavior and praise them.

4.   How does the size of the student population affect the smooth administration of school programs?

We have no total school function except when all students participate in field day.

The school population is 880 students.

School population is growing, but the faculty is not.

5.   To what extent are parents involved in dealing with disciplinary and other school policies?

The parent advisory board meets with Dr. Doss (the principal) on a quarterly basis.

Dr. Doss has an open-door policy.

Parents sign an assertive discipline form so that they can participate with the discipline program. The form gives an explanation of what role they play.

6.   What other kinds of specific awarenesses would help me to be a more effective disciplinarian?

More effort on my part as a student teacher. It takes a lot of practice.

Practice specific praise.

COMPONENT 2: Establishing a Discipline Plan

COMPONENT 2	
GENERAL FOCUS	Establishing a discipline plan
TARGET BEHAVIORS	Plan rules, consequences, and rewards
TASKS FOR STUDENT TEACHER	Complete a written discipline plan
OBSERVATION/EVALUATION STRATEGIES	Discipline Plan form

Competencies for the Student Teacher to Attain

1. Identify desirable student behaviors related to general conduct.
2. Identify undesirable student behaviors related to general conduct.
3. Identify rules, positively stated, that are most essential to classroom management and control in your class.
4. Identify rewards (both individual and group) that you can use to positively reinforce good behavior.
5. Identify consequences or penalties that you will impose when students break the rules. List four or five consequences, arranging them hierarchically.
6. Make students aware of rules, rewards, and consequences.

Tasks for the Student Teacher

1. Prior to developing your own plan, check to see whether a schoolwide or departmental disciplinary policy is in place. If so, read it carefully to be sure that any policies that you develop will not be in conflict.
2. Develop a list of desirable student behaviors and record them on the form provided (Figure 7.5).
3. Develop a list of undesirable student behaviors and record them on the same form.
4. Develop a short list of rules (four or five), positively stated, that are most essential to classroom management and control and record these on the Discipline Plan (Figure 7.6).
5. List rewards that you can use to positively reinforce individual students who demonstrate appropriate behavior and record these on the Discipline Plan (Figure 7.6).
6. List consequences (ordered hierarchically from least severe or first occurrence to most severe) that you can impose to penalize individuals who break rules and record these on the Discipline Plan (Figure 7.6).
7. Identify group rewards that you can use to reinforce appropriate behavior of entire classes or groups of students within a class and record these on the form entitled Additional Rewards for Appropriate Behavior (Figure 7.7).
8. Make a poster and place it conspicuously as a visual reminder to students of class rules, rewards, and consequences. (Note: It is not necessary to post the forms entitled Desirable and Undesirable Behaviors, Figure 7.5, and Additional Rewards for Appropriate Behavior, Figure 7.7. These simply aid teacher planning.)

9.   Teach rules, rewards, and consequences to the class and check for student under-
     standing. Remind the students of the rules consistently, paying particular attention
     to appropriate student behaviors.

Observation and Evaluation Strategies for the Cooperating Teacher

The student teacher uses three forms to develop the written discipline plan. These are Defining Desirable and Undesirable Student Behaviors (Figure 7.5), Discipline Plan (Figure 7.6),
and Additional Rewards for Appropriate Behavior (Figure 7.7).

You will use these forms to evaluate the student teacher. Discuss the forms with the student teacher, and review written materials and provide input before the student teacher
implements the plan. The student teacher can develop an alternative written disciplinary
plan to incorporate other models or philosophies. Monitor the student teacher's communication of the plan to students and the ongoing consistency of its implementation.

Figure 7.5

Defining Desirable and Undesirable Behaviors
Sample Data From Secondary Level

Desirable student behaviors (list student behaviors that you seek to develop)

Following instructions

Dressing for activity on a regular basis

Participation

Willingness to learn

Good attitude

Positive interaction with other students

Promptness

Respect for authority

Consideration for equipment and facilities

Staying in gym area until bell rings

Undesirable student behaviors (list student behaviors that you seek to eliminate)

Insubordination

Fighting

Using inappropriate language

Tardiness

Frequent failure to dress for participation

Inattentiveness

Destroying school property

Overt disrespect

Bringing food or gum into the gym

Leaving gym early

Theft

Figure 7.6

Discipline Plan
Sample Data From Elementary Level

Classroom rules

1. *Be polite and considerate to others*
2. *Take good care of equipment*
3. *Be quiet when entering and exiting class, stay in personal space*
4. *Listen when the teacher is talking*
5. *Freeze on the signal*

Rewards

1. *Verbal praise*
2. *Nonverbal praise*
3. *Stickers*
4. *Certificates*
5. *Special activities*

Consequences

1. *Verbal warning*
2. *Short time-out*
3. *Longer time-out*
4. *Phone call or letter sent home*
5. *Administrative assistance*

Figure 7.7

Additional Rewards for Appropriate Behavior
Sample Data From Secondary Level

Individual rewards

Verbal praise

Lead exercises

Squad leader

Bonus points

Good grades

Names posted in gym

Group rewards

Game day

Select an activity for 1 day

Attend a sporting event

Field trips

Hold an Olympics

Pizza party

Extra time to shower and change

A game structured around the lesson

Music in the locker room or gymnasium

COMPONENT 3: Communicating Expectations and Reinforcing Desired Behaviors

	COMPONENT 3
GENERAL FOCUS	Communicating expectations and reinforcing desired behaviors
TARGET BEHAVIORS	Cue and reinforce
TASKS FOR STUDENT TEACHER	Analyze verbal behavior from observation made by cooperating teacher
OBSERVATION/EVALUATION STRATEGIES	Systematic observation form—Communicating Expectations

Competencies for the Student Teacher to Attain

1. Provide clear cues for student behaviors through verbal communication of desired behaviors.

2. Provide verbal reinforcement of desired student behaviors through specific teacher verbal feedback.

3. Analyze data that the cooperating teacher recorded on the form entitled Communicating Expectations (Figure 7.8). Use this information to improve clarity of communications and frequency and specificity of feedback statements.

Tasks for the Student Teacher

1. Plan and teach a lesson to be observed by the cooperating teacher, who will use the systematic observation instrument entitled Communicating Expectations (Figure 7.8).

2. Analyze and interpret data obtained from systematic observation of cueing and feedback behavior. Determine to what extent you have achieved clear communication and reinforcement of desired behavior, and establish some goals for follow-up. Remember, the goal is to provide high rates of positive and specific feedback. It is not possible to prescribe ratios; this will be determined by the skill and developmental levels of the learners.

3. Plan and implement a follow-up lesson to be observed by the cooperating teacher, who will use the form entitled Communicating Expectations (Figure 7.8).

4. Analyze and interpret data obtained from the second observation, and discuss with the cooperating teacher your progress toward achieving your goals.

Observation and Evaluation Strategies for the Cooperating Teacher

The use of the instrument Communicating Expectations (Figure 7.8) is exactly the same as described for Component 1, except that the roles are reversed. Having gained some understanding of the use of the instrument, the student teacher now has an opportunity to attain data on his or her own performance in communicating expectations. During Component

3, you will observe the student teacher with the instrument and will code the data. The data will be used for self-analysis by the student teacher and as a basis for discussion between you and the student teacher. The student teacher can then reteach the lesson, using the results of the observation to adjust teaching.

An alternative approach to your observation is the use of audiotaped self-recordings. By placing a small cassette recorder in the pocket, the student teacher can record and later code and analyze teacher verbal behavior.

Figure 7.8

Communicating Expectations
Systematic Observation of Teacher Verbal Behavior
Sample Data From Secondary Level

Teacher _____*Ms. McKensey*_____ Date _*September 12, 1991*_ Grade/period _2_

Class size _____*23*_____

Expectations communicated

1. *Work full time 30 seconds.*
2. *Rotate promptly.*
3. *Stop on the whistle.*
4. *Run on the outside of the cones.*

ETC.

Feedback

Positive general ++++ ////	Corrective general ++++ ++++ ++++ ++++
Positive specific ++++ /	Corrective specific //

Number positive _____*15*_____   Number general _____*29*_____

Number corrective _____*22*_____   Number specific _____*8*_____

COMPONENT 4: Improving Classroom Management

	COMPONENT 4
GENERAL FOCUS	Improving classroom management
TARGET BEHAVIORS	Begin and end class on time; use short transitions, brief instructions, and verbal prompts
TASKS FOR STUDENT TEACHER	Develop a written plan for reducing management time
OBSERVATION/EVALUATION STRATEGIES	Plan for Improving Classroom Management; Classroom Management Observation Instrument

Competencies for the Student Teacher to Attain

1. Plan and implement strategies for reduced management time and increased student time on task.
2. Provide brief and precise instructions to get students moving quickly and to reduce management time.
3. Plan and implement lessons to minimize time spent transitioning between and within activities.
4. Incorporate verbal prompts to maintain student on-task behavior.
5. Begin and end class promptly.
6. Use a time-saving method for taking roll.
7. Teach a signal for attention.
8. Use data obtained through systematic observation of classroom management to adjust plans for reduced management time.

Tasks for the Student Teacher

1. Utilize the form Plan for Improving Classroom Management (Figure 7.9) to identify strategies for reducing management time. Pay specific attention to strategies for beginning and ending class promptly, giving brief and precise instructions, using a time-saving method for taking roll, teaching a signal for attention, and using enthusiasm, hustles, and prompts.
2. Implement the strategies in a class to be observed by the cooperating teacher. The cooperating teacher will use the Classroom Management Observation Instrument (Figure 7.10) to collect data on managerial efficiency, or may use the Management Strategies Checklist (Figure 7.11) as an alternative.
3. Analyze data obtained with the Classroom Management Observation Instrument or the Management Strategies Checklist and use this information to adjust your plan for reduced management time.
4. Plan and implement a follow-up lesson to be observed by the cooperating teacher with the same instrument.
5. Use the obtained data for follow-up comparisons, evaluating your own progress in reducing management time.

Observation and Evaluation Strategies for the Cooperating Teacher

The Plan for Improving Classroom Management (Figure 7.9) will provide a product for discussion and analysis. You can provide input and advice from the standpoint of personal experiences, helping the student teacher to shape and develop a plan. Later, the systematic observation data will provide a measure of the success of that plan.

The Classroom Management Observation Instrument (Figure 7.10) allows you to use duration recording techniques to measure the length of managerial episodes and to obtain a total class time spent in management overall. You will need the tally sheet and a stopwatch.

Coding of managerial behavior takes place throughout an entire class period, so you must be present and ready to begin at the start of the class. Failure to begin coding promptly can lead to misrepresentative data, because managerial episodes are generally frequent at the start of class. For each managerial episode you observe, record the nature of the episode (e.g., taking roll, organizing groups, distributing equipment, transitioning to an activity, transitioning between or within activities, or disciplining) in the space provided. Time the managerial episode with the stopwatch from the initiation of management (teacher verbal managerial behavior) to the initiation of another managerial behavior or an instructional (nonmanagerial) activity.

Time the length of the managerial episode continuously from the first teacher managerial behavior to the end of the segment, marked when all of the students have complied with directions or have begun a new, nonmanagerial activity. Siedentop and Rife (1989) defined three categories of managerial behaviors that can be observed. Typically, the initial managerial episode occurs when the teacher calls the students to squads or other organization formation and it ends with the start of the first content-related instructions. Interim managerial episodes occur when the teacher stops or interrupts an activity and then resumes or initiates a new activity. Terminal managerial episodes occur near the end of the class and begin when the teacher cues students to assemble for discussion or leave the gymnasium or playing area. Activities related to closure (reviewing skills, discussing progress, providing group feedback, and explaining activities for the next class) are considered instructional input and should not be included within managerial episodes.

Following are examples of new, nonmanagerial activities (Siedentop & Rife, 1989):

- The teacher explains a game.
- The teacher explains and describes a skill.
- The teacher gives group or individual feedback for student skill attempts.
- The students practice a skill.
- The students play a game.

Managerial behaviors are "any teacher behavior that includes preparation for an activity or a signal to change from one activity to another" (Siedentop & Rife, 1989, p. 163). They are distinguished from teacher reactions or feedback statements in that they precede student behavior.

In analyzing and interpreting the data, tabulate the raw data for each episode, providing a total of management time observed for the entire class. You can use the instrument to provide baseline data for managerial efficiency, to provide cues for the improvement of managerial efficiency, and to test the effects of specific improvement strategies. You will want to review and analyze the data with the student teacher. Use the data from the first observation to help the student teacher replan and establish goals for reduced management time. The general goal is for the student teacher to minimize managerial time within reasonable limits and thus maximize time for student learning.

An alternative form, the Management Strategies Checklist (Figure 7.11), may be substituted for this component. It entails a simple check-off of observed pre-class and class management indicators.

Figure 7.9

Plan for Improving Classroom Management
Sample Data From Secondary Level

During the next week I plan to emphasize the following preventive classroom management strategies to improve my managerial effectiveness.

1. Begin and end class promptly (describe facilitating factors)

   The class will begin 5 minutes after the tardy bell. Those not present in roll call order at this time will be marked as tardy.

2. Keep verbal instructions brief and precise

   Incorporate instructions on written lesson plan. Try to develop these in order to minimize wordiness.

   Identify only critical features of the skill, and then get the students moving quickly. Make sure everyone is listening before I begin to talk.

3. Use a time-saving method for taking roll

   Assign students to roll call squads in alphabetical order, six squads with six students in each squad.

4. Teach a signal for attention

   Remind the students that the whistle will be the signal to stop and listen. Provide positive reinforcement when they do this quickly.

5. Use enthusiasm, hustles, and prompts

   Verbally prompt the students to move quickly from the gym to the field.

   Provide positive feedback for good effort.

   Establish a businesslike and task-oriented pace.

Figure 7.10

Classroom Management Observation Instrument
Sample Data From Secondary Level

Teacher _____ *Kris Seigel* _____   Date *February 12, 1992* _____   Grade/period   *6* _____

Class size _____ *18* _____

Managerial episodes	Duration
1. Organizing students into squads	*1:31*
2. Taking roll	*3:21*
3. Distributing equipment	*:54*
4. Assigning students to stations	*1:16*
5. Transitioning to activity	*:17*
6. Transitioning within activity	*:21*
7. Rotating students to next station	*:11*
8. Rotating students again	*:15*
9. Instructing students to pick up equipment	*:28*
10. Assembling class for closure	*:32*
Total management	*9:06*

Total class time = <u>35</u> minutes   Management time = <u>25.9</u> percent

Note: Intervening episodes related to instruction are eliminated from this observation.

Figure 7.11

Management Strategies Checklist

Teacher _____   Date _____   Grade/period _____

School _____   Activity _____

Ø = Observed   O = Not observed   NA = Not applicable

Pre-class

_____ Exhibits proper punctuality and attendance
_____ Displays proper dress and appearance
_____ Writes lesson plans
_____ Prepares unit plan

Class management

_____ Starts activity quickly (less than 2 minutes)
_____ Ensures equipment and environment are safe
_____ Ensures equipment is easily accessible
_____ Establishes and reinforces stop and go signals
_____ Clearly communicates and reinforces behavior rules and expectations
_____ Quickly and consistently enforces consequences for inappropriate behavior
_____ Gives directions clearly and briefly
_____ Tells or demonstrates to students what to do before they get equipment
_____ Effectively uses demonstrations
_____ Observes class from the perimeter
_____ Moves around class and keeps students on task
_____ Ensures transitions are planned and efficient
_____ Speaks to students only when they are quiet and listening
_____ Conducts a lesson closure (less than 2 minutes)

Comments:

_____

_____

_____

Adapted from Ratliffe (1990) by permission.

COMPONENT 5: Establishing a Positive Classroom Climate

COMPONENT 5	
GENERAL FOCUS	Establishing a positive classroom climate
TARGET BEHAVIORS	Positive verbal behavior related to student behavior and skill attempts; use first names
TASKS FOR STUDENT TEACHER	Make audiotaped self-analysis of verbal behavior
OBSERVATION/EVALUATION STRATEGIES	Classroom climate observation form

Competencies for the Student Teacher to Attain

1. Demonstrate positive teacher behavior related to student social behavior (conduct).
2. Demonstrate positive teacher behavior related to student skill attempts.
3. Learn and use students' first names.
4. Use audiotaped self-recordings in the analysis of teacher verbal behavior.
5. Interpret data summarized from the form entitled Observation of Classroom Climate (Figure 7.12) and adjust teaching as indicated.

Tasks for the Student Teacher

1. Plan and teach a lesson to be observed by the cooperating teacher using the form entitled Observation of Classroom Climate (Figure 7.12).
2. Analyze and interpret data obtained from systematic observation of classroom climate. Determine to what extent you have achieved a positive classroom climate, and establish some goals for follow-up.
3. Plan and implement a follow-up lesson that you will record by placing a small microcassette recorder in your pocket before you teach. Or, the cooperating teacher may do live coding.
4. Use the form entitled Observation of Classroom Climate (Figure 7.12) to analyze and interpret data obtained from the self-recording or second observation; discuss with the cooperating teacher your progress toward achieving your goals.

Observation and Evaluation Strategies for the Cooperating Teacher

Use the form entitled Observation of Classroom Climate (Figure 7.12) to record observable teacher behaviors that are indicators of a positive or negative classroom climate.

Record indicators of a positive classroom climate on the left side of the instrument as they occur. Code with a tally and write examples of the teacher's actual words. Positive indicators include the following.

Use of first names—write the name within the box

Specific individual encouragement—verbal behaviors designed to motivate the student to try hard or persist at a task (given prior to the desired student behavior)

Specific individual praise—verbal behaviors designed to positively reinforce the student's efforts in skill performance or conduct (given after the desired response)

Use of amenities—verbal courtesies such as ''please'' and ''thanks''

Indicators of a negative classroom climate are recorded with tallies and words on the right side of the instrument as they occur. They include the following.

Use of sarcasm—verbal behaviors that taunt or ridicule, such as mockery or derisive humor

Specific individual criticism—verbal behaviors that berate an individual student

Negative feedback—verbal reactions to a student's incorrect skill performance or inappropriate conduct that add an element of insult or personal put-down

Figure 7.12

Observation of Classroom Climate
Sample Data From Elementary Level

Teacher _____ *Kay Pillar* _____   Date ___ *October 10, 1991* ___   (Grade)/period ___ *3* ___

Class size ___ *16* ___

Within the spaces provided, list and/or record observed indicators of positive and negative classroom climate.

Indicators of a positive climate	Indicators of a negative climate
Use of first names (place a check and write the name) *Kevin* *Jessica* *Terry* ++++ ++++ / *Danielle* *Holly*	Use of sarcasm (record examples)
Specific individual encouragement and corrective feedback—delivered in a way that respects the student's feelings (record examples) ++++ ++++ // *"Keep it up."* *"Up real high on toes."* *"Go, go faster."*	Use of ridicule or criticism of the student as an individual (record examples)
Specific individual praise (record examples) *"That's right."* /// *"Good job, Tamica."* *"That was great."* ++++ / *"That was a good answer."* ++++ ++++ *"Good job of galloping."*	Negative feedback—delivered in a way that disregards the student's feelings (record examples)
Additional comments/observations of positive climate (e.g., use of amenities—please/thanks) ++++ *Children smiling and laughing* *Teacher attentive and energetic*	Additional comments/observations of negative climate

Praise is given as feedback in response to a good effort. Encouragement is given in advance of an effort, to prompt the learner to try.

Criticism and ridicule are directed at the learner as a person. Negative feedback is directed at the learner's behavior (skill attempts or conduct) and is delivered in a way that disregards the student's feelings (e.g., "lousy shot"). Negative feedback is distinguished from corrective skill feedback (error correction) (e.g., "Your shot needs more arc").

Summary and Implications

The activities in Phase 1 focus on helping the student teacher gain confidence and establish control. This proactive approach is designed to help the teacher prevent problems through reflective planning. The student teacher accomplishes this by first learning as much as possible about the school environment and by then observing selected behavior patterns of the cooperating teacher. Attention then shifts to the student teacher's acquisition of skills related to communication, management, and classroom climate.

Although many other teaching skills may receive attention during the early weeks of the internship, the supervisor's major goal is to ease transition shock and to facilitate positive outcomes early on. The student teacher will gradually assume more responsibility for planning and teaching lessons while completing the 5 components of Phase 1. At the completion of this phase, he or she will be prepared for increased planning responsibility and attention to the mechanics of instruction.

Although the model was initially developed for student teachers, beginning teachers might benefit equally from this developmental approach. Selected strategies within Phase 1 can also help in-service teachers increase their knowledge and awareness of classroom management skills.

Chapter 8

Phase 2: Planning for Maximum Learning

Phase 2 is presented here in the form of a theoretical overview, a knowledge base for Phase 2 components, and specific steps for implementing Phase 2. The theoretical overview describes the broad scope of issues related to planning for maximum learning, whereas the knowledge base synthesizes the literature related to each of its 5 components. Specific steps for implementing Phase 2 include competencies for the student teacher to attain, tasks for the student teacher, and observation/evaluation strategies for each of the 5 components.

A Theoretical Overview

Planning is probably the area of teaching skill that erodes most quickly as teachers are inducted into the real world. Most faculty in teacher preparation consistently emphasize the need for comprehensive and written plans, both long-term and short-term, based on clear goals and objectives. Curriculum, unit, and lesson plans; goals and objectives;

instructional materials; and evaluation plans are subjected to varying levels of scrutiny by faculty as undergraduate majors pursue their methods training. However, this theoretical emphasis on planning fails to transfer to practice as beginning teachers face the struggle for daily survival. The end result is that public school physical education programs often lack direction and purpose, and teachers are unable to articulate their goals or evaluate program outcomes in any meaningful way.

A number of factors contribute to this failure of theory to transfer to practice. Initially, teachers focus on surviving the teaching environment (i.e., attending to the mechanical and managerial aspects of teaching). The dual role of teaching and coaching places conflicting demands on many physical education teachers, making it difficult for them to find enough time to plan for success in both endeavors. Unfortunately, the rewards for successful coaching are often greater than those for teaching, and excellence in teaching is too seldom recognized. The socializing influence of peers, the lack of incentive and rewards, and the absence of accountability are other interacting factors that undermine the importance of planning.

Placek (1983) provided unique insights into influences on teacher planning through a naturalistic study of teachers in a public school setting. The author observed four physical education teachers throughout the day in their natural environment for a period of 2 weeks each. The author analyzed field notes, interview data, and written lesson plans to determine what influences were potent. Two influences that appeared to have the greatest impact were student behavior and environmental unpredictability. In considering how selected activities influenced student behavior, teachers were most concerned about which activities would keep students involved, would be enjoyable, and would produce few disciplinary problems. Placek conceptualized this syndrome as "busy, happy, and good."

Up until 1975, virtually no research had examined teacher planning. Although educators generally believed planning to be important, no definitive evidence was available to show whether in fact it makes a difference. The literature predominantly contained prescriptions for planning based on the Tyler (1950) model of specifying objectives, selecting learning activities, organizing learning activities, and specifying evaluation procedures. This conceptualization, termed an "ends-means" model, entails a scientific approach to selecting activities on the basis of predetermined goals and objectives. The model has been widely prescribed for educational planning at all levels (Yinger, 1980). Also referred to as prescriptive, this model identifies goals and objectives (ends) prior to the selection of content (means).

A contrasting conceptualization of planning is the "integrated ends-means model" (Eisner, 1967; McDonald, 1965; McDonald, Wolfson & Zaret, 1973). This approach proposes that teachers first think about content (means) that is desirable for students, and that objectives (ends) arise or become integrated from activities as they are completed. Research indicates that planning is not a straightforward, prescriptive practice. In fact, the complex nature of the processes involved, the variations in teacher abilities to use the breadth and depth of available information, and individual differences in teacher planning styles do not lend themselves to a simple description of planning processes.

Teacher Cognitions

Jackson (1968) categorized cognitive or decision-making processes used by teachers as preactive (occurring outside of the classroom) and interactive (occurring "on the feet," or while the teacher is teaching). Processes involved in preactive teaching might include development of goals and objectives; curriculum, unit, or lesson planning; grading of papers; construction of evaluation materials; development of instructional materials; and selection of learning activities. Interactive decisions are split-second processes that determine how the teacher will adjust plans on the basis of what occurs in the classrooms.

Both preactive and interactive decisions involve complex processes, and variables that affect these processes are diverse (e.g., cognitive styles, conceptual flexibility, and process ability [the quality and quantity of information teachers use in making decisions] (Morine, 1976). Research on how teachers plan and what information sources they use can contribute to knowledge of effective teaching practices. However, this area of research interest is still relatively new and unexplored.

One technique that provides a protocol for investigating preactive teacher decisions is the "talk-aloud" technique developed by researchers at Stanford University (Crist, Marx, & Peterson, 1974; Peterson, Marx, & Clark, 1978). Researchers use this method to study decisions that teachers make as they plan, and verbalizations of the processes obtained from audiotape are used to code decisions into various categories. However, the technique is subject to some limitations, because teachers may vary in terms of their talkativeness during simulated planning, or with respect to their effectiveness in preactive and interactive decision making (Morine, 1976). Effective teachers must be able to integrate information from a variety of sources in preactive planning and then revise their plans as needed during interactive phases of teaching.

Twardy and Yerg (1987) used the talk-aloud technique to study the relationships between planning and instructional behaviors of preservice teachers in physical education. The researchers audiotaped teacher verbalizations in 30-minute planning sessions and analyzed these verbalizations by content analysis. Planning sessions were followed by 30-minute teaching sessions, in which the researchers conducted live coding of teacher and student behaviors and academic learning time. Following the lesson, teachers were debriefed through the use of a questionnaire focusing on evaluation of the plan.

Results of the content analysis of teacher verbalizations during the planning phase showed an emphasis on the activity dimensions of planning. The authors found little evidence of a goal focus or diagnostic (evaluative) orientation. Analysis of in-class teaching behaviors showed that feedback, lecturing, and monitoring were prevalent, although the predominant student behavior was *not-engaged/ waiting*. The authors found several significant relationships between preactive and interactive teaching behaviors.

Research on interactive teacher planning has only recently received attention, and the studies in this area are still few in number. Zahorik (1970) conducted the first empirical study of classroom planning behavior to determine how teachers would adjust plans to the individual needs of students. The results of this study do not support the use of lesson plans in increasing student learning. Observations of teacher behavior show that teachers who plan show less sensitivity to students and less ''honest'' or ''authentic'' use of student ideas than teachers who do not. Planning appears to produce inflexible teaching, locking teachers into the patterns established by their written plans. A subsequent study (Zahorik, 1975) involved preactive decisions in planning. This study revealed that the majority of preactive planning decisions (51 percent) relate to content, whereas only 3 percent relate to activities and 28 percent are based on objectives. These relative proportions indicate a strong emphasis on the content dimensions of planning, in contrast to a prescriptive, ends-means approach.

A technique for studying interactive teacher decisions is the stimulated recall method attributed to Bloom (1953). In a sense, this technique is an application of think-aloud or talk-aloud strategies, requiring the teacher to verbalize thoughts, judgments, and decisions while viewing videotapes of his or her own teaching. The videotape provides many cues and stimuli to help the teacher relive the situation with vivid reactions. In using stimulated recall, the observer replays the tape for the teacher as soon as possible after the lesson. The observer then prompts the teacher's reactions with questions such as these:

(a) What were you doing and why? (b) What were you noticing about the students? How were the students responding? (c) Were you thinking of any alternative actions or strategies at that time? and (d) Did any students' reactions cause you to act differently than you had planned? (Shavelson, Webb, & Burstein, 1986, p. 80).

Observed Planning Practices of Physical Educators

Descriptions of how physical education teachers plan have been provided by Goc-Karp and Zakrajsek (1987); Housner and Griffey (1985); Kneer (1986);

and Placek (1983). Collectively, these studies indicate that the planning practices of physical education teachers are widely disparate from theoretical models.

Placek (1982) reported that physical education teachers tend to plan informally and on a daily rather than long-term basis. Student learning is less of a concern than keeping students busy, happy, and good. The author identified similar criteria of success in a follow-up study of the perceptions of undergraduate physical education majors (Placek, 1983).

Failure to plan is one indication of the theory/ practice gap, as assessed in the descriptive study of Kneer (1986). Descriptions of the practices of a large sample of secondary physical education teachers show that only about one-third developed written lesson plans. The most common reason reported for non-use of lesson plans was that they are not necessary.

At least one study shows evidence that the planning practices of physical education teachers vary with respect to levels of experience. Housner and Griffey (1985) considered both preactive and interactive aspects of teaching in their comparison of experienced and inexperienced teachers. Through the use of think-aloud and stimulated-recall techniques, the authors analyzed the preactive and interactive thought processes and information cues used by the teachers. Results show that experienced teachers in the study requested more information and made more decisions during planning sessions. During the interactive phase, experienced teachers focused more on student performance cues and individual student behavior, whereas inexperienced teachers attended more to student interest cues and group participation.

Goc-Karp and Zakrajsek (1987) compared planning models prescribed theoretically (taught in college) and actually practiced (used by teachers). The authors obtained data through questionnaires given to college professors and questionnaires given to and ethnographic observations of junior high school physical education teachers. The obtained data show substantial differences between theoretical and actual models. Whereas professors emphasized planning for student learning, teachers emphasized planning for management. Objectives were the first consideration for professors, yet activities were the first step in teacher planning.

Stroot and Morton (1989) examined planning strategies used by effective elementary physical education teachers. Written yearly, unit, and daily plans provided data for content analysis, and questionnaires provided additional data on the extent of the plans' use. Analysis of written plans showed distinct attention to objectives, equipment and facilities, organization, activities, and evaluation. Teachers ranked goals and objectives, organization of activity, and level of student performance as the most important factors used in planning. Season of the year, evaluation of students, and student enjoyment received the lowest rankings. The teachers varied in the extent to which they implemented their plans, with inexperienced teachers seemingly more plan dependent.

Imwold et al. (1984) assessed the effect of planning on teacher behavior with preservice physical educators using Cheffers' Adaptation of the Flanders Interaction Analysis System (CAFIAS). Comparison of teachers who planned and those who did not plan revealed significant differences in two of the behavior categories. Teachers in the planning group gave more directions, whereas teachers in the no-planning group spent more time in silence. Within the parameters of CAFIAS, the authors could not directly link the value of planning to improved teacher effectiveness. However, other differences in time utilization, content coverage, and skill focus may have been operant.

Studies of teacher planning in classroom and physical education settings have produced some interesting findings and pertinent questions. Much of teacher planning is unsystematic and haphazard and tends to focus on activity and content dimensions of the planning process. Teachers do not typically identify goals and objectives for selecting content. Planning, at least as it is practiced, may not necessarily lead to improved teaching. Thus, we must begin to question what kinds of planning processes distinguish effective and ineffective teachers and what factors are salient in preactive and interactive decisions. More importantly, we need further research and intervention to determine the impact of planning on in-class teaching behaviors and to determine what conditions can best facilitate effective planning.

Summary of Research on Teacher Planning

Despite a recent surge in interest, the research base related to teacher planning is relative sparse. The majority of studies reported in the literature focus on describing the planning practices of teachers. These studies indicate that teachers tend to plan poorly and focus primarily on activity dimensions of the lesson. For this reason, it might appear that planning has little or no impact on instruction. However, emerging evidence shows that experienced and superior teachers plan in a more com-

prehensive manner and that this planning does lead to desirable changes in observable teaching behavior.

Phase 2 is designed to reinforce planning skills that should lead to improved instruction. A series of activities reinforces a prescriptive, ends-means process, mediated by diagnosis of student needs. Within this phase, specific attention is given to performance objectives, mechanical analysis and teaching cues, adaptation to meet varying skill levels, time on task, and evaluation of lesson effectiveness.

A Knowledge Base for Phase 2 Components

This knowledge base describes the conceptual foundation for the components selected for Phase 2 and synthesizes the important elements of planning for maximum learning.

Developing Performance Objectives

Three essential questions that effective teachers must ask themselves in planning are, Where am I going? How will I get there? and How will I know when I've arrived? Comprehensive written lesson plans containing performance objectives enable teachers to answer all of those questions. Performance objectives specify the performance, conditions, and criteria of desired student learning outcomes.

Performance objectives define the desired results of instruction (products) rather than the process of instruction (Mager, 1984). It is preferable to state precise performance objectives for a number of reasons. First, performance objectives enable teachers to select or design learning activities. Second, they provide a basis for determining whether students achieve the objective. And last, they provide clear direction for students in attaining the established objectives. Thus, teachers use objectives to select or design, evaluate, and direct student learning.

As applied to physical education, performance objectives are useful for defining outcomes in three domains of learning: psychomotor (movement skills), cognitive (knowledge and awareness), and affective (values, feelings, attitudes, and emotions). In most daily lesson planning, the teacher will place primary emphasis on the attainment of psychomotor objectives. However, the teacher should develop long-term objectives (yearly curricula and unit plans) to encompass all three domains of learning. The teacher must determine these in advance of actual instruction so he or she can appropriately emphasize learning activities to achieve the desired outcomes.

Simply stated, performance objectives allow teachers to teach to the test by orienting instruction specifically toward designated objectives. In addition, teachers should test what they teach by constructing tests to measure the explicitly stated objectives. It is not appropriate, for example, to evaluate students on the development of fitness if the teacher does not provide ample opportunities for improvement. In testing cognitive products (paper-and-pencil tests), the teacher must closely parallel objectives and evaluation methods. Test items should appropriately reflect the nature of the objectives and the amount of instructional emphasis the teacher places on them.

The exercises in Component 6 provide the teacher practice in developing clear performance objectives. The student teacher will use Mager's (1984) format to define performance (what the learner should be able to do), conditions (under what conditions the performance should occur), and criterion (the level of quality or quantity of performance expected). This format is suggested as a guideline for developing clear and useful objectives. However it may not always be useful to describe both conditions and criteria. For example, the condition (in a practice situation) might be implied in this objective: "Students will demonstrate traveling in different directions." Similarly, a criterion is not essential for the cognitive objective: "Students will define the concepts of health-related and skill-related fitness." It may be desirable in some instances for the teacher to use more than one sentence to describe an objective.

In order to assess mastery of performance objectives, the teacher must define performance in terms of observable behaviors. Although it is not possible to directly observe learning, it can be inferred through certain aspects of performance. For example, a teacher cannot directly observe whether a student understands the concept of health-related fitness. However, the teacher can determine whether the student can state five components of health-related fitness or write a definition of that concept.

Teachers must describe performances, therefore, with "doing" words as opposed to "being" words (Mager, 1984). *Running, solving, discriminating,* and *writing* are examples of doing words. These behaviors can be directly observed. *Happy, understand-*

ing, and *appreciating* are being words, outcomes that cannot be directly observed. The following are doing words that the teacher might use in developing performance objectives in physical education:

- doing (do)
- stating (state)
- running (run)
- writing (write)
- smiling (smile)
- listing (list)
- balancing (balance)
- throwing (throw)
- rolling (roll)

The following are conditions that the teacher may use in developing performance objectives:

- while practicing with a partner
- in a drill situation
- in a game situation
- while standing stationary
- on a written quiz
- given a list of examples and nonexamples

The teacher may define criteria of performance in terms of quantity or quality. The following are examples that may be useful.

Quantity (speed, duration, frequency)

- 5 times
- for a period of 1 minute
- for a distance of 10 feet
- within 30 seconds

Quality (accuracy, acceptable deviation)

- without stopping
- while moving in general space
- with a straight elbow

The planning form for Component 6 provides the teacher practice in developing performance objectives within three domains. It is intended to help the teacher review the characteristics of performance objectives and develop the habit of stating objectives in behavioral terms.

Incorporating Mechanical Analysis and Teaching Cues

Another important aspect of planning for motor skill learning is analyzing the skills to be taught in terms of the mechanics of desired performance. Skill analysis allows the teacher to determine the mechanical aspects or quality of performance to be developed. It also enhances the quality of teaching by allowing the teacher to give more precise instructions, clear demonstrations, and positive and specific feedback. Teaching cues, short phrases that alert the performer to certain aspects of the performance (e.g., "flat back" or "side to the net"), are also helpful in promoting skill acquisition.

In developing a lesson plan for which the primary focus is on specific skill acquisition, the teacher should first analyze the mechanics of the skill. For example, the teacher can analyze the skill of the tennis forehand in terms of the mechanical form that constitutes an effective stroke. Beginning with the most gross aspects of the skill, or movements of large body segments, the analysis might initially focus on the stance: The side of the body is to the net, and the feet are positioned about shoulder-width apart. The teacher might then analyze the grip, the preparation, the swing, and the follow-through in terms of what the positions or pathways of the body segments should look like.

In a skill analysis, the level of mechanical precision (gross/fine) and the number of factors the teacher introduces depend on the skill and maturity levels of the learners. In early stages of skill development, learners must focus attention on the gross aspects of movement and will be able to attend to fewer details. Less skilled learners may also benefit more from feedback of a more general or motivational level. Older and more skilled performers will attend to the fine aspects of performance and will benefit from more precise verbal feedback.

When teaching a lesson for which the purpose is to encourage a variety of responses (movement education approach), as opposed to helping students perform a specific skill, the teacher can use another form of skill analysis. With this approach, the teacher first identifies the skills to be performed (e.g., throwing, striking, twisting, or jumping). Next, the teacher identifies the aspects of space, body, effort, or relationship awareness that he or she wishes to combine with this skill theme (e.g., in self/general space, with different body parts, fast/slow, or alone/with a parnter). These themes will then comprise the focus for the movement tasks that the teacher designs for young children.

Once the teacher has analyzed the skill, the next step in lesson planning is to develop performance objectives. The aspects of form or quality of movement that the teacher selects for emphasis will provide keys to the criteria of effective performance that the teacher will establish. The following is an example of a mechanical analysis and performance

objective for overhand throwing. In this example, the purpose is for students to develop proficiency in the specific movement pattern.

Skill—overhand throwing

Shoulder faces target
Nonthrowing elbow is extended for balance
Trunk rotates
Oppositional stepping occurs
Note: these are some, but not all, of the characteristics of a mature overhand throwing pattern.

Performance objective:
Students will demonstrate overhand throwing, while standing stationary, with oppositional stepping.

Note: In this example, the instructor chose to work on only one aspect of mechanical form. Another performance objective might state this: Students will demonstrate overhand throwing, while standing stationary, with a mature pattern. In this case, the mature pattern is described in the skill analysis.

In the next example, the intent is for students to develop proficiency and diversity of movement patterns in overhand throwing. Therefore, the teacher has combined the skill theme with a variety of movement qualities. These movement qualities relate to selected aspects of spatial awareness.

Skill—underhand throwing

In self-space
In general space
High and low
Near and far

Performance objectives:
Standing in self-space, students will perform overhand throwing four ways: high and low, and near and far.
While moving in general space, students will perform underhand throwing four ways: high and low, and near and far.

Developing teaching cues is the next step in this lesson-planning format. The teacher should identify some short phrases or key words that will help the student develop a visual image of the skill ("flat as a pancake") or focus on a particular aspect of that skill performance ("elbows out"). Gagne (1984) explained that these teaching cues are important to motor skill learning because they remind learners of procedural steps (e.g., "step-hop," or "throw and go"). Cues also provide convenient reminders so that learners can self-teach in independent practice. Two cues that tennis beginners often recall are "side to the net" and "racket back."

The following are examples of teaching cues that the teacher might use to illustrate aspects of the tennis serve (Briddell, 1986):

Stance

"Side to the net"

"Batter's stance"

"Bisect the box"

Toss

"Ice cream cone"

"Toss a glass of water"

Backswing

"Slicing a loaf of bread"

"Backscratch position"

Component 7 incorporates a specific planning format that helps the teacher analyze skills to be taught and identify teaching cues for reinforcing correct mechanics.

Selecting Activities at an Appropriate Level of Difficulty

A very important aspect of planning for maximum learning is providing opportunities for all students, regardless of previous experience or skill level, to experience success within the tasks. A common criticism of traditional physical education programs is that they are frequently oriented toward the skilled student. Consider, for example, the old familiar standby "bombardment," also called "dodge ball." The object is for one student to quickly eliminate the other players in the game by hitting them with a ball. Some of the obvious problems of this activity are that it intimidates unskilled students, it encourages aggressive behavior, and it provides little useful transfer of skill to other game and sport situations. (Because no other games or sports require players to dodge away from the ball, it doesn't matter that the skill doesn't

transfer!) Worse yet, the game is entirely self-defeating in terms of skill development, because the students first eliminated from the game are those unskilled students who are most in need of practice.

Games of elimination are a common threat to the success of all students in physical education. Often, a variety of other practices inhibit students' success. Insufficient practice opportunities and overemphasis on competition can rob both skilled and unskilled students of opportunities to improve skills. The selection or design of activities which, by their very nature, allow few opportunities for practice is also counterproductive. A good example is the all-too-common game of "kickball," which offers almost negligible opportunities for students to practice kicking, striking, catching, throwing, and running.

Wilson (1976) graphically illustrated this problem. She determined that during the average game of kickball, third and fourth graders had only about two attempts to catch the ball per game. Almost half of the children never had a chance to throw the ball, and the average number of throws made (pitcher excluded) was approximately one. By the nature of its organization, kickball lends itself to very low time on task. In this kind of activity, low-skilled students can easily disengage from learning and further decrease their practice opportunities by moving to the periphery of the playing field, sticking close to the end of the line, and generally blending into the scenery.

The selection of activities with single skill entry levels is probably one of the most common threats to skill development. In illustrating this problem and proposing a solution, Mosston and Ashworth (1986) used the analogy of jumping over a horizontal or slanted rope. If the objective is for students to develop skill in jumping over a rope, the teacher can select the single-standard design of a horizontal rope (the concept of exclusion) or the multiple-standard design of a slanted rope (the concept of inclusion). In the first instance, some students will be eliminated immediately because of low skill in jumping, whereas others will be quite unchallenged. Thus, this task is most appropriate for students of average jumping abilities. The second choice, the slanted rope, provides multiple skill entry levels in which the students select heights at which they can be both challenged and successful.

Component 8 is designed to increase awareness of the diverse skill levels present within a given group of students and to help teachers plan for success for all of the students. The inclusion style lends itself handily to this goal. Systematic observation of student skill attempts allows the teacher to evaluate the success levels achieved by students of low and high skill levels within a given lesson.

Maximizing Time on Task

In order to maximize student learning, teachers must provide for high rates of time on task, or time in which the students are involved in the subject matter. The teacher can accomplish this by planning lessons carefully to reduce the amount of time spent in management (or noninstructional activity). It is equally important that the teacher select tasks that are appropriate for the skill level of the students in the class and organize these activities so that students spend optimal time in actual motor activity. These provisions will help to increase academic learning time (ALT), the amount of time in which students are engaged in the content at a high success rate (Fisher, Marliave, & Filby, 1979). In physical education, this variable is referred to as academic learning time in physical education (ALT-PE) (Siedentop et al., 1982).

Three important components of ALT are allocated time, student engagement, and student success rate. The allocated time in physical education is the amount of time scheduled for a given class period (e.g., 30 minutes). Student engagement time is the amount of time in which the students are actively involved in physical education content (i.e., time when they are not changing in the locker room, moving to the teaching area, transitioning between groups, or waiting for the teacher to take roll, organize groups, and distribute equipment). Student success rate is determined by the level of difficulty of the tasks or activities. Research shows that learning is enhanced when students are engaged for high rates of time at an appropriate level of difficulty (Fisher et al., 1980). The concepts of time on task and success evolved from the Beginning Teacher Evaluation Study (BTES) described in chapter 4.

Although student learning and time are positively related, high time on task is a factor frequently absent in classrooms. Research has documented this shortcoming consistently across subject matter settings. In summarizing the findings of the BTES, Fisher et al. (1980) reported average student engagement rates in reading and math ranging from 50 to 90 percent of allocated time. These rates varied significantly among teachers and among individual students. Randall and Imwold (1989) found varied rates of academic learning time in physical education settings, with estimates ranging from 15 to 85 percent. In a study that compared the relative amounts of ALT-PE provided in elementary physical education by classroom teachers and physical education specialists, Placek and Randall (1986) found no significant differences.

Students need many opportunities to practice motor skills in order to improve; thus, teachers should structure learning activities to provide for many skill attempts. Consider the objective of developing skill in overhand throwing, then consider the traditional game of kickball. Within a 30-minute game, the average student may have two or three opportunities to throw. To what extent will that activity then lead to greater skill development in overhand throwing? Obviously, the effect is negligible at best.

Component 9 emphasizes strategies for maximizing time on task and ultimately increasing student learning. A specialized planning format focuses attention on organization for optimal time use. It guides the teacher in planning for maximum participation by each student and helps the teacher match tasks with the ability levels of the learners. Observation/evaluation strategies provide feedback to the teacher about the effectiveness of these planning measures.

Lesson Effectiveness

Determining the effectiveness of a lesson requires that an observer gather data during the interactive phase of the lesson. Analysis of the data will show whether the teacher gave students maximal opportunities to practice the skills to be developed. The data will also provide a lens for viewing the extent of success achieved by skilled and unskilled students in the class.

The observer can collect data for evaluating lesson effectiveness in a variety of ways. The target of observation might be student behavior or teacher behavior (process variables), that is, what students or teachers do. Or, the observer might choose to look at product or outcome variables — changes that take place in performance. Component 15 of this model focuses more directly on assessment of student performance. For Component 10, the focus of observation is on student process variables, specifically, the extent to which students are on-task versus off-task and motor engaged versus non–motor engaged.

On-task behavior can be defined simply as student activity that is congruous with the objectives and instructions of the teacher. This may or may not involve motor activity, depending on the instructions the teacher gives. Therefore, on-task behavior might involve sitting and listening to directions, getting equipment, waiting a turn, practicing a task, helping a partner, or playing in a game, provided that the behavior is congruous with the established directions. Off-task behavior is student behavior that is not congruous with the objectives and instructions of the teacher or that interferes with student learning.

Motor-engaged behavior involves meaningful or purposeful movement activity of students. Here, the students are both on-task and engaged in motor activity — practicing a task, performing an exercise or drill, or playing in a game. Non–motor activity encompasses aspects of the lesson that largely focus on cognitive or managerial (noninstructional) tasks.

By isolating these behaviors, the teacher can obtain concrete and valuable data regarding two important aspects of lesson effectiveness: Are the students participating in the intended tasks of the lesson, and are they to a large extent motor engaged? Teachers, both novice and experienced, often become absorbed with the instructional aspects of the lesson or with what the group does as a whole. Teachers tend to ignore what individuals within the group do and the relationship of that activity to objectives.

Consider, for example, a lesson for which the objective is for students to develop improved cardiovascular fitness. Suppose the instructor spends 5 minutes taking the role, gives 15 minutes of detailed instruction, spends 5 minutes organizing groups, devotes 10 minutes to activity (interrupted by many transitions), and spends 5 minutes on closure. Within this activity phase, many students will be off-task or inactive because the structure of the task involves too much waiting (there is not enough equipment and the task is poorly designed). Given that individuals must engage in 15 to 20 minutes of moderate-intensity exercise in order to impact cardiovascular fitness, it seems unlikely that the structure of the lesson will allow students to achieve the objective.

One objective method of obtaining data on student behavior is called a planned activity check, or placheck, method (Siedentop, 1991). At regu-

larly planned intervals (e.g., every 2 minutes, or every 5 minutes), the observer scans the class from left to right and categorizes behavior according to a dichotomous variable (on-task/off-task, motor engaged/non–motor engaged). It is easiest to count the number of students engaged in the least frequently occurring behavior (we hope this will be *off-task, non–motor engaged*). The observer records the numbers on the appropriate line of the observation instrument. The observer repeats this procedure throughout the duration of the class at specified intervals and uses a formula to calculate the percentages of behaviors observed within each category.

The teacher can also use this kind of scanning technique informally as he or she conducts the class. Keeping in mind a given desired behavior, the teacher simply scans from left to right at regular intervals to obtain a picture of what is going on. Scanning can help teachers become more aware of what individual students are doing within the class.

Component 10 is intended to integrate all the components of Phase 2, providing an analysis of how general planning strategies result in increased on-task and motor-engaged student behaviors. Although many other indicators of lesson effectiveness might be selected, student involvement is a logical starting point.

Specific Steps for Implementing Phase 2

The competencies and target behaviors for Phase 2 are organized into 5 components: developing performance objectives, incorporating mechanical analysis and teaching cues, selecting activities at an appropriate level of difficulty, maximizing time on task, and evaluating lesson effectiveness. The following material defines specific competencies, tasks for the student teacher, and observation/evaluation strategies for the cooperating teacher.

COMPONENT 6: Developing Performance Objectives

	COMPONENT 6
GENERAL FOCUS	Developing performance objectives
TARGET BEHAVIORS	Planning observable and measurable objectives for three learning domains
TASKS FOR STUDENT TEACHER	Develop and analyze performance objectives and lesson plans
OBSERVATION/EVALUATION STRATEGIES	Performance Objectives Assessment Form; stimulated recall technique

Competencies for the Student Teacher to Attain

1. Distinguish between process objectives and performance (product) objectives.
2. Identify observable behaviors to indicate desired outcomes.
3. Practice developing performance objectives that specify performance (observable task), conditions, and criteria.
4. Incorporate performance objectives in the development and implementation of lesson plans.
5. Evaluate videotaped lessons using stimulated recall technique.

Tasks for the Student Teacher

1. Use the planning form Developing Performance Objectives (Figure 8.1) to develop psychomotor, cognitive, and affective objectives.
2. Develop and implement a minimum of three written lesson plans, incorporating performance objectives.
3. Obtain a videotape of one of these lessons.
4. Observe and analyze the videotaped lesson with respect to the stated objectives.

Observation and Evaluation Strategies for the Cooperating Teacher

1. Review the planning form, Developing Performance Objectives (Figure 8.1), with the student teacher. Check to see that objectives contain observable performance, conditions, and criteria.
2. Review lesson plans to determine whether the student teacher has defined performance (as opposed to instructional) objectives.
3. Videotape a lesson and arrange a time to observe and analyze it with the student teacher using stimulated recall technique.

Figure 8.1

Developing Performance Objectives
Sample Data From Secondary Level

Psychomotor Objective

Running	In a practice situation	For a minimum of 12 minutes
Observable task	Conditions	Criteria

Statement of objective: _Students will run continuously for a minimum of 12 minutes._

Cognitive objective

Locate and count pulse	After running	For a 10-second interval
Observable task	Conditions	Criteria

Statement of objective: _After running, students will locate and count the pulse for a 10-second interval._

Affective objective

Listening	During directions	Without talking
Observable task	Conditions	Criteria

Statement of objective: _Students will demonstrate cooperation by listening quietly when the teacher gives directions._

STIMULATED RECALL

The purpose of this technique, as adopted from Morine (1976), is to gain insight about how the student teacher uses information during the lesson to adjust teaching. Although stimulated recall focuses on all decisions made during teaching, it is used here as a reminder of the importance of teaching toward objectives. Before viewing the tape with the student teacher, ask him or her to look for points in the lesson at which the student teacher was conscious of making a decision, such as, "Let's see, I think I'd better do this now," or "I guess I'll try doing this." Explain that you may also stop the tape at certain points to ask questions about the teacher decisions that were made. On all occasions when the tape is stopped, ask these questions:

1. **What were you thinking at that point?**
2. **What did you notice that made you stop and think? (If necessary, add, Were pupils doing something that made you stop and think?)**
3. **What did you decide to do?**
4. **Was there anything else you thought of doing at that point, but decided against?**
5. **What was it?**

At the end of playback, discuss the decisions the student teacher made during the lesson with respect to the objectives. Try to help the student teacher focus on the extent to which he or she was successful in achieving the stated objectives, and in making the necessary adjustments to accomplish this.

COMPONENT 7: Incorporating Mechanical Analysis and Teaching Cues

	COMPONENT 7
GENERAL FOCUS	Incorporating mechanical analysis and teaching cues
TARGET BEHAVIORS	Skill analysis; use teaching cues, and skill feedback
TASKS FOR STUDENT TEACHER	Identify mechanics and teaching cues for skills to be taught in written lesson plan
OBSERVATION/EVALUATION STRATEGIES	Specialized Lesson Plan Format A; systematic observation of teaching cues and feedback

Competencies for the Student Teacher to Attain

1. Conduct a skill analysis to determine mechanical aspects of skills you plan to teach (desired form or movement quality).
2. Identify teaching cues you can use to enhance motor skill learning.
3. Develop written lesson plans incorporating mechanical analysis and teaching cues (using Lesson Plan Format A [Figure 8.2]).
4. Provide high rates of positive and specific feedback related to student skill attempts.

Tasks for the Student Teacher

1. Use Lesson Plan Format A (Figure 8.2) to develop a lesson plan incorporating mechanical analysis and teaching cues. In order to do this, you must become a student of mechanical analysis, using whatever resources you can find to help you analyze the skill.
2. Implement the plan with one or more classes; focus on using teaching cues to give instruction and provide positive, specific feedback related to student skill attempts.

Observation and Evaluation Strategies for the Cooperating Teacher

1. Your major function here is to act as a resource person as the student teacher selects appropriate skills, conducts mechanical analysis, and identifies teaching cues. Review the written lesson plans to see that the mechanical analysis is technically correct and that the selected skills are developmentally appropriate.
2. You may wish to obtain some objective data by using the instrument entitled Teaching Cues and Skill-Related Feedback: Observation of Teacher Verbal Behavior (Figure 8.3)

You will need to review a copy of the written plan before you observe a lesson with this instrument. It is hoped that, by using the specialized lesson plan format to identify mechanics and teaching cues, the student teacher will enhance certain characteristics of effective teaching. You should observe clear instructions regarding skill performance, the use of verbal teaching cues (as planned), and greater specificity of feedback statements.

To conduct the observation, use the coding form, a clipboard, and a pencil. This systematic observation instrument uses event recording of verbal feedback statements and teaching cues as they occur. Record feedback statements with a check within the appropriate boxes. Feedback is defined as information about the response (skill attempt or performance) that students use to adjust future responses. For purposes of this observation, you will be concerned only with augmented verbal feedback (that which is provided extrinsically by the teacher, as opposed to sensory feedback, which is intrinsically available to the learner). When the teacher makes a feedback statement, first determine whether it is positive (indicates that the performance is desirable, e.g., "correct," "that's it," or "nice stretch") or corrective (indicates that an adjustment is needed, e.g., "wrong," "not quite," or "too high"). If the statement is positive, place the check on the left side of the grid; if corrective, the right side of the grid. Next determine if the feedback is general in nature (does not identify what aspect is or is not desirable, e.g., "good," "yes," or "no") or specific (identifies the aspect of desired or undesired response, e.g., "good tuck" or "wrong foot"). Record general feedback at the top of the grid under the corresponding valence (positive or corrective); record specific feedback on the bottom.

Record teaching cues at the bottom of the observation instrument on the lines provided. Having read the lesson plan, you will be attuned to the teaching cues that the student teacher has planned. Write them verbatim as they occur, and place a tally beside them for each repetition.

Figure 8.2

Lesson Plan Format A
Using Mechanical Analysis and Teaching Cues
Sample Data for Fundamental Motor Skill Lesson

Teacher _____*Dave Rosenthal*_____ Date ____*April 28, 1992*____ (Grade)/period ___*3*___

Class size _____*28*_____

Performance objectives: *Students will demonstrate overhand throwing while working with a partner, with a mature pattern (side orientation, extension of throwing arm, weight transfer, differentiated trunk rotation, and follow-through).*

Equipment needed for this lesson:

Fleece balls—1 for every student

Skill analysis

Skill to be taught	Mechanics	Teaching cues
Overhand throw	*Side orientation (nonthrowing side faces the target)*	*"Side to the target"*
	Extension of throwing arm	*"Step and throw"*
	Weight transfer as hand passes above shoulder	
	Sequential hip and shoulder rotation	
	Follow-through	*"Point to the target"*

(Cont.)

Figure 8.2   (Continued)

Procedures

Set induction (introduction):

"Today we will practice throwing forcefully. At first you will throw alone at the wall. Next, we'll see if you can throw the ball to your partner, who will be standing very far away."

Explanation/demonstration:

"I'd like everyone to stand in self-space, so that you can move in all directions without touching anyone. Let me see you pretend to throw very hard, as if you had an imaginary ball. You are trying to crash the ball against the wall."

As the children practice, encourage them to stand so that their shoulders face the imaginary target. Then discuss stepping and weight transfer (step and throw) and follow-through (point to the target).

Organizational plan (How will students and equipment be organized?):

Initially, children will work alone, throwing fleece balls at a target. Later, they will find a partner to share a ball. They will begin throwing near, with partner standing about 5 feet in front. Gradually, they will increase the distance so that they must throw forcefully with a full range of motion in the throwing pattern.

Practice opportunities

Time allocation	Activities for students	Activities for teacher
1 minute	Set induction	Orient the children to the purpose of the lesson.
1 to 2 minutes	Imaginary throwing for force— Side orientation Extending the arm Stepping Follow-through	Explain and demonstrate, emphasizing mechanical factors (cues oriented toward feeling the movement—kinesthetic awareness).
5 minutes	Find a space opposite the wall, and practice throwing very hard. Try to crash the ball against the wall.	Monitor, observe, provide feedback. Observational focus is characteristic of a mature pattern. (Variations: throwing high, throwing low)
10 minutes	Stand opposite your partner across the rope and practice throwing hard. Your partner will have to stand back to catch	Reinforce mechanics and teaching cues as children increase the distance of their throws.

Closure: *Culminating activity—with all the children standing in self-space, again review the mechanics of overhand throwing for force. Reemphasize teaching cues.*

Figure 8.3

Teaching Cues and Skill-Related Feedback
Observation of Teacher Verbal Behavior
Sample Data From Tennis Lesson

Teacher _____ *Gina Rodriquez* _____ Date ___ *October 12, 1991* ___ Grade/period ___ *4* ___

Class size _____ *17* _____

Feedback

Positive general	Corrective general
++++	*/*
Positive specific	Corrective specific
++++ ++++ /	*///*

Number positive ____ *16* ____   Number general ____ *6* ____

Number corrective ____ *4* ____   Number specific ____ *14* ____

Teaching cues

Side to the net

Racket back

COMPONENT 8: Selecting Activities at an Appropriate Level of Difficulty

	COMPONENT 8
GENERAL FOCUS	Selecting activities at an appropriate level of difficulty
TARGET BEHAVIORS	Student opportunity to respond and student success rates
TASKS FOR STUDENT TEACHER	Use of Mosston & Ashworth's inclusion style to teach a lesson with multiple skill entry levels
OBSERVATION/EVALUATION STRATEGIES	Event recording of skill attempts and success rates—high- and low-skilled students

Competencies for the Student Teacher to Attain

1. Select learning activities that will allow students of varying skill levels to experience success within a lesson.

2. Incorporate Mosston and Ashworth's (1986) inclusion style of teaching to plan and implement a lesson with multiple skill entry levels.

3. Obtain estimates of opportunities to respond (skill attempts) and success rates for high- and low-skilled students.

Tasks for the Student Teacher

1. Design and implement a lesson plan using Mosston and Ashworth's (1986) inclusion style of teaching.

    In implementing Mosston and Ashworth's inclusion style, first select a skill that coincides with your current unit objectives. Next, analyze that skill in terms of the factors that determine the degree of difficulty for that skill. Mosston and Ashworth (1986) developed a factor grid for analyzing difficulty factors within a given skill. A sample of a completed grid for a volleyball serving task is included in Figure 8.4. The grid helps you identify two kinds of factors that can influence difficulty. External factors are not an inherent part of the task structure, or are externally imposed, whereas intrinsic factors are directly related to the task. You can establish the range of choices for the factors to be manipulated (e.g., small or large targets, 5 to 10 feet).

    Once you have selected a skill, determine two or three factors that you can manipulate to provide multiple skill entry levels. For example, key factors related to the skill of shooting a ball into a basket might include distance, height of the basket, and diameter of the hoop (Mosston & Ashworth, 1986). Supporting factors can include size of the ball, weight of the ball, and angle of the shot. You can rank order the key and supporting factors in terms of their abilities to influence inclusion within the task. Then, adjust the task in several ways so that students may select their own entry levels and progress at their own rates. You may then design several levels of performance within the given task. The sample Inclusion Style Lesson Plan shown in Figure 8.5 demonstrates the use of this strategy.

2. Analyze the success of the lesson in terms of the number of skill attempts and the success rates obtained by high- and low-skilled students. You can accomplish this

by studying the data from the systematic observation (event recording) instrument used by your cooperating teacher in this component.

3. Redesign and reteach the lesson according to the feedback obtained in this assessment.

Observation and Evaluation Strategies for the Cooperating Teacher

The systematic observation instrument entitled Event Recording of Student Skill Attempts (Figure 8.6) uses the technique of event recording (tallying discrete events as they occur). In order for the instrument to be relevant, you must use it to observe discrete skills (those that have a distinct beginning and ending point) as opposed to continuous skills (those for which duration is a better measure). Some examples of discrete skills are throwing at a target, bumping a volleyball, performing a forward roll, striking a ball, and catching.

In order to get a representative assessment, observe one low-skilled and one high-skilled student. You can identify these students on the basis of your previous experience. In completing this observation, you will need the observation form Event Recording of Student Skill Attempts, a pencil, a clipboard, and a stopwatch. As soon as the student teacher begins the class (first verbal directions), start the watch and begin to observe the low-skilled student for 2 minutes. Each time the student makes a skill attempt, mark a circle on the line corresponding to Interval 1. If the skill attempt is successful (e.g., the student makes a basket or catches the ball), make a diagonal slash through the circle. Continue coding throughout the 2-minute interval.

At the end of 2 minutes, locate the high-skilled student and continue this process. Observe for 2 minutes, then return to the low-skilled student. Continue this process until the conclusion of the class (teacher verbally dismisses the class).

Figure 8.4

Factor Grid for Inclusion Style of Teaching
Sample Data for Volleyball Serve

Name of the task _____ *Volleyball serve* _____

- Rank order for the key and the supporting factors _____

- Range _____

External factors	**Range**
_____ Number of repetitions	*5 to 10*
_____ Time	

Intrinsic factors

_1_ Distance	*1 to 30 feet from net*
_2_ Height	*net at 6 to 7 feet*
_3_ Weight of implements	*foam ball, leather volleyball*
_____ Size of implements	
_4_ Size of target	*whole court or selected target*
_____ Speed	
_____ ?	
_____ ?	
_____ Posture (position of the body)	

Adapted from Mosston and Ashworth (1986) by permission.

Figure 8.5

Lesson Plan
for Inclusion Style Teaching
Sample Data From Secondary Level

Teacher _____ *Linda Miskovic* _____   Date ____ *January 5, 1992* ____   Grade/period *6 and 7*

Class size _____ *30* _____

Performance objectives: *In a practice situation, students will demonstrate the volleyball overhand serve, with weight transfer and trunk rotation.*

Equipment needed for this lesson:

2 volleyball nets/standards
6 volleyballs
3 volleyball trainers
6 high-density foam balls

Skill analysis

Skill to be taught	Mechanics	Teaching cues
Overhand throw	*Trunk rotation* *Weight transfer* *Oppositional stepping*	"Rotate" "Shift" "Opposite hand and foot"
Overhand serve	*Trunk rotation* *Weight transfer* *Oppositional stepping*	"Toss - step - contact"

(Cont.)

Figure 8.5 (Continued)

Procedures

Set induction (introduction):

Overhand serving uses the same pattern as overhand throwing. Three important parts of the pattern are oppositional stepping, trunk rotation, and stepping on the opposite foot.

Explanation/demonstration:

Overhand throwing pattern—Oppositional stepping
                                    Trunk rotation
                                    Weight transfer
Overhand serve—"Toss—step—contact"

Organizational plan (how will students and equipment be organized?):

Students will select their own entry levels in this inclusion-style lesson. They may select a regulation volleyball, high-density form ball, or volleyball trainer. They may also choose one of two courts: one with a 6'6" net and one with 7' net. They may stand as close to or as far away from the net as they wish. They may choose a large or small target (whole court or self-selected segment).

Practice opportunities

Time allocation	Activities for students	Activities for teacher
5 minutes	*Observe demonstration.*	*Demonstrate the mechanics of the overhand throwing pattern, as identified in mechanical analysis.*
10 minutes	*Practice overhand pattern—begin by throwing the ball over the net.* *May select starting location.* *Design their own targets—whole opposite court or segment of it.*	*Observe movement pattern—look for weight transfer and trunk rotation.*
5 minutes	*Observe.*	*Demonstrate overhand serve.*
10 minutes	*Perform the overhand pattern, adding the striking aspect of the serve.*	*Observe performance.* *For students who are achieving success, emphasize control by striking the exact middle.*
5 minutes	*Practice the serve while increasing the distance from the net—goal is to ultimately reach the baseline.*	*Monitor and provide feedback.*

Closure: *Review elements of overhand throwing pattern and overhand serve. Provide group feedback related to common errors.*

Figure 8.6

Event Recording of Student Skill Attempts

Teacher _____ *Ellen McGuire* _____   Date ___ *April 17, 1992* ___   Grade/period   5

Class size _____ 27 _____

Select one low-skilled and one high-skilled student in the class. Alternately observe each student for intervals of 2 minutes. In the space corresponding to each interval, place a circle (O) each time the student attempts a psychomotor skill. Place a — through the circle if the attempt is successful.

Low-skilled student	High-skilled student
Interval	Interval
1. Ø O	1. Ø O O Ø
2. O	2. O
3.	3. O O O
4. Ø O O	4. O Ø Ø Ø O
5. O	5. O
6.	6. O
7. O Ø O	7. O
8. Ø O O O	8. Ø Ø Ø
9. O Ø Ø Ø O	9. Ø Ø Ø Ø Ø O
10. O O	10. Ø O

Total skill attempts __21__

Total successful skill attempts __7__

Percent success _28.6_

Total skill attempts __27__

Total successful skill attempts __14__

Percent success _51.8_

COMPONENT 9: Maximizing Time on Task

	COMPONENT 9
GENERAL FOCUS	Maximizing time on task
TARGET BEHAVIORS	Student engaged time in motor, cognitive, and management activities
TASKS FOR STUDENT TEACHER	Utilize Lesson Plan Format B to plan for maximum time on task and success
OBSERVATION/EVALUATION STRATEGIES	Duration recording of motor-engaged time; systematic observation of time management

Competencies for the Student Teacher to Attain

1. Implement a lesson-planning format for maximizing time on task.
2. Provide activities to ensure that students at a variety of skill levels can participate successfully.
3. Obtain estimates of time spent in management, instructional input, and motor activity for a sampling of classes.
4. Determine the amount of time that a target student within a given class spends in motor activity.
5. Utilize data obtained in Items 3 and 4 to restructure lessons and establish goals for maximizing time on task.

Tasks for the Student Teacher

1. Use Lesson Plan Format B (Figure 8.7) to plan a minimum of three lessons for this component. Identify steps to ensure maximum participation by each student, and provide tasks that match the ability levels of the learners.
2. Study the data your cooperating teacher obtains for duration recording of motor-engaged time and Systematic Observation of Time Management (Figure 8.8). Find out how well you've maximized time on task, and try to determine what aspects of the lesson did or did not contribute to this goal.
3. Establish some new goals for increasing time on task, and discuss these with your cooperating teacher. Then, replan and reteach one lesson, which the cooperating teacher will observe with the Systematic Observation of Time Management instrument (Figure 8.8). Compare the initial percentages of time on task (motor activity) with those occurring in the reteach phase.

Observation and Evaluation Strategies for the Cooperating Teacher

1. Observe one class using the following technique for duration recording of motor-engaged time. Using a stopwatch, record the duration of time in which a selected student is actively involved in motor activity. The target student should be someone of average ability (or someone randomly selected) so there will not be a built-in bias. Often, highly skilled students are more active in physical education classes. By contrast, a student who frequently poses disciplinary problems would not be typical. In observing, follow these procedures:

     a. Be sure that you are in the teaching area prior to the beginning of class.

     b. Select a target student prior to the instructor's beginning the class. Keep that student in view throughout the class.

     c. Begin observing at the instructor's first signal to begin class (e.g., calling the students together, taking roll, or giving directions).

     d. Start the stopwatch as soon as the target student begins to engage in purposeful movement activity (e.g., practicing a task, playing in the game, or performing a skill). Stop the watch whenever the student is not engaged in purposeful movement (e.g., listening to directions, engaging in off-task behavior, waiting a turn, transitioning to a new activity, or getting equipment).

     e. Continue observing until the class is dismissed, starting and stopping the watch in relation to the target student's activity. Do not reset the watch, because you want to obtain a total elapsed time (duration) of motor engagement.

     f. At the conclusion of the class, you will have a total elapsed time that you can record in minutes and seconds. Determine what percentage of the allocated class time this represents (e.g., 3 minutes of motor engagement during a 30-minute class period equals 10 percent).

2. Observe two classes using the Systematic Observation of Time Management instrument (Figure 8.8). After the first observation, analyze the data with the student teacher and use it to formulate goals for the next observed lesson. The second observation will allow you to see what changes the student teacher has made. Again, you will use a stopwatch for duration recording. The focus, however, will be on the nature of activity for the class as a whole (or what the teacher is doing). Procedures for using this instrument are as follows:

     a. Observe and record throughout the class any provisions the teacher makes to maximize time on task. These might include readying equipment in advance, using a time-saving method for taking roll, providing one ball per student, or setting up stations. Record these in the box at the top of the instrument.

     b. Time the duration of each episode as it occurs within the class. For example, if the student teacher begins by taking roll, which is a managerial (or noninstructional) episode, you will write *taking roll* on the first line under *Managerial episodes* and record the amount of time the class spends in this activity (e.g., 2:20). Cognitive activity is instructional input, or information the teacher provides that relates directly to the content of the lesson (e.g., demonstrating a skill, explaining how to play the game, describing a skill technique, or explaining rules for the activity). Motor-engaged time is that portion of the lesson devoted to psychomotor content or purposeful movement (e.g., practicing skills, scrimmaging, game play, or movement exploration).

     c. Time each episode as it occurs and record it under the appropriate category. Continue to do this throughout the entire class.

     d. At the conclusion of class, calculate the total time devoted to each of the three categories and convert these to percentages of total class time. Fill in the corresponding sections of the bar graphs for the three categories to provide a graphic description.

Figure 8.7

Lesson Plan Format B
Maximizing Time on Task

Sample Data From Secondary Level

Teacher _____*Curtis Napier*_____ Date ___*October 24, 1991*___ (Grade)/period _*6 and 7*_

Class size _____*35*_____

Performance objectives: *The student will demonstrate the ability to participate in a variety of recreational games.*

Equipment needed for this lesson:

Shuffleboard:
  4 sticks
  8 disks (4 different colors)
  shuffle markers

Handball:
  ball—tennis size
  wall (make service line and boundaries)

Table tennis:
  2 ping pong tables
  2 nets
  4 paddles
  2 balls

Air tennis:
  4 air rackets
  2 Nerf balls

Steps to be taken to ensure maximum participation by each student:

1. *Start class by taking complete control*
2. *Explain today's lesson briefly, yet completely.*
3. *Set up each station prior to class.*
4. *Arrange stations in order of rotation.*
5. *Set time allocations for each stateon.*
6. *Have cue to switch to next activity.*

Provisions for matching tasks with ability levels of the learners:

The selected activities require very little entry-level skill. To increase success, I will make up groups in advance of class to match groups by ability levels.

(Cont.)

Figure 8.7 (Continued)

Procedures

Set induction (introduction):

Explain the rules of each game being taught. Discuss each station and specify how to play each game; give some detail about the game, such as who plays it, where it originated, etc.

Explanation/demonstration:

The game experiences will be more recreational than sporting. The game experiences will be different because of the game requirements. Some games require four players, whereas others need only two.

Given the variety of possible skills, I will circulate during practice time to assist with basic skills required.

Organizational plan (How will students and equipment be organized?):

Students will be grouped in fours. Each station will be organized with proper equipment. Each group will start at a station when given a cue and will move to the next station when given a cue.

Practice opportunities

Time allocation	Activities for students	Activities for teacher
2 minutes	Dress for class.	
3 minutes	Participate in roll call.	Record absences.
8 minutes	Listen to games explanation.	Explain rules.
7 minutes	Play shuffleboard.	Circulate to demonstrate, observe, and give feedback.
7 minutes	Play handball.	
7 minutes	Play air tennis.	
2 minutes	Listen to closure.	Review one rule and one technique for each activity.
10 minutes	Shower and change.	

Closure: *Review one rule and one technique from each activity. Check for understanding.*

Figure 8.8

Systematic Observation of Time Management
Sample Data From Secondary Level

Teacher _____ *Ann Haves* _____   Date _*January 23, 1992*_   Grade/period   *2*

Class size _____ *32* _____

Provisions for reducing management time and increasing time on task:
- *Prepared equipment in advance*
- *Used a signal for attention*
- *Provided many stations*
- *Incorporated few transitions*

Managerial episodes		Cognitive activity		Motor-engaged time	
1. Arrange groups	1:30	2. Explains task	:45	4. Skill practice	5:00
3. Transition	:30	6. Technique	:15	7. Skill practice	5:00
5. Switch stations	:30	11. Closure	1:00	9. Skill practice	5:00
8. Transition	:25			10. Minigrame	3:00
	2:55		2:00		18:00

Percent of total time

| 100 |
| 80 |
| 60 |
| 40 |
| 20 |
| 0 |

12.73 percent

Percent of total time

| 100 |
| 80 |
| 60 |
| 40 |
| 20 |
| 0 |

8.83 percent

Percent of total time

| 100 |
| 80 |
| 60 |
| 40 |
| 20 |
| 0 |

78.54 percent

COMPONENT 10: Evaluating Lesson Effectiveness

	COMPONENT 10
GENERAL FOCUS	Evaluating lesson effectiveness
TARGET BEHAVIORS	Student rates of on-task/off-task, motor-engaged/non-motor-engaged activity
TASKS FOR STUDENT TEACHER	Conduct self-analysis of placheck data; restructure lesson for reteach phase
OBSERVATION/EVALUATION STRATEGIES	Planned activity check of student on-task/off-task, motor-engaged/non-motor-engaged behavior

Competencies for the Student Teacher to Attain

1. Calculate percentages of time in which students are on-task/off-task.
2. Use data from these calculations to restructure and reteach the same lesson plan.
3. Calculate percentages of time in which students are motor engaged/non–motor engaged.
4. Use data from these calculations to restructure and reteach a second lesson.

Tasks for the Student Teacher

1. Develop two written lesson plans using any planning format you deem appropriate.
2. Implement the first lesson while the cooperating teacher systematically observes on-task/off-task behavior.
3. Obtain data concerning on-task/off-task behavior from the cooperating teacher's observation form, entitled Planned Activity Check for Evaluating Lesson Effectiveness (Figure 8.9).
4. Use these data to calculate percentages of on-task/off-task behavior.
5. Replan and reteach the same lesson plan using this feedback.
6. Implement the second lesson while the cooperating teacher observes motor-engaged/non-motor-engaged activity.
7. Calculate percentages of this behavior and use data to restructure and reteach the second lesson plan.

Observation and Evaluation Strategies for the Cooperating Teacher

1. Use the systematic observation form entitled Planned Activity Check for Evaluating Lesson Effectiveness (Figure 8.9) to evaluate Lesson 1 for student on-task/off-task behavior.
2. Use the same form to observe and evaluate Lesson 2 for student motor-engaged/non-motor-engaged behavior.

Planned Activity Check for Evaluating Lesson Effectiveness

Conducting a planned activity check (placheck) involves scanning the group of students at designated intervals (for the instrument shown in Figure 8.9, every 5 minutes). To conduct the observation, you will need the observation instrument, a pencil, a clipboard, and a watch. At the beginning of the class, note the total number of students participating and the time at which the class begins. At the first 5-minute interval (e.g., 9:05), scan slowly from left to right and classify the students according to their designated behaviors (on-task/off-task, motor engaged/non–motor engaged). It is easiest to count the least frequently occurring behavior (e.g., off-task). Subtract this number from the total number of students to obtain the number of students on-task. Continue scanning at 5-minute intervals until the end of the class. The student teacher will use the obtained data to calculate percentages for observed student behaviors.

Figure 8.9

Planned Activity Check for Evaluating Lesson Effectiveness
Sample Data From Elementary Level

Teacher _____ *Susan Schwartz* _____   Date ___*April 15, 1992*___   (Grade)/period ___*4*___

Class size ___*21*___

Time	Number on-task	Number off-task	Number motor engaged	Number non–motor engaged
9:05	*14*	*14*	_____	_____
9:10	*28*	*0*	_____	_____
9:15	*18*	*10*	_____	_____
9:20	*22*	*6*	_____	_____
9:25	*27*	*1*	_____	_____
9:30	*28*	*0*	_____	_____
9:35	*20*	*8*	_____	_____
_____	_____	_____	_____	_____
_____	_____	_____	_____	_____
_____	_____	_____	_____	_____

Number of plachecks for on-task = *157*
Number of plachecks for off-task = *39*

Percent on-task =

$$\frac{\text{Number on-task}}{\text{Number on-task + number off-task}} \times 100 = \frac{157}{157 + 39} \times 100 = \frac{157}{196} \times 100 = 80.1 \text{ percent on task}$$

Note: Use the same formula to calculate motor engagement.

Summary and Implications

The components in Phase 2 focus on specific applications of planning for maximum learning. Having previously developed a foundation of confidence and control, the student teacher is able to revisit some planning skills that were introduced in undergraduate coursework. These skill areas include performance objectives, mechanical analysis and teaching cues, individualizing instruction, time on task, and evaluation of lesson effectiveness. Because many of the terms and strategies included in Phase 2 may be new for experienced teachers, this content may be useful as a resource for in-service training.

Although planning is critical to effective teaching, this process is frequently abbreviated or ignored. Interns and beginning teachers are particularly vulnerable to the effects of socialization as they observe the practices of their more experienced colleagues. I hope that this series of developmental tasks will help to reduce the rejection of theory by illustrating concretely the positive effects of planning for maximum learning.

Chapter 9

Phase 3: Refining Teaching Skills

Chapter 9 provides a theoretical overview, a knowledge base for Phase 3 components, and specific steps for implementing Phase 3. The theoretical overview encompasses elements of effective teaching that the supervisor can address once foundational skills are in place. Although the gross structure of the Systematic Supervision Model is sequential and hierarchical, the order of the components provides for flexibility. Therefore, the supervisor may introduce components contained in Phase 3 earlier when circumstances warrant their attention. Again, a knowledge base synthesizes the literature related to the 5 components of this phase. Specific steps for implementing Phase 2 include competencies for the student teacher to attain, tasks for the student teacher, and observation/evaluation tools for each of the 5 components.

Theoretical Overview

Having established a sound foundation of basic teaching skills, the developing teacher is now ready to fine tune aspects of professional development. The teacher at this stage has progressed beyond survival concerns, has mastered essential planning skills, and has achieved a measurable

degree of success in promoting student learning. Some of the skills in this phase, specifically those of lesson presentation and questioning, involve teaching functions normally pertinent to the classroom, thus they are not typically emphasized in physical education professional preparation programs. However, these skills can add versatility to the teaching repertoire and may be increasingly practical as physical educators become more involved in cognitive instructional activities. Practicing Phase 3 components will primarily help the teacher promote cognitive learning, which typically takes place in a classroom setting. However, application of these components is generally appropriate for instruction in movement settings. The basic principles will also apply to promoting conceptual learning in a movement setting.

In addition to reviewing lesson presentation and questioning, components included in this phase review appropriate feedback, effective modeling, and assessment of student performance. Having initially examined teacher verbal behavior with respect to student conduct, the supervisor adds the element of feedback for skill attempts. Refinement of modeling skills ensures that the teacher can make use of clear and concise demonstrations. Finally, the text emphasizes attention to process measures of skill assessment.

A Knowledge Base for Phase 3 Components

This conceptual framework addresses 5 components that extend the knowledge bases for Phases 1 and 2. The student teacher will have practiced many of these skills in earlier periods of student teaching or induction. However, specific attention is intended here to anchor skills that might have received peripheral treatment (e.g., feedback and demonstration) and to introduce some often neglected aspects of effective teaching in physical education (such as lesson presentation, questioning, and evaluation).

Skill Feedback

It is not possible to exactly prescribe appropriate feedback. Although pedagogists often recommend high rates of positive feedback, research indicates that a neutral environment is more facilitative to student learning. However, these studies have focused on achievement dimensions of cognitive learning and have not been concerned with the motivational aspects of feedback. In establishing the learning environment, educators should create an atmosphere in which students feel encouraged to take risks and to develop new skills. The ultimate goal is to develop positive attitudes toward movement, so that students will participate in movement activities throughout their lives. Therefore, teachers should encourage participation, acknowledge effort and progress with sincere (but not lavish) praise, and provide concise information to help the student improve skills.

Characteristics of Effective Feedback

The important elements of skill feedback are the degree of precision (general or specific), the valence (positive, corrective, or negative), the latency (immediate or delayed), and the congruence (relevance) to the task. In providing appropriate feedback, the teacher must consider the student's age, cognitive development, and skill level. In general, young children and unskilled performers benefit most from feedback related to the gross aspects of performance (i.e., basic mechanical elements). It is important not to overload the novice with an abundance of feedback that is related to numerous aspects of the movement. Older and more skilled performers can process more and more precise feedback. Given these variables, it is not desirable to prescribe a target ratio (general to specific) or frequency (rate per minute) for feedback. Instead, the goal here is for the student teacher to work toward giving more feedback and more precise feedback (or that which is developmentally appropriate).

In determining which aspects of skill to respond (give feedback) to the teacher must have a clear picture of the desired performance. The teacher should be able to visualize such an image by drawing upon prior analysis of mechanics and teaching cues for the given skills. The teacher must watch the skill performance long enough to observe that the error is consistent, then provide feedback that is specific to the developmental level of the performer (e.g., ''Now, John, try to step on the opposite foot,'' or ''Try to tuck at the top of the jump''). The teacher should observe the subsequent performances to see if the feedback is understood, give additional feedback, and then move on to the next performer.

With respect to precision, specific feedback that tells the performer which aspect of performance is correct or incorrect is better than general feedback or global goods. However, general feedback may be helpful as hurdle help (special assistance given by the teacher to help a student overcome a difficult obstacle) or as a means of boosting performance. The degree of precision must also match the developmental level of the performer.

Again, giving high rates of positive feedback is not supported by empirical research. Therefore, lavish and insincere praise is not desirable. However, physical educators tend to demonstrate a kind of coaching mentality, detecting and correcting errors more often than acknowledging correct aspects of performance (Darst, 1974; Fishman & Tobey, 1978; K. Hamilton, 1974; Hughley, 1973). A classroom climate that has primarily corrective (vs. positive) valence will not be very motivational. Further, negative feedback (with elements of insult or sarcasm) is counterproductive to motivation. Some evidence shows that reinforcement and encouragement will particularly enhance self-esteem in young athletes (Smoll & Smith, 1984). With these points in mind, the teacher should devote some attention to the ratio of positive to corrective feedback.

Chapter 4 discusses latency with respect to research perspectives. As a general rule, immediate feedback is superior to delayed feedback. In actual teaching, however, immediate feedback can not always be provided.

Congruency or relevance of feedback is determined by its relationship to the critical aspect of the skill, the part of the skill that relates to the objectives of the lesson. Often, teaching cues and mechanical principles explained in demonstrations will be repeated in the form of feedback. By focusing on a few relevant aspects of the lesson, the teacher avoids overloading the students with too much information. Rink (1985) contrasts focused and congruent feedback to an ineffectual "shotgun approach" in which the teacher provides random and unrelated feedback.

Increasing Feedback Opportunities for Students

A common problem in physical education is teaching large numbers of students. With some classes numbering 50 or more students, it is difficult for the teacher to monitor performance and maintain on-task behavior, which leaves little possibility for high rates of feedback. Because feedback is essential to learning, and because feedback available through intrinsic sources (i.e., visual, auditory, kinesthetic, and proprioceptive feedback) is limited, the teacher in this situation should try to augment feedback. One way is to modify the teaching style, incorporating, for example, a reciprocal or self-check (Mosston & Ashworth, 1986) style of teaching so students learn to provide feedback.

In the reciprocal style of teaching, students learn activities in pairs, alternating roles of the doer and observer. Defined criteria, usually written on a task card, help the observer evaluate the performance of the doer. The observer provides feedback to the doer in terms of the criteria, freeing the teacher to circulate and communicate with observers throughout the class. This method effectively increases the rate of available feedback for students in the class, because each has immediate and repeated feedback opportunities. In contrast, a teacher circulating within a class of 30 or more students could probably provide an average of 30 seconds of observation and feedback per student.

With the self-check style of teaching, each student evaluates him- or herself, recording his or her own progress on a task sheet. Again, precise criteria are used to indicate desired progress, and the student applies the criteria to self-performance. One restriction for this style is that the criteria must be observable through intrinsic information (i.e., the student does not rely on information from another individual). However, this style does promote self-evaluation and self-feedback, an ultimate

goal of instruction. Ideally, the learner will internalize the criteria for correct performance and remind him- or herself of these in later practice situations.

Group feedback is another valuable strategy for reinforcing learning. At the end of a lesson segment, or during closure, the teacher may address common errors of the group or review important concepts. This technique can make scrimmage or free-play situations more instructional in nature, while allowing the students occasional freedom in unstructured practice. Following are some advantages of group feedback, as identified by Mosston and Ashworth (1986, p. 40).

- It is time-efficient. The same feedback is given to all those who made the same error. To do it individually wastes time.
- The physical proximity of the teacher and the class can create a particular climate of ease different from the climate created when the teacher broadcasts the feedback (and in the gymnasium one must shout to accomplish it).
- During this time, learners can ask questions and the teacher can ascertain that more or all learners understood the correction.
- It may reinforce those who have performed correctly.

For a summary of guidelines of effective feedback, refer to chapter 5.

Demonstration

The goal of demonstration or modeling is to convey information to learners in a manner that is brief, clear, and concise. Because learners can only attend to, recall, and apply a limited number of concepts at one time, the teacher should not waste words. The teacher must explain the activity, get the students quickly involved, and provide additional information through feedback during and after the activity. Effective demonstrations do not happen spontaneously but result from careful planning.

Brevity is not a common strength of physical education teachers; they tend to provide too much information and talk for extended periods. An example I once observed was an elementary physical education teacher who was introducing a gymnastic unit to a class of sixth graders. After a short warm-up period, the teacher explained and demonstrated 15 skills, during which time the students promptly tuned out and quickly lost the effect of the warm-up. Following the 20-minute demonstration, the teacher grouped the students and sent them off to their stations with instructions to practice the tasks. Within about 2 minutes, and after one or two students at each station had practiced one or two jumps or swings, the teacher blew the whistle and dismissed the class.

This activity revealed a number of problems. First, the effect of the warm-up was negated by the lengthy discussion that followed. Second, the teacher attempted to introduce too many skills and gave far too much information for the children to process in one class period. Having different children from the class demonstrate the skills would have been at least somewhat more efficient. Sometimes, the temptation for teachers to show off their athletic skills is hard to resist. Last, the students received little opportunity to practice their skills with feedback and thereby lost the opportunity for reinforcement through doing.

The following guidelines for effective demonstrations are synthesized from Siedentop (1991) and Rink (1985).

- The demonstrator should be skillful at the particular task, and the demonstration should be accurate. An incorrect example will be counterproductive, because students tend to imitate what they see.
- It is preferable for students to demonstrate rather than the teacher. This allows the teacher to direct students' attention to specific elements of the skill.
- The teacher should ready materials required for the demonstration in advance.
- The demonstration should be at an appropriate conceptual level for the students.
- The demonstration should be visually directed at the learners.
- The demonstrator should identify and explain a limited number of the critical features of the demonstration. Identification of teaching cues or elements that are common to previously learned tasks can enhance transfer of learning.
- The demonstrator should use instructional aids only if they enhance the demonstration and do not require excessive time.
- The demonstrator should emphasize safety aspects of the skill.
- To the greatest extent possible, the conditions of the demonstrations should simulate the conditions (e.g., organizational format, spatial orientation, and equipment) under which students will perform the skill.
- Checks for student understanding (e.g., asking for questions or having a student reiterate major points) should follow the demonstration.

Lesson Presentation Skills

Many lesson presentation skills are important to effective teaching, but several of these are particularly critical. In order to capture and maintain attention, present information with clarity, and reinforce learning, the presenter should use effective set induction, pacing, structuring, and closure. Presentation of new concepts should be followed immediately with opportunities for guided practice.

The purpose of set induction, or anticipatory set, is to gain students' attention. Set induction involves any instructor activities designed to focus students' attention on selected aspects of the material to follow (i.e., Tell them what you're going to tell them). Set induction usually occurs at the beginning of the lesson, in what Hunter (1982) calls "prime time." The teacher may also use set induction to introduce a unit, or even to connect segments within a lesson. In effect, set induction provides a framework or "intellectual scaffolding" (B.R. Joyce & Weil, 1986) to which the students can anchor new ideas.

Set induction is followed by the presentation of material, typically in the form of explanations and demonstrations. The teacher can enhance the clarity of explanations by emphasizing major points, covering small amounts of material in step-by-step progressions, using concrete examples, and checking for student understanding (B. Rosenshine & Stevens, 1985). It is helpful here to recognize that different students prefer different learning modalities: some students learn best by hearing (auditory sensing modalities), whereas other benefit more by seeing (visual modalities) or doing (kinesthetic modalities). Thus, in planning demonstrations and explanations, the teacher should incorporate verbal explanations, visual demonstrations or learning aids, and movement applications (feeling or experiencing) whenever possible.

The concepts of pacing and structuring are addressed in detail in chapter 4. In essence, pacing refers to the rate of content coverage within a given lesson or over a period of time (e.g., a unit). Effective pacing requires careful planning and monitoring; the teacher must consider the variety of interest and ability levels held by the students and must observe progress and learning. Generally, a rapid pace of instruction contributes to greater learning, provided that the teacher does not cover large amounts of material at the expense of mastery. In structuring the lesson, the teacher can use verbal actions to gain student attention and to provide a conceptual framework for what is to follow. Structuring may take the form of clear directions, advance organizers, summary, or review.

Closure, or the summarization of a lesson's major points, can help to reinforce learning. It contributes to this goal by signaling the end of a lesson or a lesson component, organizing student learning, and reviewing and summarizing important information (Shostak, 1990). This is an important element that teachers frequently forget, both in movement settings and in classroom teaching. The teacher should structure the written lesson plan to provide for closure.

A variety of presentation skills, applied during the planning and implementation stages of teaching, can enhance the clarity of the lesson structure. These occur during the planning and implementation stages of teaching. Before the teaching session, the teacher must prepare written outlines, examples, questions, and summaries for the content of the lesson. This planning will allow the teacher to effectively accomplish set induction, explanation or demonstration, and closure. Pacing and structuring activities will further enhance teaching by allowing the teacher to facilitate content coverage and mastery, recognize individual differences, and help students understand the relationship between concepts.

Questioning Skills

Component 14 emphasizes the effective use of questions, specifically in classroom teaching situations, or those in which the primary purpose is to promote cognitive learning. However, teachers can also use questioning effectively in a movement setting as a way of incorporating conceptual learning. This area of teaching effectiveness has yielded a substantial amount of research. Although the findings are not yet definitive, some important guidelines can be proposed. The goals of effective questioning should include actively involving students in the learning process, enhancing subject mastery and conceptual understanding, and promoting both low-order and high-order cognitive processes.

In circumstances in which the teacher desires rote learning or memorization, it is appropriate to ask easy questions and those that require one specific answer. These low-order questions are designed to promote knowledge (recall) and comprehension (basic understanding). Low-order questions (*what? where?*) frequently take the form of drill or practice activities, in which the teacher asks few probing or follow-up questions.

To encourage abstract or higher cognitive processes (application, analysis, synthesis, and evaluation) the teacher must ask high-order questions. These questions go beyond *what?* and *where?* to challenge students as to *how?* and *why?* High-order questions are generally appropriate for students of average or high ability, and with older students when the teacher desires independent thinking.

In addition to varying the level of questions used (high and low order), the teacher must provide wait time and must use probing and reinforcing behaviors. By allowing 3 to 5 seconds of wait time after asking a question, the teacher avoids bombarding students with questions and gives them a chance to organize their thoughts. Wait time enhances both the quality and quantity of student responses.

In probing, the teacher asks follow-up questions that help the students extend, amplify, or refine their responses. A teacher's typical reactions to student responses, such as "Uh-huh" or "Yes," do not encourage participation or active engagement. Examples of good probing questions might include these: "Could you give me another example of that?" or "Why do you think that is true?"

Whereas probing extends or refines student responses, some simple reinforcement behaviors (verbal or nonverbal) can help to increase motivation. They may simply be concise feedback statements ("Yes, good" or "Correct"), or they may be extended statements that build on or amplify student ideas ("That might be an example of . . ." or "Right, I hadn't thought of that!"). When used in combination, probing and reinforcement can promote learning through extension and encouragement of student responses.

In order to best use questioning techniques, teachers must plan in advance and incorporate these strategies into written plans. In planning for effective questioning, the teacher must consider the nature of content to be mastered and the abilities and readiness of the students. It is helpful for the teacher to write down a series of questions for a particular lesson, planning appropriately for high- or low-order questions. Spontaneous questions may not be sufficient to promote the kind of learning the teacher desires.

Assessing Student Performance

Chapters 4 and 8 of this book address the mechanical aspects of skill performance, such as lesson planning (mechanical analysis) and implementation (teaching cues, feedback). An extension of these teaching competencies involves evaluation of student performance, or skill evaluation. To evaluate student performance, the teacher must understand the mechanics of correct performance and must have a clear visual image of how the skill is correctly performed. Finally, the teacher must consider the developmental readiness of the learner to determine whether a sufficient level of mastery has been demonstrated.

Typically, teachers evaluate skills in physical education with the help of product measures, skill tests that measure the outcome of performance (how high? how far? how fast?). An example of a product measure of jumping or ballistic power is the standing broad jump. This skill test measures jumping ability in terms of the distance covered (how far?). Although this information may be of some value, it does not consider the form of the movement. (Are the arms used in coordinated swinging fashion? Does the student flex the knees and incline the body forward prior to jumping to allow an explosive takeoff?)

Process measures of skill performance require the teacher to observe the form of the movement, or the "force-producing actions" of the performer (Safrit, 1981). An example of a process measure to evaluate jumping is the horizontal jump assessment included in the Michigan Educational Assessment Program (Michigan State Board of Education, 1984, p. 4). This program lists the following performance standards as evidence of a mature pattern of jumping:

1. Preparatory movement: arms at full extension behind the body at approximately the same time the knees reach maximum flexion at a 90-degree angle (± 10 degrees)

2. A forceful, forward and upward thrust of both arms and a full extension of the legs at takeoff

3. A takeoff angle of 55 degrees (± 5 degrees)

4. Simultaneous foot contact at landing ahead of the body's center of mass (point midway to back, behind navel)

5. Thighs near parallel to the floor at touchdown

6. Arms extended forward during the landing

7. A flowing movement (not mechanical or awkward)

Although a product measure such as the standing broad jump will yield quantitative data about the product of the jump (distance), this value will be largely influenced by the genetic endowment of the jumper. In short, the distance of the jump will be determined by the jumper's ratio of fast-twitch to slow-twitch muscle fibers. Individuals possessing abundant fast-twitch muscle fibers will be able to produce the ballistic muscle contractions required for explosive power. By using a process measure, the teacher can focus on the developmental aspects of the performance, those that can be more easily improved with training. By observing the form of the jump, the teacher can identify specific areas for training (e.g., preparatory movement or takeoff angle).

It may not be easy for the teacher to locate process measures for skill assessment in physical education. Process instruments that can be easily applied are limited, because most existing instruments were developed for research purposes. These instruments often require extensive training or even the use of complicated film analysis techniques, and they therefore do not contribute to reliable observations in a live setting.

The Michigan Educational Assessment Program contains a variety of process assessments for fundamental motor skills (locomotor and object control) and body management skills (body awareness, body control, and posture). The battery contains a number of product measures as well, in addition to combined process and product assessments of physical fitness (endurance, flexibility, and muscular strength).

In addition to measuring fundamental and basic movement skills, the teacher may wish to make process measures of specific sport skills. For example, a teacher who wishes to assess a tennis serve can select a product measure by counting the number of serves that land within the service court (accuracy). That measure, however, provides little or no information about the form of the tennis serve or the movement pattern that the arms, trunk, and legs demonstrate. If the teacher is sufficiently knowledgeable about the mechanics of correct performance, he or she can develop a simple process measure for correct performance. The following criteria comprise an example of such a measure (Edgley, 1986).

1. Left toe points toward right net post.

2. Racket head faces opposite service court before player begins backswing.

3. Toss is slightly in front of left toe and begins with a push from the fingers.

4. Tossed ball goes at least as high as extended arm and racket.

5. Racket reaches back-scratch position in backswing.

6. Contact is made on the backside of the ball.

7. Racket follows through across the body.

In applying process measures, the teacher may use an existing assessment instrument or devise one based on mechanics of correct performance. In order for that instrument to provide useful information, the teacher must consider the developmental readiness of the learners to be evaluated, or the level of performance expected within a given skill. For young learners or those who are at a novice level within a given skill, it may be sufficient for the teacher to focus on the gross aspects of the movement — the pattern of the large body segments. For more mature students, the teacher can incorporate the fine aspects of skill performance into the observable criteria.

With this approach, the teacher may apply a process measure to determine the level of skill proficiency obtained by students within a given fundamental motor skill. Table 9.1 identifies three developmental levels of skill proficiency. For each level, the table describes the action of the arms, trunk, and legs. For example, the child at beginning level (Level 1) will demonstrate no stepping or weight transfer, whereas a child at a mature level (Level 3) will demonstrate weight transfer and oppositional stepping.

In order to accurately apply process measures, the teacher will need some practice in carefully observing the selected movement skill with respect to the defined criteria. By concentrating on selected aspects of form, the teacher can practice clinical diagnosis (error detection) by comparing observed performance to specified criteria. The illustrations in Figure 9.1 depict children at different levels of proficiency in overhand throwing. The first child is at an immature level of overhand throwing proficiency (Level 1). He demonstrates

Table 9.1 Developmental Levels of Skill Proficiency in Overhand Throwing

Body segment	Level 1	Level 2	Level 3
Arms	a. Arm uses primarily a flinging motion from the elbow b. Elbow of throwing arm remains in front of the body c. Elbow extends early; no forearm lag d. Fingers are spread at release	a. Humerus rotates to oblique position as ball is brought behind the head b. Arm swings forward high above the shoulder c. Wrist cocks at completion of delivery d. Forearm lags behind humerus in delivery	a. Arm swings backward in preparation b. Elbow of nonthrowing arm extends for balance c. Thumb rotates medially downward d. Fingers are close together at release e. Arm has pronounced forearm lag
Trunk	a. Body faces forward throughout b. Shoulders and hips have little or no rotation (remain facing target)	a. Trunk uses block rotation (simultaneous rotation of hips and shoulders in preparation) b. Shoulders turn to face target in delivery c. Forward trunk flexion completes delivery	a. Trunk rotation is differentiated (hips-spine-shoulders) in delivery b. Throwing shoulder drops slightly in preparation c. Throwing shoulder faces target in follow-through
Legs	a. Legs do not step b. There is no weight transfer	a. Weight definitely shifts b. (Same arm and leg move ipsalateral stepping)	a. Weight is on rear foot in preparation b. Opposite arm and leg move forward (oppositional stepping)

Note. Children who are in transition between levels of skill proficiency may exhibit intersegmental variations (i.e., different levels of maturity are reflected in the action of the three body segments). From Randall, L.E. (1989). Clinical diagnosis skills for effective training. In Marlene J. Adrian and John M. Cooper, *Biomechanics of Human Movement.* Copyright © 1989, by Benchmark Press, Inc. Reprinted by permission of Wm. C. Brown Communications, Inc., Dubuque, Iowa. All rights reserved.

a forward orientation, no stepping, and a flinging action of the arm. In contrast, the second child demonstrates a mature pattern of the same movement (Level 3). He has a sideward orientation, full range of motion and follow-through in arm action, trunk rotation, and oppositional stepping.

Process measures can facilitate instruction and evaluation in a number of ways. Through visual observation of skill performance, teachers can provide clear feedback and objective assessment information. This kind of objective data can provide more useful information to parents than can simple letter grades. Teachers can also use process measures to provide formative information and task-related skill feedback to students.

Specific Steps for Implementing Phase 3

The competencies and target behaviors for Phase 3 are organized into 5 components: providing appropriate feedback, using techniques for effective demonstration, developing lesson presentation skills, enhancing questioning skills, and assessing student performance. Specific competencies for the respective components, as well as tasks for the student teacher and observation/evaluation tools for the cooperating teacher, are defined here.

Figure 9.1 Developmental levels of overhand throwing. *Note.* Illustration courtesy of Steven Barnes, Florida State University at Tallahassee. From ''Clinical Diagnosis Skills for Effective Training'' by L.E. Randall. In *Biomechanics of Human movement* (pp. 296-302) by M.J. Adrian and J.M. Cooper (Eds.), Indianapolis: Benchmark. Reprinted by permission.

COMPONENT 11: Providing Appropriate Skill Feedback

	COMPONENT 11
GENERAL FOCUS	Providing appropriate skill feedback
TARGET BEHAVIORS	Positive, specific, and task-relevant feedback related to skill attempts
TASKS FOR STUDENT TEACHER	Audiotape lessons and analyze feedback through systematic observation
OBSERVATION/EVALUATION STRATEGIES	Systematic Observation of Teacher Verbal Skill Feedback

Competencies for the Student Teacher to Attain

1. Provide high rates of positive and specific feedback related to student skill attempts.
2. Audiotape your verbal feedback behavior.
3. Apply a systematic observation method using event recording to analyze feedback behavior.
4. Use obtained data to adjust your verbal feedback behavior as indicated.

Tasks for the Student Teacher

1. Plan and implement a lesson that is designed to develop skill within a given area.
2. Audiotape the lesson while you teach, using a small tape recorder placed in your pocket.
3. Play back the tape and systematically record the feedback statements you made, using the form entitled Systematic Observation of Teacher Verbal Skill Feedback (Figure 9.2).
4. Interpret the obtained data with respect to the number of positive and corrective, general and specific statements.
5. Develop a graph that illustrates these data, using the bar graph at the bottom of the form.
6. Plan and implement a second lesson, for which your cooperating teacher will use the same instrument to code verbal feedback while you teach. Graph and compare the obtained data to the previous graphic data.

Observation and Evaluation Strategies for the Cooperating Teacher

One observation instrument, entitled Systematic Observation of Teacher Verbal Skill Feedback (Figure 9.2), is used for this component. This instrument is used for event recording of verbal behavior related to student skill attempts and does not include data related to social behavior. In the first observation, the student teacher obtains data through audiotaped self-recordings. In the second observation, you will use the instrument to collect data while the student teacher is actually teaching.

In coding data, record only those teacher verbal behaviors that occur in response to student skill attempts. Record each event with a checkmark or slash in the appropriate box (see Component 3 for definitions and procedures).

Figure 9.2

Systematic Observation of Teacher Verbal Skill Feedback

Teacher _____Valerie Thomas_____   Date __February 5, 1992__   (Grade)/period ___5___

Class size ____28____

Skill objectives:

Students will demonstrate catching a ball, thrown underhand by a partner standing 5 feet away, without trapping the ball against the chest.

Skills practiced:

Underhand throwing
Catching

Feedback

Positive general	Corrective general
++++ ///	
Positive specific	**Corrective specific**
++++ ++++	++++

Number positive ____18____   Number general ____8____

Number corrective ____5____   Number specific ____15____

Total number of feedback statements = ____23____

Percent total feedback statements

COMPONENT 12: Using Techniques for Effective Demonstration

	COMPONENT 12
GENERAL FOCUS	Using techniques for effective demonstration
TARGET BEHAVIORS	Criteria of an effective demonstration
TASKS FOR STUDENT TEACHER	Plan and implement skill demonstration to be videotaped; analyze videotape for set criteria
OBSERVATION/EVALUATION STRATEGIES	Videotape of lesson; effective demonstration checklist

Competencies for the Student Teacher to Attain

1. Plan and implement a demonstration of a selected skill that meets defined criteria of effectiveness.

2. Obtain a videotaped recording of the demonstration and use a criteria checklist to evaluate its effectiveness.

3. Review the obtained data, noting changes indicated or criteria successfully achieved, and incorporate these changes in a follow-up demonstration.

Tasks for the Student Teacher

1. Select a specific skill to demonstrate within a given context and develop a written lesson plan incorporating that demonstration.

2. In planning the demonstration, consider the criteria defined in the Checklist for an Effective Demonstration (Figure 9.3).

3. Arrange to have the lesson videotaped while you teach.

4. Review and analyze the videotaped demonstration with your cooperating teacher, looking for evidence of the specified criteria.

5. Discuss with your cooperating teacher the extent to which you have achieved the criteria; also discuss any changes that you feel are warranted.

6. Incorporate changes in a follow-up demonstration.

Observation and Evaluation Strategies for the Cooperating Teacher

1. Use the Checklist of Criteria of an Effective Demonstration (Figure 9.3) to evaluate the student teacher's written plan of the demonstration.

2. Help the student teacher arrange for the videotaping; perhaps doing the actual taping yourself. It is not necessary to record the entire class, but it may be desirable. It is also possible, in lieu of videotaping, to apply the checklist as you observe the demonstration live.

3. Optimally, you and the student teacher will review the tape simultaneously. Allow the student teacher to first apply the checklist, and provide additional input as required.

4. If the demonstration needs substantial improvements, repeat the procedure for implementation and analysis of changes.

Figure 9.3

Checklist for an Effective Demonstration

Teacher _____ Date _____ Grade/period _____

Class Size _____ Skill demonstrated _____ Activity _____

_____ The demonstrator is skillful.

_____ The demonstration is accurate.

_____ The demonstrator readies materials in advance.

_____ The demonstration is at an appropriate conceptual level for the students.

_____ Students are able to see the demonstration.

_____ The demonstrator identifies a limited number of features of the skill and explains and performs them in sequence.

_____ The demonstrator uses instructional aids only when essential for clarity and when they do not require too much time.

_____ The demonstrator emphasizes safety points, if necessary.

_____ Conditions of the demonstration are similar to those under which the skill will be performed.

_____ The demonstrator obtains feedback from the students to check their understanding.

COMPONENT 13: Developing Lesson Presentation Skills

	COMPONENT 13
GENERAL FOCUS	Developing lesson presentation skills
TARGET BEHAVIORS	Effective set induction, explanation, and closure
TASKS FOR STUDENT TEACHER	Develop a written lesson plan (Format C) for presenting cognitive content
OBSERVATION/EVALUATION STRATEGIES	Specialized Lesson Plan Format C; Lesson Clarity Observation Form

Competencies for the Student Teacher to Attain

1. Plan and implement a lesson for which the primary purpose is to promote cognitive learning.
2. Utilize Lesson Plan Format C (Figure 9.4) to develop a written plan for classroom teaching.
3. Incorporate in lesson plans written outlines, examples, questions, and summaries.
4. Demonstrate effective use of set induction.
5. Evidence four essential aspects of lesson clarity: assessment of student learning, provision of opportunities to learn, use of examples, and review and organization of content.

Tasks for the Student Teacher

1. Utilize Lesson Plan Format C (Figure 9.4) to develop a lesson for which the primary purpose is to promote cognitive learning. Submit a copy of the lesson plan to the cooperating teacher before you teach the lesson.
2. Teach the lesson to a selected group of students, preferably in a classroom situation.
3. Use data obtained from the cooperating teacher's evaluation (Systematic Observation of Lesson Clarity, Figure 9.5) to conduct a self-evaluation of the lesson. You may substitute the alternate form (Alternate Observation of Lesson Clarity, Figure 9.6) for a more in-depth analysis.

Observation and Evaluation Strategies for the Cooperating Teacher

1. Prior to teaching the lesson, the student teacher should give you a lesson plan he or she wrote using Lesson Plan Format C (Figure 9.4). This will enable you to evaluate for the congruence between stated objectives and content; the clarity of set induction, explanation, and closure; and the advance preparation of examples and questions.
2. While the student teacher conducts the actual lesson, use the form entitled Observation of Lesson Clarity (Figure 9.5) to evaluate the four aspects of lesson clarity: assessment, opportunity to learn, use of examples, and review and organization. This is in essence a high-inference rating scale, and you will note behavioral indicators of lesson clarity as you observe them. For discrete behaviors, those with a distinct

beginning and ending point (e.g., answering questions or providing examples), use a tally to note those indicators of teacher clarity that you observe. For continuous behaviors (those that reflect the lesson structure overall), record *yes* or a zero to indicate their presence or absence. As an alternative, you may wish to use the instrument entitled Alternate Observation of Lesson Clarity (Figure 9.6). For this form, place a check mark in the space provided to indicate whether the teacher used set induction, showed the relationship between parts of the lesson, provided for practice opportunities or active participation, and provided for closure. In the boxes provided for each criterion, briefly describe how the teacher facilitated lesson clarity.

Figure 9.4

Lesson Plan Format C
Promoting Cognitive Learning
Sample Data From Elementary Level

Teacher _____ *Mark Feltz* _____ Date _____ *May 3, 1992* _____ Grade/period ___ *3* ___

Class size _____ *24* _____

Objectives:

The children will compare their heart rates while exercising and while resting.

Materials:

Drum

Terms:

Heart—a muscle that pumps blood throughout the body
Pulse point—a place in the body where we can feel the blood pushing through the arteries

---

Set induction:

"Who can tell me the name of a muscle in the body?" "Good, what is another?" (discover several) *"Is the heart a muscle?" What happens to muscles when they work hard?" "Do our hearts need exercise and rest, also?"*

Outline of content and development	Examples/illustrations/questions/terms
Locate the position of the heart in the chest—its size and its action.	
Ask the children to make fists. Discuss the size of the fist in relation to the heart.	*"Your heart is about the size of your fist. Mine is about the size of my fist. How do you think my heart looks compared to yours?"*
	"How big do you imagine the heart of an elephant is?"
	"How about a bird?"
The heart is located inside the chest. (Hold fist over heart—children mimic).	*"Can you show me where your heart is?"*
Children mimic the pumping of the heart as it beats fast and slow (by opening and closing their fists).	*"What happens when the heart beats very slowly? Can you show me?"*
Demonstrate the "lub-dub" sound with the drum.	*"Can you make your heart beat in time to the drum? Very slowly, now a little faster. What if you were running very fast?"*
Children run in place for a minute to accelerate their heart rates, moving in time to the drum beat.	*"Now, stop for a moment, and feel your heart. Is it going fast or slow?"*
Have children locate the pulse points on their wrists and necks.	

Closure: *"Let's give our hearts a rest now. Sit quietly, and feel your heart beating in your chest. What happens as we relax? Breath slowly. Can you feel your heart slowing down? Is it resting now? Relax."*

Figure 9.5

Systematic Observation of Lesson Clarity
Four Factors and Behavioral Indicators
Sample Data From Secondary Level

Teacher _____*Ellen Walters*_____ Date _____*April 18, 1992*_____ Grade/period _____8_____

Class size _____25_____

	Observed	
	Yes Tally (/)	No Zero (O)
Factor 1: Teacher assesses student learning The teacher actively attempts to determine if students understand the content or the task and makes instructional adjustments as appropriate. Indicators:		
Tries to find out if learners understand content	///	
Gives specific details when teaching	//	
Answers questions	-/H/-	
Asks learners if they know what to do and how to do it	//	
Factor 2: Teacher provides opportunity to learn The teacher structures classroom activities to allow time for students to think about, respond to, and synthesize what they are learning. Indicators:		
Teaches at a pace appropriate to the topic and learners	yes	
Shows pupils how to remember or recall ideas		O
Provides examples and explanations	///	
Gives pupils time to think	-/H/-	
Gives sufficient time for practice	yes	
Determines level of pupil understanding	////	
Stays with the topic; repeats as necessary	yes	
Factor 3: Teacher uses examples The teacher frequently uses examples, especially on the chalkboard. Indicators:		
Shows examples of how to do both classwork and homework		O
Gives explanations pupils understand	yes	
Goes over difficult homework on the chalkboard		O
Stresses difficult points		O
Factor 4: Teacher reviews and organizes The teacher frequently reviews work and prepares pupils for upcoming work Indicators:		
Prepares pupils for what they will do next	/	
Describes the work to be done	/	

Figure 9.6

Alternate Observation of Lesson Clarity
Sample Data From Secondary Level

Teacher _____*Roberta Fields*_____   Date ___*January 7, 1992*___   Grade/period ___6___

Class size _____*28*_____

Place check marks in the spaces provided to indicate the teacher's use of the four aspects of lesson clarity; describe examples as applicable.

___√___ Uses set induction to introduce the purpose of the lesson or gain the interest of the students

Describe:

Teacher used photo from Sports Illustrated *and short video segment to introduce the topic of steroids; this stimulated interest.*

___√___ Shows the relationships between lesson parts

Describe:

Teacher used an outline of topics and questions, which was shown on the overhead projector and distributed on a handout.

___√___ Provides for practice opportunities: Engages students actively in the content

Describe:

Teacher used short cooperative learning segment by placing students in small groups; students completed a survey and presented their ideas.

___√___ Provides for closure (reviews, summarizes, provides group feedback)

Describe:

Teacher reviewed major points of the lesson with respect to the outline; teacher provided feedback to each of the cooperative learning groups.

COMPONENT 14: Enhancing Questioning Skills

	COMPONENT 14
GENERAL FOCUS	Enhancing questioning skills
TARGET BEHAVIORS	High-order questions; probe; prompt; provide wait time
TASKS FOR STUDENT TEACHER	Plan and implement a lesson to develop high-order thinking
OBSERVATION/EVALUATION STRATEGIES	Systematic Observation of Questioning Skills

Competencies for the Student Teacher to Attain

1. Demonstrate use of low-order and high-order questions.
2. Use probing and reinforcing behaviors to help students refine and extend their responses to teacher questions.
3. Provide sufficient wait time after asking questions.
4. Demonstrate equity of interaction by encouraging responses from boys and girls and from low-ability and high-ability students.

Tasks for the Student Teacher

1. Develop a written lesson plan (using Lesson Plan Format C, Figure 9.4) that is oriented toward attainment of cognitive learning.
2. Incorporate low-order and high-order questions into the written plan.
3. Present and audiotape the lesson.
4. Use the instrument entitled Systematic Observation of Questioning Skills (Figure 9.7) to systematically analyze questioning skills recorded on the tape.

Observation and Evaluation Strategies for the Cooperating Teacher

The student teacher will use the form for Systematic Observation of Questioning Skills (Figure 9.7) to analyze the audiotape. You may also wish to do a live coding, recording questions verbatim as you hear them. After recording each question, place a tally in the box at the bottom of the form to indicate whether the student teacher provided a minimum of 3 to 5 seconds for wait time. Also, indicate whether the question called for a choral (group, unison) response or an individual (calling on one student, before or after asking the question) response. After you complete the live coding, review the questions and determine whether they were low order (requiring singular, factual responses) or high order (requiring analysis and reasoning). In essence, low-order questions are those that relate to Bloom's (1956) taxonomy levels of knowledge and comprehension. Questions requiring application, analysis, synthesis, and evaluation are considered high order. Though it is not necessary to make discrete determinations within this instrument, the following definitions and examples are provided for clarification.

Knowledge—involves recognition or recall of information (factual response).

- "What is the definition of cardiovascular endurance?"
- "Name four components of health-related fitness."

Comprehension—goes beyond simple recall by requiring students to organize and arrange material mentally (Sadker & Sadker, 1990).

- "What does the chart tell you about recent trends in cardiovascular disease?"
- "How are health-related and skill-related aspects of fitness different in their nature?"
- "What is the purpose of warming up before exercise?"

Application—requires the student to apply previously learned information in a new context.

- "How could you increase the intensity of your workout in a swimming program?"
- "What are some activities that require flexibility of the low back and hamstring muscles?"

Analysis—requires the student to think critically and in-depth in order to (a) identify motives, reasons, and/or causes; (b) draw conclusions; or (c) find evidence to support a conclusion, inference, or generalization (Sadker & Sadker, 1990, p. 127).

- "What are some factors in contemporary society that contribute to low levels of fitness?"
- "Cite some evidence of declining fitness levels among American children."

Synthesis—requires students to combine ideas and concepts in creative and original ways (i.e., to produce original ideas, make predictions, or solve problems) (Sadker & Sadker, 1990).

- "How can we help other students in the school become more involved in active sports and games?"
- "Develop a program for improving four aspects of cardiovascular endurance."

Evaluation—requires the students to make judgments or offer opinions (Sadker & Sadker, 1990).

- "What are some of the reasons why it is important to exercise?"
- "Is is harmful to consume alcoholic beverages occasionally?"

Figure 9.7

Systematic Observation of Questioning Skills
Sample Data From Secondary Level

Teacher _____ *Ted Hughes* _____ Date *December 13, 1991* Grade/period 7

Class size _____ *27* _____

List the questions as they occur. Indicate within the boxes whether the responses required are individual or choral, whether the teacher provided 3 seconds or less of wait time, and the level of the taxonomy the questions reflect.

1. *Who can give me a definition of health-related fitness? What does that mean?*
2. *Mark, what is one component of health-related fitness?*
3. *Who can give me another component?*
4. *What kinds of sport activities require a lot of flexibility? Can you name some, Linda?*
5. *And why is flexibility important to the sport of swimming?*
6. *Now, who remembers the definition of skill-related fitness? What does that mean?*
7. *Is speed an example of a skill-related fitness component, Danielle?*
8. *Can you identify a sport skill that requires a lot of speed?*
9. *Now, is it possible for most people to increase their speed substantially?*
10. *Why do you think that health-related fitness is more important to us than skill-related fitness?*

Individual	Choral
⁄⁄⁄⁄ ⁄⁄⁄⁄	⁄

Wait	No wait
⁄⁄⁄⁄ ⁄	⁄⁄⁄⁄

Place a tally in the space that reflects the level of the taxonomy corresponding to each question.

Low order (Knowledge, comprehension)	High order (Application, analysis, synthesis, evaluation)
⁄⁄⁄⁄ ⁄	⁄⁄⁄⁄

COMPONENT 15: Assessing Student Performance

	COMPONENT 15
GENERAL FOCUS	Assessing student performance
TARGET BEHAVIORS	Error detection, clinical diagnosis, and process assessment
TASKS FOR STUDENT TEACHER	Select and implement a process measure of skill development
OBSERVATION/EVALUATION STRATEGIES	Videotape analysis

Competencies for the Student Teacher to Attain

1. Identify criteria you will use to evaluate the performance of a selected skill.
2. Apply qualitative analysis (process measures) to the evaluation of skill performance.
3. Use process measures in the process of clinical diagnosis and error detection.

Tasks for the Student Teacher

1. Select or develop a process measure (qualitative assessment) to evaluate the performance of students. (Several samples are provided in Figures 9.8, 9.9, and 9.10). In developing an instrument, begin by developing a mechanical analysis of the correct performance of the skill. You may need to refer to a sport skill reference or similar resource to get this information. Then, list the mechanics of correct performance that would be observed in a mature pattern (or, that represent a criterion level appropriate for the students). Create a simple checklist that you will use to observe the form of the movement, specifically looking for the mechanical principles that you have identified.
2. Structure a situation in which you can videotape several students (or a whole class if possible) performing the skill that you plan to assess.
3. Use the designated instrument to rate the performance of the students.

Observation and Evaluation Strategies for the Cooperating Teacher

You will assist in the selection and development of the process measure and will coordinate the videotaping if needed. There is no systematic observation tool for this component. It is important that you check the instrument that the student teacher selects to see that the defined criteria are appropriate for the developmental level of the students to be evaluated. The criteria should be objective, precisely defined, and easily observed.

Figure 9.8

Skill Test for Overhand Throwing

Teacher _____ Date _____ Grade/period _____

Class size _____

Scoring key
1 = Demonstrated
2 = Not demonstrated

	Gender (M or F)	Grades 4, 7, and 10						Grade 4			Grade 7			Grade 10			
		Side orientation and rear weight shift at windup	Near complete extension of the throwing arm	Weight transfer as hand passes above the shoulder	Sequential hip and shoulder rotation	Follow-through		Throw ball a minimum of 40 feet in air			Hit a 6-foot target from 40 feet			Hit a 6-foot target from 50 feet			
								Trials			Trials			Trials			
Name of student		1	2	3	4	5		1	2	3	1	2	3	1	2	3	

Figure 9.9

Skill Test for Traveling Skills

Teacher _____ Date _____ Grade/period _____

Class size _____

Name of student	Movement qualities					
	Starting and stopping on signal	Moving fast and slow	Moving in straight, curved, and zigzagged pathways	Traveling around obstacles	Moving in relation to a partner	Moving to a rhythmic beat

Figure 9.10

Skill Test for Tennis Serve

Teacher _____   Date _____   Grade/period _____

Class size _____

Name of student	Movement qualities					
	Left toe points toward right net post	Racket head faces opposite service court before backswing	Toss is slightly in front of left toe and begins with a push from the fingers	Tossed ball is at least as high as extended arm and racket	Racket reaches back-scratch position in backswing	Racket follows through across the body

Summary and Implications

The activities in Phase 3 focus on refining teaching skills. They are designed to provide the fine tuning of specific teaching skills that is possible when the teacher has mastered gross aspects of planning and implementation. Skill areas included in this phase include feedback, demonstration, lesson presentation, questioning, and assessment. Although some of these areas are common to movement settings, lesson presentation and questioning skills receive little emphasis in undergraduate training for physical educators. Trends of increased accountability and mastery of a core of generic teaching skills have placed new demands on our profession.

The skills in Phase 3 are germane to physical educators at all levels of experience. Recent graduates of some professional preparation programs may have been introduced to the basic concepts, but few will have had opportunities to apply these specialized competencies to actual teaching settings. The majority of in-service teachers will find the terms and strategies in this phase to be novel. This level of refinement can constitute mastery of teaching.

Part III

Implementation, In-Service Training, and Educational Reform

This final part of the book links the model and its empirical foundation to the natural constraints of reality. Three important aspects of this integration are implementation, in-service training, and educational reform. Implementation involves strategies for using the model in the training of student teachers. The ideas for implementation evolved as answers to questions and solutions to concerns that arose during the piloting of the model. In-service parameters apply the model to staff development with beginning or experienced teachers. Because several states have implemented uniform classroom observation instruments, educational reform measures are reviewed with respect to teacher evaluation.

Chapter 10 describes strategies for implementing the Systematic Supervision Model. A typical response to such a model might be, It looks very nice, but will it work in my situation? It will, pro-

vided that a planned and comprehensive approach to implementation is used. Successful implementation of the Systematic Supervision Model requires a strong foundation, including preparation of all members of the supervisory triad. It also entails several strategies for ensuring accountability. The supervisory triad can further enhance use of the model by integrating its components with seminar activities in student teaching. Some concrete suggestions are provided for structuring the seminar activities.

Chapter 11 extends the use of the model beyond student teaching, addressing research implications for effective in-service implementation. Although the model was designed initially for student teachers, it can be very useful in providing meaningful in-service training. This chapter identifies characteristics of effective in-service programs, including obstacles to, and facilitators of transfer of training. Conclusions from research provide lessons for facilitating transfer of training.

Chapter 12 reviews the pertinent literature related to systematic supervision and educational reform. The 1980s evidenced a national trend toward increasing teacher accountability. As a result, most states have adopted some form of teacher competency testing, and several have implemented classroom observation instruments. These man-dates should not preclude the use of the Systematic Supervision Model. In fact, the two approaches can be combined for optimal results in training physical educators.

Part III should provide the reader with an expanded view of implications for the Systematic Supervision Model. The extended research base and practical guidelines are intended to promote the transfer of this theoretical model into practice.

Chapter 10

Implementing the Systematic Supervision Model

Although planned and systematic supervision is generally appealing, a comprehensive approach is needed to ensure its success. In the process of implementing the model during the past several years, my associates and I have learned some valuable lessons about how to optimize the use of the model. Feeling some initial concerns about how it would be received, we gradually gained confidence and encouragement as the model gained momentum. It has been most positively received by student teachers, who welcome specific guidelines and clear expectations for their performance. The same has been true for most cooperating teachers, although some need initial reassurance that the bulk of the responsibility for reading and digesting the material is placed on the student teacher.

The Student Teacher's Handbook for Physical Education is fairly self-explanatory and can in fact be used without much advance preparation. During the evolution of the model, the first student teachers to pilot the materials were able to use them successfully with no advance preparation. However, it is desirable to make optimal use of the Systematic Supervision Model by first introducing participants to the major concepts of the model. In order to achieve meaningful results, the implementation process will require some effort to develop shared understandings and commitments. However, we know from research and practical experience that traditional supervision as it is typically practiced has little impact upon teaching outcomes. Therefore, it seems that a comprehensive approach is the only way to provide for substantive supervision.

The following sections provide specific guidelines for implementing the Systematic Supervision Model as well as some general guidelines for effective supervision. They describe techniques for developing a stong foundation through preparation of student teachers, cooperating teachers, and college and university supervisors. They address some commonly asked questions about the model and provide solutions to potential problems. An additional section provides some activities that the supervisor can use to reinforce the components through a weekly seminar in conjunction with student teaching.

Providing a Strong Foundation

This mission entails four aspects of development that lay the groundwork for systematic supervision.

These include preparing student teachers, preparing cooperating teachers, preparing college and university supervisors, and developing a system of accountability for the inclusive functions of all participants.

Preparing Student Teachers

Supervisors can use a variety of strategies to introduce student teachers to the components of the model early in their professional preparation. At the very least, the supervisor should review the contents of the handbook with the student teacher during the semester prior to student teaching. Familiarity with the model helps the student teacher to feel more confident in approaching the internship and ensures an easier transition into the tasks required in the model.

Methods classes and preservice teaching experiences provide the earliest opportunity to expose prospective student teachers to the components of the Systematic Supervision Model. The competencies defined in the model reflect a core content of essential teaching competencies. As such, they can provide continuity and consistency within and between such experiences. When the student revisits these skills in an applied setting, as in the case of student teaching, it is logical that the skills will make more sense and have an increased likelihood of transfer.

It may well be that one of the major contributors to the theory/practice gap is the lack of consistency in methods classes taught by a variety of instructors. Although students benefit from exposure to a spectrum of ideas, they are confused when the concepts do not hang together in any recognizable form. The end result is that students do whatever is required to obtain a good grade from the given professor. When students complete the course, they quickly forget or dismiss those ideas as idiosyncratic and unrelated to the real world.

Through early exposure to the model, students can increase their awareness of effective teaching skills and the related knowledge bases. They can also practice using the observation instruments by applying them to laboratory and field settings. The instruments provide a lens for objective evaluation of teaching and help to make the theoretical constructs of the model more relevant. Remember the ancient Chinese proverb: What I hear, I forget. What I see, I remember. What I do, I know.

Just prior to the semester of student teaching, the supervisor should have several meetings with student teachers. At this point, they can be introduced to *The Student Teacher's Handbook for Physical Education* and can become familiar with the format of the book and the requirements they will need to meet. The supervisor should emphasize that it is primarily each student teacher's responsibility to read and interpret the assignments for each component (essentially weekly). The student teacher will then ask the cooperating teacher to help with the specific observations. The supervisor should assure the student teachers that the actual amount of reading for each component is quite minimal, requiring approximately 15 to 30 minutes to review the knowledge base.

Preparing Cooperating Teachers

Cooperating teachers are sometimes reluctant to try new ideas if they perceive that something new will require more work or will not provide an immediate payoff. However, experience has shown that these teachers will readily "buy" the model if they have an opportunity to explore it in advance. Even without prior introduction, few cooperating teachers have resisted the model, primarily because the student teacher carries the major responsibility.

As with the range of appetites for learning displayed by in-service teachers (B.R. Joyce & McKibben, 1982), cooperating teachers display varied reactions to initial exposure to the model. Some "omnivores" devour the model readily, immediately valuing their increased knowledge base and their defined roles in the supervision process. Others require some encouragement and closer communication, primarily during the early weeks of the internship. Those who are unwilling to commit to a minimum of two focused observations of the student teacher each week should probably not be selected as cooperating teachers.

Assuming that most cooperating teachers are willing to apply the model, university supervisors can facilitate cooperating teachers' progress by making materials available and communicating with them regularly. It is best, though not essential, that the cooperating teacher own a copy of the handbook. If necessary, the supervisor can lend *The Student Teacher's Handbook for Physical Education* to the cooperating teachers and then collect it at the end of the semester. This textbook, *Systematic Supervision for Physical Education*, can provide more in-depth information for those who desire it.

In addition to making the handbook available, the supervisor must establish and maintain regular communication with the cooperating teacher. It is probably best for the supervisor to meet with the cooperating teacher personally before the beginning of the semester, presenting the handbook and providing a brief explanation of responsibilities. A visit or phone call after the first week or two can verify that the cooperating teacher is using the materials without difficulty and can address any questions that have surfaced. Regular contact throughout the semester can reinforce the application of the model.

Ultimately, the in-service training of cooperating teachers is the optimal approach to preparing them for their roles. This textbook provides a resource for in-depth training. It's possible that the supervisor can develop a systematic supervision cadre, with a network of trained and experienced cooperating teachers who understand and endorse the model. With or without formal training of in-service teachers, the continued use of the model within a given geographic area seems to result in increased understanding. By indirect observation and word of mouth, potential cooperating teachers become familiar with the model and feel more comfortable with its requirements.

Preparing College and University Supervisors

This task might entail training and in-service development of supervisors who are a part of the physical education faculty or of those generic supervisors who have less specialized content preparation. Depending on the circumstances, this preparation will vary in terms of scope and intensity. Regardless of the scenario, it is important that the university supervisor direct and monitor use of the model to ensure that it receives adequate attention.

Training in the Systematic Supervision Model is particularly important for generic supervisors, who may feel uncomfortable observing in a movement setting. For these individuals, tracking teachers down in the locker room, trekking out to the playing field, and watching large classes in a dynamic setting is somewhat overwhelming. Experience has shown that generic supervisors are very receptive to the model, welcoming the content-specific applications of a familiar research base. Indeed, many aspects of effective teaching can readily transfer across content areas. The availability of systematic observation instruments for physical education should help the generic supervisor shift from global impressions to more specific feedback on observable skills.

Supervisors can study the theory of the model by reviewing the knowledge bases for the respective components. Although the handbook provides a brief review, the textbook can supply a more detailed analysis of the research on effective teaching and effective supervision. The college supervisor must also be thoroughly familiar with the instruments contained in the model as well as with the tasks to be completed by the student teacher.

In order to optimally use the model, the college supervisor must understand how to incorporate it into the school visit. The specific components can be incorporated into preconferencing, direct observations, and postobservation conferencing. In addition, the supervisor can monitor the cooperating teacher's participation in the model.

The school visit provides the most important opportunity for the supervisor to optimally use the model. At this time, the college supervisor parallels his or her observations with the focus of the model at a particular stage. For example, a visit conducted during Week 3 would focus on how the student teacher communicates expectations (Component 3) as well as on the use of an established discipline plan (Component 2). The supervisor might use the Component 3 instruments to obtain some objective data, amplifying these observations with anecdotal records, informal analysis, or other data sources. Conversations with the cooperating teacher will address (among other topics) the specific competencies that the student teacher has practiced.

The postobservation conference can then anchor the focus of the components. Following is a typical course of events (after direct observation of teaching): (a) opportunity for the student teacher to reflect on his/her feelings about the lesson; (b) observations by the cooperating teacher about the specific lesson, the student teacher's progress with competencies, and any other general observations; (c) some focused observations from the college supervisor, addressing the student teacher's written assignments and the current teaching episode; and (d) joint goal setting to establish priorities for continued progress.

In reviewing the student's work, the college supervisor may probe specific aspects of the assignment to enhance their practical application. With respect to the focused interview questions of Component 1, the supervisor might ask, ''What have you learned about the socioeconomic composition of the school that will help you plan for teaching?'' Observations should not be limited to the structure of the model. Anecdotal records and informal analysis can tie in very nicely, for the cooperating teacher as well.

The school visits also provide an opportunity for the supervisor to determine if the cooperating teacher is making good use of the model. Some cooperating teachers may initially feel overwhelmed by the bulk of *The Student Teacher's Handbook for Physical Education*. Occasionally, the supervisor may find the book collecting dust during the early weeks of the internship when the structure of the model places more emphasis on the student teacher's observations. Some tactful guidance can help to get the cooperating teacher back on task; the supervisor can suggest a weekly half-hour meeting in which the student teacher and cooperating teacher look over the assignments for the week. The supervisor can also make it clear that the model requires only a few pages of reading and an average of two class periods of directed observation each week.

The Systematic Supervision Model requires flexibility in its implementation. It is not intended to be a lockstep approach that dictates the activities of the student teacher and cooperating teacher. Although its general nature is developmental, student teachers will vary in the rates at which they gain competence. Individual circumstances of the school setting will also require some adaptability. It may be necessary for the supervisor to eliminate some components, substituting alternative strategies or revisiting previous components. For this reason, advance planning and clear communication within the triad will help to prevent roadblocks.

Ensuring Accountability

One important remaining concern is how to ensure the quality of work done on the model so that cursory attention does not compromise its impact. The potential for abuse of the model is great, and this can occur at any level of its implementation. First, it should be recognized that the model is comprehensive. There is a danger that individuals may use fragmented portions of the model or obtain incomplete information about it. While portions of the model could be incorporated into existing practices, Systematic Supervision was designed to be a comprehensive approach.

With respect to monitoring performance, the student teacher's written materials are a key to quality assurance. The written products of the tasks for the student teacher should be reviewed by the college supervisor on a regular (preferably weekly) basis. A delay in the receipt of materials or work that is inaccurate or incomplete will signal the need for immediate intervention. Usually, very little adjustment is required to get the student teacher or cooperating teacher back on task. Again, the bulk of responsibility for carrying out the tasks is placed on the student teacher. The cooperating teacher

is a facilitator in the model, but does not carry out major responsibility.

Seminar Approach and Activities

Some internship programs are carried out in conjunction with a weekly or periodic seminar format. Others are preceded or followed by a block class, which orients the student teacher to particular important concepts or applications. These formats provide unique opportunities for the student teacher to anchor the content in a meaningful and substantive way. The following seminar activities are proposed as a framework for linking the Systematic Supervision Model to student teaching coursework. They can also provide in-service training of cooperating teachers and supervisors.

These activities can augment the regular program of systematic supervision through short, weekly meetings or longer meetings set at periodic intervals. They provide the supervisor an opportunity to reinforce concepts in a group setting, and to facilitate group problem solving. The activities also provide a support system for the student teachers, allowing them to share feedback and strategies that have been successful. The activities suggested are arranged by component, providing

- discussion items;
- questions for review;
- individual, partner, small group, and whole-group practice activities; and
- closure.

The knowledge base for each component provides a natural base for discussion. Tasks for the student teacher can also be reviewed for clarification or to synthesize what has been learned. The observation instruments provide data for analysis or a method for group analysis of videotapes or audiotapes.

Component 1: Using Guided Observation and Inquiry

Discussion

Ask the student teachers to share their observations from this component. You might begin with the interview of the cooperating teacher, listing on a blackboard some of the responses the student teachers obtained. After several student teachers have reported, try to analyze some common trends.

Repeat this procedure, this time focusing on the interview of the school counselor or administrator.

Questions

1. How would you describe the diversity of the socioeconomic groups represented in your schools? Specifically, how will that information be useful to you in planning and implementing instruction?

2. What other factors affect the school environment? Why are these important?

3. How does your philosophy of discipline match those of your cooperating teacher and the counselor or administrator that you interviewed? If there are differences, how will you reconcile them?

4. What kinds of serious disciplinary problems might occur, and how will they be handled?

5. Do you feel adequately informed of the disciplinary policies that are established in the district, school, and department?

Partner or Small-Group Activity

Ask student teachers to go over the data obtained from their cooperating teachers with the form entitled Communicating Expectations: Systematic Observation of Teacher Verbal Behavior. Have them examine the nature of expectations communicated, as well as the ratios of positive to corrective and general to specific feedback statements.

Closure

Summarize with general guidelines for clear communication of expectations, and emphasize the importance of providing positive and specific feedback related to student conduct. The goal here is to emphasize clarity and consistency in letting students know what is expected.

Component 2: Establishing a Discipline Plan

Discussion

This is an opportunity to expand upon the concepts of assertive discipline, its rationale, and the mechanics for its application. It is also useful to review the discipline plans that the student teachers have developed, noting similarities and differences within the group and planning for the smooth implementation of plans. Chapter 7 provides some general principles of effective discipline that the group can discuss.

Questions

1. Is an established discipline plan (e.g., Assertive Discipline) used consistently throughout the city or county where you are teaching? If so, what levels of plans (e.g., schoolwide or departmental) are in place? How does your plan fit into what exists? If no uniform plan exists, what other models or policies are used?

2. What desirable behaviors are you looking for? (List some of these and discuss prioritization.)

3. What undesirable behaviors do you seek to prevent? (List some of these also, and prioritize.)

4. What kinds of severe disciplinary problems might occur, and how can you avoid them? What will be the consequences for these behaviors?

5. What kinds of individual and group rewards would be reinforcing for students at given grade levels (primary, intermediate, middle school, high school)? Brainstorm a list of these.

Small-Group Activity

Student teachers will present their discipline plans and discuss their progress to date at implementing the plans. They might also discuss some of their concerns about general disciplinary issues that might arise.

Closure

Review the concepts of Assertive Discipline and select one sample disciplinary plan to summarize. If an alternative model has been used, discuss the similarities and differences of that plan.

Additional Resources

These resources are available from Canter & Canter Associates, P.O. Box 2113, Dept. MK, Santa Monica, CA 90406:

- Assertive Discipline Teacher Kit—contains text, resource materials, workbook, follow-up guide, plan book, audio cassettes, poster-size visual, teacher guide)
- Assertive Discipline Phase I Media Package—film, video, or filmstrip (rentals available)
- Assertive Discipline Phase II Media Package (Practical Applications and Advanced Classroom Techniques)
- Positive Reinforcement Activities (elementary and secondary versions)

A large variety of other resources are also available from Canter & Canter Associates.

Component 3: Communicating Expectations/Reinforcing Desired Behaviors

Discussion

After the student teachers are observed for this competency, use the data from the instruments to focus the discussion. Look at some of the expectations for student conduct that the student teachers communicated. Examine the relative proportions of positive to corrective and general to specific feedback statements. Reinforce the goal of providing clear directions and giving high rates of positive and specific feedback.

Questions

1. Did you feel successful in communicating your expectations? What were some of them? Did the students seem to understand?

2. How did the students respond to your directions? Were they primarily on-task or off-task? (Discuss some strategies for dealing with specific problems that might have occurred.)

3. Did you find that you provided enough positive feedback related to the behavior of students? Was it specific or general in nature? How will you try to modify this behavior?

Whole-Group Activities

Role Playing

1. Ask the student teachers to take turns giving their beginning-of-class directions. The participants will observe and give feedback regarding the clarity and precision of those

instructions and the manner in which the student teacher delivers them.

2. Have the student teachers role play situations in which a student persists at off-task behavior and the teacher uses the broken record technique (Chapter 7).

Analysis of Videotape

Select some segments of previously videotaped teaching episodes that included the beginning directions, and provide an opportunity for the student teachers to code feedback.

Additional Resources

Chapter 7 summarizes basic principles to help the teacher preserve a positive classroom climate while enforcing rules. Also included in the chapter are a checklist for the effective use of verbal reprimands and a list of nonverbal body cues and their meanings.

Closure

Emphasize the importance of verbal and nonverbal cues in communicating expectations and reinforcing desired behaviors. Summarize the basic principles for maintaining a positive climate while enforcing rules.

Component 4: Improving Classroom Management

Discussion

Topics might include identification of class routines (e.g., taking roll, organizing groups, or distributing equipment) and ways for student teachers to systematize and expedite these routines. The student teachers may share some of their specific plans and strategies and analyze their own success in reducing management time.

Questions

1. What are some of the class routines that are a part of each day's management activities? How much time do they ordinarily take?

2. What are some ways that you could try to reduce the amount of time spent in management activities (e.g., taking roll)?

3. What are some unpredictable environmental circumstances that might require you to

change your routines (e.g., inclement weather or scheduling changes)? How will you prepare to cope with these when they occur?

Partner Activity

Have student teachers work in pairs to refine and expand upon their own plans for improving classroom management.

Closure

Have the student teachers identify one problem area related to classroom management and take 1 minute to write down a goal for improving that situation. At a later date, follow up by determining whether goals were achieved.

Component 5: Establishing a Positive Classroom Climate

Discussion

Examine the factors that determine the nature of the classroom climate (quality of teacher–student, student–teacher, and student–student interactions). Try to identify sources of inequity that might occur. Emphasize the importance of maintaining a positive classroom climate for enhancing student motivation.

Questions

1. If you were an observer in a physical education class, what cues would help you evaluate the quality of the classroom climate? What are some observable behaviors that you would look for?

2. How will you respond to the students in order to ensure equity (boys vs. girls, athletes vs. nonathletes, attractive vs. unattractive students, racial and ethnic groups)?

3. What kinds of inequitable practices have you previously observed in physical education classes?

Whole-Group Activity

Have student teachers analyze an audiotape or videotape of teacher behavior, using the form entitled Observation of Classroom Climate. Discuss the presence or absence of indicators of a positive or negative classroom climate. Discuss recommendations for improving the lesson from this perspective.

Closure

Summarize the indicators of a positive classroom climate. Encourage the student teachers to continue to learn the names of students as quickly as possible. Suggest that student teachers try to positively reinforce each student on a regular basis.

Component 6: Developing Performance Objectives

Discussion

You cannot overemphasize this competency, and it is helpful to work through some specific examples. Student teachers still may not understand the concept of observable behaviors. Distinguish between *being* words and *doing* words, and list as many as the student teachers can identify. Discuss the scope of possibilities for determining criteria for evaluation.

Questions

1. What are three essential questions that teachers must ask in planning?

2. What is the difference between a performance objective and a process (instructional) objective?

3. What are three components of a performance objective? Can you give an example of each?

4. What are some *doing* words that you can use in performance objectives? What are some *being* words that do not involve observable behaviors?

5. What are some of the advantages of using performance objectives?

Partner Activity

Have student teachers pair up and use the planning form entitled Developing Performance Objectives to practice developing objectives in three domains. Then, have the student teachers find new partners; the pairs then determine whether the objectives developed meet the defined characteristics of performance objectives.

Whole-Group Activity

Select a videotape taken previously of one of the student teachers. Go through the process of stimulated recall, helping the students determine relationships between preactive planning decisions and interactive teaching decisions. Discuss strategies for modifying the lesson for optimal achievement of objectives.

Closure

Review the concept of stimulated recall and how it can help teachers better understand their teaching. Emphasize the need to continue to develop performance objectives (both enabling and terminal).

Component 7: Incorporating Mechanical Analysis and Teaching Cues

Discussion

Probe the student teachers' understanding of the use of mechanical analysis and its importance in effective instruction. Ask them to identify skills that they feel competent in analyzing. Then, have them briefly identify the correct mechanics of the selected skill. Discuss how mechanical analysis and teaching cues can enhance the clarity of instructions, the accuracy of demonstrations, the specificity of feedback, and the ability of students to self-teach. Ask the student teachers to identify some resources that they might use in conducting mechanical analysis. For example, how could they analyze a golf swing if they were not competent in that area?

Questions

1. Why is it important to conduct skill analysis prior to planning lessons for skill acquisition? How will it benefit your teaching?
2. Let's consider a specific skill, for example, overhand throwing. What are the mechanics of a mature pattern for overhand throwing?
3. How would you utilize the process of mechanical analysis for developing skills in young children? In skilled athletes?
4. How would the process differ for planning a lesson for a movement education (divergent) teaching approach?
5. What are teaching cues? Give me some examples. Why are teaching cues important to effective teaching in physical education?

Small-Group Activity

Assign a specific sport skill to each group. Have them first go through the process of skill analysis, identifying the mechanics of correct performance.

Then, try to identify as many teaching cues as possible.

Whole-Group Activities

Have the class observe and analyze a selected videotape to look at teaching cues, mechanics, and skill performance. Have the class examine the relationships between the process of skill analysis and the in-class behaviors of the teacher and the students.

Select a sport skill area (e.g., tennis), and direct the class to brainstorm a list of teaching cues that teachers can use.

Closure

Review Lesson Plan Format A and discuss its implications in promoting skill analysis and the use of teaching skills. Identify situations in which it would be appropriate or inappropriate to use this or a similar format.

Component 8: Selecting Activities at an Appropriate Level of Difficulty

Discussion

Use the analogy of the slanted rope versus the horizontal rope to introduce the concept of inclusion (Mosston & Ashworth, 1986). Have the class consider what would happen if a teacher held a horizontal rope 2 feet off the ground and asked all of the students to jump over at that height. Some of the children would be eliminated from the activity immediately, being unable to clear the rope at that height. Others would be bored and unchallenged, wanting to raise the height to test their own abilities. Now, have the class consider what would happen if the rope was slanted, allowing students to select their own entry level and to be appropriately challenged. Distinguish between exclusion and inclusion, and ask the student teachers to identify some activity modifications that will allow all children to be successful within a given lesson.

Questions

1. What does the concept of inclusion mean in relation to teaching in physical education? In contrast, what does exclusion entail?
2. What are some traditional activities or teaching approaches that promote exclusion? What are some better examples of facilitating inclusion?

3. Consider a specific activity (e.g., volleyball). What factors relative to this activity could you alter to modify the level of difficulty?

Partner or Small-Group Activity

Direct the student teachers to use Mosston and Ashworth's Factor Grid for Inclusion Style of Teaching to identify difficulty factors of designated skills. The student teachers will then plan a series of tasks that will allow students to select their own entry levels, and to be successful at their own levels of skill.

Whole-Group Activity

Student teachers will observe a videotape showing the use of the inclusion style of teaching. Use the form entitled Event Recording of Student Skill Attempts to determine if students were successful.

Closure

Student teachers will use the data from the instrument as a way of synthesizing the goals and processes of inclusion. They will compare the data from the skilled and unskilled student to determine if both were successful.

Component 9: Maximizing Time on Task

Discussion

Guide the student teachers through a typical scenario illustrating how the funnel effect is manifested. For example, the average duration for a secondary level class (allocated time) is approximately 50 minutes. Consider how much of that time might actually be devoted to physical education content, to movement activity, and to time on task with success (ALT-PE). Ask the student teachers to guess what might be an average percent of ALT-PE provided in an elementary or secondary level physical education class. Encourage the student teachers to think of ways to modify traditional activities or design new activities to increase student time-on-task rates and opportunities for success.

Questions

1. Think of the average elementary (or secondary) level physical education class. What do you think the percent of academic learning time typically amounts to? Are physical educators in general sufficiently aware of the need to increase academic learning time?

2. What are some traditional activities that lend themselves to a typically low rate of time on task? What specific ways could we modify those activities to increase time on task?

3. What are three important components of academic learning time? (Define allocated time, student engagement, and student success rate.)

Whole-Group Activities

Select a videotape that focuses on an individual student for a period of time. Have student teachers use stopwatches to practice the technique for duration recording of student time on task.

Use a videotape that focuses on teacher behavior throughout a short lesson, and have the class use the instrument entitled Systematic Observation of Time Management to record time spent in cognitive, management, and motor activity.

Closure

Have the class compare the graphs for the data obtained in the second observation. Help the students identify some specific changes that could improve time management in the desired direction.

Component 10: Evaluating Lesson Effectiveness

Discussion

Lead the class in brainstorming some criteria that might be used to evaluate lesson effectiveness. Ask the student teachers to share some positive and negative feelings they have had about the effectiveness of their own lessons to date. What kind of intuitive feelings did they have about the success of lessons? Now, explore group time sampling as a technique for evaluating the effectiveness of lessons. Discuss how scanning can be a useful tool for helping the teacher gain awareness and increased vigilance of student behaviors.

Questions

1. What are some criteria that you could use to determine the effectiveness of a lesson?

2. What kinds of student behaviors lend them-

selves to the technique of group time sampling?

3. Specifically, what is a placheck (planned activity check) and how would you conduct one?

Whole-Group Activity

The best way for the student teachers to practice the placheck method is to do live coding, using the instrument entitled Planned Activity Check for Evaluating Lesson Effectiveness. If this cannot be arranged, have student teachers observe a video-taped class to identify elements of the lesson that the teacher could restructure to increase lesson effectiveness.

Closure

Reinforce the importance of vigilance; teachers must be aware of student behavior, maintain "with-it-ness," and monitor the general effectiveness of the lesson.

Component 11: Providing Appropriate Feedback

Discussion

Identify the characteristics of teacher augmented feedback that can be manipulated in an instructional setting. Determine whether student teachers can distinguish between general and specific; positive, corrective, and negative; and congruent and incongruent feedback statements. Ask student teachers to provide some examples of each of the given categories. Discuss how teachers can consider factors of age and developmental level to apply feedback appropriately.

Questions

1. What kinds of feedback are available to the learner when practicing a motor skill? How might these feedback sources be categorized?

2. What is the teacher's role in providing augmented verbal feedback to the learner?

3. How will the skill level of the performer affect the kind of feedback that you provide?

4. How will the developmental (cognitive) level of the performer affect the kind of feedback that you provide?

Whole-Group Activity

Have the student teachers use an audiotape or videotape of teacher verbal behavior to code skill feedback given within a lesson. Help them analyze the proportions of positive to corrective and general to specific feedback statements. Also, direct the student teachers in computing the total number of feedback statements given and the rate per minute of feedback statements overall. Lead the student teachers in discussing implications for improving the lesson that they coded.

Closure

Conduct a review for the student teachers of the general principles for providing effective feedback, as identified in Chapter 4.

Component 12: Using Techniques for Effective Demonstration

Discussion

Present the guidelines that are synthesized on the instrument entitled Checklist of Criteria of an Effective Demonstration. Discuss the importance of each of the criteria and how they might be manifested in a demonstration. Ask the student teachers to envision and describe what an effective demonstration might look like and what an ineffective demonstration might look like. Remind student teachers of the overall purpose of a demonstration: conveying information to learners in a manner that is brief, clear, and concise.

Whole-Group Activity

With advance planning, student teachers can present a mock demonstration to the group. You may wish to videotape this for future analysis. During the demonstration, peers may evaluate effectiveness using the defined criteria.

Closure

Explain how the effectiveness of demonstrations relates to skill analysis and comprehensive written plans. Advance planning should greatly enhance the quality of the demonstration.

Component 13: Developing Lesson Presentation Skills

Discussion

Present a short demonstration lesson incorporating the concepts of set induction, pacing, structuring, and closure. The lesson can also model the use of a variety of sensing modalities (auditory, visual, and kinesthetic) and active participation. Then, ask the student teachers to discuss how you demonstrated the elements of effective lesson presentation. The discussion can expand upon these concepts, addressing additional aspects of lesson clarity and methods of evaluation.

Questions

1. What are some of the purposes of set induction or anticipatory set?
2. Give an example of how you may use set induction to introduce a lesson.
3. What are some factors that will influence the pacing of your presentation?
4. What is meant by the term *structuring*? Give some examples.
5. What are some ways that you can enhance lesson presentation by involving auditory, visual, and kinesthetic learning modalities?
6. What is the purpose of closure in the lesson? How may you use closure in a classroom setting? In a movement setting?

Small-Group Activity

Have the groups use Lesson Plan Format C to construct a hypothetical lesson for classroom teaching. Specifically, the groups should address the elements of set induction, explanation, examples and illustrations, questions, and closure.

Whole-Group Activity

Have the class review a videotaped lesson that involves presentation of cognitive content. Student teachers will use the form entitled Observation of Lesson Clarity (or the alternate) to evaluate for specified criteria.

Closure

Have the group share some ideas developed in the hypothetical lessons.

Component 14: Enhancing Questioning Skills

Discussion

Discuss the appropriate use of high- and low-order questions for teaching in classroom and movement settings. Emphasize the importance of planning questions in advance of teaching. Review Bloom's taxonomy with respect to the development of questions at six levels. Discuss how the characteristics of the learners and the objectives of the lesson will influence the kinds of questions the teacher should incorporate. Reinforce other aspects of effective questioning, including provision of wait time, use of probing or reinforcing behaviors, and ensuring equity of responses.

Questions

1. How would you distinguish between a low-order and a high-order question?
2. Under what circumstances are low-order questions desirable?
3. As a general rule, how much wait time should you provide once you have asked a question?
4. How are student responses enhanced by the provision of wait time?
5. Give some examples of probing or reinforcing behaviors that you could use to help students amplify or extend their repsonses.

Small-Group Activity

Give the groups definitions of the levels of the taxonomy and sample questions that you have developed for each level. Then have student teachers generate additional sample questions that promote low-order and high-order thinking.

Whole-Group Activity

Using the form Systematic Observation of Questioning Skills, student teachers record and classify questions occurring in audiotaped or videotaped lesson segments.

Closure

Based on the data student teachers collect during the whole-group activity, discuss the nature of questions recorded in relation to the lesson objectives and the characteristics of the learners. Point out the kinds of probing and reinforcing behaviors that were used and the effect that they had on student responses. Also, discuss the extent to which wait time was provided, and consider whether equitable opportunities for responses were facilitated.

Component 15: Assessing Student Performance

Discussion

Emphasize the distinction between process and product measures of student skill acquisition. The sample process measures in the handbook provide a good basis for this discussion. Provide the class hands-on practice in applying the criteria, which will help to anchor the concepts and their applications.

Questions

1. What is the basic difference between process and product measures of skill performance?

2. How can you use a process measure to assess fundamental motor skills of young children?

3. How can you incorporate a process measure to assess performance of the tennis serve?

4. What might a product measure of the tennis serve include?

5. What are some of the distinct advantages of process measures of skill performance?

Whole-Group Activity

Have the group practice using selected process measures by analyzing videotapes (with slow motion and stop action if possible) or slides. Or, have student teachers simulate various levels of skill proficiency (e.g., immature/mature throwing or catching) while others observe and apply the process measures.

Additional Resources

The Michigan State Board of Education has published *Essential Performance Objectives for Physical Education*, which contains a variety of process and product measures for fundamental motor skills, object control skills, body management skills, and physical fitness. The process measures for this

battery can be very useful in this component. AAHPERD's *Strategies, A Journal for Physical and Sport Educators*, also contains skill analyses of fundamental and specialized sport skills.

Closure

Reiterate the distinctions between process and product measures of skill performance, and support the rationale for the use of process measures. Discuss the implications of using process measures as a way of reporting progress to parents (perhaps in place of letter grades) in elementary school.

General Guidelines for Effective Supervision

Regardless of the model used, a number of general guidelines can enhance supervision. These guidelines are presented here within the functions of student teacher supervision and basic priniciples of supervisory effectiveness. They are not necessarily empirically based but rather are derived from practical experience and logical interpretation. When considered in combination with a systematic model, they should help the supervisor to provide a quality experience for the teachers concerned.

Selection and Preparation of Cooperating Teachers

One of the most critical aspects of student teacher supervision involves the identification of cooperating teachers and the placement of interns. This process must be supported through in-service training, development of ongoing relations, and recognition for those cooperating teachers who make significant contributions. The university supervisor, cooperating teacher, and student teacher must work to establish clear communication. These efforts should pay off for all involved.

Finding cooperating teachers who are committed to the process requires time and care. When this selection is left to random choice or the option of a principal or department head, a student teacher might fall under the supervision of a cooperating teacher who simply "should have a turn" or has earned some release time. Supervisors should especially avoid placing student teachers with cooperating teachers who are coaching in their major seasons. Although there are exceptions, this arrangement poses serious potential for conflict of time and commitment.

In general, the cooperating teacher should provide a positive role model in teaching. It's best if the cooperating teacher emphasizes teaching first and coaching second, as demonstrated by the development of meaningful learning experiences for students. The cooperating teacher can either strongly reinforce or quickly undermine the practices endorsed in undergraduate training. Therefore, she or he should support the importance of planning and implementing substantive lessons.

In order to ensure mutual understanding, the supervisor and cooperating teacher should communicate in advance of the internship. One effective method is a written contract that spells out the roles and responsibilities of the cooperating teacher. These might include provisions for a gradual induction into teaching, adequate time for conferencing and joint planning, close monitoring and supervision, ongoing evaluation and feedback, and consistent support in the process of learning to teach.

Verbal contact between supervisor and cooperating teacher throughout the semester is another important element of communication. This can include periodic phone calls or face-to-face contact. These interactions can ensure that the cooperating teacher understands and observes the written contract. Often, minor concerns and questions can be addressed before a potential major obstacle arises.

Another effective communication technique is for the university supervisor to send a letter of introduction to the cooperating teacher. This is one way for the supervisor to dispel the ivory tower image, emphasizing a desire to stay grounded in the realities of teaching and briefly reviewing the nature of one's professional background in public school teaching. This may also help to reduce the potential defensiveness of cooperating teachers who feel that the university supervisor does not understand the real world of public schools. Periodic written communication throughout the term can support mutual understanding and highlight specific functions of supervision from a developmental perspective.

At the conclusion of the student teaching experience, it is essential that the supervisor acknowledge the efforts of those cooperating teachers and other school personnel who provided a valuable service. Although the university will provide tangible rewards, some intangible incentives and recognition will be intrinsically motivating. Letters of recognition can identify specific skills and efforts that the cooperating teacher demonstrated. As a good means of public relations, the supervisor can send these letters to the superintendent or physical education coordinator, with copies directed to the principal and the individual teacher. This investment of time can enhance future working relationships within the school district.

Basic Principles of Effective Supervision

These guidelines are proposed in a general sense and do not apply strictly to the Systematic Supervision Model. They relate first to the overall functions of observing and conferencing. In addition, they address some basic factors related to supervision that can either facilitate or hinder the process. They are intended to augment the effectiveness of supervision and to help supervisors avoid some of the potential pitfalls.

Observation Strategies

Although the Systematic Supervision Model uses observation instruments, the process can easily be augmented by informal or subjective assessments. Supervisors can use anecdotal records to provide feedback related to a wide variety of teaching functions, including planning, implementation, and evaluation. In addition, supervisors can use checklists and rating scales to supplement observation, recognizing that these measures are subjective in nature. Targeted observations based on observable and measurable criteria of effective teaching, as assessed through systematic observation, will be the primary focus of the observations. Thus, the components of the Systematic Supervision Model provide a framework, and the supervisor can observe with a specific plan in mind.

In order to yield useful data, the observation must provide sufficient time for the supervisor to get a clear view of the teaching situation. Brief observations will provide only a snapshot of the performance and will likely lead to incomplete information and false assumptions. The supervisor should confer with the student teacher before the observation, discussing the focus of the observation and getting some information about the purpose of the lesson. If possible, the supervisor should secure a lesson plan to examine before and/or during the observation.

In the case of student teacher observations, it is helpful for the supervisor to observe with the cooperating teacher. The two observers may work simultaneously with the same instrument and compare data or may look at different target behaviors with different instruments. Another effective strategy is to allow student teachers to observe their peers, using systematic observation instruments to collect objective data. Often, student teachers are less threatened by feedback offered by their peers, and they may feel more comfortable in providing frank appraisals of each other.

Although the focus of the observation is planned, there may be occasions when it is appropriate to scrap the plan and focus on another aspect of teaching. It is fairly useless to assess time on task, for instance, if the teacher is having serious discipline problems. In some cases, the supervisor may abandon the systematic observation instrument in favor of anecdotal records in trying to capture a description of events. A teacher who is discouraged or upset following an observation may benefit more from emotional support and encouragement than from percentages or totals of observed behaviors. The key is to plan yet be adaptable.

Conferencing Strategies

The postobservation conference, or "postmortem," is essential for providing supervisory feedback immediately after the observation. Teachers will experience unnecessary stress if they are left in suspense about the supervisor's evaluations for an extended period of time. In addition, the discussion of incidents will have more relevance immediately after observation than several days following.

In conducting the conference, the supervisor should begin in a nondirective style, asking the teacher to reflect on how things went or to analyze how the lesson progressed with respect to what was planned. The supervisor can respond and react to the points raised by the teacher and tie in aspects of the planned observation. In the case of student teaching, the supervisor can encourage involvement from the cooperating teacher by asking him or her to provide initial input. Ultimately, analysis of the data obtained through systematic supervision will provide a focused look at one or two target behaviors. The instruments of systematic supervision can provide graphic presentation of data to further enhance application of effective teaching skills.

As a general rule, the supervisor should begin with the positive feedback and save the corrective feedback for last. By launching into a discourse of errors and omissions, the supervisor will raise the defenses of the teacher and reduce the chance for acceptance of ideas. Some teachers will inevitably be defensive when confronted with their own shortcomings, despite the supervisor's best efforts to be positive. The supervisor should distinguish constructive criticism of teaching behaviors from criticism of the teacher as an individual. The notion of unconditional positive regard is important in maintaining good human relations.

In conducting the conference, the supervisor can use a variety of interpersonal skills to promote desired interactions. Glickman (1985) identified 10 categories of supervisory behaviors, as follows:

Listening—The supervisor looks at the teacher and nods his or her head to show understanding. Gutteral utterances ("uh-huh" or "umm...") also indicate listening.

Clarifying—The supervisor asks questions and provides statements to clarify the student teacher's point of view.

Encouraging—The supervisor provides acknowledgment responses that help the student teacher continue to explain his or her position.

Reflecting—The supervisor summarizes and paraphrases the student teacher's message for verification of accuracy.

Presenting—The supervisor discusses his or her own ideas about the issue.

Problem solving—The supervisor, usually after a preliminary discussion of the issue or problem, presses the teacher to generate a list of possible solutions.

Negotiating—The supervisor moves the discussion from possible to probable solutions by discussing the consequences of each proposed action, exploring conflict or priorities, and narrowing down choices with questions.

Directing—The supervisor tells the teacher what to do.

Standardizing—The supervisor sets the expected criteria and time for the decision to be implemented. The supervisor sets target objectives and conveys expectations.

Reinforcing—The supervisor strengthens the directive and the criteria to be met by explaining possible consequences.

Depending on the circumstances, the supervisor will use varying combinations of the categorized behavior to establish the appropriate climate. A nondirective interpersonal approach emphasizes listening, clarifying, encouraging, and reflecting. The supervisor's role in that climate is primarily one of facilitator, and the teacher is clearly in control of the decision-making process. In a collaborative interpersonal approach, the supervisor applies presenting, problem solving, and negotiating skills. The goal with this approach is to promote shared decision making and to find a solution that is acceptable to everyone involved. A third pattern of behaviors, the directive interpersonal approach, involves supervisory behaviors of directing, standardizing, and reinforcing. With this approach, the supervisor subsumes all of the responsibility for decision making.

In concluding the postobservation conference, the supervisor should provide the teacher with some form of written feedback to document the points discussed. These may include both observation instruments and anecdotal records, and both objective and subjective observations. Of course, the primary focus will be on concrete and observable elements of effective teaching.

Facilitory and Nonfacilitory Factors

A number of factors can either facilitate or inhibit effective supervision. The supervisor can directly control some of these, whereas others require commitment and support from the institution. The factors described here are related to staffing and delivery aspects of effective supervision.

Descriptions of current practice show that many supervisors are inadequately prepared for their responsibilities. These supervisors often lack extensive public school teaching backgrounds and may have little or no formal training in supervision. In colleges and universities, the role of supervision may fall onto the shoulders of older faculty members who have lost enthusiasm for the classroom. In other cases, this responsibility is carried by junior faculty members who are expected to carry heavy supervision loads, teach several classes, and publish scholarly research. The impact of supervision, therefore, depends largely on the priorities given for institutional funding and staffing.

Another obstacle to effective supervision is a general failure by the university to recognize the importance of this function. Supervision of student teachers, while meeting a critical need, is carried out away from the campus and out of the view of the other faculty members. Many colleagues fail

to recognize the amount of time and commitment that is required for this process. Worse, excellence in supervision yields little tangible benefit in terms of gaining tenure, promotion, or merit and discretionary raises.

Effective supervision depends on sufficient time and training for the personnel involved. It also requires skill in human relations, specialized technical knowledge in pedagogy, a substantive background in public school teaching, and managerial skill. The effective supervisor demonstrates a blend of businesslike objectivity and demandingness, as well as empathy and flexibility. The overall goal of improved instruction, as facilitated through supervision, is best achieved in a spirit of collaboration, cooperation, and collegiality.

Summary and Implications

Several years of piloting have shown that the Systematic Supervision Model can be effectively implemented with student teachers. This experience has indicated that both student teachers and cooperating teachers favor a planned and comprehensive model of supervision. In particular, they appreciate the clarity that is facilitated when everyone knows what is expected of him or her.

Although the benefits of the Systematic Supervision Model can be great, we should note some inherent dangers and potential abuses of the model. First, the model is designed for implementation as a comprehensive approach. Individuals may become aware of fragmented parts of the model and may attempt to use isolated instruments or strategies. Although this approach can augment an existing model, the instruments and strategies are not intended to stand alone.

A second potential pitfall for the Systematic Supervision Model is failure by the supervisor to provide close communication with and monitoring for both student teachers and cooperating teachers. Although the model is quite self-explanatory, it is important that the supervisor ensure a measure of accountability for both student teachers and cooperating teachers. To the same end, the university supervisor must link his or her observations and feedback to the components of the model.

One additional understanding is essential to the adoption of the Systematic Supervision Model. The model is intended to provide formative feedback as it guides the intern or beginning teacher through the process of induction. Similarly, it can be used by in-service teachers or their supervisors to provide ongoing feedback and support in the attainment of specific teaching skills. Therefore, the data obtained through use of the various instruments should develop awareness and facilitate improved instruction. The model is not intended to be used in a prescriptive, summative, or evaluative manner, because it is impossible to completely quantify effective teaching. The Systematic Supervision Model can highlight and reinforce the scientific principles of effective teaching through formative feedback. Through the process of completing the developmental tasks, the student teacher will acquire the art of applying these principles appropriately.

Chapter 11

Beyond Student Teaching: Research Implications for Effective In-Service Applications

The preceding chapters lay the research foundation and describe the structure of the Systematic Supervision Model. Although training student teachers is the primary purpose of the model, other applications may involve induction of beginning teachers or in-service development for experienced teachers. The material in the model (knowledge bases, tasks, and observation/evaluation tools) can provide a structure for in-service programs. Such programs can also derive some general guidelines for effectiveness from the literature. The following sections review essential characteristics, elements, and processes of effective in-service programs. A summary of lessons from research describes the findings from a group of related studies.

Characteristics of In-Service Programs

In-service programs, frequently referred to as staff development, can make positive and lasting con-

tributions to the quality of school environments, teacher effectiveness, and student learning. Staff development enhances the climate and effectiveness of the school through the development of collegial norms and common goals. The goals of such programs, as related to teacher outcomes, include enhancing knowledge and performance; developing a shared understanding of rationale and purposes (Fullan, 1982); providing a source of support and renewal; and increasing job satisfaction. By expanding their repertoire of skills, teachers become more aware of curricular and instructional alternatives. Ultimately, improvements in teacher knowledge and performance and overall school climate will yield substantial gains in student learning. In turn, overall school improvements will enhance the public esteem of education as an institution.

Functions of Staff Development

By participating in comprehensive staff development programs, teachers increase job satisfaction through renewed knowledge and skills, support of peers and administrators, and evidence of improvements in teaching. One major factor in increased job satisfaction is the reduction of isolation that results naturally from the cellular nature of schools (Lortie, 1975). Teachers have historically been isolated from interactions with peers by the physical constraints of separate classrooms and organizational patterns that discourage exchanges of ideas. The ecology of the school in total provides few opportunities for collective teacher planning or professional dialogue (B.R. Joyce & Showers, 1983). One study of a New York high school showed that teachers engaged in only about 2 minutes of professional dialogue per day (DeSanctis & Blumberg, 1979).

Metzdorf (1989) identified three roles of staff development: a curriculum function, a teaching strategies/instruction function, and a quality of work life function. These functions comprise a broad perspective of responsibility, and no program can consider them simultaneously. Curriculum functions encompass the planning, implementation, and evaluation of all curriculum development projects. Teaching strategies or instruction programs include efforts ''to help teachers and administrators expand their repertoire of teaching and classroom management strategies'' (Metzdorf, 1989, p. 21). Quality of work life entails the development of leadership and consulting skills.

Teachers as individuals will vary considerably in terms of their conceptual levels, degrees of motivation, professional training, personal growth states, and personalities. Yet, research on staff development shows that virtually all teachers can learn, provided they are given opportunities to participate in high-quality in-service programs (B.R. Joyce & Showers, 1983). In-service planners should not discount anyone from this goal and should attempt to meet teachers ''where they are'' in terms of readiness to learn. Despite this potential, research does not filter down into the schools, and a large body of literature remains relatively unknown to practitioners.

Obstacles to Effective In-Service Programs

In-service programs all too often fail to impact the ecology of schools in any substantial and lasting way. In general, in-service programs fail because they lack comprehensive and long-term planning, implementation, and evaluation. They fall prey to a variety of obstacles, including undefined goals,

lack of incentive, insufficient resources and materials, failure to seek input, lack of follow-through, and barriers to effective communication.

Undefined goals are a frequent shortcoming of in-service programs, particularly in physical education. In-service programs are often planned by curriculum or staff development specialists who lack specialized training in physical education. These individuals may fail to include physical education in their comprehensive staff development planning, or they may plan random and haphazard workshops without the advice of content specialists and physical education teachers. These efforts will lack direction and purpose and will produce little substantial impact. Worse, they tend to discourage physical education specialists from participation in staff development. It is essential that in-service coordinators conduct needs assessments of specific skills and knowledge that physical educators wish to address.

Lack of incentive is a second common obstacle to effective in-service programs. Planners of programs cannot assume that all teachers are intrinsically motivated to engage in professional development. As noted previously, a variety of personal and professional factors are salient here. In addition, most experienced teachers have been exposed to an abundance of poorly planned and cursory in-service efforts that do not adequately distinguish innovation from meaningful change. To buy into change requires teachers to invest time and energy, which may not seem warranted in terms of past experiences.

Program planners can use a variety of incentives to encourage in-service participation. Material rewards such as salary, promotion, merit pay, and college credit or in-service points are the most obvious. However, support and recognition will likely be more potent sources of motivation for teachers. Administrators can recognize in-service efforts through a variety of channels; they can acknowledge efforts to peers, provide for media attention, support publication of scholarly articles and presentation of reports, provide release time, and allow attendance at professional conferences.

Productive in-service programs must be backed up with sufficient resources and materials for implementing innovations. This means that administrators must be convinced of the value of the innovation and the abilities of those involved to carry it out. For example, adoption of a new curriculum requires sufficient equipment for teaching the new skills and activities. It may also require reductions in class sizes, revisions in schedules, or other economic considerations, such as provision of consultants, release time, and substitute teachers. However, to receive this level of support, physical educators must establish credibility by doing the best possible with existing resources (i.e., by teaching responsibly).

Failure to seek input is a potential pitfall faced by those who conduct in-service. B.R. Joyce and Showers (1988) used the term "participatory governance" to describe this process of determining perceived needs and interests. This solicitation of input helps respondents feel a sense of ownership and commitment to the goals of the resultant in-service program. Failure to seek input is particularly a problem of university personnel, who often integrate preconceived notions without observing the context of the environment.

Inadequate follow-through, or the "down-and dirty" workshop, is another frequent problem of in-service programs. The average public school teacher in the United States spends about 3 days per year in in-service programs, which often consist of dull and uninspired speeches and focus on isolated skills (B.R. Joyce & Showers, 1988). Following the workshop, virtually no application of the proposed knowledge and skills is evidenced, although some teachers might make sincere but unsupported efforts to implement suggested changes. Quickly, teachers reject these innovations along with other espoused theories as impractical or unworkable.

Barriers to communication comprise the last but still important obstacle to effective in-service programs. One common communication barrier is that of "dragging anchors," when teachers cling to old clichés and excuses about why certain techniques won't work. "My classes are too large to do that," or "I don't have enough equipment" are two rationalizations frequently heard in in-service programs. Yet, those excuses perpetuate the cycle of helplessness to which many teachers resign themselves. In turn, administrative support remains low and the likelihood of evoking positive changes remains slim.

Stereotypes of those who deliver in-service programs, particularly college and university personnel, can also limit the effectiveness of staff development programs. "He is speaking from an ivory tower," or "What does she know about the real world?" are limiting thoughts that prevent teachers from viewing innovations with open-mindedness. Similarly, administrators, staff development specialists, and consultants may have preconceived ideas about the abilities and willingness of public schools teachers to learn. These stereotypes are also limiting and unfair and

will certainly diminish the benefits of in-service programs.

Lastly, displaced frustrations can weaken in-service efforts when teachers and staff development specialists fail to communicate effectively. Having experienced many ineffectual and poorly coordinated in-service workshops, and feeling frustrated about the conditions of the work environment, teachers may vent their feelings inappropriately on the unsuspecting and undeserving consultant. Or, the opposite reaction may occur; consultants may react aggressively to the well-intentioned questions and concerns of the participants, who may seem to be intentionally obfuscating when they actually lack confidence or understanding.

Facilitators of Effective In-Service Programs

In addition to eliminating liabilities, in-service program planners should focus on positive factors that will enhance the quality of programs. Such factors include administrative support, application of a current and complete knowledge base, use of a variety of resources, peer coaching, and comprehensive and long-term planning. In addition, the element of "active, formal leadership" (B.R. Joyce & Showers, 1988) is essential.

Administrative support entails budgetary considerations and rewards (incentives), but it also necessitates policy development, support, and encouragement. In order to overcome the negative aspects of in-service programs, administrators must do a considerable amount of what Metzdorf (1989) called "cheerleading." He suggested a variety of cheerleading strategies recognizing the contributions of teachers, including a faculty newsletter, reward and recognition programs (e.g., Teacher of the Month/Year), minigrants, minisabbaticals, and adjunct professorships at colleges and universities.

Application of a current and complete knowledge base requires a research-based approach to curricular and instructional changes. After needs assessment has identified important areas of focus, the program planner will need to thoroughly review the literature to determine the range and scope of alternatives available. In addition, the planner should examine the theoretical bases and rationales, essential components, and empirical foundations of selected models and strategies. Only after this process should the next steps in planning and implementation begin.

Effective in-service programs require a variety of resources and materials. In addition to money and expertise, supplementary materials can include books, journals, selected journal articles, films, videotapes, slides, and other informational media. It is worthwhile for the program planner to develop a library of current information and make this available to teachers involved in the in-service program.

Another essential factor is the development of a system of peer coaching. After studying the theoretical basis of a particular innovation, seeing it modeled, and practicing it under simulated conditions, teachers will need additional support and guidance in implementing it in the classroom. One staff development specialist or resource person cannot possibly provide concentrated support and feedback for a group of teachers. Therefore, a system that allows peers to observe, support, and provide feedback can enhance the transfer of theory into practice.

In-service development must include comprehensive and long-term planning and evaluation. Needs assessment can reveal areas of interest and concern for teachers, as well as student learning outcomes that need improvement. A thorough review of literature will provide a strong knowledge base for implementing change. Selection of personnel to contribute various areas of expertise is a critical step, as the in-service program will be only as credible as its presenters. Identification of goals and objectives, selection of activities, and development of time lines should be a collaborative process involving representatives of faculty, administration, and perhaps parents. Evaluation of the in-service program will be an ongoing effort to determine its impact on teacher, student, and school outcomes.

Active formal leadership is the final essential ingredient of effective in-service programs. Such leadership requires the commitment and involvement of administrators in establishing organizational structures and climates for successful in-service. Active formal leadership makes optimal use of administrative support; available knowledge, resources and materials; peer coaching; and comprehensive planning and evaluation.

Essential Elements of In-Service Programs

Based on extensive experience in the training of thousands of teachers, Joyce and his associates (B.R. Joyce, 1988a; B.R. Joyce, Brown, & Peck, 1981; B.R. Joyce & Showers, 1983; B.R. Joyce & Showers, 1988) developed a training model containing four essential elements. Factors essential to the transfer of training include study of the theoretical basis or rationale of the method, observation of demonstrations by experts, practice with feedback under simulated conditions, and coaching.

The study of theory helps to avoid the bandwagon effect, in which schools adopt change for the sake of innovation, failing to investigate and fully understand the theoretical basis or rationale for such a method. Most innovations in public schools are never fully implemented, and personnel often quickly reject innovations because of incomplete understanding, insufficient training, lack of resources and support, and poor follow-up and evaluation. Study of theory helps teachers develop a "high degree of skill" (B.R. Joyce & Showers, 1988) and understand the rationale behind the skill, which therefore increases the likelihood of transfer. The process of study can include lectures, discussions, readings, films, and videotapes.

One of the best examples within physical education of failure to study theory is the initial implementation of the movement education approach in elementary education. Taught by college and university faculty who themselves had insufficient understanding of the theory and rationale, beginning teachers found themselves insipidly asking "how many ways?" Eliciting poor responses from the students, and not understanding how to extend and refine movement responses, elementary physical education teachers rejected the movement education approach and returned to the familiar traditional approach. As methods courses improved, and the availability of comprehensive resources increased, the greater level of understanding led to more productive efforts to implement this style of teaching.

The observation of demonstrations by experts, or modeling, is the next essential element of effective in-service programs. Program planners can provide for this through live demonstrations in a field setting or simulated conditions in a laboratory setting. Videotapes of teachers modeling the skills can also provide a clear demonstration. As many as 10 to 15 demonstrations, using a variety of contexts, will be necessary to provide a clear model of the instructional method (B.R. Joyce & Showers, 1982). B.R. Joyce and Showers (1983) recommended that demonstrators try to simulate the work place as much as possible so that transfer can more easily follow.

Practice with feedback, involving all of the teachers in the program, should follow quickly after the demonstration by experts. Before teachers forget the salient points, they need to try out new behaviors under simulated conditions and with ample feedback. Microteaching provides a comfortable format for practicing teaching with small groups of peers for short segments of time. Videotaping of the microteaching episodes, followed immediately by directed observation and analysis, will enhance the development of skill. Participants can use specific observation instruments as a means of providing structured feedback for "fine tuning" (B.R. Joyce, 1988a).

Opportunities for practice with feedback must be ample, the guideline being 15 to 20 opportunities to practice. For some complex teaching models, teachers may need as many as 25 practice opportunities (Showers, Joyce & Bennett, 1987). Undergraduate methods courses and in-service workshops often provide only one or two opportunities for participants to practice new teaching skills for 5- or 10-minute segments. Program instructors incorrectly assume that these opportunities will allow teachers to achieve sufficient mastery to apply these skills in a new context. Research shows, however, that only a small percentage of teachers (probably those of high conceptual levels) can apply new strategies introduced in in-service programs without extensive follow-up (B.R. Joyce & Weil, 1986).

A fourth essential training condition is the availability of peer coaching in the work environment immediately following the simulated practices. Peer coaching is a system employing "colleagues, supervisors, professors, curriculum consultants, or others thoroughly familiar with the new approaches . . . to [help] teachers analyze the content to be taught and the approach to be taken, and making very specific plans to help the student adapt to the new teaching approach (B.R. Joyce, 1988a, p. 86). Teachers who receive coaching develop a level of "executive control" that allows them to apply new methods appropriately in the actual environment (B.R. Joyce, 1988a).

Peer coaching serves five major purposes related to the transfer of instructional methodology from training to practice with impact. Peer coaching provides companionship, provides technical feedback, allows teachers to analyze application and thus extend executive control, helps teachers adapt to students, and provides personal facilitation (B.R. Joyce & Showers, 1982, p. 6). Ultimately, all of these functions contribute to the major goal of helping teachers incorporate changes into their repertoire.

By providing companionship, peer coaching ensures personal interaction, emotional support, and encouragement among teachers engaged in the lonely process of implementing change. Teachers grouped in pairs or small groups can reflect jointly, problem solve, and share frustrations associated with the process. Provision of technical feedback occurs when teachers collect and share descriptive data on the presence or absence of planned changes. It may also include exchanges on the use of materials, adaptations for students, and ideas for refinement. Technical feedback is instructive for the giver as well as for the receiver. Analysis of application involves extending executive control to help teachers decide when and how to appropriately use an instructional method. Executive control "is a 'metaunderstanding' about how the model works, how it can be fitted into the instructional repertoire, and how it can be adapted to students" (B.R. Joyce & Showers, 1982, p. 6). Peer coaches help teachers adapt to students by helping teachers read cues in students' responses and by discussing alternative courses of action. Finally, personal facilitation is achieved when teachers adapt their own comfortable style for implementing a strategy.

The literature describes three models of peer coaching, which involve differentiated functions and outcomes (Garmston, 1987). Technical coaching is used to transfer a specific method or strategy from training in the workshop to full implementation in the classroom, and usually involves pairs of peers. It includes an evaluative function, because the observer considers the presence or absence of targeted behaviors. Collegial coaching is designed to promote general and long-term goals of collegiality, increased professional dialogue, reflection, and self-growth. The individual teacher selects the focus of observation, which is followed up by data collection, shared analysis, and interpretation. As compared to technical coaching, collegial coaching has no evaluative function, and a supportive function is dominant. Collegial coaching is most effective when the goal is to increase teacher efficacy and self-concept (Garmston, 1987).

A third style, challenge coaching, uses a team problem-solving approach to find solutions to a particular instructional problem. Challenge coaching begins with the identification of a desired goal and is conducted through planning, observation, and reflection in small groups. Peers observe teachers as they implement planned procedures, and the teachers ultimately adopt those that are most effective. Coaches using this method rely heavily on the literature and may employ action research in searching for solutions.

In essence, peer coaching helps teachers to arrive at a "second stage of learning" (Garmston, 1987) in which they can readily apply their learnings to varied contexts. Administrators must understand that collegial relationships must be nurtured but by their very nature cannot be imposed. The composition of collegial groups will change in a flexible manner as teachers develop new concerns and address them. Ultimately, the goal is to help teachers acquire the habit of self-coaching, applying the skills of inquiry and reflection to improving their own practices.

Regardless of the model used, peer coaching is critical to the transfer of theory into practice and will substantially improve the overall school climate. It is a particularly useful tool for helping beginning teachers adjust to the new environment. For peer coaching to be most effective, peer coaches need extensive training and follow-up, and they must observe teachers a minimum of twice per month (Moffett, St. John, & Isken, 1987). The necessary commitments of time, money, and resources are considerable, but the potential benefits are great.

In-Service Designs

The design of the in-service program is the first and most important element of the process and will ultimately impact the overall effectiveness of the program. The program must include comprehensive needs assessment, providing opportunities for prospective participants to express their priorities. After selecting specific skills and knowledge, the program designers must thoroughly review the existing knowledge base in that area. The identification of expertise in the form of consultants is another critical step. Next, the program designers should develop a long-term plan to provide for the essential training components, including review of theory, observation of demonstration, practice with feedback, and coaching. Because of the comprehensive nature of this process, implementation of the plan will take place over a considerable period of time, varying according to the level of complexity of the selected skills.

In-service program planners must consider the developmental needs of teachers at differing levels of experience. In-service participants often include large numbers of beginning teachers, for whom learning to teach is a complex process. Learning to teach has too long been viewed as a simple process, and beginning teachers have frequently been left to their own devices. These teachers need a program of planned support, evaluation, and

mentoring, to assist them in induction. However, they can add a vital dimension to in-service programs because they are versed in current theory and are (we hope) enthusiastic. Experienced teachers have different and individualized needs, based on their previous training, conceptual levels, and motivation. These group and individual differences pose unique challenges for those who deliver in-service training.

The potential of mentoring for beginning teachers is just being recognized. This is a planned and formalized process that provides support, supervision, and companionship for beginning teachers as they enter the world of teaching. This process assumes that induction into teaching is a unique and challenging transition, and that planned guidance and encouragement can optimize the unique potential that beginning teachers bring to the school environment. The mentoring process promotes the idea that experienced teachers can enhance the process of induction by sharing their wisdom, insights, and practical knowledge (Loucks-Horsley, Harding, Arbuckle, Dubea, & Williams, 1987).

The characteristics of an effective mentor encompass more than experience in teaching and include personal characteristics that facilitate a mentoring relationship. Mentors are "experienced teachers who have mastered their craft and are dedicated to promoting excellence in the teaching profession [and] are sought as mentors for beginning teachers just starting their careers" (Brzoska, Jones, Mahaffy, Miller, & Mychals, 1987, p. 6). Research conducted in business and education shows that successful mentors are secure and people oriented. They "like and trust their proteges," take a personal interest in and encourage their development, are willing to share power and expertise, and promote self-confidence (Gray & Gray, 1985, p. 39).

The functions of the mentor encompass a broad spectrum of general purposes and specific responsibilities. General functions include informal contact, role modeling, direct assistance, demonstration, observation and feedback, and assistance with a professional development plan (Brozska et al., 1987). Brozska et al. (1987) also defined the following specific responsibilities: The mentor should

- meet regularly with the beginning teacher both formally and informally;
- guide the beginning teacher through the daily operation of the school;

- arrange for the beginning teacher to visit different teachers' classes;
- demonstrate lessons for the beginning teacher;
- observe the beginning teacher's teaching and provide feedback;
- act as a role model in all aspects of professionalism;
- develop skills as a mentor as well as teacher; and
- support and counsel the beginning teacher, providing perspective when needed.

The mentoring process is supportive in nature and is not designed to take an evaluative posture. Therefore, the mentor provides support, feedback, and counseling and works to help the protégé develop competence, self-confidence, self-direction, and professionalism (Brozska et al., 1987). The goal is for the beginning teacher to achieve a desirable level of independence. The achievement of this goal requires an extensive time commitment from the mentor teacher, as well as a considerable level of training to develop the skills essential for mentoring. The following conditions are necessary for effective mentoring: a sufficient amount of time for mentors and protégés to observe and confer within the school day, a system for identifying truly competent mentor teachers, the ongoing support of administrators, and close physical proximity and similar teaching assignments for the mentor and protégé (Loucks-Horsley et al., 1987).

Although the needs of the beginning teacher center on classroom management and organizing for instruction, experienced teachers demonstrate a wide range of needs in other areas. Effective in-service and staff development programs are needed to combat burnout and job dissatisfaction, to encourage continued professional growth, to overcome knowledge obsolescence and expand current understandings, and to promote a sense of shared purpose and collegiality. Although the beginning teacher's needs may seem more urgent, the needs of the experienced teacher, and that teacher's patterned attitudes and behaviors, may pose more formidable obstacles for the staff development specialist.

Regardless of their individual experience and readiness levels, teachers as adult learners require some general conditions for successful learning. In general, adult learners demand practical relevance as they assess the ideas that are presented, and the likelihood that these learners will adopt various strategies hinges primarily on that criterion.

They enjoy opportunities to apply their experience to self-directed goals. In addition, adult learners require a positive and growth-oriented environment (Arin-Krupp, 1989). Growth-oriented environments are those that focus on developing potential strengths as opposed to remediating weaknesses.

Arin-Krup (1989) proposed the following guidelines for instructors to use in meeting the common needs for adult learners: focus on growth, serve as a model for growth, reward growth, expect and accept failures, make material relevant and practical, focus on individual interests and needs, encourage participants to write proposals for their own staff development to meet immediate need, establish (or develop contacts with) a teachers' center, focus on concerns, link individuals with resources, and provide mentoring and networking. Specific strategies for ensuring practical relevance include using both personal and professional participant knowledge, involving the learners in planning, monitoring and evaluating to assess learning, and helping teachers to link their individual needs to school and district goals.

Lessons From Research

A great deal of research has tested the effects of various in-service development strategies, programs, and models. While yielding some common findings, this research has also produced a fair amount of conflicting results. Much of the existing research has focused on teacher satisfaction as a criterion of in-service impact (Wade, 1985). Additional research is needed to identify effective staff development practices and particularly to measure the effects of these efforts on student learning.

Transfer of Training

One way to determine the impact of staff development programs is to examine the transfer of training from the workshop to actual practice in the classroom. Transfer of training occurs in teaching when the acquisition of material or skills increases the teacher's ability to acquire other new learnings (B.R. Joyce & Showers, 1983). Transfer is horizontal when the teacher can directly apply a skill from the training context to the actual setting. Vertical transfer occurs when some additional problem solving or modification is needed for the teacher to apply training to the actual setting. This distinction is important to in-service training, because innovations that are complex and require additional learning also require more comprehensive and long-term implementation.

Studies of transfer of training reveal several general findings. The first notion is that "significant changes take considerable time" (Bertani & Tafel, 1989, p. 142). In addition to time, specific components and combinations of these enhance transfer of training. Although training in information and theory alone can produce significant increases in knowledge, the combination of demonstration, practice, and feedback increases knowledge gains substantially (B.B. Bennett, 1988; B.R. Joyce & Showers, 1983; B.R. Joyce & Showers, 1988). Opportunities for practice must be ample in order for transfer to occur; the teacher may need as many as 25 teaching episodes in which to apply the innovation (Showers et al., 1987). Finally, the addition of coaching to these previous elements is most likely to ensure transfer of training (B.R. Joyce & Showers, 1988).

Structural and Administrative Factors

Research has also focused on the scheduling of training required to promote transfer and the efficacy of various training schedules. It appears that training interspersed over a period of time is more effective than concentrated, high-dose approaches. Sparks (1983) recommended a series of four to six 3-hour workshops spaced 1 or 2 weeks apart as one effective schedule. This allows teachers to process information in small segments and to make the gradual cognitive changes needed for internalizing the strategies.

Other program characteristics that have been investigated involve the nature of participation, the size of the training group, and the composition of the group. From a meta-analysis of 91 studies, Wade (1985) concluded that voluntary participation is no more effective than nonvoluntary participation. The size of the training group and the composition of the group (faculty group or unrelated individuals) also appeared inconsequential. However, this meta-analysis sparked criticism for its failure to consider the complexity of the innovations and the goals and content of the in-service program (Sparks, 1983). No additional support for these findings is evidenced in the current literature. Further research is needed to address these questions.

Strong administrative support is a salient characteristic of effective in-service programs. In a comprehensive study of hundreds of federally funded programs, Berman and McLaughlin (1978) demonstrated that administrative leadership (of both principals and superintendents) was the most important factor in implementation. Other studies support the importance of the principal's role in effecting change (Lieberman & Miller, 1981, Stallings & Mohlman, 1981).

An essential element of administrative support is the provision of incentives. College credit and release time are two participant incentives that have been linked to significant results (Wade, 1985). In general, however, administrators should emphasize intrinsic professional rewards that increase professional motivation above extrinsic or tangible rewards (Hutson, 1981). Structural and administrative factors can ultimately increase commitment of in-service participants. Research shows that commitment follows competence as opposed to preceding it (Crandall, 1983; Miles & Huberman, 1984). In the absence of knowledge, experience, and training, teachers are unable to invest the level of commitment required to effect substantial change (Showers et al., 1987).

Teacher Characteristics

Research provides some insight into the nature of teacher characteristics that promote in-service development. Three specific lines of research that yield useful findings involve teacher conceptual level, teacher states, and teacher attitudes. Conceptual level studies attempt to characterize teachers according to their abilities to grasp and apply abstract ideas. Teachers at a low conceptual level select strategies based on previous experiences and limited decisions and have difficulty in expanding their teaching repertoires to include new strategies. Teachers at a higher level of abstraction are more adept at implementing new strategies and incorporate them into a broader range of teaching repertoires.

Teacher states may be defined from the perspective of developmental readiness for change. Based on interviews, questionnaires, and group discussions involving several thousand teachers, B.R. Joyce and McKibbin (1982) proposed an interesting conceptualization of teacher growth states. Their categories of growth states are arranged hierarchically, ranging from the lowest level, *withdrawn*, to the highest active level, *omnivores*. Depending on their growth states, teachers react differently to specific aspects of staff development programs.

The authors provided the following characterizations for five teacher growth states commonly observed:

Omnivores—"actively use every available aspect of the formal and informal systems that are available to them" (p. 37). They have rich lives, close professional colleagues, and little "emotional baggage"; they pursue change actively; and they seem to overcome obstacles easily. In essence, they are positive and self-actualized people.

Active consumers—demonstrate many of the characteristics of the omnivore but not to the extent that these characteristics pervade all aspects of professional involvement. Active pursuits may be limited to one or two channels for professional growth.

Passive consumers—are "there when the opportunity presents itself but . . . rarely seek or initiate new activities" (p. 38). They rely on formal in-service development activities to spark their growth.

Resistant—are entrenched in their environment and unlikely to seek out training. They may respond positively to aspects of training in which they already feel successful. They are not likely to participate in training without material rewards. When substantial changes threaten their stability, they are likely to actively oppose, surreptitiously oppose, or withdraw.

Withdrawn—"require a great deal of outside energy if they are to become involved" (p. 39). They tend to reject formal and informal activity, and engage in a limited number of interactions.

These findings generally imply that in-service programs must accommodate all levels of teacher involvement and that individual differences pose obstacles to all aspects of planned in-service programs. Although these differences cannot be ignored, they should not be viewed as insurmountable obstacles. A comprehensive in-service program will involve participatory governance, allowing teachers to collaborate in decision making. A program of strong organizational and administrative support will provide maximal opportunities for professional growth. Individual differences in teacher responses to training should be expected,

and ongoing support and follow-up activities will be required for all teachers.

As previously discussed, the importance of coaching as a follow-up process has earned much empirical support. Participation in a formal, peer-coaching arrangement can help teachers acquire a better understanding of the teaching/learning process, gain self-analysis skills, improve teaching performance, and develop a more positive attitude toward instructional support (Loucks-Horsely et al., 1987). These outcomes have been well documented, particularly through a formal coaching model entitled *Resident Supervisory Support for Teachers* (District of Columbia Public Schools, 1986).

Follow-Up to In-Service

In a series of studies, B.R. Joyce and Showers (1988) determined that coaching contributes to the transfer of training and helps to establish "the norms of collegiality and experimentation" (p. 88). The authors summarized that coaching promotes the transfer of training in five ways: increasing the practice and application of new strategies, facilitating more appropriate use of the strategies (e.g., congruence with objectives and curricular materials), promoting long-term retention of knowledge and skill for strategies, encouraging teachers to teach new models and their objectives to students, and enhancing the teacher's understanding of the rationale for specific applications of the strategies.

Highlights of the extensive and somewhat disjointed research findings related to effective in-service training can be summarized in terms of program content and teacher characteristics. Program content must include essential components of theory, demonstration, practice, and feedback. Transfer of training will be more likely if the program provides peer coaching and follow-up. Administrative support and incentives are essential ingredients. Strategies involving greater complexity require long-term follow-up and extensive support. We know that all teachers, regardless of their differences, can benefit from quality in-service training experiences. Teachers with greater initial competency and esteem adjust more easily to innovations, but increased flexibility in teaching generally results from exposure to a variety of new strategies. Finally, a basic level of understanding is required in order for teachers to "buy" new strategies.

The ultimate goal of in-service training is to help teachers assume responsibility for their own professional development. This requires that they be prepared for dissonance, a period of discomfort that occurs when teachers try out new strategies (B.R. Joyce & Weil, 1986). Because all growth requires a period of discomfort, teachers must be encouraged to take risks, and they must be supported by collaboration and collegiality. Finally, the in-service program must retrain teachers to operate within a broader framework of teaching styles and ultimately to exhibit more diverse learning styles.

Summary and Implications

Those who plan and deliver in-service programs frequently overlook the needs of physical educators. Curriculum coordinators and in-service development specialists often fail to recognize the potential contributions of a sound physical education program. They may not realize the need for curricular and instructional innovations in physical education. Or, they may wish to plan specialized in-service programs but lack sufficient understanding to make such programs relevant for movement specialists. Nationally, there is a need for increased attention to the specific needs of physical education teachers.

In-service programs can contribute to a variety of goals for improved instruction across the curriculum. Specifically, they help teachers to en-

hance curricula, instruction, and quality of work life. Although all teachers can learn, in-service programs are most productive when they recognize teachers' developmental needs and personal growth states. Some common characteristics of adults as learners will also impact the delivery and reception of in-service programs.

Despite their potential value, innovations often fail and in-service programs fall short when the scope of the intervention is insufficient. In order to be effective, staff development programs must demonstrate a number of essential characteristics, including defined goals, incentives, resources and materials, input, follow-through, and communication. Substantive change requires time, and change will inevitably lead to a period of initial discomfort. Teachers need many practice opportunities to acquire mastery of new skills, and practice is most effective in combination with demonstration and feedback.

The litmus test of staff development is the extent to which teachers transfer applications from the clinic to the classroom. There is evidence that peer coaching, a system of collegial support and feedback, can greatly facilitate transfer. Peer coaching provides companionship, provides technical feedback, extends executive control, helps teachers adapt to students, and provides personal facilitation. The end result is that teachers achieve a higher level of mastery and are better able to adapt innovations to unique demands.

Chapter 12

Systematic Supervision and Educational Reform

A flurry of legislative activity, occurring primarily between 1980 and 1984, has signaled renewed attention to the topic of teacher competence. In response to a series of highly visible documents, position statements, and surveys indicting the performance of American students, virtually all states have enacted some version of educational reform aimed at improving the quality of teaching. Policies that govern entrance into and retention in the profession vary greatly from state to state. However, there is a clear consensus that it is the state's responsibility to protect the public from incompetent teachers.

Declining public opinion about the performance of teachers and support for teacher testing were evident in the 1986 Gallup Poll of the Public's Attitude Toward Public Schools (Gallup, 1986). In this survey, 85 percent of the respondents endorsed requirements for all prospective teachers to pass state examinations in their selected fields of study. Public responses in the 1970s in particular reflected a low esteem for teaching and a growing dissatisfaction with teacher preparation and certification processes. Ultimately, public concerns have led to legislative mandates as state governments address this salient issue.

Among the many publications that echoed this concern, the most potent impetus for educational reform was the report of the National Commission on Excellence in Education, entitled *A Nation at Risk: The Imperative for Educational Reform* (U.S. Department of Education, 1983). Citing the need to stem ''the rising tide of mediocrity'' within our educational system, the commission called for improvements in teacher preparation and teacher effectiveness. Another significant document was *A Nation Prepared: Teachers for the 21st Century* (Tucker & Mandel, 1986), a Carnegie report that led to the formation in 1987 of the National Board for Professional Teaching Standards. This board was proposed to produce valid and stringent assessments with defined standards for teacher certification. Its major goal is to increase the quality of professionalism in teaching and thus to restore public confidence in the schools.

Sweeping reforms have led to the adoption of a variety of performance-based teacher certification programs that emphasize attainment of competence. These programs assess teacher competence in terms of content knowledge (specialized subject matter mastery), basic skills (reading, writing, and math), and performance measurement (ability to teach). Although content knowledge and basic skills are assessed by paper-and-pencil tests, some state programs measure professional skills by direct observation of classroom teaching. Eisenberg and Rudner (1988) reported that 24 states measure content knowledge by certification tests, 27 states assess basic skills (reading, writing, and math), and 23 states conduct performance measurements of professional skills.

Increased emphasis on teacher competency has been approached in a variety of ways, including beefed up entrance and exit requirements for professional preparation, induction programs for the support and evaluation of beginning teachers, and in-service programs. Other reforms include incentives to attract better teachers and programs for minority recruitment. A general trend toward performance-based certification, or making permanent certificates contingent on attainment of specified levels of competence, is certain to continue throughout the next decade.

We can trace the roots of the teacher quality reform movement to 1964. From 1964 until 1977, North Carolina was the only state to require a teacher certification exam. In 1970, the New Jersey State Board of Education became the first such body to undertake a performance-based evaluation project to examine options to course credit requirements for teacher certification; New Jersey adopted requirements for National Teacher Examination scores in 1985. Louisiana initiated state-mandated teacher certification in 1977 as a means of upgrading the quality of teaching and ultimately improving the state's economy (Wise, Darling-Hammond, & Purnell, 1988). In 1978, Florida initiated its own teacher competency assessment program (Rudner, 1987).

By 1987, 32 states had mandated performance evaluation for beginning teachers, and 12 states were considering adoption (Tanney & Ortman, 1987). By 1988, 40 states had adopted some form of uniform beginning teacher induction program. Approximately half of these 40 states and the District of Columbia mandated guidelines or evaluation procedures, and the remaining states allowed local education agencies (LEAs) to adopt procedures. Uniform evaluation procedures adopted in those states range from narrative records and high-inference rating scales to low-inference classroom observation systems (Neuweiler, 1988).

Classroom Observation Systems

This emphasis on performance-based measurement has required the development of classroom observation instruments for use in evaluating teaching performance. These instruments derive their focus from empirical research on effective teaching. They define observable and measurable indicators of teaching behaviors that correlate with pupil achievement on standardized tests. Thus, these systems operationally define effective teaching in terms of the presence of specified effective teaching behaviors. Observers use classroom observation instruments in a variety of ways, most often with beginning teachers for decisions involving certification, employment retention, and merit.

Performance-based classroom observation systems are currently used in Connecticut, Florida, Georgia, Kentucky, Louisiana, Mississippi, North Carolina, South Carolina, and Texas. Virginia has implemented a classroom observation system in its Beginning Teacher Assistance Program, but funding constraints recently led to a suspension of the program. Kentucky uses a modified version of the Florida Performance Measurement System. California has conducted pilot testing of the Connecticut Competency Instrument, a high-inference classroom observation system. Kansas has piloted an observation instrument that measures 141 behaviors, but the state legislature has not approved funding for statewide implementation with beginning teachers. New Mexico specifies six essential teaching competencies for all certified teaching personnel; however, LEAs develop observation instruments used in the state. Oklahoma designates a uniform observation and evaluation process that incorporates narrative recording. These instruments are primarily used for support and evaluation of beginning teachers but may also be used for decisions of retention or promotion. Tennessee offers a unique opportunity for increased pay for experienced teachers who are systematically observed for six major areas of competence (Furtwengler, 1987).

These systems vary substantially in terms of the procedures used; for example, Who observes? When? How? What level of minimal competency is expected? However, the systems display a number of common characteristics, especially in terms of the competencies emphasized. The areas of competence on which the various instruments focus are generally supported by research. These systems consistently emphasize planning, identification of objectives, clarity and focus of lesson presentation, questioning, time on task, and classroom management. Table 12.1 identifies areas of competence assessed in Connecticut, Florida, Georgia, Louisiana, Mississippi, North Carolina, South Carolina, Texas, and Virgina.

Table 12.1

Summary of Competencies Required
in State Teacher Performance Assessments

Connecticut

Management of the classroom environment	*Instruction*	*Assessment*
Promotes a positive learning environment Maintains appropriate standards of behavior Engages students in the activities of the lesson	Presents appropriate lesson context Develops the lesson to promote achievement of the lesson objectives Uses appropriate questioning strategies Communicates clearly, using precise language and acceptable oral expressions	Monitors student understanding of the lesson and adjusts instruction when necessary

Florida

Begins instruction promptly Handles materials in an orderly manner Orients students to classwork; maintains academic focus Conducts beginning and ending reviews Questions: academic comprehension/lesson development	Recognizes response; amplifies; gives correct feedback Gives specific academic praise Provides for practice Gives directions; assigns and checks comprehension of homework and seatwork assignments; gives feedback	Circulates and assists students Treats concepts—definitions/attributes, examples/nonexamples Discusses cause and effect; uses linking words; applies law or principle States and applies academic rules

Georgia

Teaching Task I: Provides instruction	*Teaching Task II: Assesses and encourages student progress*	*Teaching Task III: Manages the learning environment*
Instructional level—The amount and organization of the lesson content are appropriate for the students based on their abilities and the complexity and difficulty of the material. Content development—Content is developed through appropriate teacher-focused or student-focused activities. Building for transfer—Lesson includes initial focus, content emphasis or linking, and summaries that build for transfer of learning.	Promoting engagement—Instructional engagement is promoted through stimulating presentations, active participation, or techniques that promote overt or covert involvement. Monitoring progress—Progress, understanding, and bases of misunderstanding are assessed by interpreting relevant student responses, contributions, performances, or products. Responding to student performance—Students are provided reinforcement for adequate performances when appropriate and specific feedback or correctives for inadequate performances.	Use of time—Use of instructional time is optimized by techniques such as providing clear directions and using efficient methods for transitions, materials distribution, and other routine matters and by techniques such as focusing on objectives and providing sufficient instructional activities. Physical setting—The physical setting allows the students to observe the focus of instruction, to work without disruption, to obtain materials, and to move about easily, and it allows the teacher to monitor the students and to move among them. Appropriate behavior—Appropri-

(Cont.)

Table 12.1   (Continued)

Georgia (continued)

Teaching Task II: Assesses and encourages student progress (continued)	*Teaching Task III: Manages the learning environment* (continued)
Supporting students—Support for students is conveyed by using techniques such as providing encouragement, lowering concern levels, dignifying academic responses, and using language free of sarcasm, ridicule, and humiliating references.	ate behavior is maintained by monitoring the behavior of the entire class, providing feedback, and intervening when necessary.

Louisiana

Preparation, planning, and evaluation	*Classroom and behavior management*	*Enhancement of learning*
Goals and objectives	Time	Lessons and activities initiation
Teaching methods and learning tasks	Classroom routine	Teaching methods and learning tasks
Allocated time and content coverage	Student engagement	Aids and materials
Aids and materials	Managing task-related behavior	Content accuracy and emphasis
Home learning	Monitoring and maintaining student behavior	Thinking skills
Formal assessment and evaluation	*Learning environment*	Clarification
	Psychosocial learning environment	Monitoring learning tasks and informal assessment
	Physical learning environment	Feedback
		Oral and written communication

Mississippi

Plans instruction to achieve selected objectives	Demonstrates a repertoire of teaching methods	Helps learners develop positive self-concepts
Organizes instruction to take into account individual differences among learners	Reinforces and encourages involvement in instruction	Manages classroom interactions
Obtains and uses information about the needs and progress of individual students	Demonstrates an understanding of the school subject being taught and demonstrates its relevance	Meets professional responsibilities
Uses instructional techniques, methods, and media to achieve the objectives	Organizes time, space, materials, and equipment for instruction	Engages in professional self-development
Communicates with learners	Demonstrates enthusiasm for teaching, learning, and the subject being taught	Communicates high expectations for learners

North Carolina

Has materials, supplies, and equipment ready at the start of the lesson or instructional activity	Assigns tasks that students handle with a high rate of success	Provides sustaining feedback after an incorrect response, or no response, by probing, repeating the question, giving a clue, or allowing more time
Gets the class started quickly	Asks appropriate levels of questions that students handle with a high rate of success	Has an instructional plan that is
Gets students on-task quickly at		

North Carolina (continued)

the beginning of each lesson or instructional activity

Maintains a high level of student time-on-task

Has established a set of rules and procedures that govern routine administrative matters

Has established a set of rules and procedures that govern student verbal participation and talk during different kinds of activities

Frequently monitors the behavior of all students

Stops inappropriate behavior promptly and consistently, yet maintains the dignity of the student

Begins lesson or instructional activity with a review of previous material

Introduces the lesson or instructional activity and specifies learning objectives when appropriate

Speaks fluently and precisely

Presents the lesson or instructional activity using concepts and language understandable to the students

Provides relevant examples and demonstrations to illustrate concepts and skills

Conducts lesson or instructional activity at a brisk pace, slowing presentations when necessary for student understanding, but avoiding unnecessary slow-downs

Makes sure that the assignment is clear

Summarizes the main points of the lesson at the end of the lesson or instructional activity

Maintains clear, firm, and reasonable work standards and due dates

Circulates during class work to check all students' performance

Routinely uses oral, written, and other work products to check student progress

Poses questions clearly and one at a time

Provides feedback on the correctness or incorrectness of in-class work to encourage student growth

Regularly provides prompt feedback on assigned out-of-class work

Affirms a correct oral response appropriately, and moves on

compatible with the school and systemwide curricular goals

Uses diagnostic information obtained from tests and other assessment procedures to develop and revise objectives and/or tasks

Maintains accurate records to document student performance

Has instructional plan that matches or aligns objectives, learning strategies, assessment, and student needs at appropriate level of difficulty

Uses available human and material resources to support the instructional program

Treats all students in a fair and equitable manner

Interacts effectively with students, co-workers, parents, and community

Carries out noninstructional duties as assigned and/or as need is perceived

Adheres to established laws, policies, rules, and regulations

Follows a plan for professional development and demonstrates evidence of growth

South Carolina

Plans learning activities to meet objectives

Objectives for the lesson are stated in observable learner outcomes

Learner objectives are compatible with content and level

Stated instructional procedures are planned to achieve each objective

Learning experiences are planned to involve students actively in the lesson

Materials supporting the achievement of objectives are stated

Procedures or materials are planned to accommodate differences in at least two areas

Fulfills instruction responsibilities

Lesson begins promptly

Instruction facilitates the students' achievement of a stated objective

At least two areas of student needs are accommodated in the learning activities

A stimulating technique is used to motivate student interest

More than one instructional approach is demonstrated

Varying organizational sizes are used for instruction

All students are provided an opportunity for active involve-

Uses professional classroom management techniques

Expectations for behavior conducive to learning are stated or have been established for students

Firmness of the teacher in managing behavior conveys confidence

Classroom procedures are directed in a confident manner

Learning experiences are provided throughout the observational period without loss of instructional time

Disruptions are addressed if they interfere with the learning of

(Cont.)

Table 12.1 (Continued)

South Carolina (continued)

Communicates acceptably (continued)	*Fulfills instruction responsibilities* (continued)	*Uses professional classroom management techniques* (continued)
of student needs	ment	other students
Assessment procedures are planned to measure each stated objective	An opportunity is provided for all students to apply or practice knowledge or skills stated in the objective	School, district, or professional codes of behavior are adhered to and enforced by the teacher
A record of individual student progress is maintained	Information is obtained from students to determine the need for clarification, assistance, or adjustment	Techniques are used to involve students who are inattentive
Communicates acceptably		Special assistance is provided to students
Instructional plan is communicated to students	Information about progress or performance is provided to	Adjustments in the lesson are made
A logical sequence is followed in the lesson	students during the lesson	Patience and poise are maintained by the teacher
Questions, descriptions, and explanations meet student level of understanding	Instruction is compatible with the physical environment	Students are treated with fairness and impartiality
Explanations are restated in different words or initial explanations are sufficient		
Demonstrations or examples are used by the teacher for illustrations		
Knowledge of subject matter is communicated with confidence and authority		
Content information communicated by the teacher is accurate		

Texas

Instructional strategies	*Presentation of subject matter*	*Professional growth and responsibilities*
Provides opportunities for students to participate actively and successfully	Teaches for cognitive, affective, and/or psychomotor learning	Plans for and engages in professional development
Evaluates and provides feedback on student progress during instruction	Uses effective communication skills	Interacts and communicates effectively with parents
Classroom management and organization	*Learning environment*	Complies with policies, operating procedures, and requirements
Organizes materials and students	Uses strategies to motivate students for learning	Promotes and evaluates student growth
Maximizes amount of time available for instruction	Maintains supportive environment	
Manages student behavior		

Virginia

Academic learning time	Consistent rules	Questioning skill
Student accountability	Affective climate	Reinforcement
Clarity of lesson structure	Learner self-concept	Close supervision
Individual differences	Meaningful learning	Awareness
Evaluation	Planning	

Support for Generic Classroom Observation Instruments

An emerging body of literature supports the application of classroom observation instruments. Collectively, these studies have applied state-mandated instruments from Georgia, Florida, Virginia, North Carolina, and Mississippi. The studies show that these instruments have made a measurable contribution to the improvement of instructional quality in these states.

Georgia's Teacher Performance Assessment Instrument

As a pioneering state in the use of performance-based assessment, Georgia has conducted a substantial amount of research to test the efficacy of its Teacher Performance Assessment Instrument (TPAI) (Georgia Department of Education, 1985). The development of the instrument began in 1976 under direction of the Georgia Department of Education and the University of Georgia. Over a 4-year period, researchers wrote versions of a competency assessment and validated these versions using the consensus method. The researchers then conducted wide-scale pilot testing of the TPAI and published the first version of the instrument in 1980. A 1985 version involved substantial modifications, and further developments transitioned to the Georgia Teacher Evaluation Program (GTEP) (Georgia Department of Education, 1989).

While the TPAI focuses on initial certification requirements, the GTEP extends peformance-based evaluation to all certified teachers in the state of Georgia. The Quality Basic Education Act mandates its use as a part of the ongoing, annual evaluation process. Principals at the individual school level administer two instruments in the new evaluation process. The Georgia Teacher Observation Instrument (GTOI) examines how the teacher provides for instruction, assesses and encourages student progress, and manages the learning environment. For each of these teaching tasks, a set of dimensions and subdimensions identify observable indicators of effective teaching behaviors. In addition, observers use the Georgia Teaching Duties and Responsibilities Instrument (GTDRI) in evaluations conducted throughout the school year.

The emphasis of the performance-based evaluation program in Georgia has changed somewhat, but we cannot overlook the impact of the TPAI. During its implementation from 1980-1989, the instrument provided a sound research base for the evaluation of teacher effectiveness. In addition, TPAI mobilized administrative training in classroom observation and promoted greater confidence in the evaluative process (Solomon, L.M., personal communication, June 12, 1991).

Research conducted since 1983 provides strong overall support for the value of the TPAI in enhancing teacher performance. These studies examined predictive validity (student achievement and teacher performance); feasibility (reliability, validity, and ease of implementation); and reports of teacher performance (descriptive and experimental) of the instrument.

Two recent studies that examined the predictive validity of the TPAI as related to student outcome measures produced inconsistent findings. In the first, Hewitt-Dortch (1986) investigated the relationship of specified teacher management behaviors (as assessed by TPAI) and achievement of elementary grade students in science. The researcher found significant relationships between student achievement and scores for both managerial behaviors and classroom behaviors overall. In contrast, C. Hunt (1987) found no relationship between achievement of third graders in math and scores on a teaching performance instrument (ET6T) based on the TPAI.

Studies show that the National Teacher Examination (NTE) is a weak predictor of classroom teaching performance as measured by TPAI (Lovelace & Martin, 1984: Southern Regional Educational Board, 1982). The absence of a relationship between content knowledge and ability to demonstrate that knowledge has provided fuel for debate. From another perspective, Raber (1985) examined the relationship of letters of recommendation and subsequent first-year performance of teachers. Results reveal a low correlation overall.

The feasibility of using the TPAI has been explored with respect to factors of validity and reliability. Researchers have analyzed the variability of TPAI scores over time, examining same-day versus separate-day scores (Yap & Capie, 1985) and day-to-day variations versus observer differences (Cronin & Capie, 1986). Time was an important factor in the findings of both studies. The first study indicated that observations on separate days produce greater validity than single-day observations. The second study found that daily differences are of greater consequence than the observer reliability factor, and validity seems to increase with additional observations.

Capie and Cronin (1986) compared subscale scores to total scores for teacher effectiveness, as determined by student achievement. This study supports the greater validity of subscale scores in determining student achievement. However, general findings support the validity and reliability of the total instrument scores.

Convergent validity was the focus of an investigation that compared scores derived by TPAI to those derived by the Classroom Observations Keyed for Effectiveness Research (COKER) (Wiersma, Dickson, Jurs, & Wenig, 1983). The two instruments produced substantially different scores, as influenced by the nature of the instruments' compositions, that is, high inference (TPAI) versus low inference (COKER). The overall results evidence little convergent validity.

Vollmer, Creek, and Vollmer (1987) investigated the efficacy of TPAI as used in self-assessment. Comparisons of scores derived by self-analysis of interns and by expert analysis of the same lessons by master teachers produced similar findings, supporting the efficacy of intern self-assessments with TPAI.

One final study of reliability and validity used a modification of TPAI to assess student teacher performance in Nevada (Trent & Gilman, 1984). The authors compared the ratings of student teachers given by university supervisors, by cooperating teachers, and by the student teachers themselves. The TPAI produced similar ratings among the three groups, indicating acceptable utility for the instrument.

A variety of studies have used the TPAI to report teacher performance of various groups, primarily from a descriptive stance. As a criterion measure, the TPAI was used to compare student teachers to experienced teachers (Dickson et al., 1984), special education teachers to regular classroom teachers (Walters, 1986), actual performance of student teachers to expected performance (Chien, 1984), relationships between locus of control and performance (Browne, 1985), and perceptions of elementary school students related to teacher performance (Ball, 1984). A longitudinal design provided important findings for the retention of TPAI competencies mastered by beginning teachers (Green, 1987). After a 5-year interim, teachers studied were generally able to demonstrate the same competencies. In addition, Ivey (1986) conducted an experimental comparison to determine the impact of in-service training on performance. Participation in in-service seemed to enhance the performance of the teachers involved.

In a report of a 3-year study conducted with the TPAI, Tanner and Ebers (1985) identified factors related to beginning teachers' successful completion of a competency evaluation. Through direct observation of beginning teachers, the researchers identified clinical factors related to successful attainment of the TPAI competencies. Those factors found to contribute significantly to success during induction included the use of TPAI during student teaching, participation in new staff orientation, and use of the "buddy" system. White beginning teachers and graduates of primarily white institutions experienced greater success in completing the assessment than did their black counterparts. Females were more successful than males, and female principals were found to be more facilitory. An important conclusion of this study was that prospective teachers should participate in competency-based assessment during their college experiences.

Florida's Performance Measurement System

The Georgia competency testing program is of primary interest because of its pioneering status in performance-based teacher evaluation. As such, it has benefited from extensive research conducted after the development of the TPAI. However, the Florida Performance Measurement System (FPMS) can boast the most comprehensive a priori review of research to identify teacher effectiveness variables strongly correlated with student achievement. Independent follow-up research has begun to generate a body of literature. These studies can be categorized as those examining predictive validity (relationship to student outcomes), descriptions of teacher performance, and studies of the effect of training interventions.

Studies of predictive validity fail to produce strong links between teacher performance on FPMS and student learning gains. As with TPAI, conflicting findings have resulted from this research emphasis. Crosby (1987) found that total teacher performance is significantly related to both student engagement and student achievement, but student engagement and student achievement are not significantly correlated. In contrast, Allen (1985) found a significant relationship between FPMS performance and student engagement, but not between teacher performance and student achievement. Again, the author found that student engagement time is unrelated to student achievement. Additional research is needed to address this issue.

Several descriptive studies add useful information to the existing research base of FPMS. The effectiveness of beginning teachers comprises one research focus. Lewis (1987) compared the performances of student teachers from Colorado colleges and universities to those of experienced Florida teachers. The student teachers excelled in overall performance as compared to the experienced group. Thomas (1985) examined the relative proportions of effectiveness scores for the four domains of FPMS. She found that Domain 3 (instructional organization and development) produced the highest scores, whereas Domain 4 (presentation of subject matter) produced the lowest.

Other studies describe FPMS performance as specifically related to planning (Twardy, 1984; White, 1986) and managerial behaviors (Farmer, 1985). Using FPMS to code planning behaviors recorded by physical education majors in think-aloud technique, Twardy (1984) found significant relationships between some planning indicators and in-class behaviors of teachers and learners. White (1986) also analyzed planning practices of selected high school teachers with respect to FPMS planning indicators. This study found that both experienced and inexperienced teachers generally demonstrate planning practices consistent with those specified by the FPMS planning domain. In a similar design, Farmer (1985) examined relationships between management behaviors and elements of academic learning time in physical education. In this study, FPMS was used to code teacher management behaviors, and student behaviors were coded with the ALT-PE-TB instrument. Results showed that effective classroom managers were able to increase learner in-class behaviors related to academic learning time.

Finally, Clark (1986) and Kessell (1988) conducted training interventions to increase observer agreement scores for the FPMS. Clark developed an interactive video tutorial to promote attainment of concepts related to Domain 4 of the FPMS (presentation of subject matter). The author compared this method to a lecture technique in assessing posttest knowledge gains of preservice teachers. Results showed no significant differences between the posttest means of the two treatment groups. Kessell's treatment entailing multiple observations of each teacher and feedback resulted in increased observer agreement among elementary and secondary school administrators.

An Extended Research Base—Virginia, North Carolina, and Mississippi

Although the combined research base for TPAI and FPMS is extensive, a smaller body of literature is available to assess the efficacy of Virginia's Beginning Teacher Assistance Program (BTAP), North Carolina's Teacher Performance Appraisal

Instrument (TPAI), and Mississippi's Teacher Assessment Instrument (MTAI). Hylton's (1985) qualitative study of 10 beginning teachers provides insights for implementation of the BTAP. T.S. Bennett (1987) determined that both administrators and teachers perceived all 14 competencies of the BTAP to be observable. Using a large sample, Durtan (1987) found relationships between certain pressage variable and five of the process variables assessed by BTAP.

One study connected with the MTAI examined affective dimensions of its administration. Strickland (1987) surveyed the attitudes of teachers, principals, and superintendents toward the use of the instruments. Results of a questionnaire show varying degrees of acceptance among the group overall and between the two groups. Whereas only 27.8 percent of teachers surveyed supported its use, 63.8 percent of principals and 77.5 percent of superintendents were in favor. This disproportion indicates that teachers are quite skeptical about the practical utility of the instrument.

The current version of North Carolina's TPAI was implemented in 1986; however, a previous version has been in use since 1982. A literature review produced two studies involving its use. Massey (1988) assessed teachers' and administrators' perceptions of the effectiveness of the North Carolina TPAI. As with the BTAP, research found substantial differences between the groups, with principals more endorsing than teachers. R.M. Brown and Wells (1988) focused on predictive validity, employing the NTE and TPAI in comparisons. As was the case with similar research that used the Georgia TPAI, the study found scores on the two instruments to be unrelated. This is not surprising, because knowledge and skill (ability to apply knowledge) are not equivalent.

Recent Developments in Assessment of Classroom Teaching

In recent years, a number of states have developed classroom observation instruments for use in a variety of evaluation programs. The Louisiana System for Teaching and Learning Assessment and Review (STAR) (Ellett, Loup, & Chauvin, 1990) was designed to evaluate beginning and inservice teachers. The Texas Teacher Appraisal System (TTAS) (Texas Education Agency, 1991) defines competencies for evaluation of five domains of observable behaviors. California recently piloted the Connecticut Competency Instrument (Connecticut State Department of Education, 1990), a high inference measure developed from 1987-1989. In addition, Arizona's career ladder program allows local districts to develop their own systems for classroom observation.

The Louisiana STAR is an innovative approach to on-going assessment of teaching and learning. Assessors use it to help the induction of beginning teachers and as a requirement for the recertification of all teaching personnel. An important aspect of STAR is its "contextually-based" approach to assessment (Ellett et al., 1990). STAR emphasizes the unique contextual characteristics of each classroom and allows assessors to make decisions based on the appropriateness of teaching and learning strategies for that environment.

The philosophic basis of STAR (Ellett et al., 1990, p. 3) embraces the following common themes:

- all students can learn
- teaching and learning are related
- teaching/learning is viewed as a total process
- students must assume self responsibilty for learning
- reflective practice involves preparation, planning, and evaluation
- knowledge of pedagogy, content, and curriculum is paramount
- time on task is essential to learning
- active involvement/engagement are important student processes
- teachers must recognize and provide for individual student differences
- quality learning environments and student growth are related
- instruction should facilitate cognitive development/thinking skills

In 1990-91 educators in Louisana implemented STAR, containing 117 assessment indicators. These indicators allow for flexible evaluation in diverse settings, thus it is not expected that all 117 will be evidenced in any given lesson. The indicators represent 22 Teaching and Learning Components, classified into four domains:

- preparation, planning, and evaluation
- classroom and behavior management
- learning environment
- enhancement of learning

A team of three assessors administer the classroom as a part of a comprehensive professional development program.

Educators implemented the Texas Teacher Appraisal System (TTAS) statewide in the fall of 1986. To develop the system, they solicited input from 30,000 Texas teachers and reviewed existing instruments and teacher effectiveness research (Texas Education Agency, 1991). The instrument is used as part of a career ladder program and involves assessment of generic teaching skills through multiple observations by multiple observers.

Researchers refined the current edition of the Connecticut Competency Instrument (CCI) following initial implementation with 36 beginning teachers in the 1989-90 academic year. The observation system is one part of the Beginning Educator's Support and Training (BEST) program. BEST is a comprehensive induction program that involves mentoring, support, and assessment for beginning teachers. The CCI is designed to allow broad interpretation of effective teaching for diverse contexts, as opposed to using a strictly low inference and prescriptive approach. The philosophic basis of the CCI instrument (Connecticut State Department of Education, 1990) encompasses the following six basic assumptions:

- Effective teaching can take many forms.
- Critical dimensions of teacher performance that promote learning can be defined across diverse educational contexts.
- Competence of beginning teachers as decision makers can be differentiated from that of experienced teachers.
- Effective teaching is essential to cultural diversity.
- Effective teaching must be judged in the context of the teacher's objectives.
- Professional judgment is vital to teacher assessment.

CCI developers incorporated this philosophy into the structure of the 10 indicators of effective teaching within the instrument. They organized the indicators into three clusters, including management of the classroom, instruction, and assessment. A preassessment information form precedes classroom observations and allows teachers to identify instructional goals and contextual variables. These are further discussed during preobservation interviews. Observers do extensive script taping of classroom events in the direct observation of classroom teaching. They synthesize the data into a one-page form for each of the ten indicators and cite positive and negative examples of each attribute. A postobservation conference follows each of the six prescribed observations for beginning teachers.

The format of the CCI was particularly attractive to researchers at the Far West Laboratory that was authorized by the California Teaching Credential Commission to develop a program of comprehensive teacher evaluation. The Teacher Credentialing Law of 1988 and the Bergeson Act (S.B. 148), encompass three components of support, evaluation, and assessment for beginning teachers, and provides impetus for the development of such a program. The Bergeson Act specifically prohibits the use of checklist formats for teacher assessment, and emphasizes assisting "beginning teachers to teach students who are ethnically, culturally, academically, and linguistically diverse" (Estes, Stansbury, Long, & Wolf, 1991, p. 1.7).

Researchers pilot tested the CCI in California in 1989 using trained assessors from Connecticut in six geographic locations. The researchers conducted assessments in a variety of subject areas in grade levels K-12. Subsequent evaluation of the pilot testing led investigators to conclude that the CCI "could serve as a fully developed prototype" for classroom observations (Estes, et al., 1990, p. 3.36).

The new generation of performance-based observation instruments evidences a number of trends. First, recent developments have extended the application of classroom observations from initial certification of beginning teachers to recertification of experienced teachers. Second, the new instruments show a movement toward more high-inference measures, avoiding the standardization of teaching and allowing teachers to make informed decisions based on sound theory. Finally, these instruments reflect the complexity of teaching and learning processes; they recognize the uniqueness of teaching and learning environments, teachers' objectives, and learner characteristics.

Future Implications for Classroom Observation Instruments

Despite their shortcomings, performance-based classroom observation instruments have had a significant impact on monitoring and upgrading the quality of teaching in the adopting states. The primary effect has been felt by beginning teachers, who must demonstrate the competencies required for initial certification. Ultimately, this increased accountability ought to be assumed by colleges and universities, which will take responsibility for establishing the requisite competencies in undergraduate training.

Optimally, induction programs that use such uniform assessments will enhance the quality of teaching and smooth the transition from student teaching to initial employment. However, a number of potential pitfalls to the use of generic instruments are apparent. Woolever (1985) summarized

a number of these problems and questioned whether one instrument can possibly capture the essence of teaching. By the scientific nature of such instruments, "effective teaching is narrowly defined" (p. 23), allowing little room for the art of teaching. Generic instruments easily ignore such influences as common sense, practical reasoning, expert opinion, and educational philosophies. A linear approach to evaluating teacher effectiveness often discounts the contextual variables that influence student learning. Although some generic principles of effective teaching can be defined, effective teaching behaviors vary greatly across subject areas and with students of varying ages and ability levels.

Further, the comprehensive nature of the instruments pressures the beginning teacher to demonstrate overall competency over a broad range of behaviors. Woolever (1985) acknowledged that "a sensitive teacher educator is chilled by the thought of a fledgling student teacher being held accountable for all of the behaviors characteristic of a 'professional teacher'" (p. 23). These and other shortcomings support the rationale for integrating generic observation instruments with a developmental and content-specific method.

Integrating Generic Classroom Observations With Systematic Supervision in Physical Education

Teacher educators can optimally support and evaluate beginning and in-service teachers in physical education through the use of generic and content-specific models. Particularly when working with beginning teachers, the teacher educator must use a developmental approach to attaining competence. Ideally, the components of the model are first introduced in undergraduate methods courses and are then reinforced throughout preinternship and student teaching. Studies of Georgia's Teacher Performance Assessment Instrument support the assumption that student teachers assessed by competencies in student teaching will perform better in competency assessments during induction (Tanner & Ebers, 1985).

Generic models of performance-based observation consist of multidimensional instruments, designed to allow the user to observe and evaluate a number of competencies within a given observation. In contrast, a developmental approach allows the teacher to focus on one competency or area of competency at a time. It also provides a knowledge base and tasks for reinforcing the competency to be measured. Unidimensional instruments allow for assessment of focused and sequential areas of competency (limited number of skills), enhancing a formative approach to evaluation.

In examining the competencies emphasized in the generic models of Table 12.1, we see some clear commonalities. These common themes also appear in the focus of the Systematic Supervision Model, except that they are presented as developmental progressions and are applied to a physical education context. Physical education, because of its dynamic and movement-oriented nature, poses unique challenges for teachers. Therefore, physical educators must consider the specific application of generic teaching skills to a movement setting. Many supervisors and administrators who conduct evaluations may be unaware of the unique demands of a movement setting; these people will benefit from instruments designed specifically for this application.

A limitation of the generic models is that they are rarely applied to teacher support and evaluation beyond induction years. Only a few states require observation and evaluation for experienced teachers, and the Systematic Supervision Model can provide a structure for in-service education and staff development. The need for including in-service teachers in such projects was supported by W.J. Bennett (1988) in *American Education: Making It Work*. The author recommended competency testing for current teachers as well as for new teachers and emphasized that such tests must be rigorous enough to screen out those who have no place within the system.

Summary and Implications

Beginning teacher induction programs may comprise a Band-Aid approach to support and evaluation, because they usually involve only a few observations and little guidance toward developmental progression. Therefore, a hierarchical model that introduces competencies within logical phases can help the beginning teacher to break down and master the competencies without feeling overwhelmed. Because the Systematic Supervision Model involves specific strategies for working on competencies, supervisors need not limit themselves to state-mandated competencies. However, the integration of the model with state programs will help provide comprehensive assistance.

Generic classroom observation instruments provide ''snapshots of behaviors,'' measuring whether the teacher can exhibit the designated competencies on demand (Rudner, 1987). To that end, such instruments may demonstrate the teacher's familiarity with the competencies more so than the teacher's ability to apply them appropriately over time. An ongoing program of support and evaluation is needed to help teachers internalize and apply the principles of effective teaching consistently and comprehensively.

Despite their inherent limitations, generic observation instruments can yield objective and useful feedback for teachers across content areas. Because the demands of a movement setting are unique, generic observation instruments are most effective when used in combination with a content-specific model. One approach to integrating generic instruments with the Systematic Supervision Model is to use the generic data for general screening purposes. Because these instruments tend to combine many aspects of teacher effectiveness in one observation, they can serve as general indicators of areas for improvement. The supervisor can also use the Systematic Supervision Model as an intact intervention, progressing sequentially through the components of the model. Or, the supervisor can select specific components of the model based on needs identified by the generic instrument.

In cases where uniform, generic instruments are mandated, the integration of a content-specific, systematic supervision model can contribute to the following goals:

- A developmental and sequential approach to support and evaluation
- Application of effective teaching skills to a movement setting
- Increased understanding through examination of the knowledge base specific to physical education teacher effectiveness literature
- A focused, unidimensional approach to evaluating competencies in hierarchical order
- Use of prescribed tasks for developing competencies
- A comprehensive approach to observation that augments the basic observation schedule of induction programs
- Opportunities for experienced teachers to increase competency in selected areas

Source Notes

Chapter 2. An Overview of Generic Models of Supervision

1. *Note.* From Dussault, Gilles, *A Theory of Supervision in Teacher Education.* (New York: Teachers College Press © 1970 by Teachers College, Columbia University. All rights reserved.), pp. 30-32. Adapted by permission.

2. *Note.* From "Trusting Teachers to Know What's Good for Them" by B. Dillon-Peterson. In *Improving Teaching* (pp. 34-35) by K. Zumwalt (Ed.), 1986, Alexandria, VA: Association for Supervision and Curriculum Development. Copyright 1986 by the Association for Supervision and Curriculum Development. Reprinted by permission.

Chapter 4. A Research Base for the Improvement of Teaching

3. *Note.* From "Teacher Expectations" by T.L. Good. In *Talks to Teachers* (pp. 168-170) by D.C. Berliner and B.V. Rosenshine (Eds.), 1987, New York: McGraw Hill. Copyright 1987 by McGraw Hill. Adapted by Permission.

4. *Note.* From "Explicit Teaching" by B.V. Rosenshine. In *Talks to Teachers* (p. 79) by D.C. Berliner and B.V. Rosenshine (Eds.), 1987, New York: McGraw Hill. Copyright 1987 by McGraw Hill. Adapted by permission.

References

Acheson, K.A., & Gall, M.D. (1987). *Techniques in the clinical supervision of teachers: Preservice and inservice applications*. New York: Longman.

Al-Duaij, A.D.-M. (1987). A study of the impact of supervisory style on teachers' job satisfaction in the secondary schools in Kuwait (Doctoral dissertation, Western Michigan University, 1986). *Dissertation Abstracts International*, **48**(1), 12-A.

Alfonso, R.J. (1977). Will peer supervision work? *Educational Leadership*, **34**(8), 594-601.

Alfonso, R.J., Firth, G., & Neville, R. (1984). The supervisory skill mix. *Educational Leadership*, **41**(7), 16-18.

Alfonso, R.J., & Goldsberry, L. (1982). Colleagueship in supervision. In T.J. Sergiovanni (Ed.), *Supervision of teaching* (pp. 90-108). Alexandria, VA: Association for Supervision and Curriculum Development.

Allen, P.B. (1985). Merit pay criteria: A study of the relationships among student outcome measures and teacher experience, attendance, degree, and classroom performance (predictive validity). *Dissertation Abstracts International*, **47**(2), 227-A. (University Microfilms No. 86-080,76)

Allison, H. (1978, March). *Rating scale format as it affects ratings in student teaching*. Paper presented at the annual meeting of the American Educational Research Association, Toronto. (ERIC Document Reproduction Service No. ED 152 857)

Anderson, L., Evertson, C., & Brophy, J. (1979). An experimental study of effective teaching in first grade reading groups. *Elementary School Journal*, **79**(4), 192-223.

Anderson, L.A. (1987). Clinical supervision concepts and implementation by elementary principals (Doctoral dissertation, Temple University, 1986). *Dissertation Abstracts International*, **48**(2), 257-258A.

Anderson, W.G. (1980) *Analysis of teaching physical education*. St. Louis: C.V. Mosby.

Andreotti, L.R. (1987). The effectiveness of clinical supervision versus videotape feedback versus a control to enhance the ability of community college instructors at involving stu-dents in classroom discussion (Doctoral dissertation, University of Oregon, 1987). *Dissertation Abstracts International*, **48**(11), 2794-A.

Applegate, J.H., & Lasley, T.J. (1982). Cooperating teachers' problems with preservice field experience students. *Journal of Teacher Education*, **33**(2), 15-18.

Arin-Krup, J. (1989). Staff development and the individual. In S.J. Caldwell (Ed.). *Staff development: A handbook of effective practices* (pp. 58-69). Oxford, OH: National Staff Development Council.

Ausubel, D. (1963). *The psychology of meaningful verbal learning*. New York: Grune & Stratton.

Ball, M.A. (1984). Relationships between ratings of teachers made by primary pupils and professional educators. *Dissertation Abstracts International*, **45**(12), 3543-A. (University Microfilms No. 85-04,580)

Bang-Jensen, V. (1986). The view from next door: A look at peer supervision. In K.K. Zumwalt (Ed.). *Improving teaching* (pp. 61-62). Alexandria, VA: Association for Supervision and Curriculum Development.

Barrett, K.R., Allison, P.C., & Bell, R. (1987). What preservice teachers see in an unguided field experience: A follow-up study. *Journal of Teaching in Physical Education*, **7**(1), 12-21.

Bartlett, B.F. (1987). Perceived effects of clinical supervision on elementary school teachers (Doctoral dissertation, Colorado State University, 1987). *Dissertation Abstracts International*, **49**(4), 791-A.

Beatty, P.J. (1977). Dialogic communication in the supervision process: A humanistic approach. *Education*, **97**(3), 226-232.

Bell, R., Barrett, K.R., & Allison, P.C. (1985). What preservice physical education teachers see in an unguided, early field experience. *Journal of Teaching in Physical Education*, **4**(2), 81-90.

Bellack, A.A., Kliebard, H.M., Hyman, R.T., & Smith, F.L. (1966). *The language of the classroom*. New York: Teachers College Press.

Bennett, B.B. (1988). The effectiveness of staff development training practices: A meta-analysis (Doctoral dissertation, University of

Oregon, 1987). *Dissertation Abstracts International*, **48**(7), 1739-A.

Bennet, T.S. (1987). Administrator and teacher perceptions of the observability of the Virginia BTAP competencies (Doctoral dissertation, University of Virginia, 1986). *Dissertation Abstracts International*, **48**(1), 12-A.

Bennett, W.J. (1988). *American education: Making it work*. Washington, DC: U.S. Government Printing Office.

Berg, M., Harders, P., Malian, I., & Nagel, A. (1986, February 24). *Partners in supervision: A clinical supervision model program*. Paper presented at the Association of Teacher Educators annual meeting, Atlanta. (ERIC Document Reproduction Service No. ED 271 436)

Berliner, D.C. (1987). A simple theory of classroom instruction. In D.C. Berliner & B.V. Rosenshine (Eds.), *Talks to teachers* (pp. 93-109). New York: Random House.

Berman, P., & McLaughlin, M.W. (1978). *Federal programs supporting educational change: Implementing and sustaining innovations*. Washington, DC: U.S. Office of Education. (ERIC Document Reproduction Service No. ED 159 289)

Bertani, A.A., & Tafel, L.S. (1989). Theory, research, and practice: Foundations of staff development. In S.J. Caldwell (Ed.), *Staff development: A handbook of effective practices* (pp. 140-155). Oxford, OH: National Staff Development Council.

Bilodeau, E.A., & Bilodeau, I.M. (1961). Motor-skills learning: Feedback. *Annual Review of Psychology*, **12**, 243-259.

Birdwell, D.M. (1980). The effects of modification of teacher behavior on the academic learning time of selected students in physical education. *Dissertation Abstracts International*, **41**(4), 1472A. (University Microfilm No. 80-22,239)

Block, J.H. (1980). Success rate. In C. Denham & A. Lieberman (Eds.), *Time to learn: A review of the Beginning Teacher Evaluation Study* (pp. 95-106). Sacramento: California State Commission for Teacher Preparation and Licensing. (ERIC Document Reproduction Service No. ED 192 454)

Bloom, B.S. (1953). Thought processes in lectures and discussions. *Journal of General Education*, **7**(1), 160-170.

Bloom, B.S. (Ed.) (1956). *Taxonomy of educational objectives, handbook I: Cognitive domain*. New York: David McKay.

Blumberg, A. (1970). A system for analyzing supervisor-teacher interaction. In A. Simon & E.G. Boyer (Eds.), *Mirrors for behavior III* (pp. 34.1-34.4). Philadelphia: Research for Better Schools.

Blumberg, A. (1974). *Supervisors and teachers: A private cold war*. Berkeley, CA: McCutchan.

Blumberg, A. (1977). Supervision as interpersonal intervention. *Journal of Classroom Interaction*, **13**(1), 23-32.

Blumberg, A. (1980). *Supervisors and teachers: A private cold war* (2nd ed.). Berkeley, CA: McCutchan.

Blumberg, A., & Cusick, P. (1970). Supervisor-teacher interaction: An analysis of verbal behavior. *Education*, **91**(2), 126-134.

Bobbitt, J.F. (1912). The elimination of waste in education. *The Elementary School Journal*, **12**(6), 259-275.

Bobbitt, J.F. (1913). Some general principles of management applied to the problems of city school systems. *Twelfth yearbook of the National Society for the Study of Education, part 1* (pp. 7-96). Chicago: University of Chicago Press.

Boehm, J.H. (1974). The effects of a competency-based intervention on student teacher and pupil behavior. *Dissertation Abstracts International*, **35**(8), 5085-A. (University Microfilms No. 75-03,013)

Bohning, G. (1978). Subjective judgment pitfalls in evaluating student teachers. *Teacher Educator*, **14**(1), 13-17.

Bowman, N. (1979). College supervision of student teaching: A time to reconsider. *Journal of Teacher Education*, **30**(3), 29-30.

Breton, W.A. (1989). The relationship between perceived supervisory practices and resource teachers' sense of efficacy (Doctoral dissertation, University of Maine, 1987). *Dissertation Abstracts International*, **49**(7), 1630-A.

Briddell, B. (1986). Unpublished lesson plans.

Briggs, L.D., Richardson, W.D., & Sefzik, W.P. (1986). Comparing supervising teacher ratings and student teacher self-ratings of elementary student teachers. *Education*, **106**(2), 150-159.

Brodbelt, S. (1976). Stereotyped behavior in supervision. *Contemporary Education*, **47**(4), 216-220.

Brophy, J.E. (1979). Teacher behavior and student learning. *Educational Leadership*, **37**(1), 33-38.

Brophy, J.E. (1981). Teacher praise: A functional analysis. *Review of Educational Research*, **51**(1), 5-32.

Brown, R.M., & Wells, N. (1988, April). *Research and policy in evaluating initially certified teachers in North Carolina*. Paper presented at the annual meeting of the American Educational Research Association, New Orleans. (ERIC

Document Reproduction Service No. ED 301 575)

Browne, C.S. (1985). A study of the locus of control relationships between supervising teachers and student teachers (achievement) (Doctoral dissertation, Indiana University, 1985). *Dissertation Abstracts International*, **46**(12), 3690A.

Brunelle, J., Tousignant, M., & Piéron, M. (1981). Student teachers' perceptions of cooperating teachers' effectiveness. *Journal of Teaching in Physical Education*, Introductory issue, 80-87.

Brzoska, T., Jones, J., Mahaffy, J., Miller, K., & Mychals, J. (1987). *Mentor handbook*. Portland, OR: Northwest Regional Educational Laboratory. (ERIC Document Reproduction Service No. ED 288 820)

Burton, W.H., & Brueckner, L.J. (1955). *Supervision: A social process* (3rd ed.). New York: Appleton-Century-Crofts.

Calhoun, E.F. (1986). Relationship of elementary school teachers' conceptual level to the utilization of supervisory services and to the classroom instructional environment (Doctoral dissertation, University of Georgia, 1985). *Dissertation Abstracts International*, **46**(7), 1822-A.

Campbell, D.T., & Stanley, J.C. (1966). *Experimental and quasi-experimental designs for educational research*. Chicago: Rand McNally.

Canter and Associates. (1987). *Abstracts of research validating effectiveness of assertive discipline*. Unpublished manuscript. (Available from Canter and Associates, P.O. Box 2113, Santa Monica, CA 90406)

Canter, L., & Canter, M. (1976). *Assertive discipline: A take-charge approach for today's educator*. Santa Monica, CA: Canter and Associates.

Capie, W., & Cronin, L. (1986, April). *How many teacher performance criteria should there be?* Paper presented at the annual meeting of the American Educational Research Association, San Francisco. (ERIC Document Reproduction Service No. ED 270 466)

Cawelti, G., & Reavis, C. (1980). How well are we providing instructional services? *Educational Leadership*, **38**(3), 236-240.

Chamberlain, D.R. (1988). A phenomenological investigation of participant perceptions of clinical supervision (Doctoral dissertation, The Pennsylvania State University, 1987). *Dissertation Abstracts International*, **49**(4), 667-668A.

Chang, M.K., & Ferre, V. (1988). An analysis of student teaching evaluations by college supervisors and cooperating teachers. *Education*, **108**(4), 493-496.

Chien, H.C. (1984). A comparison of teacher educator' perceptions of actual performance in Taiwan (Doctoral dissertation, University of Georgia, 1986). *Dissertation Abstracts International*, **48**(9), 2840. (University Microfilms No. 842, 7518)

Chiu, L.H. (1975). Influence of student teaching on perceived teaching competence. *Perceptual and Motor Skills*, **40**(3), 872-874.

Clarizio, H.F. (1980). *Toward positive classroom discipline* (3rd ed.). New York: Wiley.

Clark, K.F. (1986). Interactive video training of preservice teachers in domain IV of the Florida Performance Measurement System. *Dissertation Abstracts International*, **48**(4), 902-A. (University Microfilms No. 87-15,983)

Clark, C., & Richardson, J.A. (1986, November). *Peer clinical supervision: A collegial approach*. Paper presented at the annual conference of the National Council of States on Inservice Education, Nashville. (ERIC Document Reproduction Service No. ED 276 696)

Cogan, M.L. (1973). *Clinical supervision*. Boston: Houghton Mifflin.

Cole, J.L. (1983). Follow-up in teacher preparation programs. *Journal of Physical Education, Recreation, and Dance*, **54**(6) 59-60, 63.

Congdon, C.J. (1980). A study of the role of the principal in clinical supervision (Doctoral dissertation, United States International University, 1979). *Dissertation Abstracts International*, **40**(9), 4819A.

Connecticut State Department of Education. (1990). *Connecticut competency instrument*. Hartford: Author.

Cooper, H., & Good. T. (1983). *Pygmalion grows up: Studies in the expectation communication process*. New York: Longman.

Copeland, W.D. (1982). Student teachers' preference for supervisory approach. *Journal of Teacher Education*, **32**(2), 32-36.

Corcoran, E. (1981). Transition shock: The beginning teacher's paradox. *Journal of Teacher Education*, **32**(3), 19-23.

Coulon, S.C. (1988). The effects of self-instructional modules on the task statements of the cooperating teacher, the teaching behaviors of the student teacher, and the inclass behaviors of the pupils (Doctoral dissertation, The Ohio State University, 1987). *Dissertation Abstracts International*, **48**(9), 2273A.

Coulon, S.C. (1989). Behavioral contracts: Uniting the student teaching triad. *Physical Educator*, **46**(2), 94-98.

Cramer, C. (1977). *The effects of a cooperating teacher training program in applied behavior analysis on* teacher behaviors of physical education student teachers (University Microfilms, 1977, No. 777318847)

Crandall, D.P. (1983). The teacher's role in school improvement. *Educational Leadership, 41*(3), 6-9.

Crist, J., Marx, R., & Peterson, P. (1974). *Teacher behavior in the organizational domain.* Stanford, CA: Stanford University, San Francisco Board of Education, Stanford Center for Research and Development in Teaching, NIE Contract No. Ne-C-3-0061.

Cronin, L., & Capie, W. (1986, April). *The influence of daily variation in teacher performance on the reliability and validity of assessment data.* Paper presented at the annual meeting of the American Educational Research Association, San Francisco. (ERIC Document Reproduction Service No. ED 274 704)

Crosby, J.T. (1987). A study of the relationships among science teacher performance as measured by the Florida Performance Measurement System, student task engagement and student achievement in regular and laboratory classroom settings. *Dissertation Abstracts International, 48*(10), 2523-A. (University Microfilms No. 88-08,289)

Cruikshank, D.R. (1985). Applying research on teacher clarity. *Journal of Teacher Education, 36*(2), 44-48.

Currens, J.W. (1977). An applied behavior analysis training model for preservice teachers (Doctoral dissertation, Ohio State University, 1977). *Dissertation Abstracts International, 38*(5), 2644-A.

Darst, P.W. (1974). The effects of competency-based intervention on student teacher and pupil behaviors. *Dissertation Abstracts International, 35*(8), 5092-A. (University Microfilms No. 75-03044)

Darst, P.W., & Steeves, D. (1980). A competency-based approach to secondary student teaching in physical education. *Research Quarterly for Exercise and Sport, 51*(2), 274-285.

Darst, P.W., Zakrajsek, D.B., & Mancini, V.H. (Eds.) (1989). *Analyzing physical education and sport instruction* (2nd ed.). Champaign, IL: Human Kinetics.

Day, A.L., & Brightwell, D.S. (1978). A process model for establishing competencies for student teachers. *Teacher Educator, 14*(1), 25-28.

Deakin, W.E. (1986). An analysis of principals' attitudes towards clinical supervision as a means for enhancing communication about instructional improvement (Doctoral dissertation, University of Massachusetts, 1986). *Dissertation Abstracts International, 47*(3), 724-725A.

Denham, C., & Lieberman, A. (Eds.) (1980). *Time to learn: A review of the Beginning Teacher Evaluation Study.* Sacramento: California State Commission for Teacher Preparation and Licensing. (ERIC Document Reproduction Service No. ED 192 454)

DeSanctis, M., & Blumberg, A. (1979, April). *An exploratory study into the nature of teacher interactions with other adults in the schools.* Paper presented at the annual meeting of the American Educational Research Association, San Francisco.

Dessecker, W. (1975). The effects of audiotaped intervention on student teacher behaviors. *Dissertation Abstracts International, 36*(11), 7352A-7353A. (University Microfilms No. 76-9957)

Dickson, G.E., Wiersma, W., & Jurs, S. (1984, April). *A comparison of teaching performance as measured through observation of student teachers.* Paper presented at the annual meeting of the American Educational Research Association, New Orleans. (ERIC Document Reproduction Service No. ED 244 935)

Dillon-Peterson, B. (1986). Trusting teachers to know what's good for them. In K.K. Zumwalt (Ed.), *Improving teaching* (pp. 29-36). Alexandria, VA: Association for Supervision and Curriculum Development.

Dinkmeyer, D.C., & Dreikurs, R. (1963). *Encouraging children to learn: The encouragement process.* Englewood Cliffs, NJ: Prentice Hall.

District of Columbia Public Schools. (1986). *Resident supervisory support for teachers.* Final evaluation report, E.C.I.A., Chapter 2. Washington, DC: District of Columbia Public Schools. (ERIC Document Reproduction Service No. ED 279 638)

Dodds, P.A. (1975). A behavioral competency-based peer assessment model for student teacher and pupil behavior. *Dissertation Abstracts International, 36,* 3486-A. (University Microfilms No. 75-26570)

Dodds, P.A. (1989). Student teachers observing peers. In P.W. Darst, D.B. Zakrajsek, & V.H. Mancini (Eds.), *Analyzing physical education and sport instruction* (pp. 225-232). Champaign, IL: Human Kinetics.

Dodds, P.S. (1985). The effect of peer clinical supervision on the concerns of student teachers (Doctoral dissertation, University of Houston, 1984). *Dissertation Abstracts International, 46*(5), 1252-A.

Doebler, L.K., & Rooberson, T.G. (1987). A study of common problems experienced by secondary student teachers. *Education,* **107**(3), 234-243.

Dougherty, N.J., & Bonanno, D. (1979). *Contemporary approaches to the teaching of physical education.* Minneapolis: Burgess.

Dreikurs, R., & Grey, L. (1968). *A new approach to discipline: Logical consequence.* New York: Meredith Press.

Dreikurs, R., Grunwald, B.B., & Pepper, F.C. (1971). *Maintaining sanity in the classroom: Illustrated teaching techniques.* New York: Harper & Row.

Dunkin, M., & Biddle, B. (1974). *The study of teaching.* New York: Holt, Rinehart, and Winston.

Durtan, S.J. (1987). The relationships among selected presage characteristics and selected process behaviors of beginning secondary school teachers in Virginia. *Dissertation Abstracts International,* **48**(11), 2849-A. (University Microfilms No. 88-01,121)

Dussault, G. (1970). *A theory of supervision in teacher education.* New York: Teachers College Press.

Earls, N. (1986). Research design, data collection, and analysis. *Journal of Teaching in Physical Education,* **6**(1), 40-49.

Edgley, B.M. (1986). Tennis. In B.M. Edgley & G.H. Oberle (Eds.), *Physical education activities handbook* (2nd ed., pp. 227-258). Winston-Salem, NC: Hunter Textbooks.

Eisenberg, T.E., & Rudner, L.M. (1988). State testing of teachers: A summary. *Journal of Teacher Education,* **39**(5), 21-22.

Eisner, E.W. (1967). Educational objectives: Help or hindrance? *School Review,* **75**(3), 250-266.

Eldar, E. (1988). The effects of a self-management program on interns' behavior during a field experience in physical education (Doctoral dissertation, The Ohio State University, 1987). *Dissertation Abstracts International,* **48**(9), 2273-2274A.

Ellett, C.D., Loup, K.S., & Chauvin, S.W. (1990). *System for teaching assessment and review: Annotated guide to teaching and learning.* Baton Rouge: Louisiana Department of Education.

Emans, R. (1983). Implementing the knowledge base: Redesigning the function of cooperating teachers and college supervisors. *Journal of Teacher Education,* **34**(3), 14-18.

Embrey, L.F. (1987). A physical education student teacher in an elementary school: A case study (Doctoral dissertation, The Ohio State University, 1986). *Dissertation Abstracts International,* **47**(10), 3735-A.

Emmer, E.T., Evertson, C.M., & Anderson, L.M. (1980). Effective classroom management at the beginning of the school year. *Elementary School Journal,* **80**(5), 219-231.

Erlanger, H.S. (1974). Social class and corporal punishment in childrearing: A reassessment. *American Sociological Review,* **39**(1), 68-85.

Estes, G.D., Stansbury, K., Long, C., Wolf, K., Wheeler, P., & Quallmalz, E. (1990). *Assessment component of the California new teacher projects: First year report.* San Francisco: Far West Laboratory for Educational Research and Development.

Estes, G.D., Stansbury, K., Long, C., & Wolf, K. (1991). *Assessment component of the California new teacher project: Second year technical report.* San Francisco: Far West Laboratory for Educational Research and Development.

Evans, E. (1976). *Transition to teaching.* New York: Holt, Rinehart, and Winston.

Evertson, C.M. (1975, April). *Relationship of teacher praise and criticism to student outcomes* (Report No. 75-7). Paper presented at the annual meeting of the American Educational Research Association, Washington, DC. Washington, DC: Institute of Education (DHEW). (ERIC Document Reproduction Service No. ED 146 155)

Evertson, C.M., Emmer, E.T., Clements, B.S., Sanford, J.P., & Worsham, M.E. (1989). *Classroom management for elementary teachers* (2nd ed.). Englewood Cliffs, NJ: Prentice Hall.

Evertson, C.M., Emmer, E.T., Sanford, J.P., & Clements, B.S. (1983). Improving classroom management: An experiment in elementary classrooms. *Elementary School Journal,* **84**(2), 173-188.

Eye, G.G. (1975). Supervisory skills: The evolution of the art. *Journal of Educational Research,* **69**(1), 14-19.

Farmer, J.T. (1985). Relationships between specified managerial behaviors and student cognitive engagement, motor engagement, and units of academic learning time in a physical education environment. *Dissertation Abstracts International,* **46**(4), 232-A. (University Microfilms No. 85-133,71)

Feistritzer, C.E. (1984). *The making of a teacher: A report on teacher education and certification.* Washington, DC: National Center for Education Information.

Fiedler, F.E. (1967). *A theory of leadership effectiveness.* New York: McGraw-Hill.

Fisher, C.W., Berliner, D.C., Filby, N.N., Marliave, R., Cahen, L.S., & Dishaw, M.M. (1980). Teaching behaviors, academic learning time, and student achievement: An overview. In C. Denham & A. Lieberman (Eds.), *Time to learn: A review of the Beginning Teacher Evaluation Study* (pp. 7-32). Sacramento: California State Commission for Teacher Preparation and Licensing. (ERIC Document Reproduction Service No. ED 192 454)

Fisher, C.W., Marliave, R., & Filby, N.N. (1979). Improving teaching by increasing academic learning time. *Educational Leadership*, **37**(1), 52-54.

Fishman, S., & Tobey, C. (1978). Augmented feedback. In W.G. Anderson & G.T. Barrette (Eds.), *What's going on in the gym?* [Monograph 1] Motor Skills: Theory into Practice, 51-62.

Flanders, N.A. (1970). *Analyzing teaching behavior.* Reading, MA: Addison-Wesley.

Flanders, N.A. (1976). Interaction analysis and clinical supervision. *Journal of Research and Development in Education*, **9**(2), 47-57.

Foley, R.P. (1987). A study of the relationship between attitudes toward clinical supervision and effective teaching behaviors in elementary reading classes (Doctoral dissertation, University of San Francisco, 1986). *Dissertation Abstracts International*, **47**(8), 2821A.

Frankiewicz, L.E. (1988). A comparison of current criteria for senior elementary education student teacher evaluation with criteria supported by teacher effectiveness research (Doctoral dissertation, Northern Illinois University, 1987). *Dissertation Abstracts International*, **48**(10), 2603A.

Fredericks, T.D. (1987). The concerns of graduate student teachers: A developmental conceptualization? (Doctoral dissertation, Columbia University Teacher's College, 1986). *Dissertation Abstracts International*, **47**(11) 4063-A.

Freiberg, H.J., & Waxman, H.S. (1988). Alternative feedback approaches for improving student teachers' classroom instruction. *Journal of Teacher Education*, **39**(4), 8-14.

Freibus, R.J. (1977). Agents of socialization involved in student teaching. *Journal of Educational Research*, **70**(5), 263-268.

French-Lazovik, G. (1981). Peer review: Documentary evidence in the evaluation of teaching. In J. Millman (Ed.), *Handbook of teacher education* (pp. 73-89). Beverly Hills, CA: SAGE Publications.

Friend, M.L. (1987). Supervision of instruction: The perception of selected Idaho educators (Doctoral dissertation, University of Southern Mississippi, 1986). *Dissertation Abstracts International*, **47**(8), 2822-A.

Fullan, M. (1982). *The meaning of educational change.* New York: Teachers College Press.

Fuller, F.F. (1969). Concerns of teachers: A developmental conceptualization. *American Educational Research Journal*, **6**(2), 207-226.

Fuller, F.F. (1971). *Relevance for teacher education: A teacher concern model* (UTR&D No. 2313). Austin: University of Texas Research and Development Center for Teacher Education.

Fuller, F.F., & Bown, O.H. (1975). Becoming a teacher. In K. Ryan (Ed.), *Teacher education* (seventy-fourth yearbook of the National Society for the Study of Education). Chicago: University of Chicago Press.

Fuller, F.F., Parsons, J.S., & Watkins, J.E. (1974). *Concerns of teachers: Research and reconceptualization* (UTR&D No. 2323). Austin: University of Texas Research and Development Center for Teacher Education. (ERIC Document Reproduction Service No. ED 091 439)

Furtwengler, C.B. (1987). Lessons From Tennessee's Career Ladder Program. *Educational Leadership*, **44**(7), 66-69.

Gage, N.L. (1963). *Handbook of research on teaching.* Chicago: Rand McNally & Co.

Gagne, R.M. (1984). *Conditions of learning and instruction* (3rd ed.). New York: Holt, Rinehart, and Winston.

Gall, M.D. (1970). The use of questions in teaching. *Review of Educational Research*, **40**(5), 707-721.

Gall, M.D. (1984). Synthesis of research on teachers' questioning. *Educational Leadership*, **42**(3), 40-47.

Gallup, A.M. (1986). The 18th annual Gallup poll of the public's attitudes toward the public schools. *Phi Delta Kappan*, **68**(1), 43-59.

Gangstead, S.K. (1983, October 13-15). *Clinical supervision of the student teacher: An applied behavior analysis approach to the evaluation of teacher behavior.* Paper presented at the annual meeting of the Northern Rocky Mountain Educational Research Association, Jackson Hole, WY. (ERIC Document Reproduction Service No. ED 241 476)

Garman, N.B. (1982). The clinical approach to supervision. In T.J. Sergiovanni (Ed.), *Supervision of teaching* (pp. 35-52). Alexandria, VA: Association for Supervision and Curriculum Development.

Garmston, R.J. (1987). How administrators support peer coaching. *Educational Leadership*, **44**(5), 18-26.

George, R.L., & Cristiani, T.S. (1986). *Counseling theory and practice* (2nd ed.). Englewood Cliffs, NJ: Prentice Hall.

Georgia Department of Education. (1985). *Teacher*

performance assessment instruments. Atlanta: Author.

Georgia Department of Education. (1989). *Georgia teacher evaluation program: Evaluation manual*. Atlanta: Author.

Gerald, V.W. (1984). A case study of the implementation of the Hunter clinical supervision model (Doctoral dissertation, Northern Illinois University, 1983). *Dissertation Abstracts International*, **45**(1), 31-32A.

Gibson, R.J. (1986). The effectiveness of clinical supervision in modifying teacher instructional behavior. *Dissertation Abstracts International*, **46**(9), 2499-A. (University Microfilms No. 85-24, 547)

Gitlin, A. (1981). Horizontal evaluation: An approach to student teacher supervision. *Journal of Teacher Education*, **32**(5), 47-50.

Givner, A., & Graubard, P.S. (1974). *A handbook of behavior modification for the classroom*. New York: Holt, Rinehart, & Winston.

Glasser, W. (1965). *Reality therapy: A new approach to psychiatry*. New York: Harper & Row.

Glasser, W. (1969). *Schools without failure*. New York: Harper & Row.

Glasser, W. (1986). *Control theory in the classroom*. New York: Harper & Row.

Glickman, C.D. (1985). *Supervision of instruction: A developmental approach*. Boston: Allyn and Bacon.

Goc-Karp, G., & Zakrajsek, D.B. (1987). Planning for learning — theory into practice. *Journal of Teaching in Physical Education*, **6**(4), 377-392.

Goldberger, M. (1982). Direct styles of teaching and psychomotor performance. In T.J. Templin & J.K. Olson (Eds.), *Teaching in physical education: Big Ten symposium series* (Vol. 14, pp. 211-223). Champaign, IL: Human Kinetics.

Goldhammer, R. (1969). *Clinical supervision: Special methods for the supervision of teachers* (2nd ed.). New York: Holt, Rinehart, & Winston.

Goldhammer, R., Anderson, R.H., & Krajewski, R.J. (1980). *Clinical supervision: Special methods for the supervision of teachers* (3rd ed.). New York: Holt, Rinehart, & Winston.

Goldsberry, L.F. (1984). Realities of clinical supervision. *Educational Leadership*, **41**(7), 12-15.

Good, T.L. (1987). Teacher expectations. In D.C. Berliner & B.V. Rosenshine (Eds.), *Talks to teachers* (pp. 159-200). New York: Random House.

Good, T.L., & Brophy, J.E. (1987). *Looking in classrooms* (4th ed.). New York: Harper & Row.

Gordon, T. (1970). *Parent effectiveness training: The tested way to raise responsible children*. New York: P.H. Wyden.

Gordon, T. (1975). *T.E.T.: Teacher effectiveness training*. New York: David McKay.

Graham, G., & Heimerer, E. (1981). Research on teacher effectiveness: A summary with implications for teaching. *Quest*, **33**(1), 14-25.

Gray, W.A., & Gray, M.M. (1985). Synthesis of research on mentoring beginning teachers. *Educational Leadership*, **43**(4), 37-43.

Green, L.R. (1987). A five-year follow-up study of competencies previously mastered by Georgia teachers. *Dissertation Abstracts International*, **49**(4), 673-A. (University Microfilms No. 88-08,996)

Griffin, G., Barnes, S., Defino, M., Edwards, S., Hukill, H., & O'Neil, S. (1983). *Clinical preservice teacher education: Final report of a descriptive study*. Austin: The University of Texas Research and Development Center for Teacher Education. (ERIC Document Reproduction Service No. 240 110)

Grimmet, P.P., & Ratzlaff, H.C. (1986). Expectations for the cooperating teacher role. *Journal of Teacher Education*, **37**(6), 41-49.

Gump, P.V. (1982). School settings and their keeping. In D.L. Duke (Ed.), *Helping teachers manage classrooms* (pp. 98-114). Alexandria, VA: Association for Supervision and Curriculum Development.

Gwynn, J.M. (1961). *Theory and practice for supervision*. New York: Dodd, Mead, & Co.

Haberman, M., & Harris, P. (1982). State requirements for cooperating teachers. *Journal of Teacher Education*, **33**(3), 45-47.

Hamilton, K. (1974). The application of a competency-based model to physical education student-teaching in high school. *Dissertation Abstracts International*, **35**(5), 5191-A. (University Microfilms No. 75-03082)

Hamilton, R.S. (1987). Perceptions of entry-year teachers in Oklahoma regarding consultation topics and clinical supervision techniques of peer consultants (Doctoral dissertation, Oklahoma State University, 1986). *Dissertation Abstracts International*, **47**(8), 3005-A.

Hanna, H.J. (1988). A case study of instructional improvement through peer observation in a suburban high school (Doctoral dissertation, Portland State University, 1988). *Dissertation Abstracts International*, **49**(6), 1431-A.

Hare, D. (1987). Frequency of observation and frequency of evaluation feedback in relationship to teacher perception of the accuracy of the evaluation process (Doctoral dissertation,

Columbia University Teachers College, 1986). *Dissertation Abstracts International*, **48**(1), 18-19A.

Harris, B.M. (1976). Limits and supplements to formal clinical procedures. *Journal of Research and Development in Education*, **9**(2), 85-89.

Harrison, J.M. (1987). A review of the research on teacher effectiveness and its implications for current practice. *Quest*, **39**(1), 36-55.

Hawkins, R., & Dotson, V. (1975). Reliability scores that delude: An Alice in Wonderland trip through the misleading characteristics in interobserver agreement scores in interval recording. In E. Ramp & G. Semb (Eds.), *Behavior analysis: Areas of research and application* (pp. 359-376). Englewood Cliffs, NJ: Prentice Hall.

Heller, D.A. (1988). *Some personal thoughts and observations on the development of a peer supervision program within the English department of the Brattleboro Union High School.* Unpublished manuscript. (ERIC Document Reproduction Service No. ED 275 671)

Hewitt-Dortch, M.R. (1986). The relationship between teacher management behaviors and achievement in an activity-based elementary science class (Doctoral dissertation, University of Georgia, 1985). *Dissertation Abstracts International*, **46**(11), 3311A.

Hill, D. (1990, April). Order in the classroom. *Teacher Magazine*, pp. 70-77.

Hoffman, S.J. (1983). Clinical diagnosis as a pedagogical skill. In T.J. Templin & J.K. Olson (Eds.), *Teaching in physical education: Big Ten body of knowledge symposium series* (Vol. 14, pp. 35-45). Champaign, IL: Human Kinetics.

Holmes Group. (1986). *Tomorrow's teachers: A report of the Holmes Groups.* East Lansing, MI: Holmes Group Incorporated.

Holodick, N.A. (1989). Clinical supervision practices as reported by elementary school principles (Doctoral dissertation, Temple University, 1988). *Dissertation Abstracts International*, **49**(10), 2874-2875A.

Hoover, N.L., O'Shea, L.J., & Carroll, R.G. (1988). The supervisor-intern relationship and effective interpersonal communication skills. *Journal of Teacher Education*, **39**(2), 22-27.

Hosack-Curlin, K. (1989). Using peer coaching to improve the implementation of a process approach to writing instruction: A clinical supervision model (Doctoral dissertation, University of South Florida, 1988). *Dissertation Abstracts International*, **49**(7), 1770-1771A.

Hosford, P.L. (1984). The art of applying the science of education. In P.L. Hosford (Ed.), *Using what we know about teaching* (pp. 141-161). Alexandria, VA: Association for Supervision and Curriculum Development.

Housego, B.E., & Boldt, W.B. (1986, April), *Critical incidents in the supervision of student teaching in an extended practicum.* Paper presented at the annual meeting of the American Educational Research Association, San Francisco. (ERIC Document Reproduction Service No. ED 275 671)

Housner, L.D., & Griffey, D.G. (1985). Teacher cognition: Differences in planning and interactive decision making between experienced and inexperienced teachers. *Research Quarterly for Exercise and Sport*, **56**(1), 45-53.

Houston, W.R. (1974). Competency based education. In W.R. Houston (Ed.), *Exploring competency based education* (pp. 3-15). Berkeley, CA: McCutchan.

Houston, W.R., & Howsam, R.B. (1972). *Competency based teacher education: Progress, problems, & prospects.* Palo Alto, CA: Science Research Associates.

Howdyshell, J.A. (1987). Some effects of microteaching, cooperating teachers, university supervisors, and discussion style upon classroom teaching during student teaching (Doctoral dissertation, University of Illinois at Urbana-Champaign, 1986). *Dissertation Abstracts International*, **47**(7), 2549-A.

Hoy, W.K. (1967). Organizational socialization: The student teacher and pupil control ideology. *Journal of Educational Research*, **61**(4), 153-155.

Hoy, W.K. (1968). The influence of experience on the beginning teacher. *School Review*, **76**(3), 312-323.

Hoy, W.K. (1969). Pupil control ideology and organizational socialization: A further examination of the influence of experience on the beginning teacher. *School Review*, **77**(3), 257-265.

Hoy, W.K., & Forsyth, P.B. (1986). *Effective supervision: Theory into practice.* New York: Random House.

Hoy, W.K., & Rees, R. (1977). The bureaucratic socialization of student teachers. *Journal of Teacher Education*, **28**(1), 23-26.

Hughley, C. (1973). Modification of teaching behaviors in physical education. *Dissertation Abstracts International*, **34**(5), 2368-A. (University Microfilms No. 73-26,843)

Hummel, R.C. (1962). Ego-counseling in guidance: Concept and method. *Harvard Educational Review*, **32**(4), 463-482.

Hunt, C. (1987). Predicting student academic gain

through a competency-based teacher assessment instrument: A validation study. *Dissertation Abstracts International, 48*(9), 2233-2234A. (University Microfilms No. 87-271,98)

Hunt, D. (1977). *Assessing conceptual level by the paragraph completion method.* Toronto: Ontario Institute for Studies in Education.

Hunter, M. (1982). *Mastery teaching: Increasing instructional effectiveness in elementary schools, colleges, and universities.* El Segunda, CA: TIP Publications.

Hunter, M. (1984). Knowing, teaching, and supervising. In P.L. Hosford (Ed.), *Using what we know about teaching* (pp. 169-192). Alexandria, VA: Association for Supervision and Curriculum Development.

Hunter, M. (1985). What's wrong with Madeline Hunter? *Educational Leadership, 42*(5), 57-60.

Hunter, M. (1986). Let's eliminate the preobservation conference. *Educational Leadership, 43*(6), 69-71.

Hunter, M. (1989). "Well acquainted" is not enough: A response to Mandeville and Rivers. *Educational Leadership, 46*(4), 67-68.

Hutslar, S.E. (1977). The effects of training cooperating teachers in applied behavior analysis on student teacher behavior in physical education. *Dissertation Abstracts International, 37*(8), 4956-A. (University Microfilms No. 77-2420)

Hutson, H.M. (1981). In-service best practices: The learnings of general education. *Journal of Research and Development in Education, 14*(2), 1-10.

Hylton, J.B. (1985). Case studies of ten teachers in the Virginia Beginning Teacher Assistance Program. *Dissertation Abstracts International, 49*(11), 3336-A. (University Microfilms No. 89-04,236).

Ingraham v. Wright, 430 U.S. 651, 51L. Ed. 2d 771 (1977).

Imwold, C.H., Rider, R.A., Twardy, B.M., Oliver, P.S., Griffin, M., & Arsenault, D.N. (1984). The effect of planning on the teaching behavior of preservice physical education teachers. *Journal of Teaching in Physical Education, 4*(1), 50-56.

Ivey, R.L. (1986). Relation of inservice training to teaching performance assessment scores (Doctoral dissertation, Florida State University, 1986). *Dissertation Abstracts International, 47*(10), 3735A.

Jackson, P.W. (1968). *Life in classrooms.* New York: Holt, Rinehart, & Winston.

Jalbert, E.L. (1966). The effectiveness of training in the evaluation of classroom instruction as an aid to self-evaluation in student teaching. *Journal of Educational Research, 60*(3), 130-135.

Johns, K.W., & Cline, D.H. (1985, October). *Supervisory practices and student teacher satisfaction in selected institutions of higher education.* Paper presented at the annual meeting of the Northern Rocky Mountain Educational Research Association. (ERIC Document Reproduction Service No. ED 267 037)

Johnston, C.A. (1986). The effects of training in transactional analysis upon the interpersonal communication transactions of graduate students in supervision (Doctoral dissertation, Rutgers University, The State University of New Jersey, 1985). *Dissertation Abstracts International, 46*(9), 2502-A.

Johnston, O.P. (1969, October). The relationship of self-supervision to change in selected attitudes and behaviors of secondary student teachers. *Educational Leadership Research Supplement, 27*(3), 57-63.

Joyce, B.R. (1988a). *Improving America's schools.* New York: Longman.

Joyce, B.R. (1988b). Training research and preservice teacher education: A reconsideration. *Journal of Teacher Education, 46*(2), 32-36.

Joyce, B.R., Brown, C., & Peck, C. (1981). *Flexibility in teaching: An excursion into the nature of teaching.* New York: Longman.

Joyce, B.R., & McKibben, M. (1982). Teacher growth states and school environments. *Educational Leadership, 40*(2), 36-41.

Joyce, B.R., & Showers, B. (1981, April). *Teacher training research: Working hypothesis for program design and directions for further study.* Paper presented at the annual meeting of the American Educational Research Association, Los Angeles.

Joyce, B.R., & Showers, B. (1982). The coaching of teaching. *Educational Leadership, 40*(1), 4-10.

Joyce, B.R., & Showers, B. (1983). *Power in staff development through research in training.* Alexandria, VA: Association for Supervision and Curriculum Development.

Joyce, B.R., & Showers, B. (1988). *Student achievement through staff development.* New York: Longman.

Joyce, B.R., Soltis, J.F., & Weil, M. (1974). *Performance-based teacher education design alternatives: The concept of unity.* Washington, DC: American Association of Colleges for Teacher Education.

Joyce, B.R., & Weil, M. (1986). *Models of teaching* (3rd ed.). Englewood Cliffs, NJ: Prentice Hall.

Joyce, R.M.G. (1982). A study of the implementation of the innovations, clinical supervision and clinical instruction (Doctoral dissertation,

United States International University, 1985). *Dissertation Abstracts International, 43*(4), 995-A.

Kamiya, M. (1986). A survey of teacher responses comparing clinical supervision with existing supervisory practices and teacher evaluation in Japan (Doctoral dissertation, University of Oregon, 1986). *Dissertation Abstracts International, 47*(4), 1135-A.

Karmos, A., & Jacko, C. (1977). The role of significant others during the student teaching experience. *Journal of Teacher Education, 28*(5), 51-55.

Karweit, N. (1985). Time scales, learning events, and productive instruction. In C.W. Fisher & D.C. Berliner (Eds.), *Perspectives of instructional time* (pp. 169-185). New York: Longman.

Kay, P.M. (1975). *What competencies should be included in a C/PBTE program?* Washington, DC: American Association of Colleges for Teacher Education.

Kelley, E.J. (1974). Definition and assessment of professional obsolescence in physical education. *Dissertation Abstracts International, 35*(12), 7708-A.

Kelley, E.J., & Kalenak, A. (1975). Programs to improve medical care of athletes. *Interscholastic Athletic Administration, 1*(1), 4-5.

Kelley, E.J., & Lindsay, C.A. (1977). Knowledge obsolescence in physical educators. *Research Quarterly, 48*(2), 463-474.

Kelley, E.J., & Lindsay, C.A. (1980). Comparison of knowledge obsolescence of graduating seniors and practitioners in the field of physical education. *Research Quarterly for Exercise and Sport, 51*(4), 636-644.

Kelley, E.J., & Miller, S. (1976). The need for a certified athletic trainer in the junior/senior high school. *Journal of the National Athletic Trainers Association, 11*(3), 180-183.

Kessell, G.H. (1988). A study of the effect of training on observer agreement in the interpretation of teacher observation data (Florida). *Dissertation Abstracts International, 49*(10), 2877-A. (University Microfilms No. 88-27,699)

Kneer, M.E. (1986). Description of physical education instructional theory/practice gap in selected secondary schools. *Journal of Teaching in Physical Education, 5*(2), 91-106.

Koehler, V.R. (1984). *University supervision of student teaching* (National Institute of Education Report No. 9061). Unpublished manuscript. (ERIC Document Reproduction Service No. ED270 439)

Koehler, V.R. (1986, April). *The instructional supervision of student teachers.* Paper presented at the annual meeting of the American Educational Research Association, San Francisco. (ERIC Document Reproduction Service No. ED 271 430)

Kopecky, C.W. (1986). Clinical supervisory skills used by principals, abstracted from narrative teacher observation records (Doctoral dissertation, Northern Illinois University, 1986). *Dissertation Abstracts International, 47*(6), 2005-A.

Kounin, J. (1970). *Discipline and group management in classrooms.* New York: Holt, Rinehart, & Winston.

Koziol, S.M., & Burns, P. (1986). Teachers' accuracy in self-reporting about instructional practices using a focused self-report inventory. *Journal of Educational Research, 79*(4), 205-209.

Krajewski, R.J. (1984). No wonder it didn't work! A response to McFaul and Cooper. *Educational Leadership, 41*(7), 11.

Kyte, G. (1930). *How to supervise.* Boston: Houghton Mifflin.

Lerch, R.D. (1982). The clinical model: The optimum approach to supervision. *Clearing House, 53*(5), 238-240.

Lewis, D.R. (1987). A view of the quality of Colorado teacher candidates as measured by indicators of knowledge, performance, and other descriptive data. *Dissertation Abstracts International, 49*(7), 227-A. (University Microfilms No. 88-08,289)

Lieberman, A.L., & Miller, L. (1981). Synthesis of research on improving schools. *Educational Leadership, 38*(7), 583-586.

Little, J.W. (1985). Teachers as teacher evaluators: The delicacy of collegial leadership. *Educational Leadership, 42*(7), 34-35.

Locke, L.F. (1974, November). *Ecology of the gymnasium: What the tourists never see.* Paper presented at the Southern Association of Physical Education for College Women fall workshop, Gatlinsburg, TN. (ERIC Document Reproduction Service No. ED 104 823)

Locke, L.F. (1979). Supervision, schools, and student teaching: Why things stay the same. In M. Gladys Scott (Ed.) *The Academy Papers, No. 13. Proceedings of the 50th annual meeting of the American Academy of Physical Education* (pp. 65-74). New Orleans: American Alliance for Health, Physical Education, Recreation and Dance.

Locke, L.F. (1983). Research on teacher education for physical education in the U.S.A.: Part II. Questions and conclusions. In R. Telama (Ed.), *Research on school physical education* (pp. 285-320). Jyvasskyla, Finland: The Foundation for Promotion of Physical Culture and Health.

Long, J.D., Frye, V.H., & Long, E.W. (1985). *Making it till Friday* (3rd ed.). Princeton, NJ: Princeton.

Lortie, D.C. (1975). *Schoolteacher: A sociological study*. Chicago: University of Chicago Press.

Loucks-Horsley, S., Harding, C.K., Arbuckle, M.A., Dubea, C., & Williams, M.K. (1987). *Continuing to learn: A guidebook for teacher development*. Andover, MA: Regional Laboratory for Educational Improvement of the Northeast and Islands.

Lovelace, T., & Martin, C.E. (1984). *The revised National Teacher Examinations as a predictor of teachers' performance in public school classrooms.* (Final Report of Funded Project, Board of Regents Research and Development Program). Lafayette: University of Southwestern Louisiana. (ERIC Document Reproduction Service No. ED 251 416)

Lucio, W.H. (1967). *Supervision: Perspectives and propositions*. Washington, D.C.: Association for Supervision and Curriculum Development.

Lucio, W.H., & McNeil, J.D. (1979). *Supervision in thought and action*. New York: McGraw-Hill.

Madsen, C.H., & Madsen, C.K. (1981). *Teaching/discipline: A positive approach for educational development*. Boston: Allyn & Bacon.

Mager, R.F. (1984). *Preparing instructional objectives*. (rev. 2nd ed.). Belmont, CA: Pitman.

Mancini, V.H., Wuest, D.A., & van der Mars, H. (1985). Use of instruction and supervision in systematic observation in undergraduate professional preparation. *Journal of Teaching in Physical Education*, **5**(1), 22-23.

Mandeville, G.K., & Rivers, J. (1988). Effects of South Carolina's PET Program. *Educational Leadership*, **46**(4), 63-66.

Mandeville, G.K., & Rivers, J. (1989). Is the Hunter model a recipe for supervision? *Educational Leadership*, **46**(8), 39-43.

Martinek, T.J. (1981). Pygmalion in the gym: A model for the communication of teacher expectations in physical education. *Research Quarterly for Exercise and Sport*, **52**(1), 58-67.

Martinek, T.J. (1982). Creating Golem and Galatea effects during physical education: A social psychological perspective. In T.J. Templin & J.K. Olson (Eds.), *Teaching in physical education: Big Ten symposium series* (Vol. 14, pp. 59-70). Champaign, IL: Human Kinetics.

Martinek, T., Crowe, P., & Rejeski, W. (1982) *Pygmalion in the gym: Causes and effects of expectations in teaching and coaching*. West Point, NY: Leisure Press.

Massey, D.E. (1988). A survey on the perceptions of teachers and administrators toward the North Carolina Teacher Performance Appraisal Instrument in selected Region VI schools. *Dissertation Abstracts International*, **49**(11), 3233-A. (University Microfilms No. 88,23-382)

Mayfield, J.E. (1983). The effects of clinical supervision on pupil achievement in reading (Doctoral dissertation, Wayne State University, 1983). *Dissertation Abstracts International*, **44**(4), 940A.

McCarty, D.J., Kaufman, J.W., & Stafford, J.C. (1986). Supervision and evaluation: Two irreconcilable processes? *Clearing House*, **59**(8), 351-353.

McCormack, S. (1989). Response to Render, Padilla, and Krank: But practitioners say it works! *Educational Leadership*, **46**(6), 77-79.

McDonald, F.J. (1974). The rationale for competency based programs. In W.R. Houston (Ed.), *Exploring competency based education* (pp. 17-30). Berkeley, CA: McCutchan.

McDonald, J.B. (1965). Myths about instruction. *Educational Leadership*, **22**(7), 571-576, 609-617.

McDonald, J.B., Wolfson, B.J., & Zaret, E. (1973). *Preschooling society: A conceptual model*. Washington, D.C.: Association for Supervision and Curriculum Development.

McFaul, S.A., & Cooper, J.M. (1984). Peer clinical supervision: Theory vs. reality. *Educational Leadership*, **41**(7), 4-9.

McIntyre, D.J. (1984). A response to the critics of field experience supervision. *Journal of Teacher Education*, **35**(3), 42-45.

McIntyre, D.J., & Norris, W.R. (1980a). The state of the art of preservice teacher education programs and supervision of field experiences. *Action in Teacher Education*, **2**(3), 67-69.

McIntyre, D.J., & Norris, W.R. (1980b). *Student teaching triad communication survey*. Unpublished manuscript. (ERIC Document Reproduction Service No. ED 251 420)

McKenzie, T.L. (1976). Development and evaluation of a model behaviorally-based training center for physical educators. *Dissertation Abstracts International*, **37**(8), 4959A. (University Microfilms No. 77-024,457)

McNeil, J.D. (1971). *Toward accountable teachers*. New York: Holt, Rinehart, and Winston.

Medley, D.M., Coker, H., & Soar, R.S. (1984). *Measurement-based evaluation of teacher performance: An empirical approach*. New York: Longman.

Medrano, H.H. (1986). Effects of classroom management training on selected teaching behaviors of student teachers (Doctoral dissertation, University of Texas at Austin, 1985). *Dissertation Abstracts International, 47*(2), 507-A.

Metzdorf, J. (1989). District-level staff development. In S.D. Caldwell (Ed.), *Staff development: A handbook of effective practices* (pp. 14-25). Oxford, OH: National Staff Development Council.

Metzler, M. (1979). The measurement of academic learning time in physical education. *Dissertation Abstracts International, 40*(10), 5365-A. (University Microfilms No. 80-09,314)

Metzler, M. (1989a). The ALT-PE microcomputer data collection system (MCDCS). In P.W. Darst, D.B. Zakrajsek, & V.H. Mancini (Eds.), *Analyzing physical education and sport instruction* (pp. 225-232). Champaign, IL: Human Kinetics.

Metzler, M. (1989b). A review of research on time in sport pedagogy. *Journal of Teaching in Physical Education, 8*(2), 87-103.

Meyers, B. (1988). A model of peer supervision in pre-service teacher training with an interpretive analysis of the seminar component (Doctoral dissertation, Temple University, 1988). *Dissertation Abstracts International, 49*(5), 121-A.

Michigan State Board of Education. (1984). *Essential performance objectives for physical education.* East Lansing, MI: Author.

Miles, M., & Huberman, M. (1984). *Innovation up close.* New York: Praeger.

Millman, J. (1987). Student achievement as a measure of teacher competence. In J. Millman (Ed.), *Handbook of teacher evaluation* (pp. 146-166). Beverly Hills, CA: SAGE.

Minehart, C.H. (1986). An ethnography of evolving student teacher concerns (Doctoral dissertation, West Virginia University, 1985). *Dissertation Abstracts International, 47*(3), 872-A.

Mistretta, A.M. (1988). Decision-making in student teaching: An ethnographic study examining autonomy in the elementary school student teacher's relationship with the cooperating teacher (Doctoral dissertation, the University of Connecticut, 1987). *Dissertation Abstracts International, 48*(10), 2605-A.

Moffett, K.L., St. John, J., & Isken, J. (1987). Training and coaching for beginning teachers: An antidote to reality shock. *Educational Leadership, 44*(5), 34-36.

Morine, G. (1976). *A study of teacher planning* (Special Study C., Beginning Teacher Evaluation Study, Technical Report Series). San Francisco: Far West Lab for Educational Research and Development. (ERIC Document Reproduction Service No. ED 146 160)

Mosher, R.L., & Purpel, D.E. (1972). *Supervision: The reluctant profession.* New York: Houghton Mifflin.

Mosston, M., & Ashworth, S. (1986). *Teaching physical education* (3rd ed.). Columbus, OH: Merrill.

Neuweiler, H.B. (1988). *Teacher education policy in the states: A 50-state survey of legislative and administrative actions.* Washington, DC: American Association of Colleges for Teacher Education. (ERIC Document Reproduction Service No. 296 997)

Nisenholz, B., & McCarty, F.H. (1976). Use of Gestalt counseling in student teaching supervision. *Peabody Journal of Education, 53*(2), 76-80.

O'Cansey, R.T.A. (1986). *An effective supervision guide for supervisors: A systematic approach to organizing data generated during monitoring sessions in student teaching* (ERIC Document Reproduction Service No. ED 284 853).

O'Cansey, R.T.A. (1987). The effects of a behavioral model of supervision on the supervisory behavior of cooperating teachers and university supervisors (Doctoral dissertation, The Ohio State University, 1986). *Dissertation Abstracts International, 47*(7), 2502-2503A.

O'Cansey, R.T.A. (1988). The effects of a behavioral model of supervision on the supervisory behaviors of cooperating teachers. *Journal of Teaching in Physical Education, 8*(1), 46-62.

Oliver, B. (1983). Direct instruction: An instructional model from a process-product study. In T.J. Templin & J.K. Olson (Eds.), *Teaching in physical education: Big Ten body of knowledge symposium series* (Vol. 14, pp. 298-309). Champaign, IL: Human Kinetics.

Olsen, H.C. (1971). *The teaching clinic: A team approach to the improvement of instruction.* Washington, D.C.: Association of Teacher Educators.

Osterman, K.F. (1985). Supervision in public schools: An examination of the relationship between supervisory practices of principals and organizational behavior of teachers (Doctoral dissertation, Washington University, 1984). *Dissertation Abstracts International, 46*(3), 572-A.

Paese, P.C. (1984a). The effects of cooperating teacher intervention and a self-assessment technique on the verbal interactions of elementary student teachers. *Journal of Teaching in Physical Education, 3*(3), 51-58.

Paese, P.C. (1984b). Student teaching supervision: Where we are and where we should be. *Physical Educator, 41*(2), 90-94.

Paese, P.C. (1987). Specific teacher feedback's effect on academic learning time and on a novel motor skill. In G.T. Barrette, R.S. Feingold, C.R. Rees, & M. Pieron (Eds.), *Myths, models, & methods in sport pedagogy* (pp. 207-214). Champaign, IL: Human Kinetics.

Parker, M. (1989). Academic learning time-physical education (ALT-PE, 1982 Revision). In P.W. Darst, D.B. Zakrajsek, & V.H. Mancini (Eds.), *Analyzing physical education and sport instruction* (pp. 195-206). Champaign, IL: Human Kinetics.

Pavan, B.N. (1985, November). *Hunter's clinical supervision and instruction model: Research in schools using comparative measures*. Paper presented at the Council of Professors of Instructional Supervision. Washington, DC. (ERIC Document Reproduction Service No. ED 273 606)

Pease, D. (1975). Comparing faculty and school supervisor ratings for education students. *College Student Journal*, **9**(1), 91-94.

Peterson, P.L. (1979a). Direct instruction: Effective for what and for whom. *Educational Leadership*, **37**(1), 46-48.

Peterson, P.L. (1979b). Direct instruction reconsidered. In P.L. Peterson & H.J. Walberg (Eds.), *Research on teaching* (pp. 57-69). Berkeley, CA: McCutchan.

Peterson, P.L., Marx, R.W., & Clark, C.M. (1978). Teacher planning, teacher behavior, and student achievement. *American Educational Research Journal*, **15**(3), 417-432.

Phelps, J.D. (1985). Application of contingency theories to the supervision of student teachers. *Teacher Education*, **2**(2), 9-14.

Phelps, L.A., Schmitz, C.D., & Boatright, B. (1986). The effects of halo and leniency on cooperating teacher reports using Likert-type rating scales. *Journal of Educational Research*, **79**(3), 151-154.

Phelps, L.A., Schmitz, C.D., & Wade, D.L. (1986). A performance-based cooperating teacher report. *Journal of Teacher Education*, **37**(5), 32-35.

Pierce, D.K. (1989). The effects of interpersonal process recall and peer clinical supervision on the concern levels of student teachers (Doctoral dissertation, University of Houston, 1987). *Dissertation Abstracts International*, **49**(7), 1772-A.

Placek, J.H. (1982). An observational study of teacher planning in physical education. *Dissertation Abstracts International*, **43**(4), 1081-A. (University Microfilms No. 82-19,838)

Placek, J.H. (1983). Conceptions of success in teaching: Busy, happy, and good? In T.J. Templin and J.K. Olson (Eds.), *Teaching in physical education: Big Ten body of knowledge symposium*

series, (Vol. 14, pp. 46-56). Champaign, IL: Human Kinetics.

Placek, J.H., & Locke, L.F. (1986). Research on teaching physical education: New knowledge and cautious optimism. *Journal of Teacher Education*, **37**(4), 24-27.

Placek, J.H., & Randall, L. (1986). Comparison of academic learning time in physical education: Students of specialists and nonspecialists. *Journal of Teaching in Physical Education*, **5**(3), 157-165.

Purcell, T.D., & Seifert, B.B. (1982). A tri-state survey of student teachers. *College Student Journal*, **15**(1), 27-29.

Queen, J.A., & Mallen, L. (1982). Student teaching: A transitional approach. *Clearing House*, **56**(2), 56-59.

Raber, G.A. (1985). Source of letters of recommendation and subsequent teaching performance of first-year teachers. *Dissertation Abstracts International*, **46**(7), 1802-A. (University Microfilms No. 85-19,660)

Randall, L.E. (1989). Clinical diagnosis skills for effective training. In M.J. Adrian & J.M. Cooper (Eds.), *Biomechanics of human movement* (pp. 296-302). Indianapolis: Benchmark.

Randall, L.E., & Imwold, C.H. (1989). The effect of an intervention on academic learning time in physical education provided by preservice physical education teachers. *Journal of Teaching in Physical Education*, **8**(4), 271-279.

Redfield, D.L., & Rousseau, E.W. (1981). A meta-analysis of experimental research on teacher questioning behavior. *Review of Educational Research*, **51**(2), 237-245.

Render, G.F., Padilla, J.M., & Krank, H.M. (1989). What research really shows about assertive discipline. *Educational Leadership*, **46**(6), 72-75.

Richardson-Koehler, V. (1988). Barriers to the effective supervision of student teaching: A field study. *Journal of Teacher Education*, **39**(2), 28-34.

Rife, F. (1973). Modifications of student teacher behavior and its effect upon pupil behavior. *Dissertation Abstracts International*, **34**(8), 4844A (University Microfilms No. 64-03, 298)

Rink, J.E. (1985). *Teaching physical education for learning*. St. Louis: Times Mirror/Mosby.

Roberton, M.A. (1977). Developmental implications for games teaching. *Journal of Physical Education, Recreation and Dance*, **48**(7), 25.

Rogers, C.R. (1959). A theory of therapy, personality, and interpersonal relationships, as developed in the client-centered framework. In S. Koch (Ed.), *Formulations of the person and the social context* (pp. 184-256). New York: McGraw-Hill.

Rogers, C.R. (1961). *On becoming a person*. Boston: Houghton Mifflin.

Rogers, M.G. (1987). Teacher satisfaction with direct supervisory services (Doctoral dissertation, University of Georgia, 1986). *Dissertation Abstracts International*, **47**(11), 4260-A.

Rogus, J., & Schuttenberg, E. (1979). Redesign of teacher education: Putting the house in order. *Journal of Teacher Education*, **30**(5), 39-41.

Rolheiser-Bennett, C. (1987). Four models of teaching: A meta-analysis of student outcomes (Doctoral dissertation, University of Oregon, 1986). *Dissertation Abstracts International*, **47**(11), 3966-A.

Rosenshine, B.V. (1979). Content, time, and direct instruction. In P.L. Peterson & H.J. Walberg (Eds.), *Research on teaching* (pp. 28-56). Berkeley, CA: McCutchan.

Rosenshine, B.V. (1987). Explicit teaching. In D.C. Berliner & B.V. Rosenshine (Eds.), *Talks to teachers* (pp. 75-92). New York: Random House.

Rosenshine, B.V., & Furst, N. (1971). Research in teacher performance criteria. In B.O. Smith (Ed.), *Research in teacher education: A symposium* (pp. 37-72). Englewood Cliffs, NJ: Prentice Hall.

Rosenshine, B.V., & Furst, N. (1973). The use of direct observation to study teaching. In R.M.W. Travers (Ed.), *Second handbook of research on teaching* (pp. 122-183). Chicago: Rand McNally.

Rosenshine, B.V., & Stevens, R. (1985). Teaching functions. In M.C. Wittrock (Ed.), *Handbook of research on teaching* (3rd ed., pp. 376-391). New York: Macmillan.

Rosenthal, R., & Jacobson, L. (1968). *Pygmalion in the classroom: Teacher expectation and pupils' intellectual development*. San Francisco: Holt, Rinehart, & Winston.

Rossicone, G.A. (1985). The relationship of selected teacher background variables to teacher preferences for supervisory style and teacher perceptions of supervisory style of supervisors (Doctoral dissertation, St. John's University, 1985). *Dissertation Abstracts International*, **46**(2), 321-A.

Rowe, M.B. (1974a). Relation of wait-time and rewards to the development of language, logic, and fate control: Part II. Rewards. *Journal of Research in Science Teaching*, **11**(4), 291-308.

Rowe, M.B. (1974b). Wait-time and rewards as instructional variables, their influence on language, logic, and fate control: Part I. Wait-time. *Journal of Research in Science Teaching*. **11**(2), 81-94.

Rudner, L.M. (1987). *What's happening in teacher testing: An analysis of state teacher testing practices*. Washington, DC: Office of Educational Research and Improvement, U.S. Department of Education. (ERIC Document Reproduction Service No. ED 228 867)

Russell, T.J., & Spafford, C. (1986, April). *Teachers as reflective practicioners in peer clinical supervision*. Paper presented at the annual meeting of the American Educational Research Association, San Francisco. (ERIC Document Reproduction Service No. ED 270 410)

Rust, F.O. (1988). How supervisors think about teaching. *Journal of Teacher Education*, **39**(2), 56-64.

Sabatino, A.C. (1983). In D.A. Sabatino, A.C. Sabatino, & L. Mann (Eds.), *Discipline and behavioral management: Handbook of tactics, strategies, and programs* (pp. 29-82). Rockville, MD: Aspen Systems Corporation.

Sadker, M., & Sadker, D. (1990). Questioning skills. In J.M. Cooper (Ed.), *Classroom teaching skills* (4th ed., pp. 111-148). Lexington, MA: D.C. Heath and Company.

Safrit, M.J. (1981). *Evaluation in physical education* (2nd ed.). Englewood Cliffs, NJ: Prentice Hall.

Sage, G.H. (1984). *Motor learning and control: A neuropsychological approach*. Dubuque, IA: Wm. C. Brown.

Saldana, J.C. (1983). Discriminant analysis of the effects of inservice training in a clinical model for the supervision and improvement of instruction (Doctoral dissertation, University of Iowa, 1982). *Dissertation Abstracts International*, **43**(8), 2525A.

Sanford, J.P., & Evertson, C.M. (1981). Classroom management in a low SES junior high: Three case studies. *Journal of Teacher Education*, **32**(1), 34-38.

Schwartzberg, J.S. (1987). The impact of clarity of criteria and standards and frequency of observation and feedback on teachers' perceptions of the utility of teacher evaluation (Doctoral dissertation, Columbia University Teachers' College, 1986). *Dissertation Abstracts International*, **48**(1), 24-A.

Seaborn, M.M. (1986). An analysis of the communication behaviors utilized by student teachers in classroom management (Doctoral dissertation, Boston University, 1985). *Dissertation Abstracts International*, **47**(1), 153-154A.

Seperson, M., & Joyce, B.R. (1981). The relationship between the teaching styles of student teachers and those of the cooperating teachers. In B.R. Joyce, C. Brown, & C. Peck, (Eds.), *Flexibility in teaching: An excursion into the nature of teaching* (pp. 101-107). New York: Longman.

Sergiovanni, T.J. (1976). Toward a theory of clinical supervision. *Journal of Research and Development*, **9**(2), 20-29.

Sergiovanni, T.J., & Starratt, R.J. (1979). *Supervision: Human perspectives* (2nd ed.). New York: McGraw-Hill.

Shavelson, R.J., Webb, N.M., & Burstein, L. (1986). Measurement of teaching. In M.C. Wittrock (Ed.), *Handbook of research on teaching* (pp. 50-91). New York: Macmillan.

Shipman, M.O. (1967). Theory and practice in the education of teachers. *Educational Research*, **9**(3), 208-212.

Shostak, R. (1990). Lesson presentation skills. In J.M. Cooper (Ed.), *Classroom teaching skills* (4th ed., pp. 85-109). Lexington, MA: D.C. Heath and Company.

Showers, B., Joyce, B., & Bennett, B. (1987). Synthesis of research on staff development: A framework for future study and a state-of-the-art analysis. *Educational Leadership*, **45**(3), 77-87.

Siedentop, D. (1981). The Ohio State University supervision research program summary report. *Journal of Teaching in Physical Education*, Introductory Issue, 30-38.

Siedentop, D. (1991). *Developing teaching skills in physical education* (3rd ed.). Palo Alto, CA: Mayfield.

Siedentop, D., Birdwell, D., & Metzler, M. (1979, April). *A process approach to studying teaching in physical education*. Paper presented at the national convention of the American Alliance for Health, Physical Education, Recreation and Dance, New Orleans.

Siedentop, D., & Hughley, C. (1975). The Ohio State Teachers Behavior Scale. *Journal of Physical Education, Recreation and Dance*, **46**(2), 45.

Siedentop, D., & Rife, F. (1989). Data collection for managerial efficiency in physical education (DACOMBE-PE). In P.W. Darst, D.B. Zakrjsek, & V.H. Mancini (Eds.), *Systematic observation instruments for physical education* (pp. 161-166). Champaign, IL: Human Kinetics.

Siedentop, D., Rife, F., & Boehm, J. (1976, May). *Modification of student and student teacher responses during management time*. Paper presented at Midwest Applied Behavior Analysis Convention, Chicago.

Siedentop, D., Tousignant, M., & Parker, M. (1982). *Academic learning time-physical education: 1982 revision coding manual*. Columbus, OH: School of Health, Physical Education, and Recreation, Ohio State University.

Silverman, S., & Zotos, C. (1987, April). *Validity and generalizability of measuring student engaged time in physical education*. Paper presented at the annual meeting of the American Educational Research Association, Washington, DC. (ERIC Document Reproduction Service No. ED 285 917)

Simon, A., & Boyer, E.G. (Eds.) (1974). *Mirrors for behavior III: An anthology of observation instruments*. Philadelphia: Research for Better Schools, Inc.

Sistrunk, W.E. (1981, Novemeber). *The development of the supervisory behavior description questionnaire, Forms 1 and 2*. Paper presented at the annual convention of the Mid-South Educational Research Association, Lexington, KY. (ERIC Document Reproduction Service No. ED 212 061)

Sistrunk, W.E. (1986, August). *Studies of supervisory behavior*. Paper presented at the annual meeting of the National Conference of Professors of Educational Administration, Flagstaff, AZ. (ERIC Document Reproduction Service No. ED 276 120)

Smith, G.R. (1985). A study of the relationship between the climate of the elementary school and the clinical supervisory practices of the elementary school principal (Doctoral dissertation, Oklahoma State University, 1984). *Dissertation Abstracts International*, **46**(5), 1155-A.

Smith, L.M., & Smith, G.W. (1966). *The complexities of an urban classroom*. New York: Holt, Rinehart, & Winston.

Smoll, F.L., & Smith, R.E. (1984). Leadership research in youth sports. In J.M. Silva & R.S. Weinburg (Eds.), *Psychological foundations of sport* (pp. 371-386). Champaign, IL: Human Kinetics.

Smyth, J.M. (1982, November). *Teaching as learning: Some lessons from clinical supervision*. Paper presented at the annual meeting of the Australian Association for Research in Education, Brisbane. (ERIC Document Reproduction No. ED 238 862)

Soar, R., Medley, D., & Coker, H. (1983). Teacher evaluation: A critique of currently used methods. *Phi Delta Kappan*, **65**(4), 239-246.

Soar, R.S., & Soar, R.M. (1979). Emotional climate and management. In P.L. Peterson & H.J. Walberg (Eds.), *Research on teaching* (pp. 97-119). Berkeley, CA: McCutchan.

Sorrick, K.M. (1988). Teachers' perceptions of the effectiveness of the post observation conference (Doctoral dissertation, Loyola University of Chicago, 1988). *Dissertation Abstracts International*, **49**(6), 1433-A.

Southern Regional Education Board. (1982). *Teacher testing and assessment: An examination of the National Teacher Certification Examination (NTE), the Georgia Teacher Certification Test (TCT), and the Georgia Teacher Performance Assessment Instrument (TPAI) for a selected population.* Unpublished manuscript. (ERIC Document Reproduction Service No. ED 229 441)

Sparks, G.M. (1983). Synthesis of research on staff development for effective teaching. *Educational Leadership*, **41**(3), 65-72.

Spaulding, J.W. (1984). A study of the implementation of a clinical supervision model in the Santee (California) School District (Doctoral dissertation, Northern Arizona University, 1983). *Dissertation Abstracts International*, **44**(10), 2948A-2949A.

Spencer, H. (1885). *The principles of sociology* (3rd ed.). New York: Appleton.

Spencer, K.A. (1986). Post-observation conferences: Factors related to success (Doctoral dissertation, Iowa State University, 1985). *Dissertation Abstracts International*, **47**(1), 47-A.

Stalhut, R. (1987, Spring). *A variable supervisory strategy that includes action research.* Paper presented at the Regional Association of Teacher Educators Illinois/Indiana Mini Clinic, Terre Haute, IN. (ERIC Document Reproduction Service No. ED 279 660)

Stallings, J.A. (1985). A study of implementation of Madeline Hunter's model and its effects on students. *Journal of Educational Research*, **78**(6), 325-337.

Stallings, J.A., & Mohlman, G.G. (1981). *School policy, leadership style, teacher change, and student behavior in eight schools. Final report.* Washington, DC: National Institute of Education. (ERIC Document Reproduction Service No. ED 209 759)

Steinhaus, L.M. (1987). Clinical and nonclinical supervision practices in Wyoming Schools. *Dissertation Abstracts International*, **49**(6), 1339-A. (University Microfilms No. 88-13,316)

Stolworthy, R.L. (1986). Follow-up studies of undergraduates in teacher education to assure quality teachers. *Education*, **107**(2), 198-202.

Stone, C. (1983). A meta-analysis of advance organizer studies. *Journal of Experimental Education*, **51**(4), 104-199.

Strickland, V.V. (1987). A study of the attitudes of Mississippi educators relative to the use of the Mississippi Teacher Assessment Instruments to evaluate career teachers. *Dissertation Abstracts International*, **48**(3), 534-A. (University Microfilms No. 87-14, 286)

Stroot, S.A., & Morton, P.J. (1989). Blueprints for learning. *Journal of Teaching in Physical Education*, **8**(3), 213-222.

Sullivan, C.G. (1980). *Clinical supervision: A state of the art review.* Alexandria, VA: Association for Supervision and Curriculum Development.

Tabachnik, B., Popkewitz, T., & Zeichner, K. (1980). Teacher education and the professional perspectives of student teachers. *Interchange*, **10**(2), 12-19.

Talmage, H., & Eash, M.J. (1979). Curriculum, instruction, and materials. In P.L. Peterson & H.J. Walberg (Eds.), *Research on teaching* (pp. 161-179). Berkeley, CA: McCutchan.

Tannehill, D.L. (1988). The effects of a self-directed supervisory training program on the behaviors of cooperating teachers in secondary physical education (Doctoral dissertation, University of Idaho, 1987). *Dissertation Abstracts International*, **48**(10), 2572-A.

Tannehill, D.L. (1989). Student teaching: A view from the other side. *Journal of Teaching in Physical Education*, **8**(3), 243-253.

Tannehill, D.L., & Zakrajsek, D. (1988). What's happening in supervision of student teachers in secondary physical education. *Journal of Teaching in Physical Education*, **8**(1), 1-12.

Tannehill, D.L., & Zakrajsek, D. (1990). Effects of a self-directed training program on cooperating teaching behavior. *Journal of Teaching in Physical Education.* **9**(2), 140-151.

Tanner, C.K., & Ebers, S.M. (1985). Factors related to the beginning teacher's successful completion of a competency evaluation. *Journal of Teacher Education*, **36**(3), 41-44.

Tanney, L.A., & Ortman, P.E. (1987). *Beginning teacher performance evaluation programs: A state-by-state survey.* Unpublished research report, University of Maryland.

Taylor, L.K. Cook, P.F., Green, E.E., & Rogers, J.K. (1988). Better interviews: The effects of supervisor training on listening and collaborative skills. *Journal of Educational Research*, **82**(2), 89-95.

Taylor, S.M. (1985). Teacher perceptions of intensive supervisor/teacher relationships (Doctoral dissertation, University of Pittsburg, 1984). *Dissertation Abstracts International, 46*(4), 953-A.

Templin, T.J. (1979). Occupational socialization and the physical education student teacher. *Research Quarterly, 50*(3), 482-493.

Texas Education Agency. (1991). *Texas teacher appraisal system.* Austin, TX: Author.

Thies-Sprinthall, L. (1980). Supervision: An educative or miseducative process? *Journal of Teacher Education, 31*(4), 17-20.

Thomas, R.R. (1985). Proportion of effective teaching behaviors demonstrated by elementary level beginning teachers in an urban school district. *Dissertation Abstracts International, 47*(4), 1148-A. (University Microfilms No. 86-15,518)

Thompson, J.D. (1979). *On models of supervision in general and on peer-clinical supervision in particular.* Unpublished manuscript (ERIC Document Reproduction Service No. ED 192 462)

Tinning, R.I. (1988). Student teaching and the pedagogy of necessity. *Journal of Teaching in Physical Education, 7*(2), 82-89.

Tobey, C. (1974). A descriptive analysis of the occurrences of augmented feedback in physical education classes (Doctoral dissertation, Teacher's College, Columbia University, 1974). *Dissertation Abstracts International, 35*(6), 3497.

Tobin, K. (1986). Effects of wait time on discourse characteristics in mathematics and language arts classes. *American Educational Research Journal, 23*(2), 191-200.

Trent, J.M., & Gilman, R.A. (1984, October). *An adaptation of the teacher performance assessment instrument (TPAI) in a teacher preparation program in northern Nevada.* Paper presented at the annual meeting of the Northern Rocky Mountain Educational Research Association, Jackson Hole, WY. (ERIC Document Reproduction Service No. ED 254 532)

Tucker, M., & Mandel, D. (1986). *A nation prepared: Teachers for the 21st century.* Washington, DC: Carnegie Forum on Education and the Economy.

Twardy, B.M. (1984). Relationships among teacher planning behaviors and specified teacher and student inclass behaviors in a physical education milieu. *Dissertation Abstracts International, 45*(7), 226-A. (University Microfilms No. 84-167,29)

Twardy, B.M., & Yerg, B.J. (1987). The impact of planning on inclass interactive behaviors of preservice teachers. *Journal of Teaching in Physical Education, 6*(2), 136-148.

Tyler, R. (1950). *Basic principles of curriculum and instruction.* Chicago: University of Chicago Press.

U.S. Department of Education. (1983). *A nation at risk: The imperative for educational reform.* Washington, DC: U.S. Government Printing Office.

van der Mars, H. (1989). Systematic observation: An introduction. In P.W. Darst, D.B. Zakrajsek, & V.H. Mancini (Eds.), *Analyzing physical education and sport instruction* (pp. 3-18). Champaign, IL: Human Kinetics.

Veenman, S. (1984). Perceived problems of beginning teachers. *Review of Educational Research, 54*(2), 143-178.

Vollmer, M.L., Creek, R.J., & Vollmer, R.R. (1987, February). *The usefulness and accuracy of self-evaluation of teaching competencies.* Paper presented at the annual meeting of the American Association of Colleges for Teacher Education, Arlington, VA. (ERIC Document Reproduction Service No. ED 283 818)

Wade, R.K. (1985). What makes a difference in inservice teacher education? A meta-analysis of research. *Educational Leadership, 42*(4), 48-54.

Walters, J.T. (1986). Professional performance of special and regular education teachers from two types of preservice teacher education programs (Doctoral dissertation, Columbia University Teachers College, 1986). *Dissertation Abstracts International, 47*(1), 4066A.

Weber, W.A. (1990). Classroom management. In J.M. Cooper (Ed.), *Classroom teaching skills* (4th ed., pp. 229-305). Lexington, MA: D.C. Heath and Company.

Weller, L.D. (1984). Essential competencies for effective supervision of the student teacher. *Education, 104*(2), 213-218.

Wheeler, A.E., & Knoop, H.R. (1982). Self, teacher and faculty assessments of student teaching performance. *Journal of Educational Research, 75*(3), 178-181.

White, J.B. (1986). Planning practices of effective high school teachers in a Florida school district. *Dissertation Abstracts International, 47*(11), 3969-A. (University Microfilms No. 87-04,133)

Whitehead, R. (1984, June). *Practicum students' perceptions of teacher associates' supervisory behaviors.* Paper presented at the annual meeting of the Canadian Society for the Study of Education, Guelph, ON. (ERIC Document Reproduction Service No. ED 269 856)

Wiersma, W., Dickson, G.E., Jurs, S., & Wenig, J. (1983, April). *Assessment of teacher performance: Constructs of teacher competenecies based on factor analysis of observation data.* Paper presented at the annual meeting of the American Educational Research Association, Montreal, PQ. (ERIC Document Reproduction Service No. ED 230 586)

Wildman, T.M., Moore, S., Borko, H., Naff, B., Simmons, S., Sowers, J., & Yon, M. (1985). *Beginning teacher's handbook.* Blacksburg, VA: Virginia Polytechnic Institute, College of Education. (ERIC Document Reproduction Service No. ED 286 852)

Wilkinson, S., & Taggart, A.C. (1985). *Physical education and sport observation coding manual for basic ALT-PE.* Columbus: The Ohio State University.

Wilson, N. (1976). *The frequency and patterns of selected motor skills by third- and fourth-grade girls and boys in the game of kickball.* Unpublished master's thesis, University of Georgia, Athens.

Winne, P.H. (1979). Experiments relating teachers' use of higher cognitive questions to student achievement. *Review of Educational Research,* **49**(1), 13-50.

Wise, A.E., Darling-Hammond, L., & Purnell, S. (1988). Impacts of teacher testing: State educational governance through standard-setting (Report No. NIE-G-83-0023). Santa Monica: Rand Corporation. (ERIC Document Reproduction Service No. ED 300 350)

Wolfe, D.E. (1973). Student teaching: Toward a confluent approach. *Modern Language Journal,* **57**(3), 113-119.

Wolfgang, C.H., & Glickman, C.D. (1986). *Solving discipline problems: Strategies for classroom teachers* (2nd ed.). Boston: Allyn & Bacon.

Woolever, R. (1983). *Observing student teachers for a hierarchy of generic teaching skills.* Unpublished manuscript. (ERIC Document Reproduction Service No. ED 238 839)

Woolever, R.M. (1985). State-mandated performance evaluation of beginning teachers: Implications for teacher educators. *Journal of Teacher Education,* **36**(2), 22-25.

Woolfolk, A.E., & Woolfolk, R.L. (1984, April). *An empirical investigation in time management: Effects of specific planning and self-monitoring.* Paper presented at the annual meeting of the American Educational Research Association, New Orleans. (ERIC Document Reproduction Service No. ED 242 693)

Wynn, M.J. (1987). Student teacher transfer of training to the classroom: Effects of an experimental model (Doctoral dissertation, University of South Florida, 1986). *Dissertation Abstracts International,* **47**(8), 3008.

Yap, K.C., & Capie, W. (1985, April). *The influence of same day or separate day observations on the reliability of assessment data.* Paper presented at the annual meeting of the American Educational Research Association, Chicago. (ERIC Document Reproduction Service No. ED 265 166)

Yinger, R.J. (1980). A study of teacher planning. *Elementary School Journal,* **80**(3), 107-127.

Young, L.S. (1986). Clinical supervision—effects on student learning: A comparative study of two processes of teacher evaluation. *Dissertation Abstracts International,* **47**(6), 1977-A. (University Microfilms No. 86-19,625)

Zahorik, J.A. (1970). The effect of planning on teaching. *Elementary School Journal* **71**(3), 143-151.

Zahorik, J.A. (1975). Teachers' planning models. *Educational Leadership,* **33**(2), 134-39.

Zahorik, J.A. (1988). The observing-conferencing role of university supervisors. *Journal of Teacher Education,* **39**(2), 9-16.

Zakrajsek, D.B., & Tannehill, D. (1989). Direct instruction behavior analysis. In P.W. Darst, D.B. Zakrajsek, & V.H. Mancini (Eds.), *Analyzing physical education and sport instruction* (pp. 195-206). Champaign, IL: Human Kinetics.

Ziechner, K.M. (1980). Myths and realities: Field-based experiences in preservice teacher education. *Journal of Teacher Education,* **31**(6), 45-55.

Zeichner, K.M., & Tabachnik, B.R. (1981). Are the effects of university teacher education 'washed out' by school experience? *Journal of Teacher Education,* **32**(3), 7-11.

Zimpher, N.L., deVoss, G.G., & Nott, D.L. (1980). A closer look at university student teacher supervision. *Journal of Teacher Education,* **31**(4), 11-15.

Author Index

Subject Index

Page numbers in bold print indicate figures or tables.